ON THE ROAD

YOUR COMPLETE DESTINATION GUIDE
In-depth reviews, detailed listings
and insider tips

Accommodation p198

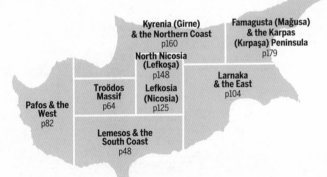

Kyrenia (Girne)
& the Northern Coast
p160

Famagusta (Mağusa)
& the Karpas
(Kırpaşa) Peninsula
p179

North Nicosia
(Lefkoşa)
p148

Troödos
Massif
p64

Lefkosia
(Nicosia)
p125

Larnaka
& the East
p104

Pafos & the
West
p82

Lemesos & the
South Coast
p48

SURVIVAL GUIDE

VITAL PRACTICAL INFORMATION TO
HELP YOU HAVE A SMOOTH TRIP

Directory A-Z 246
Transport 254
Language 261
Index 279
Map Legend 287

THIS EDITION WRITTEN AND RESEARCHED BY

Josephine Quintero,
Matthew Charles

❯ Cyprus

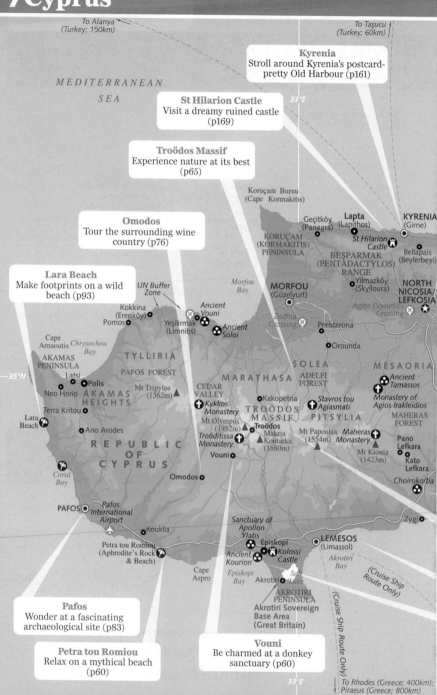

Kyrenia
Stroll around Kyrenia's postcard-pretty Old Harbour (p161)

St Hilarion Castle
Visit a dreamy ruined castle (p169)

Troödos Massif
Experience nature at its best (p65)

Omodos
Tour the surrounding wine country (p76)

Lara Beach
Make footprints on a wild beach (p93)

Pafos
Wonder at a fascinating archaeological site (p83)

Petra tou Romiou
Relax on a mythical beach (p60)

Vouni
Be charmed at a donkey sanctuary (p60)

To Alanya (Turkey; 150km)

To Taşucu (Turkey; 60km)

33°E

MEDITERRANEAN
SEA

Koruçam Burnu (Cape Kormakitis)

Geçitköy (Panagra)

Lapta (Lapithos)

KYRENIA (Girne)

St Hilarion Castle

Bellapais (Beylerbeyi)

KORUÇAM (KORMAKITIS) PENINSULA

BEŞPARMAK (PENTADACTYLOS) RANGE

NORTH NICOSIA/ LEFKOSIA

Morfou Bay

MORFOU (Güzelyurt)

Yılmazköy (Skylloura)

UN Buffer Zone

Zodhia Crossing

Agios Dometios Crossing

Kokkina (Erenköy)

Ancient Vouni

Yeşilırmak (Limnitis)

Ancient Soloi

Peristerona

Pomos

Cape Arnaoutis

Chrysochou Bay

TYLLIRIA

PAFOS FOREST

MARATHASA

SOLEA

ADELFI FOREST

MESAORIA

Orounda

AKAMAS PENINSULA

Latsi

Polis

Neo Horio

AKAMAS HEIGHTS

Terra Kritou

Mt Tripylos (1362m)

CEDAR VALLEY

Kykkos Monastery

Kakopetria

Stavros tou Agiasmati

TROÖDOS MASSIF

PITSYLIA

Ancient Tamassos

Monastery of Agios Irakleidios

MAHERAS FOREST

Lara Beach

Ano Arodes

REPUBLIC OF CYPRUS

Mt Olympus (1952m)

Trooditissa Monastery

Makria Kontarka (1680m)

Troödos

Vouni

Mt Papoutsa (1554m)

Maheras Monastery

Mt Kionia (1423m)

Pano Lefkara

Kato Lefkara

Coral Bay

Omodos

Choirokoitia

Pafos International Airport

PAFOS

Kouklia

Sanctuary of Apollon Ylatis

Episkopi

LEMESOS (Limassol)

Zygi

Petra tou Romiou (Aphrodite's Rock & Beach)

Cape Aspro

Episkopi Bay

Ancient Kourion

Kolossi Castle

Akrotiri Bay

(Cruise Ship Route Only)

Akrotiri

Salt Lake

AKROTIRI PENINSULA
Akrotiri Sovereign Base Area (Great Britain)

(Cruise Ship Route Only)

35°N

33°E

To Rhodes (Greece; 400km); Piraeus (Greece; 800km)

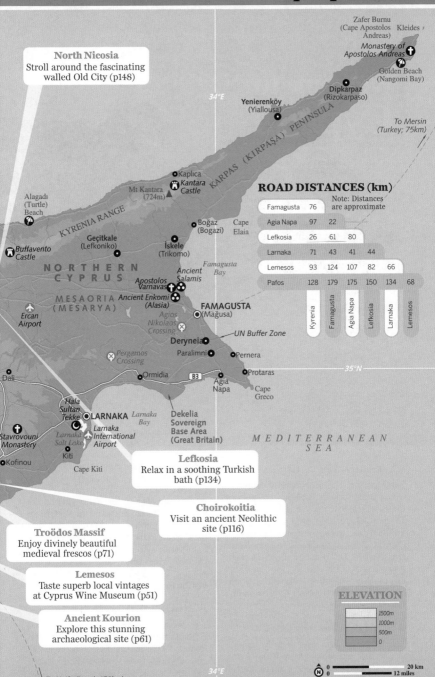

North Nicosia
Stroll around the fascinating walled Old City (p148)

Zafer Burnu
(Cape Apostolos Kleides
Andreas)

Monastery of
Apostolos Andreas

Golden Beach
(Nangomi Bay)

Dipkarpaz
(Rizokarpaso)

Yenierenköy
(Yiallousa)

KARPAS (KIRPAŞA) PENINSULA

To Mersin
(Turkey; 75km)

Kaplıca

Mt Kantara
(724m)

Kantara
Castle

Alagadı
(Turtle)
Beach

KYRENIA RANGE

Geçitkale
(Lefkoniko)

Buffavento
Castle

NORTHERN
CYPRUS

Boğaz
(Bogazi)

Cape
Elaia

İskele
(Trikomo)

Famagusta
Bay

Ancient
Salamis

Apostolos
Varnavas

Ancient Enkomi
(Alasia)

FAMAGUSTA
(Mağusa)

MESAORIA
(MESARYA)

Ercan
Airport

Agios
Nikolaos
Crossing

UN Buffer Zone

Pergamos
Crossing

Deryneia

Paralimni

Pernera

Dali

Ormidia

B3

Protaras

Agia
Napa

Cape
Greco

Hala
Sultan
Tekke

LARNAKA

Larnaka
Bay

Larnaka
International
Airport

Stavrovouni
Monastery

Larnaka
Salt Lake

Kiti

Dekelia
Sovereign
Base Area
(Great Britain)

MEDITERRANEAN
SEA

Kofinou

Cape Kiti

To Haifa (Israel; 170km)

ROAD DISTANCES (km)

Note: Distances are approximate

	Famagusta	Agia Napa	Lefkosia	Larnaka	Lemesos	
Famagusta	76					
Agia Napa	97	22				
Lefkosia	26	61	80			
Larnaka	71	43	41	44		
Lemesos	93	124	107	82	66	
Pafos	128	179	175	150	134	68
	Kyrenia	Famagusta	Agia Napa	Lefkosia	Larnaka	Lemesos

Lefkosia
Relax in a soothing Turkish bath (p134)

Choirokoitia
Visit an ancient Neolithic site (p116)

Troödos Massif
Enjoy divinely beautiful medieval frescos (p71)

Lemesos
Taste superb local vintages at Cyprus Wine Museum (p51)

Ancient Kourion
Explore this stunning archaeological site (p61)

ELEVATION

1500m
1000m
500m
0

0 — 20 km
0 — 12 miles

welcome to
Cyprus

Crossing the Line

Experiencing the intrinsically different Greek and Turkish societies of modern Cyprus is increasingly easy for visitors. To date, there are seven access points linking the Greek Cypriot and Turkish Cypriot sides, including two pedestrian crossings in Lefkosia. In theory, foreign tourists are permitted to cross and stay up to three months, although it's not currently possible to enter Cyprus on one side of the line and leave from the other.

The Great Outdoors

The landscape and overall mild climate means that outside is where it's at – and where you should be. First, there are the beaches, including everything from wild and windswept to family friendly and packed. Every conceivable water sport is also on offer, from scuba diving the watery depths to skimming the surface on a kite- or windsurf board. Tired of all that blue? Head to the interior where pine-clad mountains, sweeping valleys and densely planted vineyards offer endless scope ranging from hiking and biking to wine-tasting tours and, yes, even winter skiing.

A Sense of the Past

The story of Cyprus' tumultuous past is told through its historic sites, its Roman ruins, its multi-faceted museums and its dusty urban streets. This ease of

A fractured identity, a passionate people and a culture, landscape and lifestyle that capture the imagination and are full of surprises.

(left) Petra tou Romiou, Pafos
(below) Cypriot-style meze

accessibility is highlighted in Pafos, where one of the most important archaeological sites sprawls like an ancient theme park next to a pack-in-the-punters tourist resort. Digging into the island's past has unearthed extraordinary relics, including Neolithic dwellings, Bronze Age and Phoenician tombs and exquisite Roman mosaics while, on the streets, keep your eyes peeled for Venetian walls, Byzantine castles and churches, Roman monasteries and Islamic mosques.

A Culinary Feast

Who can resist meze? Surely this is the only way to eat...tantalising the tastebuds with a feast of small dishes, ranging from creamy hummus to spicy grilled sausage and everything in between. Heavily influenced by Turkish, Greek and Middle Eastern cuisine, Cypriot food includes some culinary stars unique to the island, like haloumi (helimi) cheese. Kebabs are also in a league of their own: sizzling and succulent with spicy red pepper or onions and black pepper. Stuffed vine leaves, lamb casseroles, juicy baked moussaka, tropical fresh fruit juices and desserts – ah, the desserts – flavoured with almonds, rose water and pistachios, creamy rice puddings, and baklava. Of course, you won't be able to sample any of the above unless you're discerning: avoid restaurants that advertise 'international cuisine' with sun-bleached photos on the sidewalk.

22 TOP EXPERIENCES

Kyrenia's Old Harbour

1 With the romantic silhouette of the mountains providing the backdrop, the slow pace of modern life in Northern Cyprus doesn't get any more idyllic than by Kyrenia's U-shaped Old Harbour (p161). Its charming elevated buildings and well-kept storehouses once stockpiled tonnes of raw carob, then considered black gold by the locals. Now these edifices proffer trendy cafes and restaurants, where you can sit for hours with a Cypriot coffee or experience the nargileh (water pipes) as Turkish gulets (traditional wooden ships) bob sporadically, moored around the harbour's landing and castle.

Pafos Archaeological Site

2 One of the island's most mesmerising archaeological sites is located in the southerly resort of Pafos. A vast, sprawling site (take a hat in summer), the ancient city (p83) dates back to the late 4th century BC and what you see now is believed to be only a modest part of what remains to be excavated. Highlights include the intricate and colourful Roman floor mosaics at the heart of the original complex, first unearthed by a farmer ploughing his field in 1962.

Meze

3 Once sampled, never forgotten: meze is a delicious and sociable way to enjoy a wide variety of different foods and flavours. In general you should expect around 30 small dishes, starting with such familiar favourites as hummus, tzatziki, taramasalata and vegetables prepared with lashings of garlic, lemon and olive oil. Next to arrive is the wide range of traditional fish and meat dishes, like *calamari* (squid) and *sheftalia* (pork and lamb rissoles). It all adds up to a lot of food, so *siga, siga* (slowly, slowly) does it.

Hiking in the Troödos

4 These mountains offer an expanse of flora, fauna and geology across a range of pine forests, waterfalls, rocky crags and babbling brooks. The massif and summit of Mt Olympus, at an altitude of 1952m, provide spectacular views of the southern coastline and welcome respite from the summer heat, with cool, fresh air you can inhale until your airways sing. Ramblers, campers, flower spotters and birdwatchers alike will be absorbed by the ridges, peaks and valleys that make up the lushest and most diverse hiking and nature trails on the island (p65).

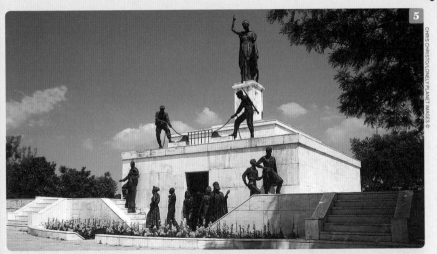

North Nicosia's Old City

5 Crossing the Green Line from Lefkosia into North Nicosia (p148), the Turkish north of the city, is an extraordinary experience. Extending like a tangled web from the Republic's smart Ledra St, old-fashioned shops selling faded jeans and frilly shirts are flanked by kebab kiosks, coffee shops and sweet stalls, their counters piled high with freshly made halva. Visit the extraordinary mosque, a tranquil hammam and the various museums, or just wander the streets, staying until the evening, when the minarets' crescent moons are silhouetted against a backdrop of twinkling stars.

Wine Villages Around Omodos

6 The far-reaching vineyards of the *krasohoria* (wine villages; p76) dominate Omodos' surrounding slopes. Navigating this region, where every house was once said to have its own wine-making tools, is an adventure that requires discipline and good use of the spittoon. Boutique wineries now number over 50 here, across six or seven traditional villages, with a vast array of wines and grapes for the connoisseur's choice. The most famous indigenous varieties derive from the mavro (dark-red grape) and xynisteri (white grape) vines, along with another 10 varieties.

Lara Beach

7 Akamas Heights is an area largely unburdened by development, and access to Lara Beach (p93) is via a rough road, backed by desert-like scrubland, tinged with dark ochre, and studded with gorse, bushy pines and seasonal wildflowers. This beach is widely considered to be the Republic's most spectacular and, thankfully, remains relatively untouched by tourism. Cupped by limestone rocks, the sand is soft and powdery and the sea is warm and calm. Tread carefully – this is prime turtle-hatching ground. It's a magical place at sunset.

Luxuriating at the Hammam Baths

8 The Omeriye Hammam Turkish baths (p134) stand in the centre of Lefkosia's Old City and offer a soothing respite from city strolling and sightseeing. Dating from the 16th century, the baths were tastefully renovated in 2004 as part of the Nicosia Master Plan project. All glossy marble, subtle scents and flickering candles, Omeriye offers a choice of massage, essential-oil, mudpack and hot-stone treatments. The baths have designated hours for men and women, as well as specified times for couples.

GRAND TOUR/CORBIS ©

Windsurfing

9 Imagine soaring across the surface of the Mediterranean, part surfing, part sailing, with nothing in front of you but the clear, bejewelled sea (p27). The eastern coast of the island, with its numerous soft, sandy beaches, inlets and coves, provides every kind of wind and wave condition a water-sports junkie could want. Once you've conquered wind-god Aeolus' lighter blows, you can upgrade to kitesurfing as well, and see about getting some real air!

Diving

10 Presenting perfectly warmed waters with outstanding visibility and a range of marine life, underwater caves, reefs and shoals, the island has picturesque diving habitats covered. Should you tire of this bounty, thanks to silted ruins, old shallow ports and bad navigating, the island offers multiple shipwrecks for you to explore (see p25). They're capped off by one of the world's top 10 wreck dives, the *Zenobia*, which foundered off the eastern coast of Larnaka Bay in 1980.

Cyprus Wine Museum

11 Taking a winery tour is becoming an increasingly attractive proposition for tourists here as Cypriot winemaking continues to improve and expand. A trip to the wine museum (p51) is a good way for novices to be introduced to the history, methods and, most importantly, the taste of leading local wines. The tour includes several options, mainly depending on how much tasting you want to do. There's also a short film and a museum that explains how the island's wine trade has developed over time. Cheers!

Shopping for Souvenirs

12 Fine lacework, embroidered silk, mosaics, pottery, leather ware, hubble-bubble pipes and decorative backgammon sets are definitely worth seeking out if you're on a souvenir-shopping mission. Stay away from the obvious tourist strips and head for the village shops, Lefkosia's backstreets or the government-sponsored Cyprus Handicrafts Centres (p142), which have fair prices, superb quality and, even better, workshops where you can watch certain products being made. The centres are located in the capital and several other major resort towns in the Republic.

11

ALX/IMAGEBROKER ©

12

ICONOTEC/IMAGEBROKER ©

Petra tou Romiou

13 Also known as Aphrodite's Rock & Beach (p60), this is possibly the most famous and mythical beach in Cyprus and it's certainly one of its most unusual and impressive. It's said that waves break over Aphrodite's Rock to form a pillar of foam with an almost human shape. For the best shot to impress the folks at home, come to the strategically positioned tourist pavilion at sunset. During the day, the sea here is delightfully cool and fresh and the beach is perfect for a picnic.

Neolithic Site of Choirokoitia

14 This Unesco World Heritage Site (p116) is one of the most important and best-preserved pre-historic settlements in the Mediterranean. It dates to around 7000 BC and offers an incredible insight into the lives and living conditions of some of the first Cypriots. Visitors can wander the ruins of the cylindrical flat-roofed huts, which sit on a protected hillside within the boundaries of an ancient wall. Using original methods, archaeologists have also helped construct five replica huts on site, which further enliven the experience.

Cypriot Folk Dancing

15 A tradition with roots in ancient religious ceremony, Cypriot folk dancing also draws on the customs of the early 19th century, when dance was vital to the celebration of marriages, holidays, harvesting and festivals. Smaller performances make up the whole, encompassing myriad meanings and including men and women, both separately and together. Initial dances symbolise harmony and gender roles, like feminine grace and humility or masculine agility and virility. Celebrations are traditionally capped off with the kalamatianos, where everyone joins in a circle to symbolise the joy of life.

Troödos Byzantine Churches

16 The proliferation of well-maintained 8th- to 12th-century churches nestling into the mountainside amaze with their vivid, timeless frescos by skilled painters. Oppression during Lusignan rule led Orthodox Cypriots, clergy and artisans to withdraw to the Troödos ranges, and these churches and chapels (p71) are the result of their dedication. Ten of them appear on Unesco's World Heritage list, truly crowning Cyprus as the 'island of the saints'.

St Hilarion Castle

17 Legend has it that this dreamy fortress (p169) was the inspiration for the spectacularly animated palace of the wicked queen in Walt Disney's *Snow White*. Its ruins now form a jagged outline across the rocky landscape, exuding the Gothic charm of the Lusignan court that once convened here during the summer. The castle's precipitous staircases and overrun gardens and paths form an arduous climb to its tower. From here, though, the spectacular views across the sea to the Anatolian coast only add to its magical quality.

Pide & Lahmacun

18 Half the fun is watching how they're made. The dough bases are kneaded over and over, topped with cheese and infused with garlic. In the case of *pide* their edges are folded. *Lahmacun*, the flatter version, is usually topped with tender little pieces of beef and seasoned with lemon juice for contrast. The Turkish 'pizza makers' then dexterously slide them into the coal ovens using 1.2m peels. Fifteen minutes later, out they come, piping hot and perfectly browned. Served on wooden tables with white tablecloths, they're a humble, mouth-watering delight.

Enjoying a Frappé

19 Don't miss the créme de la créme frappé experience during your stay in Cyprus, although be prepared to be hooked and then have to trawl through the shops for the lightest frappé maker to squeeze into your suitcase. Essentially a tall glass of iced coffee topped with several inches of froth, and drunk through a straw, it is a hallmark of Cypriot cafe life. You can vary the sweetness of your creamy beverage: ask for your frappé sweet (two tablespoons of coffee, four of sugar), medium (two tablespoons coffee, two of sugar) or straight (no sugar); they're all scrumptious.

Ancient City of Salamis

20 The once-proud beacon of Hellenic civilisation and culture on the island, Salamis (p188) was the most famous and grandiose of the ancient city kingdoms. Since antiquity, with its succession of kings dedicated to expanding the Athenian empire, the city saw great wealth and great suffering like no other. Today you can roam the expansive site taking in the ruins of grand statues, porticos, gymnasiums, pools, baths, courtyards, the agora and even what is left of the formerly prominent temple of Zeus.

Ancient Kourion

21 Founded in Neolithic times and gloriously perched on a hillside overlooking the sea, Ancient Kourion (p61) flourished under the Mycenaeans, Ptolemies, Romans and, later, the Christians. This is the most spectacular of the South's archaeological sites, including some well-preserved and fascinating mosaics, an early Christian basilica and a breathtaking amphitheatre that still hosts opera under the stars. After exploring the site, consider a dip in the sea at nearby Kourion Beach, where you can also find ruins of a port basilica dating from around the 6th century.

20

AUT/IMAGEBROKER ©

Vouni Donkey Sanctuary

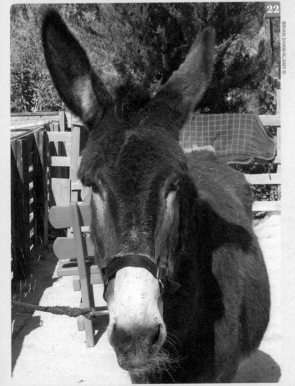

22
22 The donkey sanctuary (p60) equals a great feel-good family day out. Meet Narka, the sanctuary's oldest donkey, who was 50 years old last birthday (150 in donkey years), hear stories about how the donkeys ended up here and get the kids involved in grooming and walking them. There is also an audiovisual presentation about the history of donkeys in Cyprus and a program where you can 'adopt' a donkey for a nominal annual fee and receive regular newsletters back home.

need to know

Currency
» Republic of Cyprus: euro (€)

» Northern Cyprus: new Turkish lira (YTL)

Language
» Republic of Cyprus: Cypriot Greek, English

» Northern Cyprus: Turkish

When to Go

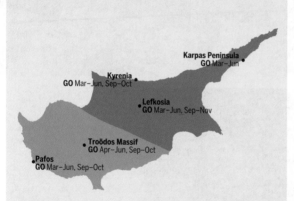

Karpas Peninsula
GO Mar–Jun

Kyrenia
GO Mar–Jun, Sep–Oct

Lefkosia
GO Mar–Jun, Sep–Nov

Troödos Massif
GO Apr–Jun, Sep–Oct

Pafos
GO Mar–Jun, Sep–Oct

Dry climate
Warm to hot summers, mild winters

High Season
(Jun–Aug, public holidays)

» Accommodation books out; prices increase up to 30%.

» Beach resorts are crowded, especially with families.

» Marked increase in local tourism.

» Temperatures can reach up to 40°C.

Shoulder Season (Mar–Jun & Sep–Oct)

» Ideal time to travel; pleasant weather and fewer crowds.

» Perfect for outdoor activities, particularly hiking and cycling in the Troödos.

» April and May are a dazzle of wildflowers inland.

Low Season
(Nov–Feb)

» Skiing in the Troödos.

» Can be wet and cool or pleasantly mild.

» Some hotels and restaurants in the main resorts are closed.

Your Daily Budget

Budget less than
€60

» Budget hotel room (with shared bathroom): €30–40

» Excellent markets and supermarkets for self-caterers

» Check out museums with free entrance, plus free tourist-office-organised walks

Midrange
€60–120

» Double room in midrange hotel: €60

» Three-course meal in decent restaurant: €25, plus wine

» Top museums, galleries and sights: average €6

Top End over
€120

» Top-end hotel room: €120

» Fine dining for lunch and dinner

» Car rental from €35 per day

Money

» ATMs widely available. Credit cards accepted in most hotels, restaurants and larger shops.

Visas

» Generally no restrictions for stays up to three months in the Republic and in Northern Cyprus.

Mobile Phones

» Pay-as-you-go mobiles with credit available from €25. Local SIM cards are easily found and can be used in European and Australian mobile phones.

Accommodation

» If you are looking for a place to stay, refer to the Accommodation chapter (p198).

Websites

» **Lonely Planet** (www.lonelyplanet.com/cyprus) Destination information, hotel bookings, traveller forum and more.

» **Cypnet** (www.cypnet.com) Information on history, accommodation, restaurants and more.

» **Cyprus Tourism Organisation** (www.visitcyprus.org.cy) Official website of the Republic's Cyprus Tourism Organisation (CTO), useful for general tourist information.

» **Go North Cyprus** (www.gonorthcyprus.com) Handy for finding flights, hotels and package holidays online.

Exchange Rates

Australia	A$1	€0.70	1.6YTL
Canada	C$1	€0.71	1.6YTL
Japan	¥100	€0.87	1.8YTL
New Zealand	NZ$1	€0.51	1.1YTL
UK	£1	€1.14	2.5YTL
US	US$1	€0.70	1.5YTL

For current exchange rates see www.xe.com.

Important Numbers

Country code (Republic of Cyprus)	☏357
Country code (Northern Cyprus)	☏90 392
International access code	☏00
Ambulance	☏199 or 112
Police	☏155

Arriving in Cyprus

» **Larnaka Airport** (p112)
Buses – up to seven daily from 6.20am to 9pm (5.45pm in winter)
Taxis – €15–20; around 10 minutes

» **Pafos Airport** (p92)
Buses – two daily from the airport at 7.30am and 6.30pm.
Taxis – €25; around 20 minutes

» **Ercan Airport**
Flights originating in Turkey only. Few facilities.

Driving in Cyprus

First, and most important: drive defensively. Cyprus has one of the highest accident rates in Europe, despite the overall good state of its roads. In the Republic of Cyprus motorways (*autopistas*) connect the airport to major resorts and towns, while secondary roads are normally well surfaced with a minimum of potholes. If you are exploring the more mountainous interior around the Troödos, consider a car of at least 1600cc horsepower for smooth handling of those steep, windy roads; they are generally among the island's most scenic as well. Aside from the coastal resorts and main cities, street parking is usually easy to find. If you're planning to rent a car in high season, book well in advance. Finally, don't forget that you drive on the LEFT in Cyprus...

what's new

For this new edition of Cyprus, our authors have hunted down the fresh, the revamped, the transformed, the hot and the happening. For up-to-the-minute reviews and recommendations, see lonelyplanet.com/cyprus

Lemesos Reborn

1 Economic crisis or not, Lemesos (p49) continues to embark on ambitious growth and development projects designed to enhance the city centre. Aside from the much-touted luxurious new marina due to splash onto the scene in 2013, the historic quarter has been pedestrianised and prettified, with the grande dame of the medieval castle quite rightly taking pride of place.

Cheap Travel

2 Bus fares are now government subsidised and fares have plummeted to €1 per ride, €2 per day, €10 per week and €30 for a month for unlimited journeys within the respective district (p143).

Mousio Theasis, Larnaka

3 This quirky Larnaka-based museum (p109) dedicated to owls is also a multi-faceted cultural space with live weekly concerts, art exhibitions and summer cinema nights.

Plateia Eleftherias, Lefkosia

4 This famous square (p132) flanking Lefkosia's historic Venetian walls will soon encompass walkways and a welcome green space right in the urban centre.

Bedesten, North Nicosia

5 Adjacent to the main mosque and reopened after years of closure, this former church (p151) has a fascinating history, an evocative interior and informative information. It's also used as a vibrant cultural centre.

Solar Car Challenge, Pafos

6 The challenge (p88) accelerated into Pafos' annual events in June 2010, with creatively constructed solar-powered vehicles racing each other. The event typically attracts local and international participants along with their ingenious inventions.

Museum of Natural History, Pomos

7 If you want to learn about Cypriot wildlife, including birds and reptiles, check out this small museum (p100) in pretty seaside Pomos, where the taxidermists have been very busy indeed.

Tricycle Power, Larnaka

8 Leave the pedalling and the patter of informative guides and hop on a tricycle (p110) for a choice of tours around town with themes that include local history and traditional handicrafts.

Pafos Marina, Potima

9 Lemesos is not the only place about to flaunt a brand-new marina. The 1000-berth Pafos Marina (p93) in Potima is scheduled to sail into the limelight in 2013 and be just as luxurious.

Larnaka Airport, Larnaka

10 Larnaka's brand-new airport (p112) cost a none-too-flighty €656 million and is large, modern and glossy with excellent amenities. An adjacent luxury hotel also opened here in 2012.

if you like...

Archaeology

Then you have definitely landed on the right island. The wealth of ancient sites in Cyprus – on both sides of the Green Line – makes it one of the most rewarding destinations for archaeology and history enthusiasts.

Ancient Salamis The island's most famous site, with impressive Roman monuments including a gymnasium, baths and a stunning ancient theatre (p188).

Pafos Archaeological Site These remains of an ancient 4th-century-BC city are mesmerising and include a collection of intricate and colourful mosaics at the heart of the original complex (p83).

Tombs of the Kings Explore these evocative and well-preserved underground tombs and chambers used by residents of the ancient city of Pafos (p85).

Ancient Kourion Founded in Neolithic times, Kourion's magnificent amphitheatre has seamless sea views and is still in use, hosting concerts under the stars (p61).

Beaches

Deciding on a beach depends on how you want your sand-between-the-toes day out: pebbly, smooth and sandy or rough and rocky. Even more crucial, do you like solitude and picnics or taverna terraces, sunbeds and easy access to ice creams?

Lara Beach Lara is the Republic's most spectacular beach, its bay cupped by limestone rocks and its sand golden, powdery and pristine, lapped by calm, warm waters. Tread carefully – this is prime turtle-hatching ground (p93).

Golden Beach (Nangomi Bay) The longest on the island, Golden Beach has miles of sand, curving dunes and feral donkeys grazing. The sunrise is spectacular and the swimming easy. Turtles hatch here too so, once again, watch out for the marked nests (p193).

Petra tou Romiou Also known as Aphrodite's Rock & Beach, this is Cyprus' most famous stretch of sand; waves breaking over the rock form a foam pillar with an almost human shape (p60).

Arts & Crafts

Cypriot culture is alive and well. Archaeology aside, the art world thrives with world-class contemporary-art museums, while more traditional craftwork includes superb embroidery, carved backgammon sets and intricate basketry. For living culture hit the festivals, in particular the Lemesos Carnival.

Cyprus Handicrafts Centre A reliable one-stop souvenir-shopping choice in Lefkosia. Good for Cypriot lacework, leather ware, mosaics and those ubiquitous backgammon boards (p142).

Chrysaliniotissa Crafts Centre Several art and crafts studios surround a central courtyard here. There's also a rare vegetarian restaurant... (p135).

Büyük Han Shop in a traditional Ottoman-style inn in North Nicosia with an enticing selection of traditional craft workshops housed in the former sleeping 'cells' (p149).

» Church in the ruins of Pafos Archaeological Site

Wine

Extremely loyal to the local drop, Cypriots invariably accompany their meals with Cypriot wine. The island's winemaking tradition goes back to antiquity and, although they're not on par with top French wines, it's well worth sampling a few choice vintages while you're here.

Republic wine routes Pick up the local Republic of Cyprus tourist information booklet outlining six wine routes you can follow, with information on winery visits and tastings along the way.

Lemesos Wine Festival This annual festival provides a suitably merry atmosphere for tasting the local tipple. A multitude of locally produced wines of every colour and vintage are available for tasting (p53).

St Hilarion winery At the time of research, there was just one winery in Northern Cyprus, but it's a good one: St Hilarion, which produces a decent cabernet shiraz red and rosé. Check out the website on www .northcypruswines.com.

Being Pampered

And who doesn't? Having your partner rub sun cream on your back is a start but not quite in the same indulgence league as a having a chocolate massage surrounded by flickering candles and wafts of incense.

Spa hotels Luxurious spa hotels, like the magnificent Ayii Anargyri Natural Healing Spa Resort, near Pafos, generally offer one-day packages. Check out www.cyprusspahotels.com for more choices.

Omeriye Hammam Keep an eye out for hammams (traditional Turkish baths) while you're travelling around Cyprus. The aesthetically restored and historic Omeriye, in Lefkosia, is one of the best, providing a welcome respite in luxurious surroundings from the city's clamour (p134).

Boat cruises There are some relaxing trips on offer in the main resorts. In Northern Cyprus, Kyrenia really pushes the boat out with barbecues at sunset and themed cruises. Check www.cyprusyacht charters.com if you want to seriously splash out on a private yacht with captain and crew.

Tantalising the Taste Buds

Cyprus is home to some delicious dishes that you may think you're familiar with – until you taste them. There are Greek, Turkish and Middle Eastern influences here, which are happily combined with an ingrained love of market-fresh ingredients.

Fruit juices Don't pass up an opportunity to try a freshly squeezed fruit juice at a juice bar here, especially the more tropical choices like papaya, mango or pineapple. Inexpensive *and* healthy.

Full kebabs Set the benchmark up a notch or two from your corner kebab house back home with this speciality of the North. Order a full kebab with grilled chunks of lambs' kidneys, baby chops and sausages; both succulent and spicy.

Pizza The Cypriot version, known as *pide,* is a lot more aromatic than you may be used to: a dough-based dish topped with spicy meat or fish with melted cheese and a squeeze of lemon. Delicious!

month by month

Top Events

1   **Lemesos Carnival**, February

2   **International Famagusta Art & Culture Festival**, July

3   **Bellapais Music Festival**, May

4   **Lemesos Wine Festival**, September

5   **Kyrenia Olive Festival**, October

January

Weather-wise January is generally mild, but the Troödos mountains can be snow-capped, so remember to pack your skis. Tourism is down and some resort-based restaurants and hotels are closed.

✦ Agia Napa Cultural Winter

Enjoy free concerts, recitals and dance performances every Thursday at 8pm at the Agia Napa Municipal Conference Hall (www.agia napa.org.cy).

February

The weather is mild, so good for cycling and hiking the trails (although it can be wet). It's also fiesta time with the high-octane annual carnival.

✦ Lemesos Carnival

Fancy-dress parades, festive floats and carafe loads of partying on the streets (p53).

March

Enjoy wildflowers, particularly orchids, with more than 32 endemic varieties. Birdwatching, hiking and the occasional sunbed on the sand make this a good month for a springtime break.

✦ Nicosia International Documentary Film Festival

View the cherry-picked international documentaries at this excellent festival; great for getting a perspective on Cypriot issues (www.filmfestival .com.cy).

April

The temperature can be perfect but you can expect crowds and a hike in flight and accommodation prices: it's school-holiday time during the Easter break.

✦ Easter Parades

Chocolate eggs take a back basket here during Easter week, when there are solemn parades with religious floats adorned with elaborate floral decorations, culminating in a spectacular firework finale.

May

A great month to visit with plenty of towel space on the sand, an average temperature of 26°C, and warmer evenings for dining alfresco.

✦ Bellapais Music Festival

Centred on Bellapais Abbey, this festival starts waving the baton on 21 May with concerts and recitals (www .bellapaisfestival.com).

June

The weather is a delight with an average of 11 hours of sunshine daily. Book accommodation well ahead: it's the start of the serious summer hols.

🏃 Classic Cars

Grab the tweed cap and don the shades – in early June the Aphrodite Classic Car Rally takes place, covering 300km across the island (www.fipa -cyprus.org.cy).

July

The mercury is rising, but the average temperature in the southern resorts is still a tolerable 32°C. This is the best month for music lovers, with several world-class festivals.

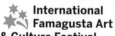

International Famagusta Art & Culture Festival

The North's biggest festival, with music, theatre and arts in Famagusta's Othello's Tower and town square, and at Ancient Salamis during the last week of the month (www.magusa.org/festival).

Paradise Jazz Festival

A fabulous location and atmosphere accompanied by excellent music make this weekend jazz festival a chart-busting hit in Pomos.

International Music Festival in Lemesos

World, classical, jazz and experimental music festival in the stunning Ancient Kourion amphitheatre.

August

This is the month you use your umbrella – for shade: the sun is at its hottest, although it still rarely sizzles above 35°C. The peak of the tourist season; expect crowded beaches and higher prices.

Countryside Documentary & Animated Film Festival

An excellent film festival in the picturesque village of Plataniskia, in the Lemesos district, with five days dedicated to animation, documentary film, workshops and open-air concerts (www.cyprusanimafest.org).

Mehmetcik Grape Festival

Wine and food feasting in this small village on the Karpas (Kırpaşa) Peninsula. Join in the 'King and Queen of Grape' contest and have a whirl at the folk dancing.

September

This is still a hot and hectic month. Escape the clamour of the coastal resorts by heading inland to the Troödos mountains for wine tasting, picnicking or gentle autumnal strolls.

Lemesos Wine Festival

Held inside the Municipal Gardens; locals and tourists alike celebrate this festival with plenty of sniffing, swirling, spitting – and tasting.

Pafos Aphrodite Festival

Opera performances are staged under the stars at the Pafos castle.

October

Enjoy autumn golds and reds in the leafy Troödos with temperatures hovering around 27°C; perfect for striding out...

Kyrenia Olive Festival

Held in Kyrenia and nearby Zeytinlik, this festival has folkloric dancing, shadow theatre and other eclectic performances. You can also taste olives and even help plant the trees.

Film Festival

Can't make Cannes? Then check out this Lefkosia film festival at the end of the month with its free screenings from international directors.

November

Expect a mix of weather, including clear summer days. It's a quiet month for annual festivities and many hotels and restaurants pull down their shutters for the winter break.

Calling All Runners

The annual Cyprus International 4-Day Challenge has four races, ranging from novice to marathon level, with routes set around the stunning Akamas Peninsula (www.cypruschallenge.com).

December

A month for family reunions, with Cypriots returning home to celebrate the festive season. The weather is changeable but, overall, mild with the occasional beach day, although the sea is very cold!

New Year's Eve

Fireworks and music into the night around Lefkosia's Plateia Eleftherias and in other towns around the island.

Life Outdoors

Best Wreck Dives

Zenobia, 17m to 43m below sea level (p120)
Vera K, 10m below sea level (p25)
Helicopter Wreck, 16m below sea level (p27)
M/Y Diana, 21m below sea level (p27)

Best Wind- & Kitesurfing Spots

Pissouri Bay, Lemesos (p60)
Protaras, Agia Napa district (p123)
Makenzy Beach (including Cape Kiti), Larnaka district (p113)

Best Hiking Zones

Aphrodite Trail and **Adonis Trail**, Akamas Peninsula (p95)
Mt Olympus, Platres and the **Troödos Massif** (p65)
Kyrenia Mountain Trail (p168)
Stavros tis Psokas forest reserve trails, Tylliria (p102)

Best Riding Connections

Kiniras Horse Riding Centre, Pafos (www.horseridingpaphos.com)
Drapia Horse Riding Farm, Tochni, Larnaka district (www.drapiahorseriding.com)
Moonshine Ranch (p124)

Best Paintball Zones

DNA Paintball, Geroskipou, Pafos
Lapatsa Paintball Ranch, Lefkosia
Souni Paintball Arena, Souni, Lemesos district

With consistently fantastic weather, a variety of terrain, and some of the warmest waters in the Mediterranean, Cyprus truly is a haven for outdoor enthusiasts. All over the island you'll find activities that suit every age and energy level.

Diving

With sea temperatures ranging gently between 16°C and 28°C, Cyprus draws flocks of tourists to dive its pristine waters, which offer ancient remains, reefs, sea shelves and even shipwrecks. Some of the best diving can be found along the Cape Greco Peninsula and Protaras bay.

Shipwrecks

Situated off the coast of Larnaka, where it sank in 1980, the *Zenobia* is rated as one of the world's top 10 diving wrecks. The 200m-long Swedish cargo ship, now home to giant tuna, barracuda, amberjack and eel, is available to fully qualified divers. For more on diving the *Zenobia* (and Cape Greco), see p120.

The *Vera K* is a fascinating wreck located 5km from Pafos harbour. A Turkish cargo vessel, it sank in the 1970s and has since been used as a romantic background for underwater photography; its submerged arches are particularly special. It's also an ideal dive for beginners.

NPR/IMAGEBROKER ©

ICONOTEC/ALAMY ©

» (above) Exploring the *Zenobia* wreck
» (left) Windsurfing in Lemesos (Limassol)

SNORKELLING

Extremely popular across the island, snorkelling is fun and safe and can be enjoyed by everyone. Some of the best areas are situated in the sheltered coves of eastern Cyprus, especially around Protaras (p123). Waters here are warm and shallow with excellent reefs and plenty of active marine life. You can also see a variety of shells, sea urchins and hermit crabs. Snorkelling equipment like masks and flippers can all be purchased easily and cheaply or hired across the island.

Officially called the Helicopter Wreck, this former British Army Air Corps helicopter is located 15 minutes by boat off Larnaka's shore. With excellent visibility to 25m, it attracts many divers and is a magnet for sea creatures such as octopus, jack and groper.

M/Y Diana, near Lemesos port, is a 15m Russian yacht that foundered in 1996. Now sitting upright on the seabed, it's frequently used for diver training and night dives. Its large squid and many fish make it popular with underwater photographers.

The *Pharses II* cargo ship sunk 800m from Lemesos port during a violent storm in 1980, when its cargo tilted. Open-decked and fully intact, it's heaving with marine life. Entry to the wreck is strictly supervised, as it's located in line with the main entrance to the port.

Sea Caves & Culture

Beautiful underwater caves such as the Big Country (23m below sea level), a multilevel cave site near Lemesos, and the Akrotiri Fish Reserve (9m below sea level), are ideal dive sites for the inexperienced but enthusiastic. You can expect to see groper and sea bass among shoals of fish.

Octopus Reef in Larnaka (10m below sea level) is another perfect spot for rookies, where you can witness the eight-legged in their natural habitat.

Serious divers should head to Mushroom Rocks (50m below sea level) near Larnaka; it offers mass fish sightings and canyons sprouting from the sea floor. Many of the rock formations are mushroom-shaped, hence the name.

Ancient history underwater is best found at the Amphorae Reef in Pafos (5m to 10m below sea level). An abundance of pottery and amphorae sit hauntingly on the sea bed, shadowed by a wreck beached on the reef.

Diving centres hiring full equipment and offering certified instruction are in Larnaka, Agia Napa, Protaras, Lemesos, Pafos, Coral Bay, Latsi, Kyrenia and Famagusta. And check out www.oceanssearch.com, to stay up to date with Cyprus' diving community.

Above the Water

Wind-, Kite- & Stand-Up Paddle Surfing

Thanks to the island's steady winds and mild weather, various forms of sea surfing have become some of the most popular and widespread of all water sports.

Windsurfing (the most popular) combines sailing and surfing techniques that can get you moving across the surface of the water with winds as gentle as 9 knots. The peak season runs from April to September; you can expect to pay about €70 a day for equipment and tutelage.

Want to take it up a notch? Kitesurfing or boarding, the younger cousin of windsurfing, is far more extreme. It involves getting pulled by a kite (or chute) while riding a smaller board across the water, sometimes getting over 10m high and doing spectacular flips and tricks. This could be you bouncing off the sea and gliding through the air with ease, as kitesurfing is considered one of the easiest (and safest-landing) extreme sports to learn. Once you've had the proper instruction you can even head out on organised kite safaris, available for beginners and advanced surfers. Travel instructors or guides take you out to experience the varying conditions that the island offers, including flat water, choppy and unadulterated waves. Go to www.windsurfingcyprus.com.

'Stand-up paddle' surfing (or SUP) has hit the island – or hopped from one island to another, as the sport originated in Hawaii. Popular with surfers, windsurfers and kite boarders, it's great fun and all you need is an SUP board, usually slightly wider than its more traditional cousins, and a paddle. People of any age and skill can participate,

MASSIMO PIGNATELLI/SIME/4CORNERS ©

BZD/DREAMSTIME.COM ©

» (above) The waters off Cape Greco
» (left) The scenic Troódos Massif

and it's a great sport for improving fitness and balance while getting a great core workout. It's also possible in any weather, so you don't need to worry about wind. The best location to try it is at Makenzy Beach, Larnaka, where you can hire everything you need, including an instructor.

Fishing

Outside of cooking and eating, the most popular activity on the island is the age-old Tao of fishing. The surrounding blue Mediterranean and a score of plentiful reservoirs make it the pastime of many who reside or visit.

The island's dams are available for angling all year round and you can expect to catch a range of fish including roach, silver bream, bass, zander, trout, catfish, tench, grey mullet, and mirror and koi carp. The quality is excellent, with usual weights anything from 1kg to 10kg.

Those who prefer the open sea won't be disappointed, with over 250 species of fish enjoying Cyprus' warm waters. Many fishing villages along the coastline hire out boats, and at the marinas of the resort towns you'll find plenty of anglers willing to take you on board or out on organised fishing excursions (kids welcome). These trips usually include a village lunch.

If you want to provide dinner for the whole village, you can charter a boat and go deep-sea fishing. Enjoy the thrill of hunting big game like bluefish, sea bass, barracuda, tuna, jack and amberjack. Wherever you're located in Cyprus, good fishing is never too far away. Go to www.fishingcy.com for the latest news.

Covering the Territory

Mountain Biking & Cycling

Tracks through terrain that once took pack mules and camel trains are now some of the best-recommended mountain-bike areas on the island. The Troödos Massif and its valleys take in both surfaced and unsurfaced roads. Long, sweeping and slowly increasing gradients lead up and down the mountains, providing riders with some of Cyprus' most scenic areas (p68). Further west, the Akamas Peninsula offers kilometres of pine-forest trails, rocky tracks and twisting roads worthy of a yellow jersey. Bikes with a good range of gears, puncture kits and maps are essential.

Mountain bikes can be hired in Troödos and Platres or you can go to www.mountainbikecyprus.com for information on training, skills courses, tours, repairs and servicing in the Akamas.

Cycling (or road biking) has become very popular in Cyprus, largely with Northern Europeans, with many international cycling teams training on the island. The relatively short distances and quieter roads that run parallel to the motorways make ideal, clean and scenic runs. These old roads connect Lefkosia with the major southern coastal towns of Larnaka, Lemesos and Pafos. Cyclists can enjoy the use of hard shoulders and well-paved roads throughout most of the island, and the weather, though hot on the tarmac, is conducive to training and fitness.

The Karpas Peninsula, in Northern Cyprus, offers some worthwhile traffic-free and flat rural roads along its cape. It has the added bonus of isolated beaches along its coastline, always available for a dip in summer. Got to www.cypruscycling.com for information on cycling clubs, races and events. Drink plenty of water and take it easy in the middle (hottest) part of the day. Aim for the spring and autumn months if cycling is your main activity while visiting the island.

Hiking

Cyprus has over 250km of well-marked trails with plenty of wilderness and unspoilt nature to discover. Its many paths span the ages and history of the island, leading to Byzantine churches, picturesque monasteries, Venetian bridges, Gothic arches, crumbling ancient ruins and waterfalls, to name just a few.

Hikers can fully immerse themselves in the expanses of the Akamas Peninsula and Troödos Massif in the South, or head north to the Kyrenia Range and Karpas Peninsula. Cape Greco on the eastern coast also offers wonderful trails, filled with spring flora, leading to its majestic sea caves.

Skiing

One of the most southerly ski resorts in Europe really comes alive over the winter months of early January to mid-March.

The spectacular 1952m peak of Mt Olympus, part of the Troödos Massif, is the

» (above) Mountain biking on the Akamas Peninsula
» (left) Hiking along the Aphrodite Trail

» (right) Exploring Cyprus by bike
» (below) Unspoilt mountain scenery near Buffavento Castle

perfect venue (p68), and its facilities have recently increased in quality and gained in popularity.

There are four ski runs close to Troödos, operated and maintained by the Cyprus Ski Club. On the north face of Mt Olympus you'll find two sweeping runs, one of 350m that's suitable for enthusiastic beginners, and a more advanced run of 500m. In the peaceful Sun Valley, on the southern side of the range, are two faster, shorter runs, each 150m long. One suits beginners and one is for intermediate-level skiers.

There's a ski shop on the southern side of the mountain with an ample supply of items for hire. The newest and best-quality equipment always goes first, though, so be sure to get in early or risk being left with slightly shabbier pieces. Check out www.cyprusski .com for ski-club information and snow updates.

Horse Riding

The island's diverse range of landscapes and scenery make it an exhilarating place for horseback riding. Cypriots' love and respect of the big animal have led to well-organised riding facilities and networks across the south of the island. The various clubs and centres offer everything from sunset rides, scenic treks, skills improvement and kids' lessons to even letting you be a cowboy (or cowgirl) for a day.

Rates usually run from €25 to €40 per hour. Trails often take in ruins and the island's ancient history, which makes riding an unforgettable way to get to know Cyprus, so pony up.

Paintball

Perhaps it's the Cypriot penchant for a good hunt, or maybe it's the adrenaline rush of split-second strategy while you avoid the onslaught of paintballs whizzing by your mask. Whatever it is, paintball, both as a serious team sport and as recreational shooting at friends and family members, has taken off across the island, and with good reason.

The exhilaration of teaming up and stalking your prey through a variety of fields (both human-made and natural) makes this sport exciting and just flat-out awesome fun.

The island now has a host of safe and well-equipped paintball-dedicated arenas, offering every kind of scenario you could want, for experienced gamers and novices alike. It's a great activity to do with a group of friends (both girls and guys). Some of the most enjoyable settings include capturing the opposing team's flag, last man standing, and night battles under lights.

It can hurt a little (think smack on the hand) if someone breaks the proximity rule, but with the fully protective suit and goggles, it's almost safer than tanning. All fitness levels can play, and no experience or special training is needed.

The paintballs or pellets themselves are easily fired from your light airgun. They're softly constructed, with brightly coloured water-based paint inside that splatters harmlessly on impact, except for showcasing you've been hit and are out of the game. So don't fear, jump right in, and be prepared to get addicted.

itineraries

Whether you've got six days or 60, these itineraries provide a starting point for the trip of a lifetime. Want more inspiration? Head online to lonelyplanet.com /thorntree to chat with other travellers.

Two Weeks
Top Spots in the Republic of Cyprus

Fly into **Larnaka** and kick back on the beach, then visit the Pierides Museum and explore the town. Day three, head for **Lefkosia**, to spend a couple of days getting to know the historical centre with its museums, shops and traditional restaurants. Reward yourself with a soothing massage at the hammam (Turkish baths). Day five, go to the mountainous **Troödos** to trek, cycle, stroll, explore the tavernas or admire the exquisite Byzantine churches.

Roll down to **Lemesos**, stopping off at Neolithic **Choirokoitia**. Spend a couple of nights enjoying the varied sights and superb restaurants of the island's second city. Next day, visit nearby **Ancient Kourion**. Make sure you take a dip at the mythic **Petra tou Romiou** (Aphrodite's Rock & Beach).

On day 11, head to **Pafos**, with its mosaics and mysterious Tombs of the Kings. Base yourself in traditional agrotourism accommodation on the **Akamas Peninsula**, near some of the loveliest stretches of sand in the South, such as **Lara Beach**. Fly home from Larnaka or Pafos.

10 Days
From Karpas to Akamas: Spanning the Peninsulas

From **Larnaka** airport head for the **Karpas (Kırpaşa) Peninsula**, somewhere that will linger in your memory for years to come. This 'tail end' of the island has positively the best beaches, deserted and clean, with soft, golden sand. Turtles hatch at **Golden Beach (Nangomi Bay)**, where there's an official turtle-hatching programme, and wild donkeys, once Cyprus' equivalent of a lorry and even a currency, roam the endless fields. Spend at least two days here, including visiting the eco village at **Büyükkonuk**, climbing **Kantara Castle** and bedding down at one of our recommended hotels.

Head back to the South via **Ancient Salamis**, the North's most impressive archaeological site. Dip into the sea at the adjacent beach before lunching at one of nearby **Famagusta's** atmospheric restaurants in the heart of the walled city, overlooking the Lala Mustafa Paşa mosque. Move on and stay overnight in **Larnaka**. Spend a day exploring the city, not forgetting the fascinating salt lake, a magnet for migrant birds, including flamingos. The next day, hightail it to **Lemesos** for some of the most sophisticated dining choices on the island. Stay overnight and make an early start heading inland to the **Troödos Massif** to work off all those calories with some scenic striding out. This region offers some of the island's best hiking opportunities, with four marked trails. After a night or two in bucolic surroundings, continue on the nature trail via the **Cedar Valley**, taking a soul-searching culture break at the **Kykkos Monastery** en route.

Stop at pretty **Fyti** for a meal at the central taverna; pick up some souvenir stitchery and stay at one of the nearby agrotourism accommodation options, surrounded by greenery and birdsong. Continue this point-to-point peninsula tour by stopping at traditional villages, like Simou, Drouseia and **Ineia**, from where you can drive westwards to the **Lara Beach**, the South's best beach and, like the Karpas beaches, also a turtle-hatching zone. You are now on the **Akamas Peninsula**, ideal for trekking, swimming and getting to know the region's rural life. The rocky Mediterranean landscape is home to the area's typical juniper bushes and low pines and, together with Lara, some wonderfully wild and windswept beaches.

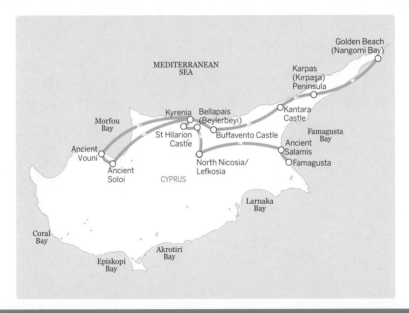

10 Days
A Journey Through Northern Cyprus

Providing you fly into Ercan airport, the first most obvious port of call will be **Famagusta**. And a suitably evocative first stop it is too, with its Venetian walls, looming and ruined Gothic buildings and Cyprus' best-preserved Lusignan monument, the magnificent Lala Mustafa Paşa mosque. Enjoy at least one meal at the Ginkgo Cafe & Restaurant, one of the best of the sprawling terrace restaurants here. From Famagusta, dig deeper into the past by heading north to **Ancient Salamis**, a spectacular ancient site which you'll need at least two hours to explore. After the exertion of absorbing all that ancient history, head to the adjacent beach and cool down with a dip in the sea.

Follow the highway to the capital, **North Nicosia**, and spend a day or two exploring its Old City. Take in highlights like the Büyük Han and Selimiye Mosque then, time permitting, enjoy a rejuvenating massage at the Büyük Hammam. Next, base yourself in pretty **Bellapais (Beylerbeyi)**, appreciating why Lawrence Durrell made this village his home for so many years. Admire the ruins of Bellapais Abbey, then visit nearby, equally dreamy **St Hilarion Castle**. Spend a day or two in picturesque **Kyrenia**, eating excellent seafood, exploring the dark caves of Kyrenia Castle and seeing the oldest shipwreck in Cyprus. Consider a boat cruise, a fishing trip or scuba-diving to the watery depths with one of the many seafaring companies operating from the harbour.

Next, head west to **Ancient Soloi** and **Ancient Vouni**. Return to Kyrenia and drive east, hiking up to **Buffavento Castle**, one of the three Lusignan castles perched atop the Kyrenia Range. Continue eastwards down the coast and take the winding road up to **Kantara Castle**, from where there are stunning views. Wind up your tour with a drive down to the most beautiful part of the island, the **Karpas (Kırpaşa) Peninsula**, ideal for lovers of wild landscapes. This area has the island's best beaches, such as **Golden Beach (Nangomi Bay)**, where turtles come to hatch. Fly home from Ercan airport, via the Turkish mainland.

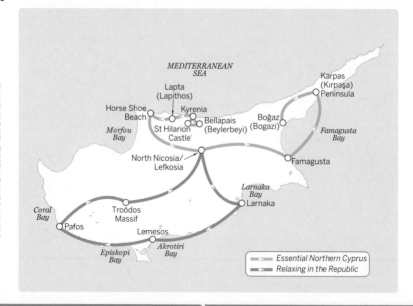

MEDITERRANEAN SEA

Lapta (Lapithos)
Horse Shoe Beach
Kyrenia
Morfou Bay
Bellapais (Beylerbeyi)
St Hilarion Castle
Boğaz (Bogazi)
Karpas (Kırpaşa) Peninsula
Famagusta Bay
North Nicosia/ Lefkosia
Famagusta
Larnaka Bay
Larnaka
Coral Bay
Troödos Massif
Lemesos
Pafos
Akrotiri Bay
Episkopi Bay

Essential Northern Cyprus
Relaxing in the Republic

One Week
Essential Northern Cyprus

Fly into Ercan and make your first stop **Kyrenia**; this is the Mediterranean as it used to be – a picturesque stone harbour, ending abruptly at a looming Byzantine castle. Splash out and stay at a waterfront hotel for two (or even three) nights. Before moving on, consider getting up close and personal with the natural beauty of the region by hiking part of the spectacular Kyrenia Mountain Trail. For the best overview of your surroundings, head for **Bellapais (Beylerbeyi)**, home of a lovely Augustinian monastery with endless views of the surrounding mountains. Stay overnight, then backtrack to Kyrenia, via **St Hilarion Castle**, and travel the northwest coast, stopping at pretty **Lapta (Lapithos)**, and windswept **Horse Shoe Beach** for some superb fresh seafood at the beachside restaurant here. History buffs can make an archaeological detour southwest to visit Ancient Vouni and Ancient Soloi; otherwise, hit the road to **North Nicosia**, spending a day here visiting the sites, before continuing to **Famagusta** and the captivating surrounds of the **Karpas (Kırpaşa) Peninsula**. Enjoy the beaches and stay overnight at the unspoilt fishing village of **Boğaz (Bogazi)** before returning to Ercan, via Ancient Salamis, for your flight home.

One Week
Relaxing in the Republic

Fly into **Pafos** and head north for a flop on the unspoilt sandy stretch of Kissonerga Bay. Next day, dig deep into the island's past at the extraordinary Pafos archaeological site and nearby Tombs of the Kings. After dark, dine alfresco and head for the latest hot spot for a drink and a dance. Day three, set off across country northeast for a day of wine tasting in the **Troödos** region and stay in tranquil agrotourism accommodation overnight. Then, leave all that nature behind and head for the fascinating capital, **Lefkosia**, for a day exploring the historic old city with its traditional cafes, intriguing museums and hubble-bubble whiff of the Middle East. Continue your journey by stopping in **Larnaka**, absorbing its workaday bustle and filling your hand baggage with crafts bought direct from the workshops in the atmospheric former Turkish district. Continue your circular tour with a visit to **Lemesos**, with its stylish and compact old town that's home to some of the island's finest restaurants. Take a hiccup west for a visit to the Cyprus Wine Museum before continuing on to **Pafos** and your flight back home.

Eat & Drink Like a Local

When to Go: Food Seasons

October–December Kick-start this serious foodie season with the olive harvest at the annual Kyrenia Olive Festival (p24), then look for freshly harvested wild mushrooms, artichokes, avocados and winter greens on your meze menu. Closer to Christmas, bakeries overflow with *kourabies* and *melomakarona* (almond and honey cakes), while strawberry guavas and pomegranates are, justifiably, the fruity favourites.

January–April A good season for warming *kleftiko* (oven-baked lamb), while mid-spring sees the emergence of wild fennel and asparagus as well as *koupepia* (meat and fish wrapped in young vine leaves).

July–September Figs, mangos, peaches, pears, plums: there's plenty of fresh fruit around, and in September the Lemesos Wine Festival (p24) is an appropriate toast to autumn.

One of the best things about Cyprus is its varied and flavoursome cuisine. Cypriots love their food and take it very seriously. Celebrations and family get-togethers are never without an army of little plates crowding the long tables. There are endless meze, fresh fish, flavoursome vegetables and fruit dripping with juice. It would be limiting to say that Cypriot food is only a combination of Greek and Turkish cuisine (although these are its pillars); Middle Eastern influences are also powerful here, the flavours of Syria and Lebanon hard to miss.

For an explanation of the price codes we used for the restaurants featured in this guide, see p247.

Where to Go: Regional Specialities

While there's not much difference between the regions *within* the Republic and Northern Cyprus, the overall Turkish and Greek influences of the North and the South mean plenty of variety.

Republic of Cyprus

Stay away from anywhere obviously geared towards tourists and make sure that a healthy percentage of the restaurant's customers are locals. For the best seafood and fish, head for the Akamas Peninsula.

» *dolmades:* stuffed vine leaves (other similarly stuffed veg, including tomatoes, onions, peppers, aubergines and marrows, are also popular).

» *guvech:* a combination of meat (traditionally beef or lamb), courgettes, aubergines, potatoes, garlic and onions.

» *koupepia:* young vine leaves rolled around meat and rice, generally baked in a tomato sauce.

» *louvia me lahana:* greens cooked with black-eyed beans and served with olive oil and fresh lemon juice; a fantastic dish that's a good choice for vegetarians.

» *melintzanes yiahni:* tasty bake of aubergines, garlic and fresh tomatoes.

» *mucendra:* a side dish that combines lentils with fried onions and rice.

» *ofto:* a simple meat and vegetable roast.

» *pilaf:* cracked wheat steamed with fried onions and chicken stock and served with plain yoghurt; particularly common at lunchtime, accompanied by meat and vegetables.

» *souvla:* large chunks of meat (usually lamb) cooked on long skewers over a charcoal barbecue.

» *spanakopita:* a combination of spinach, feta cheese and eggs, wrapped or layered in paper-thin filo pastry.

» *stifado:* a rich stew made with beef or rabbit and lots of onions and simmered in vinegar and wine.

» *tava:* a lamb and beef casserole cooked with tomatoes, onions, potatoes and cumin; named after the earthenware pots in which it's cooked.

» *trahana:* a mixture of cracked wheat and yoghurt; traditionally eaten for breakfast.

» *yemista:* courgettes stuffed with rice and meat.

Northern Cyprus

Again, in the more touristy resorts, like Kyrenia, be discerning with your restaurant choice; if you're opting for seafood, watch the cost: menus in the resorts frequently quote the price in grams.

» *adana kebab:* kebab laced with spicy red pepper.

» *adana köfte:* spicy, grilled ground veal or lamb patties with parsley, cumin, coriander and onions.

» *dolmades:* the Turkish variety is meatless, stuffed with rice, currants and pine nuts.

» *kebab:* meat (usually lamb, although there are also chicken and fish variations) wrapped in flat bread with salad; often accompanied by *ayran,* a cool, salty, refreshing yoghurt drink.

» *lahmacun:* a kind of pizza equivalent, with a crispy, thin base topped with fragrant minced lamb and fresh parsley.

SWEET DELIGHTS

Cypriot desserts carry in them the rich flavours of Turkey and the Middle East.

» *Baklava* is filo pastry layered with honey and nuts.

» *Galatopoureko* is sweet, sticky pastry filled with custard.

» *Irmik kurabiyesi* are nut-stuffed semolina pastries.

» *Kandaifi* (in Greek; *kadaif* in Turkish) are strands of sugary pastry wound into a roll.

» *Katméri* is a kind of crêpe filled with bananas, honey and cream.

» *Lokma* are doughnuts in syrup.

» *Mahalepi* (in Greek; *muhallebi* in Turkish) is an aromatic Middle Eastern rice pudding sprinkled with rosewater and pistachios.

» *Shammali* is yoghurt and semolina cake.

» *Tahinli* are tahina buns.

Despite these sweet delights, fruit is the most common Cypriot dessert in both parts of the island.

» *patlıcan:* meatball and aubergine kebab.

» *pide:* a dough base topped with aromatic meat or fish and cheese and baked in a wood-fired oven.

» *şiş köfte:* barbecued meat on a flat skewer.

» *urfa kebab:* kebab with plenty of onions and black pepper.

How to Eat & Drink Like a Local

When to Eat

Cypriots generally eat three meals daily; dinner is the main meal.

» **Breakfast** Eaten around 8am; normally a combination of olives, grilled or fresh haloumi (in Greek; helimi in Turkish), bread and tomatoes and, of course, coffee. It's a wonderful combination to start your day.

» **Lunch** Usually eaten at around 2pm or 3pm; meals don't usually last for more than an hour or so. Sunday lunch is the exception: on both sides of the island, this is when you will find entire families gathering, either at home or in restaurants, and staying for a good three to four hours, eating, drinking and chatting.

» **Dinner** Generally eaten late, from around 9pm, which is when restaurants start to seriously fill up. This is the meal where the meze is typically served. Always shared between at least two, it's usually more like 10, and dishes are passed around vociferously, so don't be shy to ask if you're dining with Cypriots and want to try something from the other end of the table.

Choosing Your Restaurant

The taverna is where Greek Cypriots go to eat whenever they don't eat at home, and there is one in every Cypriot town and village. A taverna can be a no-frills village eatery, or a more upmarket restaurant with a leaning towards the traditional. The *psistaria* specialises in souvlaki, while the *psarotaverna* mainly serves fish. The Greek word for restaurant is *estiatorio,* although every restaurant in Cyprus has an English 'restaurant' sign displayed and a menu in English.

The *kafeneio* is central to any self-respecting Greek Cypriot village's existence. Traditionally, *kafeneia* serve coffee and snacks of haloumi, tomatoes and olives, and they are frequented only by (older) men.

Meyhanes are Turkish taverns where you can eat meze, meat, fish and anything else, swilled down with plenty of *raki.* In the North, a *lokanta* is an informal restaurant and a *restoran* is a more upmarket version; again, English-language signs are everywhere. *Hazir yemek* ('ready food') restaurants specialise in dishes that are best eaten earlier in the day when they're fresh. You'll see signs for *kebapči* (kebab shops) and *oakbaş* (fireside kebab shops) where you can watch your kebab being prepared.

MAKE YOUR OWN MEZE

The following websites can help you with the ingredients and recipes necessary to create your own meze.

» www.eatgreektonight.com

» www.epicureantable.com/turkish .htm

» www.greekcuisine.com

» www.greekfood.about.com

» www.greek-recipes.com

» www.greekrecipes.gr

» www.ottomancuisine.com

» www.turkishfoodandrecipes.com

Don't miss the *pastanes* (patisseries) selling sugary treats, such as *kiru* (biscuits), cakes and sweet, sweet baklava. Beware of the difference between *pasta* (pastry) and *makarna* (noodles).

Quick Eats & Drinks

Traditional fast food on both sides of the island is the kebab or souvlaki, justifiably popular with locals. The meat is barbecued, stuffed into a pitta or rolled in a flat bread and accompanied by a large salad, garnished with lemon juice.

Don't miss out on the fabulous juice bars, as well. Mango, papaya, strawberry, guava: endless combinations are whizzed up on the spot and packed full of all those five-a-day fresh-fruit essentials, at a very reasonable price.

The Meze Match

Prepare yourself for an assault by food: a pleasant assault, a sampling of and gorging on around 30 dishes. The small plates may look unthreatening, but they keep on coming, promising a night of indigestion laced with wonderful tastebud-tantalising memories.

The word meze is short for *mezedes* or 'little delicacies', and is shared by the Greeks and the Turks equally. Meze is almost never served for one: two is the minimum, and three's never a crowd but the beginning of a beautiful feast. Try to dine in a larger group, since sharing meze is as integral to the experience of eating it as the variety of the dishes themselves. All the passing this and passing that and shouting across the table for more tahina or bread is a true bonding experience that Cypriots share many nights a week.

Think of eating meze as a boxing match, although an extremely enjoyable one that's not painful at all.

Round one: the waiter brings shiny olives, a salad and fresh bread, along with tahina, taramasalata, *talatouri* (tzatziki) and hummus for dipping. Pace yourself, go easy on the bread, suck on an olive or two, and crunch on a salad leaf.

Round two: the vegetables. Some are garnished with lemon, some are raw, a few are pickled or brought with haloumi. Sausages and Cyprus' own *lountza* (smoked loin of pork) follow. Again, eat the vegies, sample a coin of sausage and a strip of cheese, but remember, a bite of each will suffice because the biggies are still to come.

Round three: roll up your sleeves, the meat is here (this doesn't apply to vegetarians, who may be able to order vegetarian meze). A meat meze is a parade of lamb, chicken, beef, pork, souvlaki, *kleftiko*, *sheftalia* (spiced, grilled sausage), meatballs and smoked meat. If you're having fish meze, then expect everything from sea bass to red mullet, prawns and octopus, and, of course, *calamari* (squid).

By round four you should already be near knock-out time, and the waiter approaching with fresh fruit and pastries will start looking like an enemy of your gut. Assess the situation carefully, and, if possible, try some prickly pears – they're a real delicacy.

Be sure not to have any lunch before you go for a meze dinner. Pace yourself and eat slowly, or *siga siga,* as the Cypriots would say. Taste the dishes, smell them, feel their texture – there's a lot of food here and you don't want things to end before they've even started, with a full belly and no space for the mains. As with every good meal, a nice wine is recommended, so choose a bottle and *kali orexi – bon appétit!*

Dare to Try...

Don't worry: if you want to play it safe with familiar ingredients, you can in Cyprus. But if you fancy being just a tad bolder, consider the following. You could also try Greek or Turkish coffee served *sketos* (in Greek) or *şekersiz* (in Turkish), which is without sugar, so very bitter and strong.

» *mialle arnisha vrasta* (boiled lambs' brains) Halved and served with olive oil, chopped parsley, lemon juice and salt.

» *amelitita hirina vrasta* (boiled pork testicles) Cooked with onions and celery and served with a dressing of garlic, cloves, thyme, olive oil and lemon juice.

» *karalous keftedes* (fried snail balls) Minced and boiled with chopped onions, potatoes and eggs, then coated in flour and deep-fried.

» *karaolous me pnigouri* (snails with bulger wheat) Boiled snails which are then fried with chopped onions and tomatoes and served on a bed of bulger wheat.

» *kokorets* (offal wrapped in intestines grilled over charcoal) Lamb liver, lungs, heart, spleen, glands – you get the picture – chopped into medium-size pieces, wrapped in intestines and grilled over charcoal for approximately 1½ hours.

» *zalatina* (jellied pork) Ingredients include one small pig's head, two pig's trotters, eight oranges and a few red-hot peppers.

CYPRUS' TOP FIVE PLACES TO EAT

» Mattheos, Lefkosia (p137). Where the locals come for home-style Cypriot food, with a gutsy *kleftiko* (oven-baked lamb), *stifado* (beef or rabbit stew) and similar.

» Argo, Pafos (p89). Has all the charm of a village taverna with specialities such as moussaka and *kleftiko*.

» Kyrenia Tavern, Kyrenia (p165). Enjoy traditional Turkish Cypriot food in a pretty garden setting.

» Platanos, Pedoulas, Troödos Massif (p72). Sit under the plane tree enjoying dishes like *afelia* (slow-cooked pork with wine and herbs).

» Voreas, Oroklini, Larnaka (p110). Located in a hilltop village, this restaurant is famed for its superb meze.

Holiday Food

New Year's Day Every family will bake a special cake called a *vasilopitta*, with a hidden coin for good luck.

Epiphany (6 January) A religious holiday when *loukoumades* (doughnuts served with honey) are the most popular sweet of the day.

Carnival (February) Specialities include *bourekia* (pastries filled with mint and cheese) and sticky sweetmeats like *daktyla* and *kandaifi*. The last day of Carnival is called Green Monday (the first day of Lent), when locals pack a picnic and head for the countryside.

Lent Features *klokopitta*, made from red pumpkin, raisins and cracked wheat; *tahinopitta*, with sesame-seed paste; and *spanakopita*, a combination of spinach and egg wrapped in filo pastry.

Easter *Avgolemono* soup, made with eggs and lemons, is a traditional Easter dish, along with savoury cakes like *flaounes* (pastries made with cheese, eggs, spices and herbs). The main dish, however, is *souvla* (barbecued meat) cooked outside on a spit in the springtime sunshine.

Christmas In the relatively recent past, Cypriot families would slaughter a pig at this time of year and salt, smoke and cure the meat to last through the winter. These days this tradition has been downsized to families making and smoking their own *loukanika* (sausages made from lamb and pork). Brits will feel very at home with the traditional Cypriot Christmas cake, which is based on the English version with dried fruit and marzipan.

Travel with Children

Best Regions for Kids

Pafos & the West

Pafos overflows with watery activities: boat rides, fishing trips, snorkelling and a water park. Or there's the spine-tingling trip to the Tomb of the Kings.

Lemesos & the South Coast

The city beaches offer shallow waters and plenty of activities. Horse-riding, a donkey sanctuary and an expansive sports centre all keep adrenalin up.

Larnaka & the East

Older kids will really enjoy the underwater activities, plus sandy beaches, sea caves, a water park and a fascinating museum on, you guessed it, the sea.

Kyrenia & the North Coast

Fairy-tale castles, deserted beaches, nature strolls and the hulking Kyrenia shipwreck in the town's main museum should blow their little socks off.

Famagusta & the Karpas Peninsula

Famagusta's medieval walled city captures the imagination. On the peninsula, stride out on endless beaches, enjoy a cycling trip, visit an eco village and see turtles in the wild.

Cyprus for Kids

Cyprus is definitely a family-friendly destination. The culture revolves around the (extended) family and children are adored on both sides of the island. Stripped back to basics, beaches, castles, ancient sights and virtual year-round sunshine are pretty good raw ingredients. Add to this water sports, museums, parks, boat rides and loads of ice cream, and it becomes serious spoil-them-rotten time. Note that the majority of theme parks and man-made entertainment for children is in the Republic.

Always make a point of asking staff at tourist offices for a list of family activities, including traditional fiestas, plus suggestions on hotels that cater for kids.

For further general information about travelling with children, see Lonely Planet's *Travel with Children* or visit the websites www.travelwithyourkids.com, www.oddizzi .com and www.familytravelnetwork.com.

Children's Highlights

Wildlife

» **Vouni Donkey Sanctuary**, Vouni, Pafos. An excellent outing for children, with opportunities for them to help groom these rescued donkeys, plus watch an audio-visual educational presentation.

» **Pafos Bird Park**, Pafos. A superb park where children can enjoy plenty of feathered friends, as well as other animals, including giraffes and giant tortoises.

CHILD-FRIENDLY ICON

A child-friendly icon (🏠) has been added to sights and sleeping options in this book that seem to be particularly appropriate for children or go out of their way to welcome kids. This does not imply that other places in the book are not child-friendly. As most restaurants are child-friendly, but few make any special effort to, say, cater for infants, we have not used such icons in Eating reviews.

» **Mazotos Camel Park**, Mazotos, Larnaka. Ride on camels, then freshen up in the swimming pool.

» **Ostrich Wonderland Theme Park**, Lefkosia. Said to be the largest ostrich farm in Europe, with lots of educational info about these large, leggy birds.

Activities

» **Zet International Karting Circuit**, North Nicosia (www.zetkarting.com). An excellent go-kart circuit for kids of all ages.

» **African Queen**, Kyrenia (www.sailcyprus.com). Family boat rides with the option of water sports and swimming.

» **Amphora Diving**, Kyrenia (www.amphoradiving.com). Beginner scuba-diving courses for children aged eight years or older.

» **Santa Marina Retreat**, Lemesos. Offers many activities, including horse riding.

Parks & Theme Parks

» **Extreme Park**, Lefkosia (www.extremepark.com.cy). An enormous playground with indoor and outdoor spaces encompassing everything from trampolines to obstacle courses, mini bowling lanes to giant inflatable slides.

» **Parko Paliatso**, Agia Napa (www.parkopaliatsocy.com). A traditional funfair with plenty of head-spinning rides, candy floss and crowds of excited youngsters.

» **Eleouthkia Traditional & Botanical Park**, Anarita, Pafos (www.eleouthkia.com/cy). Botanical garden, plus traditional games, arts and crafts, music and cookery, a playground and a plunge pool.

Water Parks

» **Water World**, Agia Napa (www.waterworldwaterpark.com). It's big, it's splashy and it's been the recipient of a tidal wave of international awards.

» **Octopus Aqua Park**, Kyrenia. A great place to cool down on those dusty hot summer days with plenty of rides, plus a pool bar and restaurant.

» **Fasouri Watermania Waterpark**, Fasouri, Lemesos (www.fasouri-watermania.com). Large water park with landscaped gardens and options ranging from paddling pools for tots to kamikaze slides for teens – and everything in between.

Museums & History

» **Kyrenia Castle & Shipwreck Museum**, Kyrenia. The real-life shipwreck here dates back some 2300 years and is sure to fire up young imaginations – together with a circuit of the castle walls.

» **Ancient Salamis**, Famagusta. The advantage of this fascinating archaeological site is that, if it fails to thrill, you're still in front of a tempting sandy beach.

Fairy-tale Castles

» **St Hilarion Castle**, Northern Coast. Walt Disney apparently drew inspiration from this castle for his *Snow White;* it's that sort of place.

» **Buffavento Castle**, Northern Coast. Older kids should enjoy the hilly hike to this lofty castle, with its corners to explore and sensational views.

» **Kantara Castle**, Karpas Peninsula. Again a castle for older children, especially as there are some dangerous drops. But it also has a real magical appeal with turrets, towers and lookouts.

Beaches

Overall, beaches in the main resorts have shallow waters, bucket-and-spade worthy pebbles and sand, various activities (pedalos, boat rides, volleyball or similar), plus family-friendly restaurants and ice-cream vendors within tottering distance of the sand.

Planning

This is an easy-going, child-friendly destination with little advance planning necessary. Note that July and August can be very busy with tourists and hotels in the main tourist resorts are often block-booked by tour companies. Late spring is a good time to travel with young children as the weather is still warm enough for beach days, without being too hot, and attractions are not too crowded – until the Easter holidays, that is.

regions at a glance

This is an island where the word diversity takes on a whole new meaning. While the South has robustly developed its beachside towns and historical sites, the North's main attractions remain the quintessential Med-style resort of Kyrenia and the wild beaches north of Famagusta.

On both sides of the Green Line there are great opportunities for hiking, particularly in the Troödos Massif and on the northwest coast. For more gourmet pursuits, consider Lemesos with its sophisticated restaurants or enjoy the delicious simplicity of a North Nicosia kebab. History buffs have plenty to ponder as well, with some inspiring archaeological sites, particularly around Famagusta, Pafos and Lemesos. For a slice of rural life head to the interior where mountain villages around Lemesos and the Troödos Massif provide tranquil respite from the clamour of the coast, as well as superb agrotourism accommodation.

Lemesos & the South Coast

Restaurants ✓✓✓
History ✓✓
Villages ✓✓✓

Superb Dining
Lemesos is famed for its innovative and sophisticated dining, particularly in and around the historic centre; check out the expertly renovated Old Carob Mill.

Digging into the Past
Ancient Kourion was one of Cyprus' former four kingdoms and is one of several magnificent archaeological sites in this region. Plus there are museums, monasteries – and a castle.

Lovely Villages
Some of the region's prettiest traditional villages lie near Lemesos in the foothills of the Troödos and offer a tranquil respite from the crowds on the coast.

p48

Troödos Massif

Hiking ✓✓✓
Churches ✓✓✓
Activities ✓✓✓

Striding Out
There are a growing number of signposted nature trails here, ranging from a half-hour stroll to tumbling waterfalls, to climbing the dizzy heights to the peak of Mt Olympus.

Lavish Frescos
Many of the Byzantine churches located here have extraordinarily vivid frescos with a clarity of detail and colour that has remained largely unchanged for centuries.

Activities
Cycling, birdwatching, horse riding, picnicking or just touring the villages – this region's appeal lies in its lack of commercialism, compounded by an abundance of natural beauty.

p64

Pafos & the West

Beaches ✓✓✓
Sites ✓✓✓
Nature ✓✓

Best Beaches
You can still find unspoiled beaches here, especially on the Akamas Peninsula. Closer to Pafos, there are more pleasant stretches, many with adjacent tavernas, where you can grab a bite overlooking the surf.

Magnificent Mosaics
The Pafos Archaeological Site, with its superb mosaics, should be your first stop, but don't make it your only one; visit the other sites, including the Tombs of the Kings and the catacombs.

Wild Countryside
For a glimpse of untamed Cyprus, consider one of the Akamas Peninsula's treks, visit the villages in the western foothills or wonder at the towering trees in the bucolic Cedar Valley.

p82

Larnaka & the East

Activities ✓✓✓
Nightlife ✓
Beaches ✓✓

Water Sports & Swimming
One of the world's top-10 diving wrecks is just off the coast at Larnaka, plus there is plenty of scope for snorkelling, windsurfing, kite-boarding, boat rides and swimming (particularly around the sea caves).

Nightlife
Although it has tamed down a double measure, or more, since its wild heyday, Agia Napa still has the most concentrated (and spirited) nightlife on the island.

Beaches & Capes
The east of the island has some good beaches, particularly around Agia Napa, where you will find sweeps of golden sand instead of the more usual pebble and shingle.

p104

Lefkosia (Nicosia)

Museums ✓✓✓
Shopping ✓✓
Restaurants ✓✓

Museums & Galleries
The island's best, the Cyprus Museum, should not be missed. Folk art, local history, Ottoman memorabilia and world-class art can also be enjoyed in the culturally rich capital.

Superb Shopping
Shift your credit card into overdrive with the New City's extensive choice of classy shops. For more unusual finds, head for the idiosyncratic small shops in the backstreets of the Old City.

Capital Dining
This is a foodie city with restaurants ranging between spit-and-sawdust style tavernas serving just one main home-style dish, and ultra-sophisticated places with menus that never seem to end.

p125

North Nicosia (Lefkoşa)

Buildings ✓✓✓
Kebabs ✓✓✓
Souvenirs ✓✓

Architectural Gems
The city is studded with sometimes crumbling, sometimes renovated but always fascinating historical buildings. Highlights include the mosque, the Bedesten and the Büyük Han.

Best Fast Food
Forget the corner kebab house back home, this is the place to enjoy the succulent, spicy, unforgettable real thing. Head to Girne Caddesi for several good meaty choices.

Souvenirs
A former Ottoman inn, the Büyük Han is now home to two floors of exceptional arts and crafts shops selling items like embroidered silk, hand-painted cards, fruit preserves, ceramics and jewellery.

p148

Kyrenia (Girne) & the Northern Coast

Famagusta (Mağusa) & the Karpas (Kırpaşa) Peninsula

Castles ✓✓✓
Beaches ✓✓✓
Hiking ✓✓

Sites ✓✓✓
Nature ✓✓✓
Buildings ✓✓

Castles

Kyrenia's castle is home to the fascinating shipwreck museum, while nearby are the crowning glories of St Hilarion and Buffavento castles.

Beaches

For wild deserted beaches head for the coastal tip of Koruçam, while west of Kyrenia there are more tempting stretches of sand, including Çatalköy Beach, situated on a pretty protected bay.

Hiking

The Kyrenia Mountain Trail is a well-mapped out path that follows the entire crest of the Kyrenia range and is surrounded by deserted beaches and beautiful scenery.

p160

Archaeology

One of the island's prime and most extensive archaeological sites, Ancient Salamis, is located here and should not be missed.

Wild Nature

The Karpas Peninsula is wonderfully wild and isolated and where you can enjoy hiking, cycling and swimming surrounded by a uniquely beautiful landscape.

Architectural Legacy

Once seen, never forgotten, the historical centre of Famagusta is an extraordinary, albeit harrowing, landscape of Frankish and Venetian ruins, with gap-toothed frontages and looming facades.

p179

> Every listing is recommended by our authors, and their favourite places are listed first

> **Look out for these icons:**

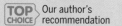 Our author's recommendation

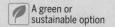 A green or sustainable option

 No payment required

LEMESOS & THE SOUTH COAST 48

LEMESOS (LIMASSOL) ... 49

AROUND LEMESOS 58

Pissouri Bay & Village 60

Petra tou Romiou (Aphrodite's Rock & Beach) 60

Ancient Amathous 61

Episkopi 61

Ancient Kourion 61

Sanctuary of Apollon Ylatis....................62

Kolossi Castle............62

Akrotiri Peninsula.........63

TROÖDOS MASSIF 64

Troödos 65

Platres 69

Around Platres 70

Marathasa Valley 71

Solea Valley..............76

Pitsylia 78

Agros 80

Around Pitsylia & Agros 80

PAFOS & THE WEST 82

PAFOS 83

AROUND PAFOS 92

Coral Bay................92

AKAMAS HEIGHTS 93

Dhrousia, Kritou Terra & Around 93

See the Index for a full list of destinations covered in this book.

On the Road

Kathikas............... 94

Pano Akourdalia & Kato
Akourdalia.............. 94

Avgas Gorge 94

AKAMAS PENINSULA..... 95

Polis 97

Baths of Aphrodite....... 99

TYLLIRIA...............100

Pomos 100

Pahyammos 101

Kokkina (Erenköy) 101

Kato Pyrgos............101

Psokas 102

Kampos 102

WESTERN TROÖDOS 103

Pano Panagia 103

Cedar Valley 103

**LARNAKA &
THE EAST.........104**

LARNAKA 105

AROUND LARNAKA 113

Kamares Aqueduct 113

Hala Sultan Tekke
(Tekkesi) 114

Larnaka Salt Lake 114

Kiti & Around 114

Stavrovouni Monastery...114

Choirokoitia.............116

Lefkara.................116

AGIA NAPA 117

AROUND AGIA NAPA 122

Palaces & Sea Caves.....122

Cape Greco 122

Paralimni 122

Deryneia................122

Dekelia Sovereign
Base Area...............123

The Kokkinohoria.......123

Pyla....................123

Protaras................123

Pernera.................124

**LEFKOSIA
(NICOSIA).........125**

LEFKOSIA (NICOSIA) 126

AROUND LEFKOSIA 144

Ancient Tamassos 144

Monastery of Agios
Irakleidios 145

Agios Mamas Church
at Agios Sozomenos 146

Maheras Monastery......146

Mesaoria Villages........147

**NORTH NICOSIA
(LEFKOŞA) 148**

**KYRENIA (GIRNE)
& THE NORTHERN
COAST 160**

KYRENIA (GIRNE) 161

AROUND KYRENIA &
THE RANGES 167

St Hilarion Castle.......169

Bellapais (Beylerbeyi)....170

Buffavento Castle 172

Panagia Absinthiotissa
Monastery.............172

Alevkaya Herbarium.....172

KYRENIA WEST 174

Lapta (Lapithos)........174

THE NORTHWEST....... 174

Koruçam (Kormakitis)
Peninsula...............175

Morfou (Güzelyurt) 176

Gemikonaği
(Karavostasi)...........176

Lefke (Lefka)...........176

Ancient Soloi...........177

Ancient Vouni 178

**FAMAGUSTA (MAĞUSA)
& THE KARPAS
(KIRPAŞA)
PENINSULA........179**

FAMAGUSTA (MAĞUSA).. 182

AROUND FAMAGUSTA ... 187

Ancient Salamis........188

Ancient Enkomi
(Alasia)................191

İskele (Trikomo) 191

Boğaz (Bogazi).........193

KARPAS (KIRPAŞA)
PENINSULA 193

Kantara Castle 194

Yenierenköy (Yiallousa)...195

Sipahi (Agia Triada).....195

Dipkarpaz
(Rizokarpaso) 196

Agios Filon &
Afendrika..............196

Monastery of Apostolos
Andreas 196

Zafer Burnu (Cape
Apostolos Andreas)......197

ACCOMMODATION ..198

Lemesos & the South Coast

Includes »

Lemesos (Limassol) 49
Around Lemesos 58
Pissouri Bay & Village 60
Petra tou Romiou
(Aphrodite's Rock &
Beach) 60
Ancient Amathous 61
Episkopi 61
Ancient Kourion 61
Sanctuary of Apollon
Ylatis................................62
Kolossi Castle.................62
Akrotiri Peninsula...........63

Best Places to Eat

» Dino Art Cafe (p53)
» Noodle House (p54)
» Syrian Arab Friendship Club (p54)
» Il Gusto (p63)

Best Places to Stay

» Chrielka (p200)
» Curium Palace (p200)
» Apokryfo (p201)
» Bunch of Grapes Inn (p201)

Why Go?

The physical heartland of the Republic, Lemesos and the south coast is one of Cyprus' most diverse regions, encompassing archaeological remains, beaches, a lively nightlife and the verdant proximity of the Troödos mountains.

The second-largest town in Cyprus, Lemesos is an increasingly sophisticated city, fast gaining a reputation for its exciting and innovative restaurants. The luxurious, long-awaited marina is due to open in 2013 and the historic centre has plenty of atmosphere, with pedestrian shopping streets that are only truly busy when the cruise ships disgorge their passengers.

Among the region's important archaeological sites, Ancient Kourion is the most impressive, perched on a bluff overlooking the azure waters of Episkopi Bay and significant for its role in the spread of Christianity throughout the island.

The area makes a great central base for visitors wishing to explore Cyprus away from the well-trodden tourist trail of Pafos and Agia Napa.

When to Go

Springtime is an ideal season here, when the Troödos mountains are blanketed with a dazzle of wildflowers and the sun can still be warm enough for beach days. The height of the holiday season is July and August, so beaches are crowded. Summer is also festival time, with lots going on, culminating in the International Music Festival and the Wine Festival, both taking place in Lemesos in September. The late-autumn and winter months are the wettest, with more changeable weather and varying temperatures, as well as snow on the highest Troödos peaks.

LEMESOS (LIMASSOL)

POP 228,780

Lemesos, still known to many as Limassol (Limasol in Turkish), is one of Cyprus' most underrated cities. Modelled on what seems to be an American seaside cityscape, the long stretch that is Lemesos has its busy main road running across the entire city, with cafes, shops, restaurants and general life going on to the north, while a long, popular beach is lapped by the Mediterranean to the south.

The historic old town, the former Turkish area, has undergone a tasteful revamp with an extensive pedestrian zone now surrounding the castle, studded with a wide range of eating and drinking choices, from traditional tavernas and coffee shops to sophisticated restaurants and designer-style bars. As part of the overall urban project (that includes the new marina), the waterfront here is similarly being enhanced with more green spaces and an expansive new promenade.

Lemesos has a gritty yet cosmopolitan individuality. Cyprus' international business centre, the city is also at the heart of one of the island's richest areas for exploration, with archaeological remains, beaches and the verdant mountains of the Troödos region all within easy reach.

History

In 1191 the crusader king, Richard the Lionheart, put Lemesos on the map when he defeated the then ruler of Cyprus, Isaak Komninos, and took Cyprus and Lemesos for himself.

The city prospered for more than 200 years with a succession of Knights Hospitaller and Templar as its rulers until earthquakes, marauding Genoese (1373) and Saracens (1426) reduced Lemesos' fortunes to virtually zero. The city was still creating a bad impression in the mid-20th century: Lawrence Durrell, writing in 1952 in *Bitter Lemons of Cyprus*, noted upon arrival in Lemesos that '...we berthed towards sunrise in a gloomy and featureless roadstead, before a town whose desolate silhouette suggested that of a tin-mining village in the Andes'.

Lemesos grew up quickly following the Turkish invasion of Cyprus in 1974, replacing Famagusta (Mağusa) as the nation's main port. It also needed to expand to keep up with the Republic's growing tourist boom. Originally comprising what is today known as the old town, radiating out from the historic fishing port, Lemesos has outgrown its original geographic limits to now encompass a sprawling tourist suburb. Signposted as the 'tourist centre', this is a riotous confusion of hotels, bars and restaurants, and you could be excused for forgetting that the sea is there at all.

Sights & Activities

Most of the main sights are within walking distance of the old port. The principal shopping artery is Agiou Andreou, one street back from the waterfront. Beach lovers will have to head west out of town, where several popular beach resorts are strung along the coast. Less commercialised, more attractive beaches are located further west, including Kourion, Melanda and Avdimou.

ROAD DISTANCES (KM)

	Vouni	Pissouri	Petra tou Romiou	Ancient Amathous
Pissouri	32			
Petra tou Romiou	37	8		
Ancient Amathous	43	36	51	
Governor's Beach	59	61	66	15

LEMESOS & THE SOUTH COAST LEMESOS (LIMASSOL)

DON'T MISS

MEDIEVAL MUSEUM

In order to fully appreciate the castle, don't miss its **Medieval Museum** (adult €3.40; ⊙9am-5pm Mon-Sat, 10am-1pm Sun). The building is an intriguing collection of vaults and air shafts, and the museum's interior is divided into a series of rooms and chambers on varying levels. All have thematic displays of Byzantine and medieval objects, including Ottoman pottery, gold religious objects, tombstones, suits of armour and weapons. In the Grand Hall, to the right and on a lower level as you enter, there are displays of black-and-white photos of Byzantine sites all over Cyprus. Climb up to a rooftop terrace for sweeping views over the city.

Lemesos & the South Coast Highlights

1 Enjoying an evening concert or play at the classical Roman theatre of **Ancient Kourion** (p61)

2 Swimming and picnicking at **Petra tou Romiou** (Aphrodite's Rock & Beach; p60), the legendary spot where the goddess Aphrodite emerged from the sea

3 Eating in one of Lemesos' old-town restaurants (p53)

4 Taking the family for a memorable day out at the Vouni **Donkey Sanctuary** (p60)

5 Checking out the **Cyprus Wine Museum** (p51) and learning how the island's favourite tipple is made

6 Relaxing in wonderfully peaceful surroundings at unspoilt **Avdimou Beach** (p58)

7 Crossing the drawbridge and being king of the castle at **Kolossi Castle** (p62), with its intriguing abandoned appeal

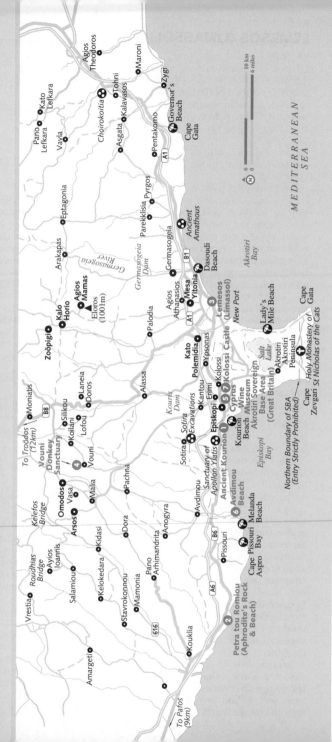

HAVE YOUR SAY

Found a fantastic restaurant that you're longing to share with the world? Disagree with our recommendations? Or just want to talk about your most recent trip?

Whatever your reason, head to lonelyplanet.com, where you can post a review, ask or answer a question on the Thorntree forum, comment on a blog, or share your photos and tips on Groups. Or you can simply spend time chatting with like-minded travellers. So go on, have your say.

FREE **Lemesos Medieval Castle**   CASTLE
(⊙9am-5pm Mon-Sat, 10am-1pm Sun; ⊛) The castle and its gardens, on the west side of the old town, are a shady haven in the summer heat. The surrounding area has been transformed into an attractive pedestrian zone.

The 14th-century structure, built over the remains of a Byzantine castle, has been used and plundered by many throughout Cyprus' turbulent history. The Venetians vandalised it, the Ottomans gave it a face-lift for military use and the British used it as a colonial prison. Apparently, Richard the Lionheart married Berengaria in the chapel of the original castle in 1191, where he also grandly crowned himself King of Cyprus and his wife Queen of England.

Although the castle doesn't appear a particularly grandiose structure, it's worth exploring. The gardens hide an old **olive oil press** that dates from the 7th to the 9th centuries.

Archaeological Museum   MUSEUM
(cnr Vyronos & Kaningos; admission €1.70; ⊙9am-5pm Mon-Sat, 10am-1pm Sun) Includes an extensive collection of pottery, and a selection of items dating from Neolithic and Chalcolithic times (primarily shards and implements for domestic use), through to Mycenaean pottery. A multitude of terracotta figures on show are thought to be the remains of votive offerings. There is a display of classical pottery, jewellery and oil lamps, as well as curiously modern-looking glass bottles and vials. Although it pales in comparison to Lefkosia's Cyprus Museum, it's well worth a browse.

Cyprus Wine Museum   MUSEUM
(www.cypruswinemuseum.com; Pafos 42, Erimi; admission €4-7; ⊙9am-5pm) Just west of town, off the Lemesos–Pafos highway, the Cyprus Wine Museum offers an insight into the history of winemaking on Cyprus. It sits in a tastefully restored stone house and offers three options for visitors; the difference in price essentially relates to how much wine tasting you fancy. The most expensive option includes four wines, accompanied by haloumi cheese. Museum exhibits include medieval drinking vessels and jars, as well as explanatory information on all aspects of winemaking. There's also a short audio-visual presentation.

FREE **Grand Mosque**   MOSQUE
(Kebir Camii; Genethliou Mitella) At the heart of the old Turkish quarter, the Grand Mosque is surrounded by palms almost as tall as its minaret. It is used by the remaining Turkish Cypriot population and Muslims from the Middle East who live in Lemesos. As with any mosque, visitors are requested to dress conservatively, leave shoes by the door and avoid visiting at prayer times. There are no fixed opening hours; if the gate is open, step within and take a look.

Hammam   STEAM BATHS
(⊡9947 4251; Loutron 3; steam bath & sauna €15; ⊙2-10pm Mon-Sat) This tiny hammam is located near the mosque. It isn't really a tourist site, since many count on privacy when going in for a steam bath. If you do decide to indulge, don't come here expecting anything too luxurious; it's a very basic place where people go to relax. Keep in mind that all sessions are mixed. Also on offer are full-body massages, shiatsu, Swedish massage, Indian head massage and anti-stress massages from €20.

Lanitis Art Foundation   EXHIBITION CENTRE
(www.lanitisfoundation.org; Old Carob Mill; ⊙10am-6pm Mon-Sat) Interesting and edgy temporary exhibitions. Check the website for what's currently on show.

☞ Tours

There are three walking tours in Lemesos, all organised by the CTO. They're free, but it's wise to book in the high season.

'A Stroll in Neapolis, Nemesos, Limassol', at 10am on Monday, takes you around Lemesos' historic centre, its monuments, markets and main sights.

Lemesos (Limassol)

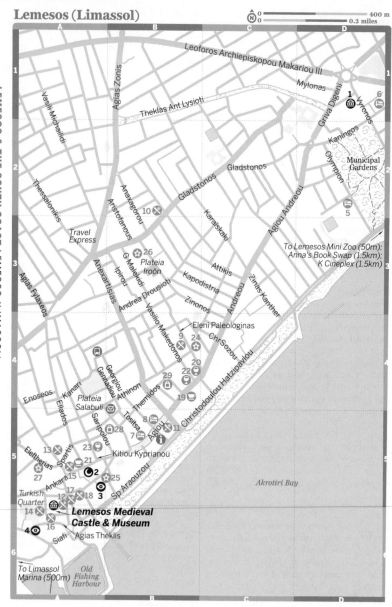

At 10am every Wednesday, from October to April, there are alternating tours: the first, 'Germasogeia: A Village Blessed by Water', goes to Germasogeia village, where the water theme is covered by a visit to the village dam. You also get to see the architecture and street life of the village itself. The second is the 'Discover the Natural Environment of Germasogeia', which is a walk in the hills (some fitness required)

Lemesos (Limassol)

◉ Top Sights
Lemesos Medieval Castle &
  Museum A6

◉ Sights
1 Archaeological Museum D1
2 Grand Mosque A5
3 Hammam A5
  Lanitis Art Foundation .... (see 16)
4 Natural Sea Sponge Exhibition
  Centre A6

◎ Sleeping
5 Chrielka D2
6 Curium Palace D1
7 Luxor Guest House B5
8 Metropole B5

◎ Eating
9 127 Cafe B4
10 Antonaros Tavern B2
  Artima Bistro .... (see 16)
11 Bono B5
12 Castello A6
13 Dino Art Cafe A5

14 Karatello A6
15 Noodle House A5
16 Old Carob Mill A6
17 Ousia A5
18 Rizitiko Tavern A5

◎ Drinking
  127 Cafe .... (see 9)
19 Adiexodo B4
  Draught .... (see 16)
20 Moyo B4
21 Pi A5
22 Rogmes Piano Bar B4
23 Sousami A5
  Stretto Cafe .... (see 16)

◎ Entertainment
24 7-Seas B4
25 Alaloum B5
26 Rialto Theatre B3
27 Sesto Senso A5

◎ Shopping
28 Pana's Patchwork B5
29 Violet's Second Hand Shop B4

following a nature trail laid out by the forestry department.

✦ Festivals & Events

Lemesos Carnival CARNIVAL
(www.limassolmunicipal.com.cy/carnival) Lemesos is the only town in Cyprus with a full-blown carnival atmosphere, enjoyed particularly by children. The 11-day carnival, held 50 days before Easter, starts with the 'King of the Carnival' entering town, escorted by a motley parade. There's also a children's carnival parade; the festivities close with a fancy-dress extravaganza.

Lemesos Wine Festival WINE FESTIVAL
(www.limassolmunicipal.com.cy/wine) Held in the Municipal Gardens annually from 30 Augustto 11 September, this festival provides a chance to sample a wide range of local wines. As you might predict, the festival is extremely popular with young, fun-seeking tourists, here for the Cypriot food, traditional music and dancing, and did we mention the wine?

✖ Eating

Eating in Lemesos equals a culinary combo of variety, quality and modern cuisine, particularly in the old town (most of the tourist area's eating options are fairly forgettable). The aesthetically restored Old Carob Mill, next to the castle, is home to several restaurants and bars sharing a cool, sophisticated vibe. Rumbling tummies should also head for the pedestrian Plateia Salabuli next to the recently refurbished municipal market, which is surrounded by inexpensive kebab houses, traditional coffee shops and similar.

 Dino Art Cafe MEDITERRANEAN €€
(☏2576 2030; Irinis 62-66; mains from €8; ☎) Dino's has a great reputation and a loyal local following thanks to its smart decor, friendly owner (Dino Kosti) and great food. The massive salads are excellent and include unusual choices like duck and orange. There's a good pasta choice with some zesty sauces, and some delicate sushi, too. Dino's also exhibits photography and other works by Cypriot artists. Reservations recommended.

Noodle House
ASIAN FUSION €€

(www.thenoodlehouse.com; Agiou Andreou 3; mains €10; 🔌) A welcome addition to Lemesos' eating scene, this is the first branch of the popular Gulf Arab chain to open in Europe. It combines an open-plan kitchen and stylish decor with a menu of dishes that includes Singaporean and Thai favourites like Tom Yam soup, Thai green curry, Asian sea bass and roasted duck, Singapore style. If you like spicy – ask; they tend to tame down the heat for the Cypriot palate. Sunday lunch is kids' time, with face-painting and balloons.

Syrian Arab Friendship Club
CYPRIOT €€

(SAFC; Iliados 3; meze €15) Sister of the Lefkosia restaurant and just as good, the SAFC is a delight to all lovers of Arab cuisine, rich with chickpeas, beans, herbs, spices, grilled and marinated meats, and sweet desserts. Try the superb meze. A nargileh (Middle Eastern water pipe) after eating is an additional puff-worthy treat. To find the Syrian Club (as it's known by locals), head east of the centre via the coast road for around 3.5km. The restaurant is located across from the Apollonia Beach Hotel.

127 Cafe
MEDITERRANEAN €€

(Eleni Paleologinas 5; salads & sandwiches from €7.50) This place has a late-night lounge atmosphere with its edgy artwork, black sofas, high ceilings and elegant terrace out the back. There's a choice of 10 innovative salads, including the suggestively named 'Orgasmic', with parmesan cheese, avocados, mushrooms and spicy tomato sauce, as well as hot dishes – and cool cocktails.

Bono
INTERNATIONAL €€

(Anexartisias 3; breakfasts from €4.50, salads from €8; ⊘closed Sun) Bono's owner spent several years in the US, where he learned how to whip up the best cheesecake in town. The breakfasts, burgers, quesadillas, salads and homemade soups are similarly a couple of notches above the norm. There's live music on Friday night and 50 choices of beer.

Ousia
MEDITERRANEAN €€

(Irinis 30-32; mains from €8) Reopened in May 2011 after a necessary extension, this place ticks all the boxes, with a fashionable arty decor and a menu that includes brunch dishes, sandwiches, classy burgers, and mains like octopus carpaccio, teriyaki chicken and souvlaki in a barbecue sauce. Mains are typically served with wild rice and roasted vegetables.

Castello
INTERNATIONAL €€

(Irinis 22; salads €8.50-12.50) Don't be put off by the touristy look of this place: it has some superb dishes, especially if you're after a greenery fix, with a choice of some 25 salads, including such delectable ingredients as papaya, hazelnuts, salmon, sun-dried tomatoes and smoked turkey.

Artima Bistro
FUSION €€

(Old Carob Mill; mains €12; ☎) This is where Queen Sofia of Spain chose to eat during an official trip to Cyprus in March 2011 (to open the Miró exhibition). The cuisine includes meat, fish and pasta-based dishes, as well as sushi choices, including innovative ingredients like mango and roasted sesame seeds.

Trata Fish Tavern
SEAFOOD €€€

(📞2558 6600; Ioanni Tompazi 4; seafood meze €20) This is arguably one of Lemesos' best fish restaurants, particularly famed for its seafood meze. Despite the plain-Jane decor and unassuming atmosphere, the place attracts shoals of locals, particularly at weekends, when booking is essential. It's just behind the prominently located Debenhams department store, around 400m east of the Municipal Gardens.

Rizitiko Tavern
CYPRIOT €€

(Tzamiou 4-8; mains from €8; ⊘dinner) Tucked away by the mosque on a newly pedestrianised street, this is a reliably good, low-key establishment with tables that spill out onto the cobbles at night. The *afelia* (pork cooked in red wine and coriander) and *kleftiko* (oven-baked lamb) are homemade quality – or better.

Karatello
CYPRIOT €€

(Vasilissis 1; mains from €8.50; ⊘dinner) The lofty ceiling of this former historic mill, coupled with a massive interior space, equals a stylish, modern canvas for Karatello's innovative, arty cuisine. Dishes that stand out are rabbit in yoghurt and lemon sauce, seasonal greens baked with feta cheese, and a delicious and neatly presented *kleftiko*.

Antonaros Tavern
MEZE €€

(Attikis 1; meze €14-16; ⊘dinner Mon-Sat) Come here for a no-frills, genuinely Cypriot, local-style evening meal. Choose between the grill meze or full meze with a wide range of dishes such as snails and mussels, as well as fish. The handwritten notes on the wall are Greek philosophical sayings.

🍷 Drinking

Most places in Lemesos are quiet until at least 10pm. Bars on the seafront strip are predictably tourist-geared with bitter on tap accompanied by football on the big screen. For a more authentic Cypriot experience, head for bars in and around the Old Carob Mill and the historic centre. The city also has a handful of contemporary, upbeat cafes, the sorts of places where you can surf the net (along with the froth on a frappé) while checking out the effortlessly stylish locals.

TOP CHOICE **Stretto Cafe**   CAFE

(Vasilissis; 🛜) Cafes in Lemesos don't come any more stylish than this. Part of the Old Carob Mill, it has tall ceilings, comfy sofas and beautiful people. Fear not: the atmosphere is still good and relaxed. You can plump out your visit with some fashionable eats like carob-crusted chicken, and chocolate ravioli with ice cream.

Draught   BAR

(Vasilissis) Draught is a pleasant place to have a drink, with a lively buzz, particularly with ace bartender Krisztian Gyokeres, who represented the island in the world bartending competition in 2010. It serves a full range of lagers, ales and wheat beers, as well as (of course) flamboyantly shaken cocktails and light munchies, like fajitas. There's a resident DJ at weekends.

Moyo   BAR

(Agiou Andreou 244; ⏰11.30am-2am) Think dark burgundy and charcoal-washed walls, intimate corners, music videos on giant screens, comfy seats, antiques and a delightful back garden with fabric gazebos and a DJ spinning the late-night discs. Light eats include vegie burgers and kebabs.

CHILDREN'S CYPRUS: LEMESOS

If your children are growing weary of ice-cream cones and sandcastles, and point blank refuse to go anywhere near another pile of archaeological excavations, never fear; there is a good selection of kiddie-geared entertainment here, although watch those admission prices, as they can quickly tot up.

Fasouri Watermania   WATER PARK

(☎2571 4235; www.fasouri-watermania.com; adult/child €29/€16; ⏰10am-6pm; 👶) Sitting in the Fasouri area, a 15-minute drive out of Lemesos, this place has all the usual watery options including a kamikaze slide, the 'big orange wet bubble', 'lazy river', a wave pool, and both children's and adult pools. There are also sunbeds and parasols for run-off-their-feet parents.

If you're driving, the park is off the Lemesos–Pafos highway, 5km northwest of town. If you don't have your own wheels, there's a shuttle to the park; phone for pick-up times and location.

Natural Sea Sponge Exhibition Centre   MUSEUM

(Agias Theklis; ⏰9am-7pm Mon-Fri, to 3pm Sat; 👶) It may not be the most obvious exhibition for the family, but sponges do have a life of their own and there's a whole cartoon duly dedicated to a talking sponge, so the kids may well connect with that. The exhibition goes through the process of sea-sponge harvesting, and how the living creatures become the soft things we use in our baths. Naturally enough, you can purchase sponges here, too.

Santa Marina Retreat   OUTDOOR ACTIVITIES

(☎9954 5454; www.santamarinaretreat.com; Pareklisia village; admission €3; ⏰9am-7pm Tue-Sun; 👶) Offers horse riding, archery, quad biking, mountain biking, wall climbing, nature trails (via battery-run buggies) and a lot more besides – including golf for the grown-ups.

Lemesos Mini Zoo   ZOO

(Municipal Gardens; admission €1; ⏰9am-noon & 3-7pm May-Sep, 9am-6.30pm Oct-Apr; 👶) Also worth considering for children is this recently renovated, albeit modest, zoo, although it has not much more than an aviary, ostriches and some cheeky cheetahs.

Sousami BAR
(Kitiou Kyprianou 8) There's a youthful, boho vibe at this simple bar-cafe, with its secluded garden and tables set under the pomegranate trees. Enjoy the weekend DJ, who ups the laid-back tempo a notch or two.

Rogmes Piano Bar BAR
(Agiou Andreou 197) A highly praised bouzouki bar touting a mad, wonderful tempo on weekend nights, when the musicians stay and play as loud and as late as the crowd wants.

127 Cafe BAR
(Eleni Paleologinas 5) Come for the food or to drink colour-coordinated cocktails, lounging in the pretty back garden.

Adiexodo CAFE
(Salaminos 8) Grab a table under the ancient ficus tree and challenge one of the elderly regulars to a backgammon game.

Pi CAFE
(Kitiou Kyprianou 27; snacks €5) A relaxed, gay-friendly cafe with a lovely garden, light meals, 10-plus choice of beer, good (mainly Italian) wines and elaborate cocktails.

☆ Entertainment

Tepee Rock Bar NIGHTCLUB
(www.tepeerock.com; Ampelakion) Chomp on Mexican burritos while enjoying live rock bands at this popular restaurant-bar-nightclub with its cowboy-and-Indian-themed decor, exposed-brick walls and great foot-stomping atmosphere. The same owners run the popular Club 11 nightclub next door. Both clubs are located in the heart of the tourist centre, around 3km east of the historic quarter on the coastal road. Check the website for a map.

7-Seas NIGHTCLUB
(www.7seaslive.com; Agiou Andreou 223, Columbia Plaza) Absolutely no beachwear is allowed at this sophisticated new live-music venue, which attracts a well-heeled clientele and is located in a state-of-the-art multifunction centre. There are regular Latin music nights, as well as some cutting-edge new acts.

Guaba Beach Bar NIGHTCLUB
(Agia Varvara Beach) This popular bar has seats right on the beach and is located 5km east of the historic centre next to the Aquarius Hotel (see p201). There are parties, as well as relaxed evenings, with DJs who play anything from reggae to electro, depending on the night and their fancy.

Alaloum NIGHTCLUB
(Loutron 1) Situated near the hammam in a renovated old mansion, this is the town's longest-standing and favourite gay club. Gay, lesbian, bi: everyone parties hard and stays up very, very late.

For more gay choices, check the www .cyprusgaybars.com website.

Sesto Senso NIGHTCLUB
(Eleftherias 45) One of the most fashionable places in town, with stunning decor, scintillating fashions – and extremely expensive drinks.

A MARINA LIKE NO OTHER

Lemesos' decrepit former fishing harbour is undergoing a €300-million facelift. The competition for the new **Limassol Marina** was won in 2007 by Lefkosia-based architects Dickon Irwin and Margarita Kritioti from Irwin & Kritioti Architects. The company's innovative and lush idea for Lemesos' marina sees the harbour's shape mimic the sea with a series of steel, wavelike shapes. But aside from its impressive aesthetics, the marina is meant to bring life back to the city centre year-round so that, when the high-tourist season wanes in the early winter months, the harbour will turn into a vibrant conference and lecture centre.

All this is being completed in stages, with the latest completion date set for 2013 – the project has been fraught with delays. The marina is expected to be the most luxurious place on the island and is so far the only Cypriot project of its size. It will hold 1000 yachts, and there'll be living spaces, shops, bars, restaurants, cafes, wi-fi access and a number of other super-exclusive areas. A park will encircle the marina and the buildings inside the new space will all cohere with traditional Lemesos architecture.

Check out the flashy website www.limassolmarina.com, and make sure you bring your yacht or, at the very least, your deck shoes.

LIFE'S NO CABARET

We don't recommend visiting any of the city's 'cabarets', but if you do decide to go, keep in mind that many of the women working in the clubs may be there under duress. Also bear in mind stories of customers being charged several hundred pounds for a couple of beers at the end of the night – and woe betide those who refuse to pay.

Rialto Theatre THEATRE
(☎2534 3900; www.rialto.com.cy; Andhréa Dhroushióti 19) Exquisitely restored to its former art-deco glory, the Rialto is the main venue in town for theatre, concerts and film festivals.

K Cineplex CINEMA
(www.kcineplex.com; Ariadnis 8, Mouttagiaka; ⏱5-10.30pm) As in Lefkosia and Larnaka, the cinema scene in Lemesos is dominated by the multiscreen K Cineplex, which features many new-release movies. It's located in the tourist centre and best reached by taxi. See the website for current screenings.

 Shopping

Most of Lemesos' clothes, shoe and appliance shops are clustered along the pedestrian street of Agiou Andreou in central Lemesos. Head for the backstreets here for more idiosyncratic gift shops, boutiques and similar.

Cyprus Handicrafts Centre SOUVENIRS
(Themidos 25) As in other cities across Cyprus, this government-sponsored store is the best place for seeking out authentic, traditional and fairly priced handmade crafts. It's about 3km east of the centre.

Anna's Book Swap BOOKS
(Oktovriou 28) A small bookshop based on the ingenious idea of 'recycling' your books. You buy the first one at full price, and once you've read it and come back to return it, you get 40% towards the price of the second book. It's located by the Debenhams department store.

Violet's Second Hand Shop CLOTHING
(Salaminos 10) A great place for clothes and jewellery, including some interesting Cypriot vintage pieces.

Pana's Patchwork ACCESSORIES
(www.panas-creations.com; Saripolou 21) Crammed with a colourful jumble of ornaments, tapestries, dolls and embroidered pieces, all made by the owner, Pana.

 Information

The regional tourist authority website is www.visitcyprus.com.

CyberNet (Eleftherias 79; per hr €2.50; ⏱1-11pm Mon-Fri, 10am-11pm Sat & Sun) Internet access in a convenient old-town location.

Cyprus Tourism Organisation (CTO; ⏱8.15am-2.30pm & 4-6.15pm) town centre (cnr Nikolaidi & Spyrou Araouzou); tourist centre (Georgiou 1, 22a) Has several branches in Lemesos. Opening hours outside of summer are subject to change.

Salamis Tours (☎2535 5555; www.salamisinternational.com; Salamis House, Oktovriou 28) Maintains its head office here, close to the CTO, and issues tickets to transport your vehicle by boat to Greece or Israel.

 Getting There & Away

AIR Lemesos is more or less equidistant from Pafos and Larnaka airports. Service or private taxis are the only way to reach either and the latter will charge you around €20.

BOAT Expensive two- and three-day cruises depart from Lemesos all year. They go to Haifa (Israel), Port Said (Egypt), a selection of Greek islands and sometimes (in summer) to Lebanon. You can book at most travel agencies.

BUS InterCity (www.intercity-buses.com) has regular buses to Lefkosia (€4, one hour), Larnaka (€3, 45 minutes) and Pafos (€3, one hour) from its bus stop north of the castle.

SERVICE TAXI Travel & Express (☎7777 7474; www.travelexpress.com.cy; Thessalonikis 21) has regular service taxis to Lefkosia (€11, 1½ hours), Larnaka (€11, one hour) and Pafos (€10, one hour). They will also drop you off at Larnaka airport (€13) and Pafos airport (€13).

 Getting Around

BUS Emel (www.limassolbuses.com) provides an urban-wide as well as regional network of buses. Fares cost €1 per journey, €2 per day or €20 per week within the district of Lemesos, including rural villages. Frequent bus lines from the city bus station include:

Bus 1 10 minutes; to the port.

Bus 17 20 minutes; to Kolossi Castle.

Bus 30 35 minutes; northeast along the seafront to Ancient Amathous.

CAR There are convenient car parks all along the waterfront.

AROUND LEMESOS

There's plenty to do and see in the area around Lemesos, ranging from excellent beaches for sun-and-sand seekers to ancient ruins for archaeological buffs.

❶ Getting There & Around

Apart from a handful of sights, reaching any of the areas described in this section is going to require rented transport or expensive taxis. Cycling in and around Lemesos is fairly easy once you have cleared the confines of the city and the surroundings. The terrain is reasonably flat until you encounter the first slopes of the Troödos Massif.

🏖 Beaches

Lemesos' city beaches are popular enough and decent for a quick swim. But if you'd like to lounge on a quieter strip of sand you may want to consider the following.

Lady's Mile Beach   BEACH

This 7km stretch of hard-packed sand and pebble is a popular weekend beach. Named after a horse owned by a colonial governor who exercised his mare here, it runs south beyond Lemesos' New Port along the eastern side of the British-controlled Akrotiri Peninsula. Keep driving away from the blight of cranes at the port, as the beach and the view improve the further south you go. On summer weekends, the citizens of Lemesos flock here in large numbers to relax in the fairly shallow waters. A couple of beach taverns serve the crowds and provide some respite from an otherwise barren beachscape. Bring your own shade if you plan to sit on the beach all day, as well as mosquito repellent if you are staying here until dusk – the nearby salt lake provides a ripe breeding ground for these little nippers.

Governor's Beach   BEACH

Lemesos' tourist appeal starts 30km east of the city, at Governor's Beach, with several coves of dark sand contrasting with the white, chalky rocks. On the downside, the Vasilikos power station looms 3km to the east, blighting the otherwise seamless sea views. A good restaurant choice (signposted from the approach road) is Panayiotis (www.panayiotisgovernorsbeach.com), which has had the same ebullient owner, Andreas, since 1963. Order the speciality, fish meze, and sit surrounded by lush, mature gardens, with eucalyptus, pines, oleanders and olive trees,

overlooking the sea below. Andreas also has a couple of reasonable apartments to rent.

Kourion Beach   BEACH

This is a lovely beach of sand and small pebbles; the area is windy and attracts windsurfers and kite-boarders, as well as the general public, who come here for the unspoilt setting and backdrop of white cliffs.

The beach is around 17km west of Lemesos, within Great Britain's Akrotiri Sovereign Base Area (SBA), which is the reason for the lack of development in this pocket of the island. The beach can be reached by public transport from Lemesos, although the locals like to drive their cars and 4WDs practically up to the water's edge. There's no natural shade, but the adjacent tavernas rent sunbeds and parasols for the day (€4).

Locals rate the Blue Beach Bar & Restaurant as the best on this short culinary strip. You can select your fish or tentacled choice from the large tank, or go for a fish meze (€21 per person). Vegetarians are thoughtfully catered for with vegie burgers and various salad choices. The eastern end of the beach is unsafe for swimming (see the sign), so head west if you fancy a dip. This beach is best combined with your trip to Ancient Kourion. (You can get a taster here: the remains of a 6th-century **port basilica**, complete with 11 columns, back on to the centre of the beach.)

The beach is also home to the well-respected **Curium Beach Equestrian Centre** (☑9956 4232; www.curiumequestrian.com; classes from €25; 🐎), which offers guided horse treks and classes, including dressage.

Avdimou Beach   BEACH

The opening of the Zigs Beach Club, with its dining area and classy wooden sun loungers, signals an inevitable increase in tourism to this hitherto unspoilt stretch of beach. It's part of the nearby Aphrodite Hills Resort Hotel; you can rent a sunbed and parasol and they will throw in a main course for €15 – or bring a picnic and pay just €3.20. The adjacent longstanding (and probably somewhat disgruntled) Kyrenia Beach Restaurant offers a combination of international and Cypriot meals. Consider a snack like haloumi and *lountaza* (smoked ham) followed by that all-time Brit favourite – sticky toffee pudding.

Melanda Beach   BEACH

This is one of the loveliest beaches in the region: an arc of fine pebbles and sand

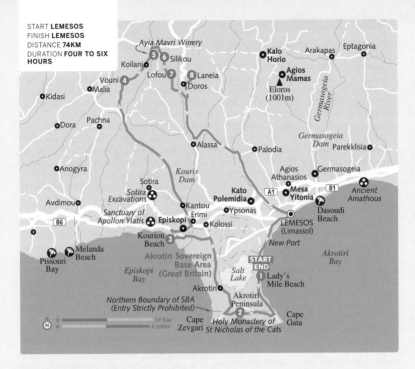

Driving Tour
Cats, Donkeys...& Wine

❯ From Lemesos, head west towards Pafos on the E602, passing the KEO winery and turning left to the signposted **1 Lady's Mile Beach**. After a quick dip in the sea, take the long loop with the beach on your left to visit **2 St Nicholas of the Cats Monastery**; see the exquisite small chapel and pick up some fruit or biscuits for your journey. Continue past the salt lake to dramatically located **3 Kourion Beach** for a coffee and mid-morning snack. Visiting Ancient Kourion takes a good two to three hours, so you may want to save this for another day. Get an inkling of what's to come by checking out the remains of the 6th-century port basilica backing Kourion Beach.

Next, double back towards Lemesos on the B6 and take the Erimi E601 exit heading north towards Omodos, passing a dam to the east. Follow the signs to **4 Vouni**, stop at the charming donkey sanctuary and have a stroll around this pretty town, pausing for lunch at Takis, part of the Vakhis scheme (see the box, p146). Continue north for 5km and

swing by the **5 Ayia Mavri Winery**, with an excellent cabernet sauvignon and a sweet muscatel that has won the prestigious French Moscats du Monde award four times. The village is also home to Cyprus' leading producer of organic wines, Gaia Oinotechniki, which offers weekday tastings.

Around 2km after this hiccup of a detour, turn towards **6 Silikou** and **7 Lofou**; the road passes through dramatic mountain scenery and terraced agriculture with distant sea views. Wander the streets of Lofou, its cobbled lanes bordered by traditional warm limestone buildings. The village is also home to three more Vakhis restaurants.

The next stop is lovely **8 Laneia**, arguably the prettiest village in these parts (see p61). Enjoy a Cypriot coffee in the leafy courtyard of Kapudia restaurant (next to the car park) and have a leisurely stroll through the cobbled backstreets before returning to Lemesos on the speedy, well-signposted B8.

WORTH A TRIP

CHILDREN'S CYPRUS: VISIT A DONKEY SANCTUARY

A good way to holistically entertain children is to take them on a ride to this **Donkey Sanctuary** (☏2594 5488; www.thedonkeysanctuarycyprus.org; Vouni; admission free; ⏱10am-4pm), situated in the foothills of the Troödos Massif 36km northwest of Lemesos. The best time to visit is after 1.30pm, when children usually have the opportunity to partake in donkey grooming and walking; advance notice is not essential but is recommended. The sanctuary holds 120 donkeys, mainly rescued from farms and isolated villages – visitors are encouraged to hear the (often heartbreaking) stories of the donkeys' lives. A brand-new visitors' centre includes a presentation providing some donkey background and facts. If you feel like expanding the family, you can also adopt a donkey for just €20 a year and receive a regular newsletter braying about your offspring.

To get to the sanctuary, leave the Lemesos–Pafos highway at the Vouni E601 exit. Approaching Vouni, follow the 'Donkey Sanctuary (Cyprus)' signs.

sheltered by low white cliffs and backed by olive trees. It's signposted off the B6; the approach road is fairly rough, but still accessible, and passes by vines and lush agricultural land. The Melanda Beach restaurant has a terrace on the beach, and rents sunbeds and parasols for €4. July and August are months to avoid, but otherwise Melanda is a good choice for a beach day out.

Pissouri Bay & Village

Pissouri Bay resort, 10km west of Avdimou, has jet skis, surfing, banana rides and other entertaining sea activities. A reputable diving outfit is **Kembali Diving** (☏2522 2468; www.kembali-diving.com; Columbia Hotel; half-day dives €55).

Despite the tourists (and the fact that Pissouri is a free wi-fi zone), the original village still has some authentic corners. An atmospheric place for a meal is the **Bunch of Grapes Inn** (☏2522 1275; Ioannou Erotokritou 9; mains from €8), which also offers excellent accommodation (p201). Dine under the thick shade of figs, grapevines and plane trees on dishes such as crispy roast duck in apricot and brandy sauce, and red mullet in garlic. Cypriots flock here; reservations recommended.

Down by the beach, the best place to eat is **Limanaki** (☏2522 1288; mains from €8; ⏱closed Mon), once a carob mill. The restaurant is famous for its homemade curries and more elaborate Middle Eastern dishes, such as lamb cooked in yoghurt sauce, garnished with dried mint and pine nuts, and served with basmati rice. Reservations recommended.

Two Friends (☏2522 2527; mains from €8) prides itself on its homemade cuisine. Everything is made from scratch, including the cheese ravioli, filled with fresh cheese and mint, and the tahini dip with freshly ground sesame seeds, garlic and olive oil. It's located on the main road to the beach, just outside the village.

Petra tou Romiou (Aphrodite's Rock & Beach)

Possibly the most famous beach in Cyprus, Aphrodite's Beach is distinctive for its two upright rocks, which are easy to spot, particularly as swimmers are generally perched somewhat precariously on top of them. To get here, take the old B6 road from Lemesos to Pafos (a recommended scenic journey).

The reason the spot is called the Rock of Aphrodite in English is because legend has it that Aphrodite, ancient patron goddess of Cyprus, emerged from the sea at this point in a surge of sea foam before, no doubt, going off to entertain some lovers. The same thing is claimed by the residents of Kythira island in Greece. But who's to say she didn't do it in two places? She was a goddess, after all.

Most visitors either stop when en route to somewhere else and have a swim, or come for the sunset, best seen from either the Petra tou Romiou tourist pavilion, or from a roadside car park about 1.5km further east. Skip any kind of eating at the tourist-pavilion cafeteria, where you'll be overcharged for indifferent snacks; bring your own food and have a picnic instead.

A pedestrian underpass leads to the beach from the kiosk and car park on the other side of the road, around 500m further on towards Pafos from the tourist pavilion; it's well signposted.

Ancient Amathous

(admission €1.70; ⊘9am-7.30pm Jul & Aug, to 5pm Sep-Jun) This archaeological site, about 11km east of Lemesos, belies its original importance: ancient Amathous was one of Cyprus' original four kingdoms (the others were Salamis, Pafos and Soloi). Legend has it that the city was founded by Kinyras, the son of Pafos. It is also said that Kinyras introduced the cult of Aphrodite to Cyprus. Founded about 1000 BC, the city had an unbroken history of settlement until about the 14th century, despite depredation at the hands of corsairs during the 7th and 8th centuries. However, in 1191, when Richard the Lionheart appeared on the scene, the city was already on the decline. Since its harbour was silted up, King Richard was obliged to disembark on the beach to claim the once proud and wealthy city. He promptly applied the royal *coup de grâce* by destroying it, and Amathous was no more.

The site can seem baffling without visual guidance, since much of the stone and marble has long been looted and carted away for other building projects. As you enter, there are several explanatory pedestals that include a schematic map of the area and explanations (in English). This will help you to understand how the city was originally laid out. Excavations only started in earnest in 1980.

Occasional free summer concerts are held within the grounds. Look for posters at the site or check with the CTO in Lemesos.

Episkopi

POP 3170

One of the main reasons for visiting the village of Episkopi, 14km west of Lemesos, is the **Kourion Museum** (admission €1.70; ⊘8am-7.30pm Jul & Aug, 9am-2.30pm Mon-Wed & Fri, 9am-2.30pm & 3-5pm Thu Sep-Jun). The collection mainly comprises terracotta objects from Ancient Kourion and the Sanctuary of Apollon Ylatis, and is housed in what used to be the private residence of archaeologist George McFadden. The museum is signposted off the Lemesos–Kourion road, as well as in Episkopi itself.

For dining, try the **Old Stables** (☑2593 5568; kleftiko €10; ⊘dinner Mon-Sat). The *kleftiko* is tender and juicy, and the mezes are good. Takeaway is also available. It's out on the Lemesos–Pafos road opposite the Eko petrol station and looks like the kind of place that was established many generations before there were roads here, with a small and shady front terrace that deserves a better view than this.

Ancient Kourion

Defiantly perched on a hillside with a sweeping view of the surrounding patchwork of fields and the sea, **Ancient Kourion** (admission €1.70; ⊘8am-7.30pm; 🚻) is a spectacular site, which means it is firmly on the

LEMESOS & THE SOUTH COAST ANCIENT AMATHOUS

WORTH A TRIP

LANEIA VILLAGE

Some of the prettiest Cypriot villages are located north of Lemesos in the mountainous Mandaria region. Vouni, Silikou and Lofou are all worth visiting and within easy distance of each other, but the prettiest village here is arguably Laneia, signposted off the B8 road, just beyond Doros – another gem. Popular with artists and foreign residents, the flower-filled cobbled streets and warm limestone buildings have real picture-postcard appeal. There are several tavernas where you can enjoy a simple meal, and a couple of superb art galleries and craft shops. Pleiades, next to Kapudia restaurant, sells local pottery, jewellery and owner Phoebe's exquisite glassware and mosaics. She also runs a cafe here (consider indulging in a piece of her homemade caramel cheesecake).

Professional painter Michael Owen (www.michaelowengallery.com) has a well-signposted gallery and produces work that is alive with the spirit of the Cypriot landscape. The village is also home to a couple of modest agricultural museums displaying historic olive oil and grape presses. But the real joy here is just wandering the streets with your camera at the ready, stopping for a drink at the traditional coffee shop and fantasising about buying that hideaway holiday home for regular, annual escapes.

coach-tour and school-excursion trail. Come early in the morning or late in the afternoon, when the site is usually less crowded.

There's a small visitor's centre beside the ticket desk where you can see a scale model of the whole site, which can help orientate your visit. Note that Ancient Kourion is close to two other attractions in the immediate vicinity: the Sanctuary of Apollon Ylatis and Kolossi Castle; all three can be visited in the same day. As a cooling break, incorporate a swim at Kourion Beach, spread out temptingly below the ancient site of Kourion itself.

Ancient Kourion was most likely founded in Neolithic times because of its strategic position high on a bluff overlooking the sea. It became a permanent settlement in about the 13th century BC, when Mycenaean colonisers established themselves here.

The settlement also prospered under the Ptolemies and Romans. A pre-Christian cult of Apollo was active among the inhabitants of Kourion in Roman times, as evidenced by the nearby Sanctuary of Apollon Ylatis. Christianity eventually supplanted Apollo and, despite the disastrous earthquakes in the region, an **early Christian basilica** was built in the 5th century, testifying to the ongoing influence of Christianity on Kourion by this time. Pirate raids 200 years later severely compromised the viability of the Christian bishopric; the Bishop of Kourion was obliged to move his base to a new settlement at nearby Episkopi (meaning 'bishopric' in Greek). Kourion declined as a settlement from that point on and was not rediscovered until tentative excavations at the site began in 1876.

The early Christian basilica displays all the hallmarks of an early church, with foundations clearly showing the existence of a narthex, diakonikon (a storage area for agricultural products used by priests and monks), various rooms, a baptistery and an atrium. Some floor mosaics are also visible among the remains.

The site is dominated by its **classical Roman theatre**. This is a reconstruction of a smaller theatre that existed on the same spectacular site, high on the hill overlooking the sea, but which was destroyed by earthquakes during the 4th century. Nevertheless, it gives a good idea of how it would have been at its peak. Today it's used for cultural events, such as Shakespeare plays and music concerts, by Cypriot and visiting Greek singers and bands.

Nearby is the **Annexe of Eustolios**, originally a palace dating from the 5th century BC, but subsequently altered in the 3rd century AD and made a more communal space for the local residents, with extensive baths, courtyards and halls. Its colourful, Christian-influenced mosaic floors are well preserved and make a mention of the builder, Eustolios, and the decidedly non-Christian patron, Apollo. Look for the Christian motifs of cross-shaped ornaments and fish.

Northwest is the **House of the Gladiators**, so called because of two fairly well-preserved floor mosaics depicting gladiators in combat dress. Two of these gladiators, Hellenikos and Margaritis, are shown practising with weapons.

Sanctuary of Apollon Ylatis

About 2km west of Kourion's main entrance, and prominently signposted off the highway, is the **Sanctuary of Apollon Ylatis** (admission €1.70; ◎9am-7.30pm), which is part of the larger site of Kourion. The precinct was established in the 8th century BC in honour of Apollo, who was considered god of the woods (*ylatis* means 'of the woods' in Greek). The once woody site now has far less vegetation but retains a good scattering of remains that give a reasonable idea of the layout of the original sanctuary. The remnants that you see are Roman structures that were levelled by a large earthquake in AD 365.

Apollon Ylatis' **main sanctuary** has been partly restored; the beautiful, imposing columns mark the extent of the restoration. Also discernible are the **priests' quarters**, a **palaestra** (sports arena) and **baths** for the athletes, and a rather depleted **stadium** 500m to the east, which once seated up to 6000 spectators.

Kolossi Castle

Less of a castle and more a fortified tower house, **Kolossi Castle** (admission €1.70; ◎9am-7.30pm Jul & Aug, to 5pm Sep-Jun) perches incongruously between the vineyards and houses of the village of the same name. It's an interesting reminder of the rule of the Knights of St John in the 13th century, who started producing wine and processing sugar cane at a commandery that stood on this land. The current structure dates from 1454 and was probably built over the older fortified building.

Kolossi Castle is accessible by a short drawbridge that was originally defended by a machicolation (a parapet for protecting the castle) high above, through which defenders would pour boiling oil on the heads of unwanted visitors. Upon entering, you come across two large chambers, one with an unusually large fireplace and a spiral staircase that leads to another two chambers on the second level. The only tangible remnant of occupation is a mural of the crucifixion in the first-level main chamber. The spiral staircase continues onto the roof, where the battlements, restored in 1933, lend a final touch.

To the east of the castle is a large outbuilding, now called the **sugar factory**, where cane was processed into sugar.

Akrotiri Peninsula

AKROTIRI SOVEREIGN BASE AREA

Cyprus' past is full of stories of colonisers, raiders and armies generally coveting the small island's strategic position. So when Cyprus finally and belatedly received its independence from colonial administration in 1960, Britain negotiated terms that saw the newly formed Republic of Cyprus ceding 158 sq km (99 sq miles) of its territory to its former colonial master. This territory, now known as the sovereign base areas (SBAs), is used for military purposes by the British.

The only indication that you are on 'foreign soil' is the odd sight of British SBA police, who patrol the territory in special police vehicles. To the immediate west of the peninsula, along the old Lemesos–Pafos road (beyond Episkopi), you'll come across green playing fields, cricket pitches and housing estates more reminiscent of Leicester than Lemesos.

The lower half of the peninsula is out of bounds since it's a closed **military base**, complete with its own large airfield. The village of **Akrotiri** itself is the only true settlement within the SBA (borders were set in order to exclude most settlements). British military personnel often eat here at the several tavernas; they may be seen on their days off riding flashy mountain bikes and tackling the dirt tracks surrounding the large salt lake in the middle of the peninsula.

They also have easy access to one of the region's best restaurants: **Il Gusto** (☑2529

2638; Akrotiri Vasilissis Elisavel 11; mains €10), definitely something to write home about, with superb cuisine that's an innovative twist on classic Italian cooking. Reservations are essential. Easy to find, it is situated among the strip of restaurants on the main street here, wedged in between Chinese, Indian and fish-and-chips restaurants, but vastly superior to them all.

The area is also known for its **Fasouri plantations**, a swathe of citrus groves across the north of the peninsula, interwoven with long, straight stretches of road overhung by tall cypress trees. They create wonderfully cool and refreshing corridors after the aridity of the southern peninsula.

HOLY MONASTERY OF ST NICHOLAS OF THE CATS

A wonderful and bizarre story lies behind the name of this place. The **monastery** (☺8am-2pm & 3-6.30pm) and its original little church were founded in AD 327 by the first Byzantine governor of Cyprus, Kalokeros, and patronised by St Helena, mother of Constantine the Great. At the time the Akrotiri Peninsula, and indeed the whole of Cyprus, was in the grip of a severe drought and was overrun with poisonous snakes, so building a monastery was fraught with practical difficulties. A large shipment of cats was therefore brought in from Egypt and Palestine to combat the reptilian threat. A bell would call the cats to meals and the furry warriors would then be dispatched to fight the snakes. A Venetian monk visiting the monastery described them all as maimed, one missing a nose, another an ear, and some completely blind as a result of their selfless battles.

The peninsula was in fact known for a time as 'Cat Peninsula'. A delightful small chapel here dating from the 13th century has noteworthy icons painted by the original two nuns in residence. The actual monastery building has recently received a modern (and somewhat bland) refurbishment. The many cats that you'll find snoozing in the shade of the monastery colonnades far outnumber the six solitary sisters who now look after the place. You can buy the sisters' preserves, jams, honey and sweets, plus some fresh herbs and bags of oranges (in season).

Positioned on the edge of the salt lake with its back to the SBA fence, the monastery can be reached by a good dirt road from Akrotiri or via a not-so-obvious route west from Lady's Mile Beach.

Troödos Massif

Includes »

Troödos 65
Platres 69
Around Platres 70
Marathasa Valley 71
Solea Valley 76
Pitsylia 78
Agros 80
Around Pitsylia
& Agros 80

Best Places to Eat

» Linos-Mesastrato Tavern (p77)

» Skylight Restaurant, Bar & Pool (p70)

» Platanos (p72)

» Village Tavern (p70)

» Psilo Dendro Restaurant (p70)

Best Places to Stay

» Semiramis (p202)

» Linos Inn (p203)

» Mill (p203)

» To Spitiko tou Arhonta (p202)

» Elyssia (p203)

Why Go?

Home to Mt Olympus (1952m), the island's highest peak, this forested mountain range overlooks the valleys of Lemesos, Larnaka and the greater Mesaoria plain. In 1992, over 90 sq km of the forest was made a national park, safeguarding wildlife, ecology and geology. The region's diverse landscape makes it ideal for camping, picnicking, hiking, cycling and birdwatching. Spring is perfect for enjoying the numerous nature trails and wineries, while summer is well spent in the cool shade of black pines amid the fresh mountain air. In winter skiers and snowboarders populate the ski resorts of the northern slopes.

If its vast array of natural offerings aren't enough, Troödos also has a variety of charming villages with cobbled streets, terraced slopes and folk architecture. The region's peaks and valleys also hide some of the island's most important medieval frescoed churches, along with unexpected mansions, monasteries and museums.

When to Go

From January to April you can ski and board the slopes by day and enjoy a hot tavern meal by night.

April to September is ideal for wine tasting; explore some of the many fine wineries hidden among the sprawling vineyards and steep, breezy valleys.

Ramble over 65km of diverse nature and hiking trails in 13 locations in early summer (May and June).

Beat the July and August heat by camping 1000m above sea level at verdant sites in the ranges.

Troödos

POP 24

Located near the summit of Mt Olympus (known as Chionistra in Greek), Troödos village is the focal point for all hiking, cycling and snow-related activities in the region. At over 1900m above sea level, it's far cooler than the plains below and offers superb views of the surrounding valleys.

The village itself is minimal, centred on a simple square *(plateia)* known as Central Troödos (Kentriko Troödos in Greek). The square has a playground with some benches and a handful of souvenir shops selling everything from wind chimes to *soujoukko,* a traditional sweet made from almonds and sun-dried grape juice.

Opposite the park is the Troödos Hotel, with a couple of neighbouring restaurants and cafes. (Nightlife here is practically non-existent, as most travellers are generally exhausted from the day's activities and head to bed early.) A further 200m downhill to the west is Troödos Visitor Centre (see p69). The skiing facilities (open in winter) are just to the north near the Jubilee Hotel.

From the square the road north heads towards the Solea Valley and Lefkosia. To the west is the road to Prodromos and the Marathasa Valley. The third approach (and most common) is from the south, which takes in Platres (sometimes Pano Platres on maps), and the *krasohoria* (wine villages) of the Kommandaria region.

Central Troödos is best reached from Lemesos (via the B8) or Lefkosia (via the B9). It can also be accessed from Pitsylia, in the east, and from Pafos in the west, via good but slow winding roads. On Sunday evening traffic can be very heavy on all the roads off the mountain, as weekend visitors head home to Lefkosia and the coast.

History

The Troödos ocean crust, created over 90 million years ago, was the first part of the island to emerge from the sea around 15 million years ago. Rocks such as serpentinite, dunite, wehlite, pyroxenite, plagiogranite, gabbro, diabase and volcanic rock can be found at high altitudes in the region.

According to Strabo, the Greek geographer (born c 63 BC), Mt Olympus was the site of a temple to the goddess Aphrodite during the Hellenistic period. It was said to be not only unapproachable for women but completely invisible to them.

ROAD DISTANCES (KM)

	Plano Platres	Kakopetria	Pedoulas	Agros
Kakopetria	25			
Pedoulas	18	15		
Agros	25	50	46	
Omodos & the Krasohoria	8	35	29	31

In AD 1571, Venetian generals built a fort on the mountain to keep invading Ottomans at bay, according to Cypriot nobles who visited the surrounding monasteries and summer recreation areas.

In the late 1800s Troödos became the summer residence of the island's British governors, who came to avoid the scorching sunshine, and the area was considered the summer seat of government during British rule. At different points in its history it has provided a refuge for religious communities, freedom fighters and outlaws, as well as the wealthy of the Levant.

Nowadays, nature lovers, natural-history buffs and activity-seekers flock here for the camping, hiking trails and skiing during the winter months.

⊙ Sights & Activities

Hiking

Troödos has 13 nature trails, varying in length from 1.6km for novices to 14km for the more experienced. Together they provide an excellent insight into the diversity of the region. Most trees and plants on the trails are marked with their Latin and Greek names, and there are frequent wooden benches positioned beneath trees to allow you to take breaks and admire the views.

Booklets outlining the flora, fauna and geology of each trail are available from the Troödos Visitor Centre (p69).

Artemis Trail
(Chionistra Circular Trail) HIKING
Ideal for a first hike, this trail goes around the summit of Mt Olympus in a roughly circular loop, beginning and ending in the little car park off the Mt Olympus summit road. The track runs alternately through shaded and open areas with spectacular views to the south. It takes in vegetation like St John's wort, Troödos sage, alyssum

Troödos Massif Highlights

1 Visiting all 10 of the famous painted churches on the Unesco World Heritage–listed **Byzantine churches route** (p71)

2 Breathing in the fresh air while **hiking** (p65) and **cycling** (p68) in the shadow of Mt Olympus, and the region's natural beauty

3 Staying in some of the island's most authentic accommodation and getting a taste of traditional Cypriot rural life in villages such as **Treis Elies** (p74), **Kakopetria** (p76) and **Pedoulas** (p71)

4 Sampling the best in Cypriot wines and visiting the **vineyards** (p76) along the wine routes of the mountain slopes

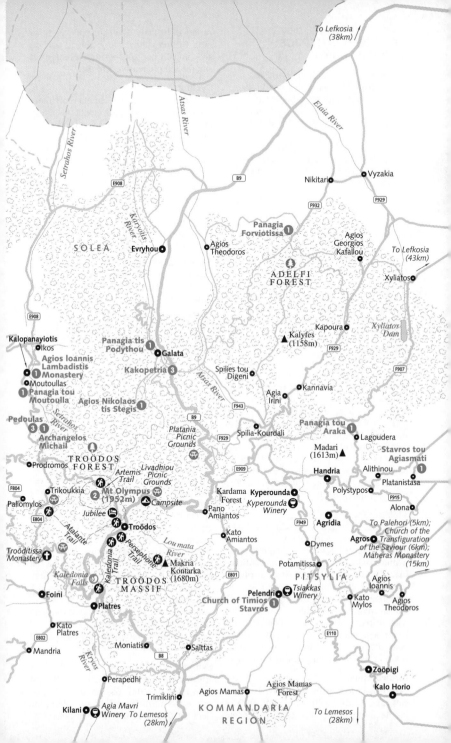

CHILDREN'S CYPRUS: HORSE RIDING

The small horse- and donkey-riding outfit that operates from the south side of the village (near the public toilets) is ideal if you want to give your kids an introduction to riding. The beasts are very friendly and gentle, so don't expect any galloping chases. A 10-minute escorted ride around Troödos costs €6, 20 minutes will set you back €10, half an hour €15.

and barberry, and the geology includes a chromite pit and veins of pyroxenite and dunite. The route also features the 'Walls of the Old Town', which legend says are remnants of the Venetian fort (see p65). The ski lift is also located on this trail, should you come in winter. The 7km trail is fairly flat and takes three to four hours to complete. Come prepared with drinking water and a hat.

Persephone Trail   HIKING
Named after the mountain it ascends, this trail takes you on an attractive out-and-back hike through tall pines, rich vegetation and open areas with views to the horizon. The trail is 3km long and takes about an hour and a half to complete. There's a lookout at the top of **Makria Kontarka**, where you can see the spread of vineyards and wine villages as far as Lemesos port to the south. On the northern side you can see the enormous scar in the earth left by the now-closed asbestos mine at Pano Amiantos.

Atalante Trail   HIKING
Starting at the square in Troödos, this trail is great for walkers as it's relatively easy-going and well marked. Named in honour of forest nymph Atalante, it runs at a lower altitude than the Artemis trail but follows nearly the same route. While the views are not as spectacular as those from the higher trail, it's still an enjoyable walk. There's a fresh spring with drinking water about 3km from the trail's beginning. To get back to the village take the main Prodromos–Troödos road. Allow around five hours for this 12km walk.

Birdwatching
Cyprus is blessed with nearly 400 bird species, and many visitors come to Troödos for its tranquillity, excellent visibility and variety of habitats. You can spot everything from Griffon vultures to warblers, wagtails and pipits. Check out www.natureofcyprus .org for comprehensive bird lists.

Cycling
Troödos has a growing number of routes dedicated to cycling and mountain biking, including several forest tracks. The booklet *Cycling Routes* is available at the visitor centre and CTO offices, and has detailed information on bike tracks in the mountain range. Troödos' most common cycling route comprises three tracks making up one large circular run of the Mt Olympus summit:

Psilo Dendro (Platres)–Karvounas
A 16.2km flat ride through easy terrain including good-quality tarmac, forest and dirt track.

Karvounas–Prodromos A 22.7km ride with a decent incline, a medium to hard degree of difficulty and good all-surface conditions.

Prodromos–Psilo Dendro An 18.2km simple ride downhill with good roads mixed with stony tracks that can be tough on tyres.

Check out www.cypruscycling.com for information on bike runs and events held on the island.

Picnicking
With nine well-organised sites ranging in capacity from 250 to 2000 visitors, Troödos Forest Park attracts flocks of picnickers. You can set up practically anywhere and all sites have facilities such as wooden tables, fresh drinking water, toilets, playgrounds and parking. Barbecuing is allowed in the pits provided if you wish to join the locals in grilling chops or spit-roasting *kontosouvli* (chunks of lamb).

Kampos tou Livadi, a great little picnic ground among the pine trees, is located 3km down the Troödos–Lefkosia road (B9). A further 8km along this road is the popular **Platania** (Plane Trees) picnic ground and camp site. It can get busy with weekend visitors, but it offers plenty of shade and includes a children's adventure park, making it ideal for families.

Skiing
Troödos has four slopes, ranging in length from 150m to 350m. The two longer slopes are on the north face of the mountain; the Hera lift takes you to the 350m beginners'

slope, and the Zeus lift takes you to the peak for the advanced 500m-long Jubilee run and the racing runs. The **North Face Ski Centre** (☏2542 0105) is located here at the Dias Restaurant.

On the southern shoulder are the ski lifts to the shorter Aphrodite and Hermes runs, great for beginners and intermediates. The **Sun Valley Centre** (☏2542 0104) and a ski shop are located here. Surf www.skicyprus .com for snow reports and the latest information on slope conditions.

Eating

Choice here is not great unless you're after a simple snack. If so, **Fereos Park Restaurant** (mains €8) for a good-sized kebab or souvlaki is your best bet. Otherwise, head for Platres, where there are many more restaurants with a variety of food and far better quality.

❶ Getting There & Away

Buses to the Troödos Massif run from Lefkosia or Lemesos regularly. You can call the companies below to confirm routes and times and even request a stop at an in-between village.

Clarios Bus Co (☏2246 5546; 1 way/all day & return €5/8) Buses run from Constanza Bastion, Lefkosia, to Central Troödos at 10.20am weekdays, 11.30am Saturday; the return trip is at 7pm Monday to Saturday.

Emel (☏7777 8121; www.limassolbuses.com; 1 way/all day & return €3/5) Buses run from Lemesos to Central Troödos at 9am daily; the trip back is at 3.30pm daily.

TROÖDOS VISITOR CENTRE

Just south of Troödos' main street and well worth a look, the **visitor centre** (admission €1; ☺10am-4pm) includes a small museum with displays dedicated to examples of all the region's flora, fauna, geology and wildlife. A great mini-theatre plays an informative 10-minute video detailing the park's history, and a geographic display in the foyer outlines the park's boundaries, mountains and environs. Importantly, all maps, brochures and published information about the region, including hiking trails and vegetation, are available here. The 250m botanical and geological trail surrounding the centre is an easy introduction to the area's attractions for children and adults alike.

Service taxis don't operate out of Troödos. A standard taxi will take you there, but it can be expensive due to the time it takes to drive up the mountain.

❶ Getting Around

The best way to explore the expanse of Troödos is to get your own car, so that you can see all the wonderful little villages without being at the mercy of the limited public transport. The roads, although windy, are good.

Platres

POP 280

> The nightingales won't let you sleep in Platres.
> *Georgos Seferis, Eleni, 1953*

Platres (formerly Pano Platres) is the highest of the mountain communities, with an altitude of approximately 1200m. Located in a lush and fertile pocket of dense forest, it receives some of the highest rainfall in Cyprus.

A popular health retreat with British colonialists and personalities of the past, Platres has hosted Nobel Prize–winning Greek poet Georgos Seferis, who spent many days in the village and wrote famous poems about it, and King Farouk of Egypt, who crossed the Mediterranean to seek summer refuge here. Modelled somewhat on the hill stations of colonial Asia, it has all the trappings of a cool mountain retreat: forest walks, bubbling streams, relief from the heat of the plains, and gin and tonics on the balconies of old-world hotels.

Nowadays it's popular with hikers, retirees and travellers who prefer the hills to the beaches. Platres has now merged its former charm with modernised restaurants and hotels to become a delightful place to stay while visiting the mountains.

Platres is off the main Lemesos–Troödos highway (B9) and consists of a series of snaking roads, an upper road that's home to a number of hotels, and a lower road populated with restaurants, shops and bars. Check out www.platres.org to keep up with local information.

◉ Sights

Platres is a perfect retreat during the heat of summer with its dry climate, nature and tranquillity. In winter it converts into the

BUG BEACON

Make sure you bring bug or insect repellent. The mountains are wonderfully picturesque, but they do have their share of creepy-crawlies. Many of the big flies and tree bugs appear to be especially attracted to white T-shirts and skirts, so consider wearing alternative colours, particularly during the hotter months and around the summit.

perfect ski resort, with cosy restaurants and roaring log fires.

Traditional buildings NOTABLE BUILDINGS
The village has some wonderful examples of traditional stone buildings, now mostly held (and still used) by the municipality. As you walk around the streets look out for examples like the **police station** (built by the British) near the CTO office, the **old gymnasium** (now the Platres Hospital) 600m south of the village centre, the two-storey **community council offices**, and the well-kept building of the **Electricity Authority**, built in 1930 using local stone.

🏃 Activities

Only 10km from Central Troödos and its various nearby hiking trails (p65), Platres has some good hikes, such as the downhill route to Foini, 9km to the west, the slightly easier 7km route to Perapedhi, and an excellent 3km uphill ramble to Pouziaris. These hikes and others are mapped in the CTO brochure *Platres,* available at the Troödos Visitor Centre (p69).

✖ Eating

Enjoy local dishes with some incredible wines from the nearby *krasohoria* valley and Kommandaria region.

TOP CHOICE Skylight Restaurant
Bar & Pool MEDITERRANEAN €€
(Leoforos Archiepiskopou Makariou III 524; www.skylight.com.cy; mains from €8, pool admission per day €5; ⊘9am-6pm;) This modern restaurant combined with a cool bar and swimming pool offers an excellent choice of grills, salads and seafood dishes. And you can enjoy the outstanding service between swims and lounging on the sunny terrace.

Village Tavern CYPRIOT €€
(Leoforos Archiepiskopou Makariou III; mains €8) Open views from the terrace, blended with simple traditional food served in good-sized portions, make this a pleasant spot to recharge after a hike. Try the fresh Greek salads with the lightly browned moussaka.

To Anoi CYPRIOT €€
(Olympou 37; mains from €9) A large stone building, this family tavern serves traditional dishes like *kleftiko* (oven-baked lamb) and *souvla* (skewered meat, usually lamb) cooked over hot coals.

Psilo Dendro Restaurant CYPRIOT €€€
(Aïdonion 13; trout €14; ⊘11am-5pm) Close to the southern end of the Kaledonia Trail from Troödos, this restaurant receives many hungry hikers. It has an adjoining trout farm, from which it serves some of the freshest fish on the island.

ℹ Information

The **Cyprus Tourism Organisation** (CTO; 📞2542 1316; platresinfo@cto.org.cy; ⊘9am-3.30pm Mon-Fri, to 2.30pm Sat, closes 30 min earlier Jul & Aug) has information on the Troödos hiking trails.

To report a **forest fire** call 📞1407.

ℹ Getting There & Away

All public transport arrives at and departs from the area adjoining the CTO office. You can call the bus companies below to confirm routes and times and even request a stop at an in-between village.

Emel (📞7777 8121; www.limassolbuses.com; 1 way/all day & return €3/5) buses run from Platres to Lemesos at 7.20am, 9.05am and 3.45pm Monday to Saturday, 7.20am and 3.45pm Sunday; the run back is at 9.30am, 1.30pm, 3.30pm and 6pm weekdays, 9.30am, 12.30pm and 5pm Saturday, 9.30am and 5pm Sunday.

Service taxis (📞2542 1346) run from Lemesos to Platres at €11 per person.

Around Platres

Platres is a great base for day trips to surrounding sites like the monasteries at Kykkos and Troöditissa, the Byzantine churches and the wine villages of the Kommandaria region. You'll definitely need a car or suitable alternative to explore the greater area.

THE FRESCOED BYZANTINE CHURCHES OF CYPRUS

Many visitors come to the Troödos region to see the remarkable Byzantine churches, built and decorated with stunning frescos between the 11th and 15th centuries. Ten of these churches are Unesco World Heritage sites. In viewing order they are Archangelos Michail, Agios Ioannis Lambadistis Monastery (p72), Panagia tou Moutoulla (p73), Agios Nikolaos tis Stegis (p77), Panagia tis Podythou (p77), Panagia Forviotissa (Asinou; p78), Stavros tou Agiasmati (p80), Panagia tou Araka (p80), Church of Timios Stavros (p81) and Church of the Transfiguration of the Saviour (p81).

When the French Catholic Lusignan dynasty took control of Cyprus in 1197, work on a series of small churches in the mountains had already begun. But it was the repression and discrimination exercised by the Lusignans against the Orthodox Greek Cypriots that prompted the Orthodox clergy, along with artisans and builders, to retreat to the northern slopes of the Troödos Massif. Here they built and embellished private ecclesiastical retreats where Orthodoxy flourished undisturbed for 300 years.

The culmination of this activity was many churches built in a similar fashion. Most were little bigger than small barns; some had domes, some did not. Because of the harsh winter weather, large, steeply inclined overhanging roofs were added to protect the churches from accumulated snow. Inside, skilled fresco painters went to work producing a series of vivid images.

Not all churches were lavishly painted, but the Unesco-designated churches represent the finest examples. The frescos are remarkable for their clarity of detail and the preservation of their colour. The later didactic-style frescos are unusual in that they are painted like a movie strip, ostensibly to teach illiterate villagers the rudiments of the gospels.

You will need at least two days to visit all the churches. A number of them are kept locked, so you'll have to track down their caretakers. Donations of €1 to €3 are appreciated and commonly expected. A car is the easiest way to visit most of the churches, as public transport is sporadic.

Marathasa Valley

This scenic valley to the northwest of Troödos cradles some of the mountain's most important and impressive sights, like the splendid Kykkos Monastery, the beautifully frescoed church of Archangelos Michail in Pedoulas; and the humble Agios Ioannis Lambadistis Monastery in Kalopanayiotis.

Spring and autumn, when wildflowers display their colours like fireworks, are particularly lovely times to visit. There's also some excellent agrotourism accommodation to be found in the valley, mostly in restored traditional houses (see p203).

PEDOULAS
POP 190

Pedoulas (pedoulasvillage.com) is the main settlement and tourist centre in the Marathasa Valley. Famous for its spring water (sold all over Cyprus), it's particularly cool and breezy in summer. It has some great eating and sleeping options.

◉ Sights

Archangelos Michail CHURCH
(admission by donation) Most people visit Pedoulas to see this Unesco-listed church. Dating from 1474, the gable-roofed building sits in the lower part of the village. Its **frescos**, restored in 1980, show a move towards the naturalism of the post-Byzantine revival, and are credited to an artist known only as Adamos. Depicted are, of course, the Archangel Michael, looming above the faithful, the denial of Christ, the sacrifice of Abraham, the Virgin and Christ, and a beautiful baptism scene where an unclothed Christ is exiting the River Jordan with fish swimming at his feet.

The key to the church is held at the Byzantine Museum on the opposite side of the street.

Byzantine Museum MUSEUM
(admission €1.70; ⊙10am-1pm & 2.30-5pm) The museum's rich collection of 12th- to 15th-century icons includes the late-13th-century **icon of the Virgin Vorinis**. Many pieces have featured in world exhibitions.

DON'T MISS

NIGHTINGALES & WATERFALLS

A perfect summer hike, the **Kaledonia Trail** is well shaded and well marked. Around 3km long, it starts approximately 1km downhill from Central Troödos and ends just outside the town of Platres. The trail winds down through a thickly wooded valley alongside the Kryos River, a gurgling stream with stepping-stone crossings and log bridges. The track is steep in parts and is best tackled from north to south, as it drops about 400m in altitude. It offers a variety of vegetation like black pines and Cyprus mint and an abundance of little birds like Cyprus and Sardinian warblers and nightingales. The last kilometre brings you to picturesque **Kaledonia Falls**, a 15m drop of cascading water from an immense gabbro-rock precipice. Allow yourself two hours for an uplifting and relaxing hike.

Folk Art Museum MUSEUM
(admission €1.70; ⊘10am-1pm & 2-4pm) Near the village centre, this museum houses clothing, furniture and agricultural tools that provide a snapshot of the culture, customs and history of the Marathasa region.

✗ Eating

TOP CHOICE Platanos CYPRIOT €€
(Vasou Hadjiioannou; mains €9) In the cool shade of the *platano* (plane tree), this restaurant serves traditional dishes such as *souvlakia* (souvlaki) and *afelia* (slow-cooked pork with wine and herbs). Cypriot coffee is a must, prepared the time-honoured way using a tray of hot sand between the *brikki* (a small saucepan) and the open flame. This method allows the coffee to heat gradually, giving a richer and fuller taste.

ⓘ Getting There & Away

Clarios Bus Co (☑2246 5546; 1 way/all day & return €5/8) buses go from Constanza Bastion, Lefkosia, to Pedoulas at 12.30pm and 4.15pm weekdays, 12.30pm Saturday; the return journey is at 5.20am and 6.30am weekdays, 6.30am Saturday.

KALOPANAYIOTIS
POP 290

Famous for its monastery and Byzantine museum, Kalopanayiotis is a relaxing place to stop for a few days, with natural **sulphur springs** (dedicated to the ancient god of healing, Asclepius) and good-quality agrotourism accomodation.

◉ Sights

Agios Ioannis Lambadistis Monastery CHURCHES
(by donation; ⊘8am-noon & 1.30-6pm May-Sep) This Unesco-listed site is a complex of three churches in one, dating from the 11th century and built over 400 years. The original Orthodox church has a double nave, to which a narthex and a Latin chapel were later added. Now under one huge pitched wooden roof (in typical Troödos-mountain style) they represent one of the most wonderfully preserved churches in the region.

The main domed Orthodox church exhibits colourful and intricate 13th-century **frescos** dedicated to Agios Irakleidios. These include Jesus' entry to Jerusalem on a donkey, with children climbing date trees to get a better look. Other featured frescos include the Raising of Lazarus, the Crucifixion and the Ascension, with vivid colour schemes suggesting artistic influence from Constantinople.

The antechamber and Latin chapel have more frescos, dating from the 15th and 16th centuries. Those in the chapel are considered the most comprehensive series of Italo-Byzantine frescos in Cyprus. The scenes representing the Akathistos hymn (praising the Virgin Mary in 24 verses) are shown as 24 pictures, each carrying a letter of the Greek alphabet. The Arrival of the Magi depicts the Magi on horseback, wearing crusader armour and grandstanding red crescents (a Roman symbol for the Byzantines and later the Turks).

Photographs of the iconography are not permitted. The monastery is reached by following the main street to the opposite side of the valley. The keys are held by the village priest, who is usually found at the central *kafeneio* (coffee shop) during the summer months.

Byzantine Museum MUSEUM
(admission €1; ⊘9.30am-5pm Mar-Jun, to 7pm Jul-Sep, 10am-3.30pm Oct-Feb) Part of the monastery, this museum displays a

collection of 15 icons discovered in 1998. Dating from the 16th century, the icons were hidden underground for many years by Orthodox priests escaping the invading Ottomans. The iconostasis (screen that holds icons) is covered in carvings of local ferns found at the river in Kalopanayiotis, confirming its origins.

MOUTOULLAS

This small village, on the road between Pedoulas and Kalopanayiotis, is the site of another Unesco-listed church, **Panagia tou Moutoulla** (admission free; ⊙dawn-dusk), with frescos dating to 1280.

Believed to have been a private chapel, it has the steep aisle and pitched roof common to the region. Its rare unrestored paintings include depictions of St Christopher, St George and the Virgin. You will need to seek out the key, held at the village coffee shop. While there, you can browse and buy some of the locally made traditional woodcarvings. The village also has (and sells) wonderful apples and cherries, thanks to the vast orchards surrounding it.

KYKKOS MONASTERY

The island's most prosperous and opulent Orthodox **monastery** (admission free; ⊙dawn-dusk), Kykkos was founded in the 11th century by Byzantine emperor Alexios I Komninos after a bizarre series of events. It all started with a hermit called Esaias (Isaiah), who lived in a cave close to the site. One day in the forest, Esaias crossed paths with a hunter from Lefkosia, Manouil Voutomytis, who was also the Byzantine governor of Cyprus.

Voutomytis was lost and asked directions from the recluse, only to be ignored because of Esaias' ascetic vows. The self-important hunter became outraged at what he perceived to be the hermit's insolence, cursing at him and shoving him as a lesson.

Upon returning to Lefkosia, Voutomytis began to suffer incurable lethargy. He recalled how he had mistreated Esaias and set out to beg forgiveness, in the hope of restoring his failing health.

Meanwhile, a vision from God appeared to Esaias, telling him to charge Voutomytis with the task of bringing the Icon of the Virgin Mary from Constantinople to Cyprus.

At the hermit's request, and after much soul-searching, Voutomytis was eventually able to bring the icon to Cyprus. He convinced the Byzantine emperor in Constantinople, whose daughter suffered the same lethargic affliction, that she would be saved if they did what the hermit (and therefore God) had asked.

The icon, said to be painted by St Luke, is one of only three that survive. For the last four centuries it has sat in a sealed, silver-encased box in Kykkos Monastery.

Over the centuries, a series of fires all but destroyed the original monastery. The surviving building is an imposing and well-maintained structure dating from 1831. It's located about 20km west of Pedoulas. To enter you will need to dress conservatively and cover your arms and legs. Stalls outside hire out trousers and shawls in summer.

Byzantine Museum   MUSEUM
(☐2294 2736; www.kykkos-museum.cy.net; admission €3.40; ⊙10am-6pm Jun-Sep, to 4pm Oct-May) This museum houses much of the monastery's fabulous wealth, including Byzantine and ecclesiastical artefacts.

On the left when you enter is an antiquities display. In the large ecclesiastical gallery are early Christian, Byzantine and post-Byzantine vestments, vessels and jewels. A small circular room houses old manuscripts, documents and books, and a rich display of icons, wall paintings and carvings can be found in the larger circular chamber.

Comprehensive guidebooks are available from the ticket office for €5 – they're well worth the price.

TOMB OF ARCHBISHOP MAKARIOS III

The tomb of the first president of Cyprus is located on Throni Hill, 2km past Kykkos Monastery where the road bends right and heads upwards. Makarios was buried here at his request, close to the place where he served as an apprentice monk in 1926. The simple stone sepulchre is overlaid with black marble and covered by a round, stone-inlaid dome. Its humble look is partly accounted for by its hasty construction following Makarios' sudden death.

A huge bronze statue of the archbishop, moved from Lefkosia's Archepiscopal Palace in 2008, now stands on the hill, adding to its grandeur.

Higher up on the path is the **Throni Shrine** to the Virgin Mary. It has spectacular, endless views of the valleys and roads leading to Kykkos from the east.

A **wishing tree** is located just near here, where the pious tie paper and cloth

ARCHBISHOP MAKARIOS III – PRIEST & POLITICIAN

The ethnarch and religious leader of Cyprus during its brief period of independence as a united island, Makarios was born Michael Christodoulou Mouskos on 13 August 1913, in the small mountain village of Pano Panagia in Pafos.

He studied in Cyprus and at the University of Athens, and graduated from the School of Theology at Boston University. Ordained Bishop of Kition in 1946, he became archbishop four years later.

Initially a supporter of the enosis (union with Greece) movement for Cyprus, he later opposed its notions of independence, commonwealth status, and *taksim* (the Turkish objective for separation). However, during the three-year uprising of the 1950s, the British suspected him of collaboration with the rebel pro-enosis movement Ethniki Organosi tou Kypriakou Agona (EOKA; National Organisation for the Cypriot Struggle) and he was exiled to the Seychelles.

Still, Makarios was a politician, not an insurgent, and he was welcomed back to Cyprus in 1959. Negotiating an independence agreement with the British, he was elected president of the newly independent Republic of Cyprus in a landslide victory on 13 December of that year.

Indirectly merging religion and state, he formalised the tradition of ordinary people relying on their clergy for leadership and guidance. This was a role that had previously been forced upon Cypriot religious leaders during the island's domination by foreign powers.

Now distancing himself from the enosis movement in favour of independence, Makarios tried to appease the Turkish Cypriot minority on the island and forge a foreign policy of nonalignment. However, he was seen by some Turkish Cypriots as anti-Turkish, and serious sectarian violence broke out in 1963. The US saw his disinterest in the west as being too communist and pegged him as the 'Castro of the Mediterranean'.

The Greek junta, abetted by the American CIA and pro-enosis EOKA-B (the post-independence version of EOKA) radicals, launched a coup in 1974 behind Greek general Grivas with a view to assassinating Makarios and installing a new government.

The coup backfired: Makarios escaped, and Turkey (already preparing for partition) used the coup as a reason for invasion, politically sabotaging any hope of peace between the two communities. Turkey started bombing villages and invaded the north of Cyprus.

The junta fell and Makarios returned from England to preside over a now truncated state. He died unexpectedly on 3 August 1977 aged 63. Today he is remembered by many as a leader, a statesman and the embodiment of the people's aspirations for independence and identity.

---

messages in the hope that the Virgin Mary will grant their requests.

TREIS ELIES

Southwest of Prodromos via the F10 and F811 is Treis Elies (www.triselies.org), a quiet hamlet perfect for relaxation. There's a small river and nature trail around the village and just outside is the Iamatikes (signposted as 'Ιαματικές') **sulphur spring**, spurting through large rocks. Its location is ideal for hikes to the Kelefos, Elies and Roudhias medieval bridges, which were built during Venetian rule in an effort to streamline the camel-caravan route near the village. The camels transported copper from Troödos to Polis and Pafos, where it was traded. Unfortunately the original path is now all but lost.

The three bridges are connected by European Long Distance Path E4 (see p76), which is perfect for walking.

Closest to Treis Elies is **Elies Bridge**, just after the village of Kaminaria. Set in dense forest, with a fresh stream flowing underneath, it is the smallest of the three, and was believed to be the easterly link of the caravan route.

Kelefos Bridge is the most elegant, with a strong single-pointed arch over a wide waterway. It takes about two hours to hike from Elies to Kelefos, where you'll find an excellent picnic spot. You can also reach Kelefos Bridge by car, following the signs towards Agios Nikolaos.

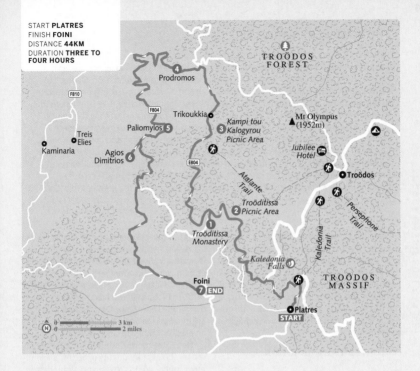

Driving Tour
Monasteries & Mountain Villages

❯ Take the E804 from Platres for a peek at some of the valley's hidden villages. This route includes the 13th-century **1 Troöditissa Monastery**, located amid thick pines at the top of a steep gorge.

The monastery was founded after the discovery of a priceless silver-plated icon of the Virgin that was brought from Asia Minor. Believed to assist fertility, the icon had been guarded in a nearby cave by two hermits until their deaths. The monastery's existing church, built in 1731, is currently closed to the public as it is part of a working religious order. However, if you are polite and patient the monks may let you in.

Continuing along the mountain road, you pass the shaded picnic areas of **2 Troöditissa** and **3 Kampi tou Kalogyrou** in the cool pine forests. From there you reach the village of **4 Prodromos** (www.prodromos .org.cy). This small village still has some hill-station clientele but is not as well known as Troödos and Platres. At 1380m, it's Cyprus' highest village and has incredible orchards with apple, peach, plum, almond and chestnut trees.

Looping back towards the south brings you to **5 Paliomylos** (paliomilos.org) and **6 Agios Dimitrios**, a pair of timeless villages barely touched by tourism, buried beneath the greenery and grapevines.

A little further on is **7 Foini**, a great place to stop for some *loukoumades* (Cypriot honey balls) and a strong coffee. It's also very popular for its handmade pottery and *pitharia* (earthenware storage jars). For lunch, a good choice is Neraida, which has fresh trout and delicious meze (€17). On the western side of the village, near the stream, it's open Thursday to Tuesday for lunch, and for dinner Friday and Saturday.

THE ROAD LESS TRAVELLED

Treis Elies is a fantastic base from which to explore **European Long Distance Path E4**, an incredible trail that starts at Gibraltar and passes through Spain, France, Switzerland, Germany, Austria, Hungary, Bulgaria, Greece and, since late 2005, Cyprus. An inauguration party was held in the Maheras Forest to celebrate the extension of the path to the island and the expectation of more visitors exploring the area. The E4 is linked to Cyprus by air and sea, starting at Larnaka and Pafos airports, and covering the Troödos Massif. It continues on to the Akamas Peninsula and stretches across to the eastern regions of the free areas of Famagusta. The Cyprus Tourism Organisation (CTO) booklet *European Long Distance Path E4 & Other Cyprus Nature Trails* gives an overview of the Cypriot walks, stating lengths, degrees of difficulty, starting and ending locations, and points of interest. The path is a rambler's delight, with detailed maps an essential. Conquering the Cypriot portion is a terrific start to being part of the greater project, so give it a shot.

The third, **Roudhias Bridge**, is impressive but far more remote. It's a long-distance four-hour hike away, along the trail past the Pera Vassas forestry station and picnic ground. The bridge can be difficult to find, so take a good map. If you choose to drive, the direct road is a narrow track with limited access. There is also a river crossing that requires a 4WD.

OMODOS & THE KRASOHORIA
POP 30 (OMODOS)

The extensive vineyards of the *krasohoria* (wine villages) occupy the slopes around Omodos village (www.omodos.org). It makes for a mesmerising landscape on the southwest flank of the Troödos Massif.

The village itself is built around the Byzantine **Moni Timiou Stavrou** (Monastery of the Holy Cross), making it unique in the Greek world as settlements do not customarily centre on a monastery. Built around 1150, the monastery was extended and remodelled in the 19th century. The town centre has a cobblestone pedestrian area, which is geared towards tourists, with souvenir stalls and shops. **Socrates Traditional House** (admission free; ⊘9.30am-7pm) is located in the backstreets and is a great spot to visit if you want to taste or buy bottles of homemade Kommandaria (Commandaria) wine. It also has a traditional display of presses, looms, a corn mill and objects from rural life.

It was said that every house in the *krasohoria* had its own winemaking tools. With so many vineyards in the region, you'll find that many villages sell a variety of traditional grape products like *soujoukos* (grapes blended with almonds), *espima* (grape honey) and *palouze* (grape sweets).

Agia Mavri Winery (☑2547 0225; www.ayia mavri.com), with award-winning whites, and **Domane Valassides** (☑9944 1574), offering aromatic, full-flavoured reds, are both located in Kilani village. **Yiaskouris Winery** (☑2594 2470), in Pachna village, has great shirazes and dry whites, and **Gaia Oinotechniki** (☑2594 3981; www.gaia.com.cy), in Agios Amvrosios, has an excellent range of organic wines.

There are more than 50 boutique wineries in the region, many open by appointment only; go to www.cypruswineries.org for profiles and seasonal opening times.

Solea Valley

The Solea Valley, bisected by the Karyotis River, has significant frescoed churches built during the late Byzantine era, when the area was revered for its importance as a stronghold.

The valley's reputation as a strategic refuge was furthered in the 1950s, when it served as the prime hideout area for Ethniki Organosi tou Kypriakou Agona (EOKA; National Organisation for the Cypriot Struggle) revolutionists during their anti-British campaigns. With its concealed terrain and proximity to Lefkosia it was an ideal location.

Today it's still perfect for accessing the mountains and beyond, with roads to both the east and west. The main village in the valley is Kakopetria, fantastic for day trips and longer stays, with decent hotels and fantastic facilities.

KAKOPETRIA
POP 1200

Kakopetria, or *kaki petra* (meaning 'bad rock'), gets its name from the line of huge rocks along the ridge around the village that were clearly a hindrance to the first settlers. Situated across both banks of the Karyotis River, the village is filled with steep roads, hanging trees and the sound of natural storm drains.

The area is very popular with wealthy Cypriots, who retire to their homes in the mountains for the summer months. The old quarter of the village is heritage listed, and many of the houses have been restored accordingly, enabling it to retain its charm.

Kakopetria has two excellent hotels and some good eateries. It's also another ideal place to base yourself while exploring the frescoed churches and the surrounding area.

🍴 Eating

Linos-Mesastrato Tavern   CYPRIOT €€
(☑2292 3161; www.linos-inn.com.cy; Palea Kakopetria 34; meze per plate from €5) An atmospheric restaurant with excellent meze and great local reds like Ktima Malia (€20), a rich cabernet. There's also a relaxing cafe and bar (open in summer) where you can try smoking the *nargileh* (water pipe). This is a very popular venue, so book in advance.

Mill Restaurant   MEDITERRANEAN €€
(☑2292 2536; www.cymillhotel.com; Mylou 8; mains from €10; ⊙closed 20 Nov-20 Dec) Ideally situated next to the river, with a slow-turning mill wheel and a shady terrace. Trout is a big thing here, served either grilled or 'special' (herbed). In winter they light up the old fireplace inside. You'll need to reserve on weekends.

Village Pub   CYPRIOT €
(mains from €6) This place has a wooden terrace overlooking the village, and provides good and simple summer meals like fresh salads, *fassolia* (white beans) and *faggi* (lentils). Try the well-prepared daily specials.

❶ Getting There & Away

There's no direct public transport to the Unesco-listed churches in the valley.

Clarios Bus Co (☑2246 5546; 1 way/all day & return €5/8) runs from Constanza Bastion, Lefkosia, to Kakopetria about every hour from 6am to 6pm weekdays, 11.30am to 5.30pm Saturday. There are two buses on Sunday in summer. Buses make the return trip at 5am, 5.45am, 6.10am, 6.30am, 6.45am, 8am, 1.30pm and 2.30pm weekdays, 6am, 6.45am, 8am and 2.30pm Saturday.

All public transport arrives at and departs from the area adjoining the CTO office.

AROUND KAKOPETRIA

These valleys are filled with Unesco-listed churches and hiking trails.

AGIOS NIKOLAOS TIS STEGIS

This Unesco-listed **church** (donations welcome; ⊙9am-6pm Tue-Sat, 11am-4pm Sun), known in English as St Nicholas of the Roof because of its large, heavy-pitched top, was founded in the 11th century.

Situated 5km north of Kakopetria, it was originally part of a monastery complex. The dome and narthex were added in the 15th century, along with the roof, to protect against the region's snowfall.

The arts of iconography and fresco painting flourished here in the Middle Ages, while the Orthodox hid from the then dominant Latin administration. The **frescos** at Agios Nikolaos are a mix of images and styles, the best being a depiction of the Virgin Mary breastfeeding Jesus, the Crucifixion, the Nativity, and the Myrrh Carriers, which shows an angel on Christ's empty tomb.

Photos (without flash) may be permitted, if you're polite, and make a donation in the collection box.

PANAGIA TIS PODYTHOU

In the village of **Galata**, on the Lefkosia road, is another Unesco-listed **church** (☑2292 2393; ⊙by request). It was established in 1502 by Dimitrios de Coron, a Greek military officer, in the service of James II (King of Cyprus). Once belonging to a monastery, it was occupied by monks until the 1950s.

KOMMANDARIA

Homer made mention of its amber colour and rich sweetness in his writings. The Knights Templar were so fond of it they named it after their Commanderie (headquarters) in Lemesos, exporting it to the royal courts of Europe. Upon Richard the Lionheart's marriage in Lemesos he declared it 'the wine of kings' and 'the king of wines'. For over 4000 years it has been made at the vast vineyards in the Kommandaria valley, exposed to the southerly sun. Made from dark and white grapes, Kommandaria is as excellent as ever, with over a dozen villages still producing it. Try **Revecca Spirits** (www.reveccaspirits.com) in Agios Mamas for a large selection. You can also visit a number of the wineries and sample their produce.

The church is rectangular, with a semi-circular apse at the eastern end and a portico (built later) that surrounds it on three sides. It also has the characteristic pitched roof you would expect.

Internally, its **frescos** cover the pediment of both the east and west walls and its floor is enclosed with terracotta tiles.

The two 17th-century frescos on the north and south walls appear to have never been completed. They depict the apostles Peter and Paul, in a Renaissance-influenced (Italo-Byzantine) style, with vivid colours that give it a three-dimensional appearance.

PANAGIA THEOTOKOU (ARHANGELOU)

Dating from around 1514, this smaller chapel is just near Panagia tis Podythou. It's quite dark inside, so you may want to bring a torch. It has vivid didactic-style (teaching) panels with **frescos** depicting an interesting panoply of images from Jesus' life.

To access the church you will need to ask for (and probably hunt down) the caretaker at the Galata village coffee shop.

PANAGIA FORVIOTISSA (ASINOU)

This Unesco-listed **church** (☑9983 0329; donations welcome; ☺9.30am-12.30pm & 2-4pm Mon-Sat, 10am-1pm & 2-4pm Sun) is on the perimeter of the Adelfi Forest 4km southwest of Nikitari village. Dedicated to the Virgin of 'Phorbiottissa', it arguably the finest set of Byzantine **frescos** in the Troödos Massif.

Its images date from the 12th to the 17th centuries, displaying motifs across several artistic styles. It has similar themes to those of the other Unesco-listed churches, but their vibrancy and colours make the Asinou frescos unique.

To view the church, you'll need to ask its priest and caretaker, Father Kyriakos, who can usually be found at Nikitari's *kafeneio*.

The church can be reached by following the signs off the B9 from Lefkosia, via Vyzakia. There's also a forest hike from the village of Agios Theodoros to the west (off the B9), where you can take advantage of the surroundings and picnic in the adjoining forest.

Pitsylia

This wide-reaching region stretches east from Mt Olympus and Troödos, encompassing around 40 villages across to the Maheras Monastery. Its northern slopes are covered

in tall, aromatic pines and its valleys are full of vines and nut and fruit trees.

Pitsylia has a number of Byzantine churches, as well as challenging walks for long-distance hikers.

Agros is the hub of the region. Other villages with significant sites include Kyperounda, Platanistasa, Paliaiochori and Pelendri.

Hiking

Pitsylia has some well-marked hiking trails, including two short circular trails. Most take an out-and-back approach, unless you're hiking to the next village.

The CTO's pamphlet *Cyprus: Nature Trails* provides good maps of these trails, but it's still advisable to take detailed maps of the greater region.

Routes traverse forests, orchards, villages, valleys and mountain peaks, offering some of the best recreational hiking on the island.

Doxasi o Theos to Madari Fire Station (3.75km, two hours) A panoramic ridge-top hike with excellent views. The trail starts 2km outside Kyperounda.

Teisia tis Madari (3km, 1½ hours, circular) A continuation of the first route, this involves a circular cliff-top hike around Mt Madari (Adelfi; 1613m) with first-rate views.

Panagia tou Araka (Lagoudera) to Agros (6km, 2½ hours) A longer hike through vineyards and orchards, with a great viewpoint from the Madari-Papoutsas ridge.

Panagia tou Araka to Stavros tou Agiasmati (7km, 3½ hours) Takes in two of the most important Byzantine churches and weaves through forests, vineyards and stone terraces. This is the longest hike.

Agros to Kato Mylos (5km, two hours, circular) A gentle hike through cherry and pear orchards and past vineyards and rose gardens.

Petros Vanezis to Alona (1.5km, 30 minutes, circular) A shorter hike around the village of Alona, passing through hazelnut plantations.

Agia Irini to Spilies tou Digeni (3.2km, 1½ hours) A simple out-and-back hike to the concealed Digenis caves, where EOKA members hid during the insurgency of 1955–59.

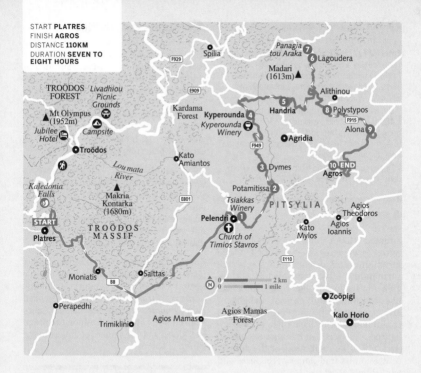

Driving Tour
Wine Route 6

❯ Wine Rte 6 takes in over 14 villages, two wineries and some of the best family-owned vineyards in the region. It is well signposted the whole way: look out for the green and burgundy signs that have a grape symbol and the number six on them. Take the B8 south from Platres, then turn onto the E806 to Pelendri. Here you can stop at ❶ **Tsiakkas Winery**, where you'll be offered some excellent dry whites and a commendable cab sav. Continue on the F949 past ❷ **Potamitissa** and ❸ **Dymes** villages until you reach Kyperounda and the ❹ **Kyperounda Winery**. This contemporary winery has a large range of whites and reds and a particularly palatable red blend called Andessitis. Next stops are the high-altitude villages of ❺ **Handria** and ❻ **Lagoudera**, on the F915, with abundant vineyards. Here you can stop and see the Unesco-listed 12th-century Byzantine church of ❼ **Panagia tou Araka**. Double back a short way then wind past ❽ **Polystypos** and ❾ **Alona** on the F915, then turn onto the E903 to reach the village of ❿ **Agros**, home of many mavros grapevines. Here you can finish the day at Dionysos Restaurant and stay the night at the lovely Rodon Hotel. The wine route is one long, winding loop, so make lots of rest stops, allocate a designated driver or watch the amount of wine you consume. Visiting times at the wineries are fairly loose, so it's a good idea to call beforehand. The wineries offer vineyard tours and are happy for you to taste freely. You ought to buy at least one bottle, though, which isn't much of a hardship.

❶ Getting There & Away

Public transport to the Pitsylia region is limited. **Emel** (☎7777 8121; www.limassolbuses.com; 1 way/all day & return €3/5) buses run from Agros to Lemesos at 5.15am, 6am, 7am, 9am and 2.30pm weekdays, 6am, 7am and 9am Saturday, 9.30am and 4pm Sunday.

Buses depart Lemesos at 7.30am, noon, 1.40pm and 4.15pm, weekdays, 7.30am and noon Saturday, 11am and 5pm Sunday, running to Agros, Agios Nikolaos tis Stegis, Kyperounda, Pelendri and Kato Mylos.

Buses run to Lefkosia from Agros at 6.40am daily; the journey back is at 12.50pm daily.

Agros

POP 840

Situated 1100m high in a cool valley, Agros (www.agros.org.cy) is well placed for hiking and driving forays into the surrounding hills. Renowned in the region for its locally made rose products like rosewater and Cypriot delight, it also specialises in preserved fruit and traditional Cypriot meats like *loukanika* (spiced sausages) and *lountza* (smoked pork fillet). As such, most of the activity centres on its traditional warehouses and workshops.

NECTAR OF THE GODS

Archaeologists have traced the island's winemaking history back to around 4000 BC, with amphorae, wine jugs and even grape pips excavated in the Lemesos region, suggesting Cyprus could be the oldest wine manufacturer on earth. Wine god Dionysos is making his presence felt once more, as Cypriot wines are growing in stature and popularity, perhaps regaining their former glory.

Troödos, with its fertile hills and valleys, is where some of the island's finest grapes are cultivated. Indigenous mavro (with dark red grapes) and xynisteri (with white grapes) vines are cultivated here, along with 11 other varieties. They contribute to red wines such as ofthalmo, maratheftiko, cabernet franc, cabernet sauvignon, mataro, mavro, lefkada and shiraz, and to whites such as xynisteri, sauvignon blanc, malaga and chardonnay.

◉ Sights & Activities

CNT – House of Roses TRADITIONAL WORKSHOP
(www.rose-tsolakis.com; Anapafseos 12; ⊕8am-5pm Mon-Fri, 10am-5pm Sat & Sun) At this rose-product and pottery store you can check out the workshop for a glimpse of the many ways roses can be used. Great examples include flower water, rose brandy, skin cleanser, candles, rose liqueur and even rose-infused wines. This is an excellent place for gifts.

Niki's Sweets TRADITIONAL WORKSHOP
(www.nikisweets.com.cy; Anapafseos 5; preserves €3-5) Selling her products all over Cyprus, and exporting as far as Australia, Niki makes marmalades, fig preserves and walnut sweets. Many of her preserves offer natural soothing and healing properties.

Kafkalia Sausages TRADITIONAL WORKSHOP
(Agros; prices by weight) Here some of the tastiest Cypriot meat products, including *lountza, hiromeri* (traditional smoked ham), *loukanika,* and *pastourmas* (spicy smoked beef) are made fresh on the premises. Check out the smoke room next to the store.

Around Pitsylia & Agros

STAVROS TOU AGIASMATI

This Unesco-listed Byzantine **church** (donations welcome) is famous for its 15th-century **murals** by Orthodox Syrian painter Philippos Goul.

In two tiers, upper and lower, the images decorate the ceilings and interior beams of the gabled roof, depicting scenes such as the discovery of the Holy Cross.

If the priest cannot be found, ask for the key to the church at the coffee shop in Platanistasa village (www.platanistasa.org). The church itself is 5km from the village, concealed slightly along the closed road off the Orounda–Platanistasa route (E906). Follow the Unesco signposts.

PANAGIA TOU ARAKA

This frequently visited 12th-century Unesco-listed **church** (donations welcome; ⊕9am-6pm) is located on the outskirts of Lagoudera village. From the outside it appears enormous, its pitched roof and wooden trellis concealing the church within.

Inside, it has some of the finest examples of late Comnenian style (1192) **frescos** in the Orthodox world. Its wide selection of neoclassical works, by artists from Constantinople, display images like the incredible Pantokrator featured in the tholos (beehive-shaped stone tomb).

Its other excellent frescos include the Annunciation, the Four Evangelists, the Archangel Michael and the Panagia Arakiotissa (patron of the church).

The unusual name of the church derives from *arakiotissa* (meaning 'of the wild pea') and owes its origins to the vegetable that grows profusely in the district. The church's priest and caretaker can usually be found next door. You should check with him before you take any photos of the frescos; if you receive permission to take pictures, be sure not to use a flash.

CHURCH OF TIMIOS STAVROS

Built sometime in the 12th century, the stone Church of the Holy Cross (donations welcome; ☺10am-5pm), as it is known, was originally dome shaped with a single aisle. In the 13th and 14th centuries it was added to, then destroyed, burnt and repaired again. Only the apse is original.

Another of the Unesco-listed churches of Cyprus, its uncovered frescos (1178) painted on the apse make it unique. Jesus is depicted (rather oversized) in prayer from the waist up, with the Virgin Mary and John the Baptist, painted as miniatures, flanking him.

Other depictions include the altar and the grail near the small window in the apse and St Stephen on the north side. These frescos (painted by the same hand) are considered a preface to the great works found in other Troödos churches, with simple straight lines and shiny earth colours.

The rest of the images are from the 14th century, when the church was completely repainted. They make up the more visually impressive frescos, especially the Descent to Hades in the upper section of the chapel.

The church is at the southern end of the village of Pelendri (www.pelendri.org), which was ruled by Jean de Lusignan while he was regent of Cyprus in the 13th century. If the church is closed (which is likely) ask at the village *kafeneio* for the whereabouts of the priest.

CHURCH OF THE TRANSFIGURATION OF THE SAVIOUR

Perched on the slope overlooking Palaichori village (www.palaichori.com), 14km from Agros, is this Unesco-listed early-16th-century chapel (☎9997 4230; donations welcome; ☺10am-1pm Tue & Wed). It has the wooden slanted roof common to other mountain churches, and one of the island's most complete groups of late Byzantine wall paintings.

The paintings, by an unknown master, depict complete figures like St Mamas upon the lion. The church also holds a series of iconostases painted by Mt Athos monk Mathaios. To see inside the church you may have to call the custodian or ask in the village centre at the Byzantine Heritage Museum.

SPILIA-KOURDALI
POP 460

These two traditional villages, situated in the Adelfi Forest, were established in the 16th century near the monastery and church of Virgin Mary Chrysokourdaliotissa (Kourdali). Like many villages in the region, they grew as refuges from constant invasions by conquerors like the Francs and later the Turks.

Kourdali's (www.kourdali.org) narrow valley saw it expand towards the village of Spilia, which got its name from the Roman graves (*spilioi* in Greek) found in the area. Local asbestos mining was the main proficiency of the villagers for many years, but after this they became skilled tailors and cobblers. Now the villages' cafes and craft shops are the main attraction.

Olive Mill of 'Paphitaina'   HISTORICAL SITE
In operation until 1955, the well-preserved olive-stone mill and wooden press are now housed in a traditional building in Spilia's village centre.

The mill, originally privately owned, was usually turned by a donkey, with the broken olives later being crushed by the presser. Olive oil was then extracted into *tzares* (clay urns) through the groove in the presser's base. Eventually the mill was superseded by modern presses in nearby villages. You can obtain the key to the olive mill house from the Friends of Spilia-Kourdali, in the building right next door.

Pafos & the West

Includes »

Pafos 83
Coral Bay 92
Akamas Heights 93
Dhrousia, Kritou Terra
& Around 93
Kathikas 94
Pano Akourdalia
& Kato Akourdalia 94
Akamas Peninsula 95
Polis 97
Baths of Aphrodite 99
Tylliria 100
Pomos 100
Kato Pyrgos 101
Psokas 102
Cedar Valley 103

Best Places to Eat

» Old Town Restaurant (p99)

» Kiniras Garden (p88)

» Argo (p89)

» Imogen's Inn (p94)

Best Places to Stay

» Axiothea Hotel (p204)

» Bougainvillea Hotel Apartments (p206)

» Amarakos Inn (p205)

» Ayii Anargyri Natural Healing Spa Resort (p205)

Why Go?

Pafos is packed with historical relics...and tourists. If you find the beach strip at Kato Pafos too developed, head up to Ktima on the hillside, which has an atmospheric Cypriot feel and a good choice of shops, restaurants and cafes. More beach resorts are strung out north along the coast towards Agios Georgios.

To seriously sidestep the crowds, consider renting a car and heading for the unspoilt Akamas Peninsula, where there are traditional villages, remote beaches and some of the best walks on the island. To the east, the vast Pafos Forest is equally enticing, melting almost imperceptibly into the sombre tracts of the Tyllirian wilderness.

Pafos itself has some of the island's most important archaeological sights, such as the extensive Pafos mosaics and the mysterious Tombs of the Kings. The small, pretty town of Polis, still untouched by package tourism, makes a perfect base for the independent traveller.

When to Go

Pafos is the island's top tourist destination, which is worth bearing in mind when planning your visit. July and August are, obviously, when you find the most sunbeds on the sand, the most sunburned noses – and the highest hotel prices. May-June and September-October are less crowded, with plenty of long sunny days. Spring and autumn can also be pleasantly warm, although evening temperatures cool down considerably. In winter, some restaurants and hotels close down altogether; if you head to the Western Troödos, you may even see some snow.

PAFOS

POP 67,432

Linked by a traffic artery, Kato Pafos (Lower Pafos) and Ktima (Upper Pafos, 3km to the northeast) form a schizoid whole. Kato Pafos, the tourist centre, is blatantly geared towards English tourists, with the inevitable all-day English breakfasts and bars. It could be worse: construction along the palm-fringed seafront is low-rise and, as well as being home to a vast archaeological site, Kato Pafos has backstreets hiding other historic gems, like medieval baths, catacombs and a simple fishermen's church. The official Pafos Archaeological Site is the grand-slam sight, however, being one of the South's richest archaeological locales. When you're standing (relatively) alone here, surrounded by acres of history, a vast blue sky and the wild fennel and caper plants that grow on the Mediterranean's edges, you feel a thousand years away from Guinness on tap.

Ktima, the old centre of Pafos, is overall a calmer place, where locals go about their daily business much as they have for decades. The neighbourhoods are rich with handsome colonial buildings that house government institutions and many of the town's museums. Ktima is also home to some good hotels.

○ Sights

Pafos Archaeological Site
ARCHAEOLOGICAL SITE

(Map p86; Kato Pafos; admission €3.40; ⊘8am-7.30pm) Nea Pafos (New Pafos) is, ironically, the name given to the sprawling Pafos Archaeological Site, which occupies the western segment of Kato Pafos. Nea Pafos was the ancient city of Pafos, founded in the late 4th century BC. Palea Pafos (Old Pafos) was in fact Kouklia, southeast of today's Pafos, and the site of the Sanctuary of Aphrodite. At the time of Nea Pafos, Cyprus was part of the kingdom of the Ptolemies, the Greco-Macedonian rulers of Egypt whose capital was Alexandria. The city became an important strategic outpost for the Ptolemies, and the settlement grew considerably over the next seven centuries.

The city was originally encircled by massive walls and occupied an area of about 950,000 sq metres. Despite being ceded to the Romans in 58 BC, it remained the centre of all political and administrative life in Cyprus, reaching its zenith during the 2nd

ROAD DISTANCES (KM)				
Polis	21			
Kato Pyrgos	69	46		
Fyti	36	17	66	
Pano Panagia	47	33	61	13
	Lara Beach	Polis	Kato Pyrgos	Fyti

or 3rd century AD. It was during this time that the city's most opulent public buildings were constructed, including those that house the famous Pafos mosaics.

Nea Pafos went into decline following an earthquake in the 4th century that badly damaged the city. Subsequently, Salamis in the east became the new capital of Cyprus, and Nea Pafos was relegated to the status of a mere bishopric. Arab raids in the 7th century set the seal on the city's demise and neither Lusignan settlement (1192–1489) nor Venetian and Ottoman colonisation revived Nea Pafos' fortunes.

The archaeological site is still being excavated since it is widely believed that there are many treasures still to be discovered. The following sections detail the major sights.

Pafos Mosaics

This mesmerising collection of intricate and colourful mosaics is located in the southern sector of the archaeological site, immediately to the south of the Agora. Found by accident in 1962 by a farmer ploughing his field, these exquisite mosaics decorated the extensive floor area of a large, wealthy residence from the Roman period. Subsequently named the **House of Dionysus** (because of the number of mosaics featuring Dionysus, the god of wine), this complex is the largest and best known of the mosaic houses.

The most wonderful thing about the mosaics is that, apart from their artistic and aesthetic merits, each tells a story, mostly based on ancient Greek myths.

The first thing you'll see upon entering is not a Roman mosaic at all but a Hellenistic monochrome pebble mosaic showing the monster **Scylla**. Based on a Greek myth, this mosaic was discovered in 1977, a metre underground in the southwestern corner of the atrium.

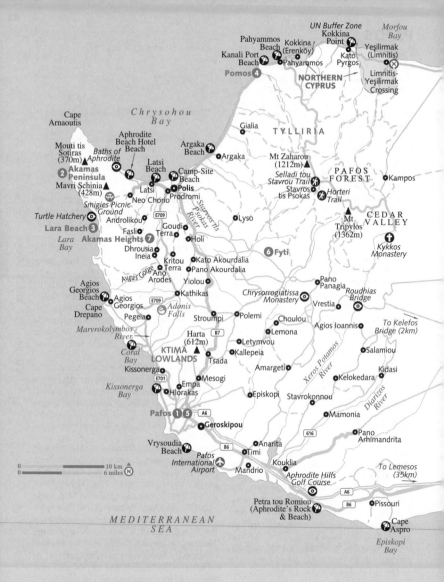

Pafos & the West Highlights

1 Exploring Pafos' ancient past by visiting its Roman **mosaics** (p83) and the **Tombs of the Kings** (p85) necropolis

2 Wandering the wild and rugged **Akamas Peninsula** (p95)

3 Swimming on **Lara Beach** (p93), the Republic's wildest stretch of sand

4 Hearing some first-class jazz at the **Paradise Jazz Festival** (p101) in Pomos

5 Enjoying delicious *kleftiko* at **Argo** (p89), a long-time Pafos restaurant that has built its reputation on this traditional oven-baked lamb dish

6 Watching the weavers at work in **Fyti** (p102), a scenic village famous for its cotton and silk craftwork

7 Relaxing in lovely **Akamas Heights** (p93) and spending time in its simple traditional villages

The famous tale of **Narcissus** is depicted in a mosaic in Room 2, while the wonderful **Four Seasons** mosaic (Room 3) depicts Spring crowned with flowers and holding a shepherd's stick, Summer holding a sickle and wearing ears of corn, Autumn crowned with leaves and wheat, and Winter as a bearded, grey-haired man.

Phaedra and Hippolytos (Room 6) is one of the most important mosaics in the house. It depicts the tragic tale of a stepmother's bizarre love for her stepson.

Another stunning mosaic in the house is the **Rape of Ganymede** (Room 8). Ganymede was a beautiful young shepherd who became the cupbearer of the gods. The mosaicist had apparently miscalculated the space allowed to him, which is why the eagle's wings are cropped.

In the Western Portico (Room 16) is a mosaic based on a tale familiar to any lover of Shakespeare: the story of **Pyramus and Thisbe**, first narrated by Ovid in his *Metamorphosis,* and adapted in *Romeo and Juliet* (and badly staged in *A Midsummer Night's Dream*).

For in-depth details on these and the other mosaics, buy the excellent official *Guide to the Pafos Mosaics,* on sale for €6 at the ticket kiosk.

A short walk away are the smaller **Villa of Theseus** and the **House of Aion**. The latter, a purpose-built structure made from stones found on the site, houses a 4th-century mosaic display made up of five separate panels. The house was named after the pagan god Aion, depicted in the mosaics. Although the image has been damaged somewhat, the name Aion and the face of the god can still be clearly seen.

The Villa of Theseus is thought to have been a 2nd-century private residence and is named after a representation of the hero Theseus fighting the Minotaur. The building occupies an area of 9600 sq metres and, so far, 1400 sq metres of mosaics have been uncovered. The round mosaic of Theseus and the Minotaur is particularly well preserved and can be seen in Room 36. Other mosaics to look out for are those of Poseidon in Room 76 and Achilles in Rooms 39 and 40.

Allow at least two hours to see the three houses properly.

Agora, Asklipieion & Odeion

The Agora (or forum) and Asklipieion date back to the 2nd century AD and constitute the heart of the original Nea Pafos complex.

TOMB TIPS

» Allow at least two hours for the Tombs of the Kings site.

» Try to visit during the early morning as it can get very hot walking around the sprawling necropolis later in the day.

» Bring a hat and bottled water.

» Be very careful when descending into some of the tombs, as the stone steps are large and can be slippery.

Today, the Agora consists mainly of the Odeion, a semicircular theatre that was restored in 1970 but does not look particularly ancient. The rest of the Agora is discernible by the remains of marble columns that form a rectangle in the largely empty open space. What is left of the Asklipieion, the healing centre and altar of Asklepios, god of medicine, runs east to west on the southern side of the Odeion.

Saranta Kolones Fortress

Not far from the mosaics are the remains of the medieval Saranta Kolones Fortress, named for the '40 columns' that were once a feature of the now almost levelled structure. Little is known about the precise nature or history of the original fortress, other than it was built by the Lusignans in the 12th century and was subsequently destroyed by an earthquake in 1222. A few desultory arches are the only visual evidence of its original grandeur.

Tombs of the Kings   ARCHAEOLOGICAL SITE
(off Map p86; Kato Pafos; admission €1.70; ⊙8.30am-7.30pm) Imagine yourself surrounded by ancient tombs in a desert-like landscape where the only sounds are waves crashing on rocks. The Tombs of the Kings, a Unesco World Heritage site, is indeed a fascinating and mysterious place. The tombs are also unique in Cyprus, being heavily influenced by ancient Egyptian tradition, when it was believed that tombs for the dead should resemble houses for the living.

Located 2km north of Kato Pafos, the site contains a set of well-preserved underground tombs and chambers used by residents of Nea Pafos during the Hellenistic and Roman periods, from the 3rd century BC to the 3rd century AD. Despite the name, the tombs were not actually used by royalty; they earned the title Tombs of the Kings for their

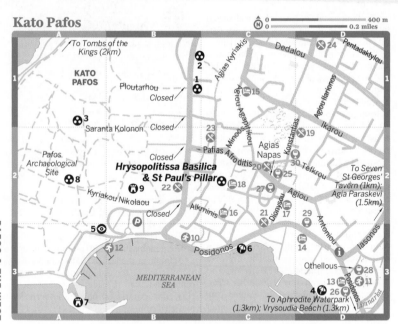

Kato Pafos

To Tombs of the Kings (2km)

KATO PAFOS

Ploutarhou *Closed*

Saranta Kolonon *Closed*

Pafos Archaeological Site

Closed

Agias Kyriakis

Dedalou

Pentadaktylou

Agiou Aeapitikou

Agias Napas

Minoos

Pafias Afroditis

Hrysopolitissa Basilica & St Paul's Pillar

Kyriakou Nikolaou

Closed

Alkminis

Posidonos

MEDITERRANEAN SEA

Othellous

To Aphrodite Waterpark (1.3km); Vrysoudia Beach (1.3km)

To Seven St Georges' Tavern (1km); Agia Paraskevi (1.5km)

Agiou Ilarionos

Ikarou

Konstantias

Tefkrou

Agiou

Dionysou

Antoniou

Iasonos

Larnaka

grand appearance. Members of the higher social classes were, however, buried here.

The seven excavated tombs are scattered over a wide area; the most impressive is No 3, which has an open atrium below ground level, surrounded by columns. Other tombs have niches built into the walls where bodies were stored. Most of the tombs' treasures have long since been spirited away by grave robbers.

FREE Hrysopolitissa Basilica
& St Paul's Pillar ARCHAEOLOGICAL SITE
(Map p86; Stassándhrou, Kato Pafos) This fascinating and extensive site was home to one of Pafos' largest religious structures. What remains are the foundations of a Christian **basilica**, built in the 4th century, which aptly demonstrates the size and magnificence of the original church; it was ultimately destroyed during Arab raids in 653. Marble columns from this church lie scattered around the site and **mosaics** are still visible. Further incarnations of the basilica were built over the years, leading to the present small **Agia Kyriaki** church, now used for Anglican and Greek Orthodox services. Pathways crisscross the site with explanatory plaques in English. Look also for the **tomb of Eric Ejegod**, the 12th-century King of Denmark

who died suddenly in 1103 on his way to the Holy Land.

On the western side of the basilica is the so-called **St Paul's Pillar**, where St Paul was allegedly tied and scourged 39 times before he finally converted his tormentor, the Roman governor Sergius Paulus, to Christianity.

On the northwest side of the site is a tiny **early-Christian basilica**, the entrance to which has been almost completely taken over by the gnarled root of an ancient olive tree.

FREE Agia Solomoni & the
Christian Catacomb ARCHAEOLOGICAL SITE
(Map above; Kato Pafos) This modest tomb complex just off Leoforos Apostolou Pavlou is the burial site of the seven Machabee Brothers, who were martyred around 174 BC during the time of Antiochus IV Epiphanes. Their mother was Agia Solomoni, a Jewish woman who became a saint after the death of her sons. It is thought that the space was a synagogue in Roman times. The entrance to the catacomb is marked by a collection of votive rags tied to a large tree outside the tomb. There are more rags surrounding the tombs, some attached to copies of icons. This ostensibly pagan practice is continued by Christian visitors today.

Kato Pafos

◎ **Top Sights**
Hrysopolitissa Basilica & St
Paul's Pillar C2

◎ **Sights**
1 Agia Solomoni & the Christian
Catacomb B1
2 Agios Lambrianos Rock-Cut
Tomb B1
3 Agora, Asklipieion & Odeion.................. A1
4 Alykes Beach D3
5 Entrance to Pafos
Archaeological Site.......................... A3
6 Main Municipal Beach C3
7 Pafos Castle... A3
8 Pafos Mosaics A2
9 Saranta Kolones Fortress..................... B2

◎ **Activities, Courses & Tours**
Bubble Maker ....(see 10)
10 Cydive.. B3
11 Mickys Tours D3
12 Paphos Sea Cruises B3

◎ **Sleeping**
13 Alexander the Great............................... D3
14 Annabelle... D3
15 Crystallo Apartments C1
16 Daphne... C2
17 Dionysos.. C2
18 Pyramos Hotel.. C2

◎ **Eating**
19 Almond Tree D2
20 Argo.. C2
21 Chloe's No 1... C2
22 Hondros... B2
23 Kyra Frosini C2
24 Nikos Tyrimos Fish Taverna D1

◎ **Drinking**
25 Baywatch.. C2
26 Deck Cafe & Bar D3
27 Different Bar.. C2
28 Kouskous.. D3
29 La Place Royale....................................... D2
30 Zen.. C2

Be wary of the lowest section at the base of a set of steep stairs; entering from the bright sunlight, it is hard to discern the water-filled cave and deep well which constitutes a potentially dangerous hazard.

FREE **Agios Lambrianos
Rock-Cut Tomb** ARCHAEOLOGICAL SITE
(Map above; Kato Pafos) A little further north, on the side of Fabrica Hill, are a couple of enormous underground caverns dating from the early Hellenistic period. These are also burial chambers associated with the saints Lambrianos and Misitikos. The interiors of the tombs bear frescos that indicate they were used as a Christian place of worship. There are ongoing excavations here which have, more recently, revealed remains of a classical theatre.

FREE **Agia Paraskevi** CHURCH
(off Map opposite; Geroskipou; ⊙8am-1pm & 2-5pm) One of the loveliest churches in the Pafos area is this six-domed Byzantine church in Geroskipou, east of Pafos. Most of the surviving frescos date back to the 15th century AD. The first frescos visible when entering are the **Last Supper**, the **Washing of Feet** and the **Betrayal**. A primitive but interesting depiction of the **Virgin Orans**

(the Virgin Mary with her arms raised) can be seen in the central cupola.

Pafos Castle CASTLE
(Map opposite; Kato Pafos; adult/child €1.70/free; ⊙9am-6pm; ⊕) This small, empty fort guards the harbour entrance and is entered by a small stone bridge over a moat. Most visitors climb to the roof to enjoy the sweeping harbour views. The castle also serves as an event venue during the Aphrodite Festival.

The castle is all that remains of an earlier Lusignan fort built in 1391; the rest of it was destroyed by the Venetians less than a hundred years later. The Ottomans subsequently used the ground floor as dungeons.

Archaeological Museum MUSEUM
(Map p89; Leoforos Georgiou Griva Digeni, Ktima; admission €1.70; ⊙9am-5pm Mon-Fri, 10am-1pm Sat & Sun) Essentially for admirers of archaeological minutiae, this small museum houses a varied and extensive collection of artefacts from the Neolithic period to the 18th century. Displayed in four rooms, exhibits include jars, pottery and glassware, tools, coins and coin moulds. Hellenistic and Roman artefacts include a limestone grave stele, marble statuettes, votive objects, pottery from the House of Dionysus and terracotta figures of dogs and stags.

Byzantine Museum
MUSEUM

(Map p89; Andrea Ioannou 5, Ktima; admission €2; ⊙9am-4pm Mon-Fri, to 1pm Sat) This noteworthy museum is worth visiting for its ecclesiastical vestments, vessels, copies of scripture and collection of impressive icons, including a 9th-century representation of Agia Marina, thought to be the oldest icon on the island, and an unusual double-sided icon from Filousa dating from the 13th century.

Ethnographical Museum
MUSEUM

(Map p89; Exo Vrysis 1, Ktima; admission €3; ⊙9am-6pm Mon-Sat, to 1pm Sun) This privately owned museum houses a varied collection of coins, traditional costumes, kitchen utensils, Chalcolithic axe heads, amphorae and other assorted items. There's more of the same in the garden, including a Hellenistic rock-cut tomb. The €5 guidebook available at the entrance helps you sort out the seemingly jumbled collection.

FREE Agios Georgios Museum
MUSEUM

(Hlorakas; ⊙9am-6pm) Buffs of recent Cypriot history may find this somewhat bizarre and nationalistic museum of interest. It's located on the spot where the caïque *Agios Georgios* (now the museum's prime exhibit), captained by EOKA rebel Georgios Grivas, landed in November 1954 with a large supply of arms and munitions, with the aim of overthrowing British colonial rule. His rebels were finally arrested two months later while attempting another landing. The museum walls document the capture and subsequent trial, including the rebels' mug shots, as well as some of the seized rifles and ammunition.

The site, known as 'Grivas' Landing', is 4km north of Kato Pafos on the E701 and is easily identified by the large Agios Georgios church, built to commemorate the event, as well as the adjacent St George Hotel.

✦ Activities

Aside from the organised tours offered by myriad companies (look for the flyers all over town), most activities here are centred on the sea. Apart from those mentioned below, there are boat trips, pedalos and (if you must) the ubiquitous banana ride. Alternatively, head for the harbour, where around a dozen kiosks advertise glass-bottom-boat rides, waterskiing, fishing trips, cruises and boat charters. The promenade is also good for strolling, with plans afoot eventually to extend the promenade from Pafos airport to the new marina due to be completed at Potima by 2013.

Paphos Sea Cruises
BOAT TRIPS

(Map p86; ☑8000 0011, www.paphosseacruises .com; Pafos harbour, Kato Pafos; ⚓) A reputable choice; most cruises include extras such as an onboard barbecue, snorkelling gear, children's entertainment and canoes. Day trips cost from €33 per person. Children under 12 are free or pay half, depending on the cruise.

Cydive
DIVING

(Map p86; ☑2693 4271; www.cydive.com; 1 Posidonos, Myrra Complex 33, Kato Pafos) The waters off Pafos are ideal for diving, with around 50 sites to explore. This is a professional, longstanding company. Single dives, including all equipment, cost €50; a package of 10 dives costs €435.

✦ Festivals & Events

Pafos Aphrodite Festival
MUSIC FESTIVAL

(www.pafc.com.cy) Enjoy opera under the stars every September when a world-class operatic performance takes place in the suitably grandiose surroundings of Pafos Castle. Recent operas include Puccini's *Madame Butterfly* and Offenbach's *The Tales of Hoffmann*.

Solar Car Challenge
CAR RACE

(www.cyi.ac.cy/solar_race/intro; Geroskipou) This annual solar car race revs into action every June, attracting local teams and international participants who compete in creating and racing their solar-powered cars with some truly ingenious results.

✗ Eating

Pafos' food scene varies considerably. In general, stay away from restaurants along the front-line strip in Kato Pafos, especially those with HP sauce and ketchup bottles on the tables. Instead, wander back a street or two for more genuine local food. Tafon Ton Vasileon (Tombs of the Kings Rd) and the harbour also have some good choices, while Ktima has quality over quantity, including a couple of superb options.

KTIMA

✐ Kiniras Garden
CYPRIOT €€

(Map opposite; ☑2694 1604; Leoforos Archiepiskopou Makariou III 91; mains €8-15; ⊙dinner) This restaurant is a small green oasis with

Ktima

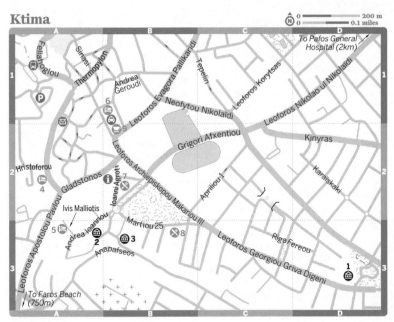

Ktima

◎ Sights
1 Archaeological Museum D3
2 Byzantine Museum.............................A3
3 Ethnographical Museum....................B3

🛏 Sleeping
4 Agapinor Hotel....................................A2
5 Axiothea Hotel A3
6 Kiniras...B1

🍴 Eating
7 Fetta's...B2
Kiniras Garden ....(see 6)
8 Politia..B3

🍷 Drinking
9 Kafé...B2

trees, statues and trickling waterfalls. Fourth generation, Georgios is passionate about his traditional cuisine; most of the recipes have been passed down from his grandmother and the produce comes from his own 60-hectare gardens. A member of the Vakhis scheme (see the box, p146), the restaurant's *kleftiko* (oven-baked lamb) is a house speciality. There are homemade desserts and the wine list includes excellent vintages from family-owned local vineyards. Reservations recommended.

Fetta's CYPRIOT €€€
(Map above; ☎2693 7822; Ioanni Agroti 33; meze €16; ⊘evenings) Fetta's specialises in classic regional fare made with salutary (and salivatory) attention to detail. A *yaya* (grandma) prepares a fantastic meze of grilled meats, serving out of a low, smoky window on the side of the house, while efficient waiters dart between the kitchen and the sprawled-out tables. Reservations recommended.

Politia MEDITERRANEAN €€
(Map above; Martiou 25; mains from €7) Housed in a historic stone building overlooking a park of pines, this chilled-out cafe and restaurant has regular live music and art exhibitions, combined with comfy sofas and a menu of tasty light eats, including crêpes, kebabs and salads.

KATO PAFOS
Argo CYPRIOT €€
(Map p86; ☎2693 3327; Pafias Afroditis 21; mains €10; ⊘dinner) Located in the (relatively) quiet part of Kato Pafos, this place has all the charm of a village taverna with its natural stone, original wooden shutters

PAFOS TOWN BEACHES

» In the centre of Kato Pafos, the **Main Municipal Beach** (Map p86) is not your standard holiday brochure–style sweep of sun-kissed sand: the beach area is paved and partly pedestrianised. Comprising a collection of wooden decks, rocks, sand and diving points, it's still pleasant and the water is sparkling clean. Facilities include showers, toilets and a cafe-restaurant.

» Heading east, you come to **Alykes Beach** (Map p86), which is better known locally as Sopab Beach after a factory that once stood here. Wedged between the Deck Cafe and Bar and the Alexander the Great hotel, this is a perfect spot for families with paddling tots, with rock pools and shallow, clear water, as well as sufficient sand for sandcastles. The sprawling terrace of the overlooking cafe is also convenient for refreshments and drinks (including grown-up cocktails at sunset).

» Continuing east from Alykes Beach, you come to **Vrysoudia Beach** (off Map p86), the pleasant sandy stretch behind the Anabelle Hotel where you can rent sunbeds and parasols (€5 per day).

» You will need wheels to reach **Faros Beach** (off Map p89), located north of the archaeological site. It's an exposed, sandy beach with some sandstone rocks and a couple of on-site snack bars. Keep in mind, however, that the open sea often develops a swell, which can be dangerous for swimming.

» Even further out, around 8km north of Kato Pafos, is the long, sandy undeveloped beach of **Kissonerga Bay**, where you can find banana plantations and solitude. There are almost no facilities, so bring a book, food and water, and relax.

and walls washed in warm ochre. The specialities, such as moussaka, are similarly authentic, as is the twice-weekly (Tuesday and Saturday) *kleftiko;* on these days it's advisable to book.

Hondros   CYPRIOT €€
(Map p86; www.hondros.com.cy; Leoforos Apostolou Pavlou 96; mains €10) This is the oldest traditional restaurant in Pafos, dating back to 1953, so it's spent a long time getting it right. Highlights include a meaty *stifado* (rabbit or beef stew) and a variation on the tasty Turkish dish *imam bayildi,* here known as *imam* (aubergines and courgettes in a tomato and garlic sauce).

Almond Tree   FUSION €€
(Map p86; Konstantias 5; mains from €8; ☉dinner; 🖉) Features unusual Thai-Cypriot tastes to titillate the palate – try the chicken satay or salmon cakes with mango – along with a smattering of stock Cypriot and international dishes. Vegetarians are also well catered to with stir fries and similar.

Nikos Tyrimos Fish Taverna   SEAFOOD €€€
(Map p86; Agapinoros 71; seafood meze €14) This is the place in Pafos to come for a taste of the creatures of the sea, caught daily from the owner's own boats. Choose from the ones on display or push the boat out

with the seafood meze, consisting of 22 fishy dishes.

Kyra Frosini   CYPRIOT €€
(Map p86; Pafias Afroditis & Filoktitou 4; mains €7) Kyra Frosini is relaxed, with a pretty courtyard shaded by palm trees and a cosy winter interior. There are regular art exhibitions and the food ranges from fetta pies to pork chops, though it's the home-style cakes that truly excel.

Chloe's No 1   CHINESE €€
(Map p86; ☎2693 4676; Posidonos 13; mains €10) The best Chinese restaurant in town.

 Drinking

Most bars and pubs are clustered along Agiou Antoniou in Kato Pafos, known locally as Bar St. Places like Blues Brotherz and Robin Hood adorn the once-quiet streets, and Bubbles stays true to its name by shooting bubble guns outside to lure customers. English pubs are just like back 'ome, but with the added treat of Robbie Williams impersonators (and similar) entertaining the sunburnt crowds. There is a handful of more sophisticated places in town.

Kouskous   BAR
(Map p86; Othellous 5, Kato Pafos) There's a wonderful over-the-top opulence about

this place, with its glittering chandeliers, smoochy purple-and-black colour scheme, plush lilac seats, circular mirrors and fresh orchids – and let's not forget the strawberry-and-kiwi spiked mojitos.

Baywatch BAR
(Map p86; cnr Konstantias & Agias Napas, Kato Pafos; ⏱8am-late) Comfortable cushioned chairs, billiards, 30-plus cocktails and a congenial owner, Antonis, equal a winning combination. All the tables are facing the street for maximum people-watching potential and the cocktails just keep on coming, as well they should, at just €2 a tipple.

La Place Royale CAFE-BAR
(Map p86; Posidonos, Kato Pafos) This is one of the classiest cafe-bars, right on the busy pedestrian strip at the eastern end of Posidonos. This little oasis of glass, cane, wrought iron and mini waterfalls in a shaded paved patio is perfect for a pre-clubbing cocktail.

Kafé CAFE
(Map p89; cnr Leoforos Archiepiskopou Makariou III, Ktima; snacks €6; 🛜) This place has an edgy contemporary feel despite its claim of being 'the oldest cafe in Paphos'. Enjoy dynamic abstract prints, a mounted motorbike on the wall (!) and a short, sharp menu including cocktails and coffees, plus lightweight snacks.

Different Bar BAR
(Map p86; Agias Napas, Kato Pafos) Popular gay bar.

Zen BAR
(Map p86; Tefkrou 2, Kato Pafos) Slick minimalist decor with a black-and-white colour scheme; popular with well-heeled locals.

Deck Cafe & Bar BAR
(Map p86; Posidonos, Kato Pafos) Kick back on this vast terrace overlooking the sand and rocks, listening to feel-good lounge music while sipping a (feel-good) cocktail.

☆ Entertainment

If you're into clubbing, head for Agiou Antoniou in Kato Pafos, near the tourist office, home to the best-loved music bars and clubs (as well as the previously mentioned bars). Don't confuse ordinary clubs with 'cabarets', which are basically brothels.

ℹ Information

Wi-fi is widely available in Pafos hotels, as well as in a number of cafes and bars, where you can generally connect free with a drink. There's a handful of internet cafes; the tourist office can provide a list.

Cyprus Tourism Organisation (CTO) airport (☎2642 3161; Pafos International Airport; ⏱9.30am-11pm); Kato Pafos (☎2693 0521; Posidonos; ⏱8.15am-2.30pm & 3-6.30pm Mon-Sat, closed Wed & Sat afternoons); Ktima (☎2693 2841; Gladstonos; ⏱8.15am-2.30pm

---

CHILDREN'S CYPRUS: PAFOS

Children will not be bored in Pafos. Like the rest of Cyprus, the town is extremely child-friendly and there are various options for them to use up all that energy and be entertained at the same time.

Pafos Bird Park (☎2681 3852; www.pafosbirdpark.com; Agios Georgiou; adult/child €15.50/8.50; ⏱9am-8pm; 👶) Located on the road to Coral Bay, this may be Cyprus' best zoo and best children's attraction rolled into one. Apart from birds, there are giraffes, antelopes, deer, gazelles, mouflon, reptiles, giant tortoises, emus and ostriches. There's also a restaurant and snack bar, and a playground.

Aphrodite Waterpark (off Map p86; ☎2691 3638; www.aphroditewaterpark.com; Posidonos, Kato Pafos; adult/child €28/15; ⏱10am-5.30pm; 👶) A place for all-day entertainment – at a price to match – where the adults can have a massage while the kids battle the mini volcano. A wristband can keep track of all your daily expenses, which you then pay at the end of the day.

Bubble Maker (Map p86; Cydive; ☎2693 4271; www.cydive.com; 1 Posidonos, Kato Pafos; €40-45; 👶) Bubble Maker is a full–scuba gear diving experience for children between eight and 10 years old. There are two programmes: the first in a pool, the second taking that grand leap to the sea. It's a great watery way to get youngsters interested in diving, and this PADI-trained team ensures a safe and confined environment at all times.

TOP PICKS FOR THE TEENS (& THEIR PARENTS)

Parents, if you're on holiday with your teenage kids – or equally, teenagers, if you're on holiday with your parents – and you want a break from incessant sunbathing and bickering beach time, get over to **Zephyros Adventure Sports** (2693 0037; www.enjoycyprus .com; The Royal Complex, Shop 7, Tafon Ton Vasileon) and take your pick of activities. You can choose from mountain biking, kayaking, climbing, trekking, snorkelling, scuba diving and, in the winter months, skiing. It's the perfect way to a happy family holiday. Alternatively, go on one of the **hikes** around the Akamas peninsula recommended on p95. Plenty of outfits offer 4WD safaris, but bear in mind their environmental impact, including soil erosion, excessive fossil-fuel use and noise pollution, and resist if you can.

& 3-6.30pm Mon-Sat, closed Wed & Sat afternoons) Has decent maps, useful brochures and booklets on hiking, biking and agrotourism, a hotel guide, transport information and tons of other useful information about Cyprus. It also organises free guided tours around Ktima every Thursday at 10am from the Ktima office. You need to book in advance.

www.paphosfinder.com Lists a lot of useful services for visitors to the city.

www.visitcyprus.com The regional tourist authority website.

www.visitpafos.org.cy Specific information about Pafos and the surrounding region.

❶ Getting There & Away

TO/FROM THE AIRPORT Bus 613 runs to the airport from the Karavella Bus Station (Map p89)in Ktima at 2pm and 7pm, while buses from the airport to Ktima run at 7.30am and 6.30pm. Bus 612 runs half-hourly between 10.30am and 10.30pm to/from the airport, with stops or pick-up points including Coral Bay and Posidonos in Kato Pafos. A single journey is €1.

A taxi between the airport and Pafos costs about €25.

AIR Pafos International Airport is 8km southeast of the town. Many budget airlines and some scheduled planes fly here.

BUS InterCity (www.intercity-buses.com) has five daily buses weekdays to Lefkosia (€5,

1½ hours) and eight daily buses weekdays to Lemesos (€3, 45 minutes) departing from Karavella Bus Station in Ktima. There is a reduced service at weekends.

SERVICE TAXI Travel & Express (0777 7474; www.travelexpress.com.cy; Leoforos Evagora Pallikaridi 9, Ktima) operates service taxis to Lemesos (€10, one hour), to Larnaka (change at Lemesos; €21, 1½ hours) and to Lefkosia (change at Lemesos; €22, 1½ hours).

❶ Getting Around

Pafos Buses (www.pafosbuses.com) provides an urban-wide and regional network of buses. Fares cost €1 per journey, €2 per day or €10 per week within the district of Pafos, including rural villages.

Frequent services from Ktima:

Coral Beach Bus 610; 25 minutes.

Geroskipou Beach Bus 615; 25 minutes. (The beach is 3km southeast of Kato Pafos.)

Kato Pafos Bus 611; 15 minutes.

Polis Bus 645; one hour.

In Kato Pafos, there's a large free car park near the entrance to the Pafos Archaeological Site. In Ktima, there are car parks on the main square (cnr Gladstonos and Leoforos Georgiou Griva Digeni) and by Karavella Bus Station.

If you need a **taxi** (2693 3301), you can call, flag one down or head for one of the plentiful taxi stands across the city. Be aware that taxi drivers will charge an extortionate €10 for the 3km Kato Pafos–Ktima ride.

AROUND PAFOS

The area around Pafos is superb for beaches, walks, traditional villages and overall exploring. To visit, however, you'll generally need to take a tour or organise your own transport. While a scooter is great for pottering around beach resorts, a car is preferable, especially for visiting the western Troödos, the wild and desolate Akamas Peninsula or the sparsely populated Tyllirian wilderness of northwest Cyprus.

Coral Bay

Coral Bay is located 12km northwest of Pafos, with several different stretches of beach, all accessible from different parts of the approach road. Although rows of umbrellas and crowds of bathers are no longer conducive to finding coral on this lovely beach, the atmosphere is lively and the facilities are good for families, although the restaurants are largely indifferent unless you like burgers and chips.

One exception is **Neo's Sports Club** (2662 2900; Panayias Agridiotissas 38), where owner Stavros cooks a perfect steak at your table. The coconut-baked sea bream is another winner. Resembling a private colonial club, the place has billiard tables, a rooftop cocktail bar and a traditional bowling green. While the club unabashedly attracts the local silver-haired set, the food is very good indeed. Reservations are essential for dinner. Neo's is signposted off the E701 just beyond the main Coral Beach roundabout.

The construction of the luxurious new 1000-berth marina in nearby Potima may well give Coral Bay a welcome touch of class. After some lengthy legal wrangling, a completion date for the **Pafos Marina** (as it will be known) has been set for late 2013.

AKAMAS HEIGHTS

If you're spending any time in the Pafos area, make sure you check out the Akamas Heights region. Most of the villages have great agrotourism-restored traditional houses for rent (check www.agrotourism .com.cy); the food in the taverns, cooked for the locals, is generally delicious; the atmosphere is peaceful; and the hiking possibilities are fantastic. And did we mention the beaches? This area has some of the best in the South.

The villages of Akamas Heights can be visited en route to Polis, on the picturesque western road (E701/709). There's no public transport to get to these villages, the beaches or Avgas Gorge. The climb to the heights starts at Pegeia, populated mainly by well-heeled Brits. From here you can head northwest towards the southern approach to the Akamas Peninsula.

🏖 Beaches

There is a real treat on the southwestern side of the Akamas Peninsula. Approached by a rough but driveable track from Agios Georgios, around 21km north of Coral Bay, the famous Lara coastal area is mercifully undeveloped. Backed by desert-like scrubland, tinged with dark ochre, and studded with gorse, bushy pines and seasonal wildflowers, it is set against a distant backdrop of low-lying hills. Look for the signs to Lara Restaurant, where you can stop for a

drink or snack on the vast terrace overlooking pristine **Lara Bay**, with its shingle and dark sand.

The more famous **Lara Beach** lies in the next cove, separated by a headland and cupped by lime rocks. Aside from the modest cafeteria-bar that recently opened near the entrance, there is no development here; the beach is sandy and the water is clean and calm. Also serving as a **turtle hatchery**, this is one of the few remaining havens for green and loggerhead turtles to nest, so sun loungers and umbrellas are not allowed. Monk seals also dwell in the sea caves around the peninsula.

The path towards the beach is a dirt track but can be driven on by 'normal' (2WD) cars, although you should take care when parking not to get stuck in the sand. If you would rather not retrace your path to Agios Georgios, take the signposted paved road to **Ineia** (8km) near the entrance to Lara Restaurant; this is a pretty drive which winds between pine-clad hills and valleys.

Agios Georgios Beach can be reached by conventional vehicle from Polis (via Pegeia) or Pafos (via Coral Bay). It is a 100m stretch of shadeless sand and rock with a little harbour, but beach umbrellas and loungers are available for hire. There is a small beach bar and, up on the bluff, one of the region's most popular seafood restaurants, **Saint George's Fish Tavern** (Agios Georgios; 2662 1888; mains €13). Due to the restaurant's location next to the harbour, the fish here is the best in the region – and you know it's good when it's just grilled, with nothing but some olive oil and lemon. The squid and octopus are similarly superb. Weekends get busy and, despite the vast terrace, you may have to queue for a table, but you can enjoy the sea views while you wait. It also has a few rooms to rent.

The adjacent large open space is popular at sunset. There is also a modest archaeological site nearby, with ruins of a 6th-century basilica church, including a partly visible mosaic floor, and several rock-hewn tombs dating from the Roman period. Access times are a hit-and-miss affair.

Dhrousia, Kritou Terra & Around

POP 390 & 90

Once you are up in the heights, you will come across a series of villages that enjoy a

WORTH A TRIP

GOURMET GEROSKIPOU

A pretty, traditional village with a striking 9th-century Byzantine church, Geroskipou nonetheless has its main appeal in the meze at **Seven St Georges' Tavern** (off Map p86; ☎2696 3176; www.7stgeorgestavern.com; meze €25; ☺closed Mon). Owner George, together with his wife, Lara, have grown, dried or pickled (organically) everything you eat and drink in this place. There is a herb garden and a meat-smoking cabin at the back. Even the wine is produced here, from organic home-grown grapes. Your meze, the house speciality, comes in the usual trickle of olives and capers, beetroot and carrot salads, cold meats, casseroles and smoked ham. Everything is seasonal, so you might get hand-picked wild asparagus, wild mushrooms with fresh herbs, aubergines in tomato, or tender *kleftiko* (oven-baked lamb). The restaurant is in an old house with a vine-and-palm-leaf-covered terrace, in the centre of the village near the church.

cool climate, grow fine wine grapes and are prettier than most Cypriot villages. They also make a useful alternative base for travellers wishing to avoid the busy beach scene of the coast further south.

Particularly beautiful are the villages of Dhrousia and Kritou Terra. Few tourists spend their time here, but each village has a lovely place to stay and makes a good base for a relaxing holiday.

Dhrousia is a village of winding streets, moustached men sitting outside the *kafeneio* (coffee shop), large fig trees offering their fruit to passers-by, and an occasional donkey standing by the road. There are several tavernas in town, including well-signposted **Finikkas** (☎2633 2336) with its traditional dining room and menu of meaty mains including grilled souvlaki and lamb kebabs.

Kritou Terra, a little east from Dhrousia, is an unspoilt village with some splendid traditional houses tastefully renovated by their inhabitants; several have been reborn as atmospheric places to stay. The late-Byzantine church of Agia Ekaterini, at the southern end of the village, is worth whipping your camera out for.

Two other villages, not far from Dhrousia and Kritou Terra, are unspoilt **Inia** (population 350) and **Goudi** (population 160), both of which also have places to stay. For more details, see p205.

Kathikas

POP 335

This is the most easily accessible village from Pafos, midway between Pafos and Polis on the E709. Famous for its vineyards and wine, it is home to several popular restaurants. You can also spy one of Cyprus' so-called tree monuments located just outside the village here: the Cypress tree of Agios Nikolaos is a lofty 14m high, with a pensionable age of more than 700 years.

There are several traditional tavernas offering reliably good, if unexceptional, food. For something different, head for **Imogen's Inn** (☎2663 3269; meze €16.50), which resembles a French bistro, with the sounds of jazz and blues tinkling into the garden that sprawls out under a large fig tree. There is the usual meze fare here, but there is also a vegetarian option which includes spinach and feta pie, falafel and *ful medame* (broad beans). Consider chocolate fudge cake for afters.

Pano Akourdalia & Kato Akourdalia

POP 35 & 30

From Kathikas you can detour onto the B7 (the direct road between Pafos and Polis) via these two picturesque villages, where you have the option of staying overnight or just stopping for a relaxing lunch. **Amarakos Inn** (☎2231 3374; Kato Akourdalia; mains €10; ☺restaurant lunch & dinner) is a delightful agrotourism hotel (see p205) with an excellent restaurant where much of the produce is grown organically by the owners. Enjoy palate-pleasing fare such as village sausages with grilled mushrooms and *afelia* (pork cooked in red wine). It's a good idea to reserve in advance.

Avgas Gorge

Also known as the Avakas Gorge, this narrow split in the Akamas Heights escarpment is a popular hiking excursion. The gorge is reached by vehicle from its western end via Agios Georgios Beach. You can drive or ride more or less up to the gorge entrance, though low-slung conventional vehicles will have to take care. The hike up the gorge, which becomes a defile with cliffs towering overhead, is easy and enjoyable. There is usually water in the gorge until at least May, hence the lush streamside vegetation (keep an eye out for tree frogs). The walk will take no longer than 30 to 40 minutes one way, although some groups do press on upwards – with some difficulty – emerging on the escarpment ridge and then finding their way to the village of Ano Arodes (not much use if your vehicle is at the gorge entrance).

AKAMAS PENINSULA

This part of western Cyprus, jutting almost defiantly into the Mediterranean, is one of the island's last remaining wildernesses. Visitors can still traverse the Akamas as long as they're prepared to walk, ride a trail bike or bump along in a sturdy 4WD. Those with less stamina can take tour boats that sail the Akamas coastline from Latsi, west of Polis. The peninsula can be approached from two sides: from the east via Polis, or from the south via the little village of Agios Georgios. Tracks linking the two entry points are very rough, perhaps deliberately so to discourage traffic.

The peninsula's big attraction is its abundant flora and fauna, resulting from Akamas' position as the easternmost point of the three major plant-life zones of Europe. There are around 600 plant species here, and 35 of them are unique to Cyprus. There are also 68 bird species, 12 types of mammals, 20 species of reptile and many butterflies, including the native *Glaucopsyche pafos,* the symbol of the region.

The only public transport to the area is the bus from Polis to the Baths of Aphrodite.

Hiking

Easily the most popular way to get a taste of the Akamas is to spend a few hours hiking one of the following trails, which run through the northeastern sector of the peninsula. All can start and end at one of two points: the Baths of Aphrodite, or Smigies picnic ground, which is reached via an unsealed road 2.5km west of Neo Chorio.

The two most popular trails are those that start and end at the Baths of Aphrodite. They are both longer than the Smigies trails

and offer better views. The first is the **Aphrodite Trail**, a 7.5km, three- to four-hour loop. It heads inland and upwards to begin with; as this can be tiring on a hot day, make an early start if you can. Halfway along the trail you can see the ruins of **Pyrgos tis Rigainas** (Queen's Tower), part of a Byzantine monastery. Look for the huge 100-year-old oak tree nearby before you head up to the summit of **Mouti tis Sotiras** (370m). At this point you head east and down towards the coastal track, which will eventually lead you back to the car park.

The second hike, the 3½-hour, 7.5km **Adonis Trail**, shares the same path as the Aphrodite as far as Queen's Tower but then turns left (south) before looping back to the car park. Note that, in order to complete its circular path, the trail follows the main road connecting the Baths of Aphrodite and Polis for about 400m. Alternatively, you can turn right (south) just after the village of Kefalovrysi and continue on to Smigies picnic ground if you have arranged a pick-up beforehand.

Water is usually available at Queen's Tower and, on the Adonis Trail, at Kefalovrysi, but don't count on it in high summer. In any case, these trails are best attempted in spring or autumn; if you must do it in Cyprus' extremely hot summer, stride out at sunrise.

The CTO produces a step-by-step and plant-by-plant description of these two

> **DON'T MISS**
>
> ## FOOD FIT FOR A KING
>
> If you haven't taken a picnic with you, excellent food is available close to the entrance of Avgas Gorge at **Viklari** (☑2699 6088; mains €12; ⏰1.30-4pm), more famously known as the **Last Castle**, with its stunning views of citrus and banana groves leading down to the sea. Owner Savvas Symeou has been greeting customers here since 1989, providing lunch for hungry hikers. For €12 you get a delicious *kleftiko* barbecue, accompanied by salad and a baked potato. You eat at heavy stone tables under grapevines, surrounded by petrified-rock 'sculptures', lovingly nurtured pot plants and a garden. Look for signs to the 'Last Castle' from the coastal road.

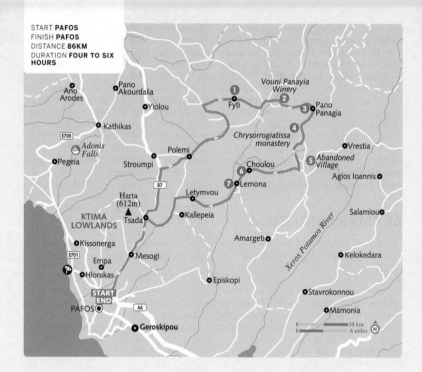

Driving Tour
Wineries, Weaving & Abandoned Villages

❯ From Pafos, take the B7 north towards Polis. After around 17km head towards Fyti on the signposted E703; this pretty country road winds between vineyards and agricultural land. Pass through Polemi and Psathi, then take the signposted left turn towards Milia and Fyti (F725). Head for the centre of **①Fyti** and park by the church. Stop at the Fyti Village Tavern (also known as Maria's Place), duck into the Folk Art Museum and then leave on the F725 towards Pano Panagia via Kritou Marottous and Asprogia; the scenery is lovely, with vineyards, citrus groves and distant mountains.

Watch for the sign for the **②Vouni Panayia Winery** and stop for a wine tasting; the Barba Yiannis dry red, matured in oak for a year, comes particularly recommended. Continue on to **③Pano Panagia**, the birthplace of Archbishop Makarios; have a quick nose around his childhood home, a typical peasants' house with just two rooms (one of which was formerly used for stabling animals).

Head south out of town on the F622, stopping at the well-signposted **④Chrysorrogiatissa monastery** for lunch on the terrace, accompanied by beautiful countryside views. Pick up a bottle of organic wine from the monks, take a look at their atmospheric 18th-century chapel, then follow signs to the E702 and Choulou. After around 5km you will pass through a fascinating **⑤abandoned village** where just a couple of residents, one donkey and several goats remain after a 1969 earthquake forced the vast majority of villagers to relocate.

In **⑥Choulou** have a look at the simple whitewashed mosque (this was a Turkish village before 1974) and enjoy a coffee at the traditional Antoyaneta Taverna across the way. Make the last stop on your tour the village of **⑦Lemona**, home to an excellent micro-winery: Tsangarides Winery. Continue back to Pafos on the B7, via Letymvou and Tsada.

trails in a booklet entitled *European Long Distance Path E4 and other Cyprus Nature Trails,* available from the main CTO offices. Two other trails to consider (also outlined in the booklet) commence from Smigies picnic ground: the circular 2.5km or 5km **Smigies Trail** and the circular 3km, 1½-hour **Pissouromouttis Trail**. Both afford splendid views of Chrysohou Bay to the northeast and the Akamas coastline to the west.

Polis

POP 1890

Polis is mainly visited by Cypriots on their August holidays. It's an appealing small town, with a beach, a good camp site, and some decent hotels and restaurants. It makes an ideal base for hiking or mountain biking in the Akamas and touring the Akamas Heights winemaking villages. The sand-and-sea package-tour agencies have left Polis alone for the time being, allowing it to remain free of the overdevelopment and decay of quality that plagues Pafos town. However, a holiday village has opened near the centre, and a new highway linking Pafos to Polis has been proposed (but has been fraught with controversy and delays).

Polis lies on wide Chrysohou Bay, on the northwestern sweep of Cyprus from Cape Arnaoutis at the tip of the Akamas Peninsula to Pomos Point at the start of the Tyllirian wilderness.

◉ Sights & Activities

Polis' main attractions are its relaxed atmosphere, its proximity to the Akamas Peninsula and the region's lovely beaches, which are among the most attractive on the island. There is also plenty of scope for water sports at **Latsi Harbour**, located 2km west of Polis.

Archaeological Museum   MUSEUM
(Leoforos Archiepiskopou Makariou III; admission €1; ⊙8am-2pm Mon-Wed & Fri, to 6pm Thu, 9am-5pm Sat) Includes finds from the nearby graves at Marion and Arsinoe. There is an old **olive tree** close to the museum; its trunk is almost split in two, but it still produces olives after 600 years.

FREE **Agios Andronikos**   CHURCH
(Iouliou) This 16th-century church was previously a mosque and the centre of local Turkish Cypriot religious life. It has recently had some fine Byzantine frescos revealed that were formerly hidden behind whitewash. Sitting on the western side of town, by the car park, the church can only be visited in groups of 10 or more. The key is held at the Archaeological Museum.

Latsi Watersports Centre   WATER SPORTS
(☏2632 2095; www.latchiwatersportscentre.com; ⛵) Offers diving courses (from €65), boat hire (from €45), parasailing (from €43) and windsurfing (from €35 per hour, including equipment rental).

Ride in Cyprus   HORSE RIDING
(☏9977 7624; www.rideincyprus.com; from €30; ⛵) For hour-long horse-riding treks, overnight safaris and picnic day rides, contact this company in Lysos, 12km southeast of town, on the road to Stavros tis Psokas.

THE MUCH-MALIGNED CYPRIOT MOUFLON

Featured as a stylised graphic on the tail fin of Cyprus Airways planes, the Cypriot mouflon (*Ovis orientalis ophion*), known as *agrino* in Greek, is Cyprus' de facto national symbol. Similar to a wild sheep and native to the island of Cyprus, it has close cousins on the islands of Sardinia and Sicily, and in Iran. Today, Cyprus' mouflon population is limited to the dense vegetation of the Pafos Forest on the western side of the Troödos Massif.

Once treated as vermin, the mouflon was fair game for trigger-happy hunters – by the 1930s there were only 15 alive in Cyprus. Since then an enlightened preservation programme has seen numbers rise to around 3000. The mouflon is a shy, retiring animal and is rarely seen in the wild, as it will disappear into the forest long before your arrival. The male mouflon sports enormous curved horns and, while not aggressive to humans, uses its horns in mating battles with other males.

While numbers have reached stable levels, the mouflon is still considered an endangered species. The main threats nowadays come from forest fires and poachers. For more mouflon info, check the www.moa.gov.cy/forest website.

Polis

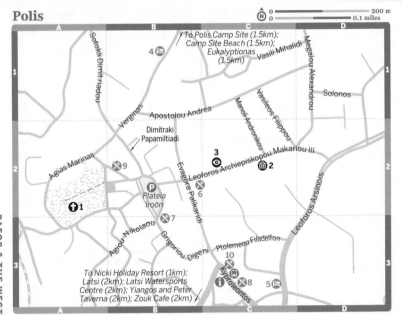

Polis

◉ Sights
1 Agios Andronikos	A2
2 Archaeological Museum	C2
3 Olive Tree	C2

◉ Sleeping
4 Bougainvillea Hotel Apartments	B1
5 Stephanos Hotel Apartments	C3

◉ Eating
6 Archontariki Restaurant-Tavern	B2
7 Arsinoe Fish Tavern	B3
8 Mosfilo's Tavern	C3
9 Nave	B2
10 Old Town Restaurant	C3

🏖 Beaches

The best beaches easily accessible from Polis are those on the eastern side of Latsi, 2km west of Polis. These beaches tend to be mixed sand and pebble, and are somewhat exposed to the vagaries of the weather, but they are popular enough and well serviced with restaurants.

Camp site beach BEACH

The nearest stretch of sand is a good beach and convenient if you don't want to move far from Polis and fancy a picnic, or are camping there. It's sandy, with natural shade from fragrant eucalyptus trees. There's a beach restaurant and lifeguards.

Aphrodite Beach Hotel beach BEACH

This lovely, calm beach is clearly signposted on the way to the Baths of Aphrodite. It's good for children, with its clear, swimmable waters and comfortably small pebbles.

👉 Tours

Wheelie Cyprus BICYCLE TOURS
(☎9935 0898; www.wheeliecyprus.com; from €60) Organises bike tours on little-known trails throughout the area. The price includes bike rental, all equipment and pick-up from your hotel.

Mickys Tours SIGHTSEEING, BOAT TOURS
(☎2694 2022; www.mickystours.com; Posidonos, Kato Pafos; ⛵) Organises tours and boat trips of the Akamas Peninsula.

🎉 Festivals & Events

Summer Nights in Polis CONCERTS
In summer the Plateia Iroön (Town Hall Sq) hosts various free concerts ranging

from traditional dancing, music and folkloric events to classical-music and jazz performances.

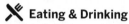 Eating & Drinking

You'll find plenty of restaurants and bars in Polis.

Old Town Restaurant MODERN CYPRIOT €€€
(☑9963 2781; Kyproleontos 9; mains €16; ☺dinner) This is a discreet and relaxing place with a leafy, secluded garden and a stripped-back stone-clad dining room with crisp white tablecloths, shelves of wine and plants. The menu changes according to what is in season, but you can expect dishes like rabbit *stifado* with wild mushrooms and juniper berries, crispy duck spring rolls with honey and chilli and lobster pasta. Reservations recommended.

Mosfilo's Tavern CYPRIOT €€
(Kyproleontos; mains €8) This place exudes a traditional ambience with its high ceilings, original tiles and columns, and gallery of historic pics of Polis. The menu includes classics like spinach and lamb, and grilled chicken. The location is less aesthetic – across from the petrol station on the B7 main road to Pafos.

Archontariki Restaurant-Tavern CYPRIOT €€
(☑2632 1328; www.archontariki.com.cy; Leoforos Archiepiskopou Makariou III 14; mains €11; ☺dinner) This is a popular and atmospheric tavern where the service is attentive and the food top class. Dine in an old renovated stone house and try chicken stuffed with haloumi and mushrooms, or *kathisto* (octopus cooked in wine and oregano). There's live music on Friday. Reservations recommended.

Zouk Cafe FUSION €€
(Latsi Harbour; mains €10) Sit here and face the sea and harbour (and a bit of a car park), and relax on the rattan chairs and sprawling sofas. It's a popular place for locals, expats and visitors, with music and fashion videos, snacks, sushi (on Friday) and cocktails.

Nave FUSION €€€
(Plateia Iroön; mains €8-20; ☑) Looking a tad out of place among all the culinary old-timers in the main square, Nave has a menu that takes in Italian, fusion and soul food, plus vegetarian options like fresh ricotta with avocado and sweet gorgonzola. There

are tables outside and a smoochy musical backdrop of swing and jazz.

Yiangos & Peter Taverna SEAFOOD €€€
(Leoforos Latsi; mains from €12) Across from the harbour, with a large terrace; most (though not all) of the fish on display here is freshly caught on the day.

Arsinoe Fish Tavern SEAFOOD €€€
(Grigoriou Digeni; fish meze €14; ☺dinner) An atmospheric place. Try the succulent fish meze.

☆ Entertainment

Stop by the CTO office for details of events. Ticketed concerts, often given by top-name Greek artists, take place in the Eukalyptionas (Eucalyptus Grove) at the Polis camp site. These outdoor events can be magical on a hot summer night. Tickets cost between €10 and €20.

❶ Information

CTO (www.visitcyprus.org.cy; Vasileos Stasioikou 2; ☺9am-1pm & 2.30-5.30pm Sun-Tue, Thu & Fri, 9am-1pm Sat) Very central.

❶ Getting There & Around

Pafos Buses (www.pafosbuses.com) has daily service to/from Polis leaving from Karavella Bus Station in Ktima. All buses from Polis depart from Osypa Bus Station; destinations:

Baths of Aphrodite Bus 622; 30 minutes, €1. Hourly 8am to 5pm weekdays, five on weekends.

Latsi Bus 623; 20 minutes, €1. Two daily.

Pafos Bus 645; one hour, €3. Up to 11 on weekdays, five on weekends.

Pomos Bus 643A; one hour, €1. Three on weekdays, two on weekends.

Baths of Aphrodite

The myth surrounding the cool cave that is the Baths of Aphrodite (Loutra tis Afroditis) is great advertising. Aphrodite, goddess of love and patron of Cyprus, came to the island in a shower of foam and nakedness, launching a cult that has remained to this day. Legend has it that she came to this secluded spot to bathe after entertaining her lovers.

The baths attract a steady crowd, but it is easy to wonder if the visitors expect more than they find. Surrounded by fig trees and filled with the relaxing sound of running water, the grotto is a nice spot away from

THE CULT OF APHRODITE

Cyprus is indelibly linked to the ancient worship of the goddess Aphrodite (known as Venus in Roman mythology). She is known primarily as the Greek goddess of sexual love and beauty, although she was also worshipped as a goddess of war – particularly in Sparta and Thebes. While prostitutes often considered her their patron, her public cult was usually solemn and even austere.

The name Aphrodite is thought to derive from the Greek word *afros*, meaning 'foam'. Cypriot legend has it that Aphrodite rose from the sea off the south coast of Cyprus. She was born out of the white foam produced by the severed genitals of Ouranos (Heaven), after they were thrown into the sea by his son Chronos (the father of Zeus, king of the Greek gods). The people of Kythira in Greece hold a similar view to that expressed in the legend; an enormous rock off the south-coast port of Kapsali is believed by Kytherians to be the place where Aphrodite really emerged.

Despite being a goddess, Aphrodite has a predilection for mortal lovers. The most famous of them were Anchises (by whom Aphrodite became mother to Aeneas) and Adonis (who was killed by a boar and whose death was lamented by women at the festival of Adonia).

The main centres of worship on Cyprus for the cult of Aphrodite were at Pafos and Amathous. Her symbols included the dove, the swan, pomegranates and myrtle.

Greek art represented her as a nude-goddess type. Ancient Greek sculptor Praxiteles carved a famous statue of Aphrodite which later became the model for the Hellenistic statue known as *Venus de Milo*.

the heat, but it's far from the luxurious setting that may be associated with a goddess of such amorous prowess. The surrounding botanical garden is pretty, however, with labelled plants and trees, including carob trees, red gum and the slightly less exotic dandelion.

The baths are 11km west of Polis, along a sealed road. From the baths' car park with its adjacent gift shop, follow the well-marked paved trail for 200m. You are not allowed to swim in the baths.

There are various nature trails you can take from the grotto; for more details, see p95.

TYLLIRIA

If you love untouched, tranquil nature, head for Tylliria. It's a sparsely populated, forested territory with a few desultory beach resorts nestling between Chrysohou and Morfou Bays. Enjoying its wilderness, even if just for a few days, is highly recommended.

The only public transport in this area is the bus connecting Pomos with Polis and Pafos.

Pomos

POP 570

The trip up the coastal road from Polis towards Tylliria becomes gradually more scenic, although it doesn't really unfold in all its glory until beyond Pomos, which is the first village you come to (at 19km). This is a lush agricultural area with olive trees, citrus groves and vines, and precious little development.

Sights & Activities

FREE **Museum of Natural History** MUSEUM (☉7.30am-2.30pm Mon-Fri, to 4pm Wed, 8am-1pm Sat; ♿) Signposted clearly off the main street, this museum is an unexpected attraction to find here, with its two large galleries of animals and birds endemic to the island, as well as a modest display of rocks and minerals. While taxidermists may not be impressed with some of the mildly moth-eaten exhibits, the comprehensive display includes some surprises, like pelicans, a mouflon, the large Caretta turtle and a prehistoric-looking *gyps fulvos* vulture – all native to Cyprus. Don't miss the photo of the skeleton of a hippopotamus found in caves in the Akrotiri area, along with skeletons of the pygmy elephant, both dating back to Neolithic times.

✷✷ Festivals & Events

Paradise Jazz Festival JAZZ FESTIVAL
(www.paradiseplaceproductions.com) Pomos, small though it may be, creates musical waves every year with this jazz festival, which takes place in July at Paradise Place restaurant.

✕ Eating

Paradise Place INTERNATIONAL €€
(☎2624 2537; mains from €8; ⊙lunch & dinner Apr-Dec; ⫟) Paradise Place is located at the entrance to the village on the right-hand side. Outside festival time (July), this is an outdoor bar-restaurant with a positively loungey, decadent feel – but in a good way. A hammock here, wooden chairs there, local photographers' exhibitions, fantastic music, chicken curry, zucchini-and-cheese fritters...and sunsets. No wonder they called it Paradise.

Kanali Fish Restaurant SEAFOOD €€€
(Pomos Harbour; mains from €12) Easy to find, beside the harbour, Kanali has as its main draw the stunning holiday-brochure view from the terrace of steep forested slopes running down to the turquoise bay; romantics should head here at sunset. The kitchen specialises in fresh fish, namely sea bass, bream, red snapper and red mullet.

Sea Cave SEAFOOD €€
(mains from €8) A more informal option, 500m further east along the coast, with an outside terrace shaded by pomegranate trees, and a classic seafood menu.

Pahyammos

Located just 5km east of Pomos along a lovely stretch of highway flanked by colourful oleander bushes, Pahyammos means 'broad sand'. Its beach is indeed broad and sweeps around a large bay up to the UN watchtowers that mark the beginning of Kokkina, a Turkish Cypriot enclave.

The beach is made up of darkish sand and there's no natural shade, but the swimming is reasonable. There are no facilities on the beach, but there are one or two places to eat in the town, which is strung out along the main through-road.

Kokkina (Erenköy)

Tylliria really felt the pinch when it was partly isolated from the rest of Cyprus following the Turkish invasion in 1974. Since that time, this small Turkish enclave, known in Greek as Kokkina and in Turkish as Erenköy, has been surrounded by Greek Cypriot territory. Don't risk driving off the road trying to spot the place; it's hidden behind mountains and guarded by a couple of UN and Greek Cypriot army lookout points, with signposts forbidding photography.

Kato Pyrgos

POP 1135

This remote beach resort is as far out of the way as you can get in the Republic, yet it attracts a regular summer clientele of Cypriots who come for its laid-back ambience. Don't expect palm-fringed promenades and white sandy beaches; Kato Pyrgos has a mildly shabby, old-fashioned appeal, and many Cypriots come here just to get away from the rampant commercialism that they recognise has overwhelmed the more popular coastal resorts of their island. Since the opening of the border crossing here in 2010, the resort has attracted still more visitors, who stop here en route to the North.

The breezy village is strung out along a wide bay running from Kokkina Point to where the Green Line meets the sea. The border's proximity is emphasised by the frequent chatter of UN helicopters that fly in and out of the nearby base. You can bathe at a number of locations along the bay, though the most popular spot seems to be the far eastern end, close to the Green Line, which is also where the most attractive part of town is, its main street lined with leafy trees and a couple of traditional coffee houses.

Kato Pyrgos has a sprinkling of bars and tavernas. **La Sera** (Ayaniou 20; snacks from €6; ⊙10.30am-midnight) has a contemporary feel with its giant screen and menu of cocktails, coffees, salads and crêpes. Come here for live music in summer or a DJ spinning the discs. Down on the beach at the far eastern end of town, follow the signs to **La Mare Beach Bar** (⊙summer) for the best beachside atmosphere, accompanied by reasonable, if unexceptional, food.

Psokas

From Kato Pyrgos or Pahyammos you can strike out south into the Tylliria hinterland. Make sure you detour slightly to the lovely forest reserve of **Stavros tis Psokas**, also accessible from Pafos (51km) via a picturesque road that is unsealed for a considerable distance. This vast picnic site is a forest station responsible for fire control in the Pafos Forest. Nature-loving Cypriots come here to walk and enjoy the peace, and it can get quite crowded in summer. In a small enclosure, signposted from the main parking area, you can get a glimpse of the rare and endangered native Cypriot mouflon (see the box, p97). Move quietly and slowly if you want to see them, as they get rather skittish at the approach of humans.

You can do some hiking from the Stavros tis Psokas forest station. The **Horteri Trail**, a 5km, three-hour circular hike, loops around the eastern flank of the Stavros Valley. The trail starts at the Platanoudkia Fountain, about halfway along the forest station's approach road, which turns off the main through-road at Selladi tou Stavrou (Stavros Saddle). The hike involves a fair bit of upward climbing and can get tiring in the heat of summer, so tackle the walk early in the day if you can.

The second trail is the **Selladi tou Stavrou**, a 2.5km, 1½-hour circular loop of the northern flank of the Stavros Valley. The start is prominently marked from Stavros Saddle (at the junction of the forest station approach road and the main through-road). A longer option (7km, 2½ hours) is to tackle the trail anticlockwise and then branch south to the heliport. From there you can walk along a forest road to the forest station proper.

The CTO should be able to provide you with more information on these trails. Alternatively, consult www.visitpafos.org.cy.

You will need your own car to get here. There's a small camp site at Stavros tis Psokas with capacity for 60 people.

Kampos

POP 430

Few tourists make it to Kampos, the only substantial habitation in Tylliria. The scenery is beautiful and the locals may stare; they don't get to see many foreigners in these parts.

Although technically part of the Kykkos Monastery sector of the Troödos, Kampos is stuck out on the southern edge of the Tyllirian wilderness with – these days – only one road out. The road that leads north from the village now comes to an ignominious end after 12km, at the Green Line.

However, this part of Tylliria is now less isolated than it was, thanks to the completion of the good sealed road that leads across the Tyllirian hinterland and northern extent of the vast Pafos Forest, linking the Kykkos Monastery with Kato Pyrgos and Pahyammos. Take it slowly, though; the

---

WORTH A TRIP

THE WEFT & WARP OF VILLAGE LIFE

Easily accessible from Pano Panagia or Pafos, the pretty self-contained village of **Fyti** is known for its distinctive weaving, with patterns passed down through generations. Park outside the church and have a mid-morning snack or lunch at the welcoming Fyti Village Tavern, the most popular place in town with villagers, including the local priest. Courgettes with eggs, couscous with yoghurt and an excellent €12 meze are among the culinary treats. The interior is all beams and stone arches, with examples of local handwoven cloth on the wall, although the shady terrace is where you really want to be.

Next, amble across the square to the **Folk Art Museum** (⊙8am-1pm & 2-5pm) where former school teacher Charalambos will explain the exhibits, ranging from live silkworms munching on their bed of mulberry leaves to centuries-old donkey saddles and farm implements. Meanwhile, his cheerful wife, Theano, is busy at the loom, weaving exquisitely patterned silk-and-cotton fabrics. There are interesting historical photos here as well, including some of camels, which were used as pack animals until the late '50s. You can buy the hand-woven pieces, including cushion covers, runners and bags. At the very minimum, pick up a €2 embroidered bookmark memento. If you don't make a purchase, a small donation is appreciated.

road, while good, is very winding and tiring to drive. Most maps still show it as unsealed. It's a much shorter, if more challenging, route into the Tyllirian wilderness than the traditional road from the southeast, via Polis.

WESTERN TROÖDOS

The sparsely populated area flanking the western foothills of the Troödos Massif is home to few attractions other than several delightful villages, where traditions hold fast and the local Cypriot dialect is just that bit more impenetrable. If you're looking for a route to central Troödos from the west coast you can now easily follow a mixture of good sealed and unsealed roads into the mountains. The best route takes you to the Kykkos Monastery via the village of Pano Panagia.

Pano Panagia

POP 560

This village is the **birthplace of Makarios III**, the island's famous archbishop-president (see the box, p74, for more about his life). The **Makarios Cultural Centre** (admission €0.50; ☺9am-1pm & 2-5pm) is a place for hardcore fans only, containing memorabilia from Makarios' life as a politician and priest, including plenty of photos. Housed in just one room, the exhibits include his overcoat, slippers and dressing gown (from the famous London department store Selfridges).

Carrying on in the same vein, the **childhood house of Makarios** (admission free; ☺10am-1pm & 2-6pm) is quite a large building, considering his family's peasant status. It contains more photos and memorabilia from the life of the young Makarios. If the house is locked, you can obtain the key from the nearby cultural centre.

A few tavernas and cafes on the main street provide very average (and overpriced) snacks and meals to the day trippers.

Cedar Valley

This cool valley is the highlight of the western Troödos hinterland, home to a large number of the unusual indigenous Cypriot cedar (*Cedrus brevifolia*), a close cousin of the better-known Lebanese cedar. The valley is approached via a winding, unsealed forest road from Pano Panagia on the Pafos side of the Troödos Massif, or along a signposted unsealed road from the Kykkos side of the Troödos. There is a picnic ground here and the opportunity to hike 2.5km to the summit of **Mt Tripylos**.

You'll need a vehicle to see these places, as public transport is patchy or nonexistent. Alternatively, you could join a tour from Polis or Pafos.

Larnaka & the East

Includes »

Larnaka 105
Around Larnaka 113
Kamares Aqueduct 113
Kiti & Around.................. 114
Stavrovouni
Monastery..................... 114
Choirokoitia 116
Lefkara 116
Agia Napa...................... 117
Around Agia Napa.......... 122
Deryneia........................ 122
The Kokkinohoria 123
Protaras 123
Pernera.......................... 124

Best Places to Eat

» Voreas (p110)

» Zephyros (p110)

» Militzis (p110)

» Karousos Beach (p120)

» La Cultura Del Gusto (p124)

Best Places to Stay

» E-Hotel (p206)

» Alkisti City (p207)

» Eleonora (p207)

» Aeneas (p208)

» Brilliant (p208)

Why Go?

With a lower profile than her bustling neighbours, Larnaka has a tranquil character that mimics the gentle pace of old Cyprus. However, a refurbished seafront and an extravagant new marina in the works have Larnaka gaining ground as a legitimate coastal city. Its central location also makes it an ideal base while touring the island.

Authentic taverns, traditional handicrafts and shallow beaches blend seamlessly with ancient city-kingdoms, historic churches, flamingos, salt lakes, and aqueducts that stretch into the distance.

The wider district hosts agrotourism and remarkable Neolithic sites. Coastal roads wind around to the celebrated resort town of Agia Napa, with white sandy beaches and hundreds of clubs and bars. Further along the coast are echoing sea caves, natural rock formations and tombs dating to the Hellenistic period. Round the cape you'll find even more stunning beaches at Protaras bay, ideal for family getaways.

When to Go

Migratory birds like waterfowl, flamingos and wild ducks find respite in the salt-lake habitat from February to April.

From May to September you can lounge on the beach all day and cool down with watermelon and haloumi at night.

Agia Napa's music scene reaches its peak from June to August, with beach parties and all-night clubbing.

LARNAKA

POP 46,700

Larnaka lives through its connection to the sea. As such, the main promenade on the seafront, known universally as the Finikoudes ('little palm trees', which line its beach) is the main hub. The town has fared better than others in its quest to keep family-owned businesses and restaurants over big business. It's truly a working town; the people know each other and care about community.

This atmosphere has kept the tradition of arts and crafts alive especially in the old Turkish quarter. The rest of Larnaka faces the common conundrum of blending past and present. Traditional houses are interspersed with replica developments springing up for the next wave of Europeans chasing a better work-life balance.

History

Larnaka, originally known as Kition, was established during the Mycenaean expansion in the 14th century BC. An influential Greek city kingdom of the late Bronze Age, Kition prospered as a trading port through the export of copper. Withstanding rule by the Phoenicians and then the Persians, the city flourished into the Hellenistic period, even adopting the Phoenician fertility goddess Astarte, who was perhaps a precursor to Cypriot patron goddess Aphrodite.

During the Greek-Persian wars, Athenian general Kimon attempted to liberate the city from Persian rule in 450 BC. He died during the siege, urging his captains to conceal his fate from both enemies and allies. The episode is famously told as *'Kai Nekros enika'* (Even in death he is victorious!). His bust now stands on the Finikoudes as a tribute.

Under Ottoman rule between the 16th and early 19th centuries, Larnaka attracted merchants, dignitaries and foreign consuls. Many of these participated in amateur archaeology, prevalent at the time and spirited away much of Larnaka's artefacts. The city's importance slowly decreased during Britain's 88-year rule as trade moved through the port at Lemesos.

In 1974 the Turkish invasion of Northern Cyprus forced thousands of Greek Cypriots south, dramatically increasing Larnaka's population. Today Larnaka has Armenian, Lebanese, Pontian Greek and Palestinian settlers living alongside Cypriots and Europeans with mixed backgrounds of their own. Tourism is now the town's primary industry.

ROAD DISTANCES (KM)

	Lefkara	Agia Napa	Protaras	Makenzy
Agia Napa	61			
Protaras	70	9		
Makenzy	29	32	41	
Pernera	73	12	3	44

◉ Sights & Activities

FREE **Agios Lazaros**   CHURCH
(Agiou Lazarou; ⊘8am-12.30pm & 3.30-6.30pm Apr-Aug, 8am-12.30pm & 2.30-5.30pm Sep-Mar)
This 9th-century church is dedicated to Lazarus of Bethany, whom Jesus is said to have resurrected four days after his death. Shortly afterwards, Lazarus was forced to flee Bethany. His boat landed in Kition, where he was ordained as a bishop and canonised by Apostles Barnabas and Paul. He remained a bishop for a further 30 years and when he died for the second time was buried in a hidden tomb.

In 890 the tomb was discovered, bearing the inscription 'Lazarus friend of Christ'. Byzantine Emperor Leo VI had Lazarus' remains sent to Constantinople and built the current church over the vault to appease the Christians. The remains were moved again, to Marseille, in 1204.

The church itself is an astounding example of Byzantine architecture and was further restored in the 17th century. It exhibits Latinate and Orthodox influences, most prominently in the bell tower, which was replaced after being destroyed by the Ottomans. The church was ransomed back to the Christians in 1589 and inscriptions in Latin, French and Greek can be seen in its portico. Unique Catholic woodcarvings and skilled gold-plated Orthodox icons grace its interior.

Tomb of Lazarus   TOMB
The tomb is under the church apse. It is accessible by descending stone stairs to the right and contains only a few of the several sarcophagi found in the catacomb.

In 1972 human remains were found under the altar. Some believe that the remains are those of St Lazarus, possibly hidden here by priests in anticipation of any theft.

Larnaka & the East Highlights

1 Unwinding with beach life on the main promenade in **Larnaka** (p105) or strolling the picturesque Turkish quarter with its ceramics and handicrafts studios

2 Meandering through the intimate streets of **Lefkara** (p116) searching for the perfect piece of handmade lace

3 Bathing in the island's finest waters at **Nissi Beach**

(p119) and **Protaras** (p124)

4 Visiting the eastern peninsula's natural sea caves and lookout at **Cape Greco** (p122)

5 Viewing the tomb of St Lazarus beneath the bulb

of the church honouring his name, **Agios Lazaros** (p105)

6 Diving the **Zenobia Wreck** (p120), rated as one of the world's 10 best dives

7 Letting the kids splash in

the sun and slip on the slides at **Water World** water park (p119)

8 Exploring one of the earliest human settlements in the world at the Neolithic site of **Choirokoitia** (p116)

Byzantine Museum
MUSEUM

(admission €1; ⊘8.30am-1pm & 3-5.30pm Mon, Tue, Thu, Fri & Sun, 8.30am-1pm Wed & Sat) Located in the courtyard of the Agios Lazaros complex, the museum originally contained many priceless relics and artefacts. Unfortunately, the collection was moved by order of the Turkish insurgents to the Larnaka fort for safekeeping between 1964 and 1974. It was later discovered that the entire collection had disappeared and only the original catalogue of items now remains. The museum has tried to rebuild its collection over the years with Byzantine ecclesiastical artefacts, icons and utensils. Several exhibits were donated by Orthodox Russian clergy.

Pierides Archaeological Foundation
MUSEUM

(Zinonos Kitieos 4; admission €1.70; ⊘9am-4pm Mon-Thu, to 1pm Fri & Sat) This museum was established in 1839 by Demetrios Pierides as a protective answer to the region's notorious tomb raiders and illegal selling of precious artefacts from the area.

The collection, expanded by Pierides' descendents, is housed in Pierides' family mansion, built in 1825. It features artefacts from all over Cyprus, with detailed explanations in English. The museum's six rooms are arranged chronologically and present a comprehensive history of Cyprus, taking in the Mycenaean and Achaean periods, the Iron Age, the Roman occupation, and Byzantine, Crusader, Lusignan, Venetian and Ottoman periods.

The Pierides houses Neolithic exhibits like the famous ceramic **howling man**, dating to c 5500 BC. If water is poured into the seated figure's mouth it will drain from his phallus. Archaeologists have debated whether the figure had a religious or a secular function, but no consensus has been reached.

The collection also showcases intricate Greek and Roman glassware and offers fine examples of weaving, embroidery, woodcarvings and traditional costumes associated with Cypriot folk art.

Larnaka Archaeological Museum
MUSEUM

(Plateia Kalogreon; admission €1.70; ⊘9am-2.30pm Mon-Fri & 3-5pm Thu Sep-Jun) A stop on the Aphrodite Cultural Rte, Larnaka's second museum houses a wide collection of pottery from ancient Kition and a reconstructed **Neolithic tomb** from Choirokoitia. Spread out over five rooms, the collection's highlights are its terracotta votive figures.

Larnaka Fort
HISTORICAL SITE, MUSEUM

(Leoforos Athinon; admission €1.70; ⊘9am-7pm Mon-Fri) Built in the Lusignan era, the fort stands at the water's edge and separates the Finikoudes promenade from the old Turkish quarter. Its present form is a result of remodelling by the Ottomans around 1605.

Nowadays, all there is for visitors to enjoy of the building itself is its architecture and the coastal views from the turrets. On the upper floor is a small **Medieval Museum** with displays from the Hala Sultan Tekke (p114) and ancient Kition.

During summer, the impressive courtyard is used for concerts and cultural events, which are heavily advertised on the Finikoudes.

FREE Ancient Kition
ARCHAEOLOGICAL SITE

(⊘9am-2.30pm Mon-Fri) A lot of the original city kingdom of Kition is still covered by present-day Larnaka. What is unearthed of the ancient city, referred to as Area II, is about 1km northwest of central Larnaka. The site appears sparse as you walk the raised runway that takes you over the remains of Cyclopean walls. Most remarkable is what remains of the five temples (from the 13th century BC) and ship depictions etched into the walls of the nearby ancient port. These confirmed that the city was founded by sea-trading Mycenaeans.

Municipal Cultural Centre
MUSEUMS, GALLERY

(Leoforos Athinon, Plateia Evropis) Made up of five adjoining colonial-style stone warehouses built by the British in 1881, the cultural centre is located on Finikoudes promenade, opposite the marina.

CHILDREN'S CYPRUS: CAMEL RIDES

At **Mazotos Camel Park** (☎2499 1243; www.camel-park.com; Mazotos; rides adult/child €9/6) the kids can enjoy 15-minute camel rides on the well-trained and affable humped residents. The park also offers a pool, a play area with games and a restaurant, allowing you to make a day of it.

Mazotos Camel Park is 20 minutes from Larnaka by car. The €3 entrance fee is deducted from activity fees.

Larnaka

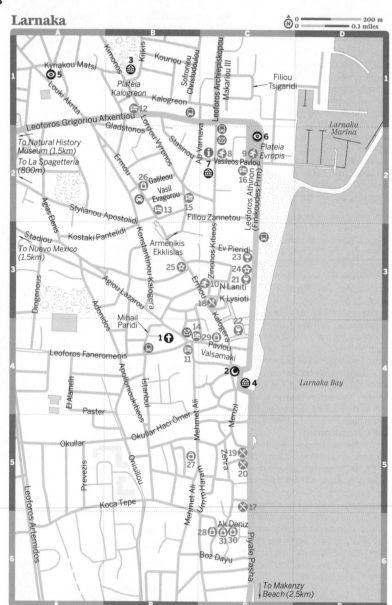

Municipal Art Gallery

(admission free; ☉9am-2pm Tue-Fri, to noon Sat & Sun) The gallery features old and contemporary works of art from local artists. It also has regular monthly exchanges of international exhibitions with various European galleries.

Palaeontology Museum

(admission €1.70; ☉9am-2pm Tue-Fri, to noon Sat & Sun) This museum's rare collection of fossils spans 500 million years. The best exhibits, though, are the bones (including skulls) of the now extinct pygmy

Larnaka

◎ Sights
1 Agios Lazaros B4
  Byzantine Museum.......................(see 1)
2 Grand Mosque (Büyük
  Camii).. C4
3 Larnaka Archaeological
  Museum..B1
4 Larnaka Fort & Medieval
  Museum... C4
5 Mousio Theasis.................................A1
6 Municipal Cultural Centre.................... C2
7 Pierides Archaeological
  Foundation.................................... C2
  Tomb of Lazarus...........................(see 1)

● Activities, Courses & Tours
8 CTO... C2
9 Larnaka City Cruisers
  Departure Point C2
10 Yoga Room....................................C3

⊜ Sleeping
11 Alkisti City B4
12 Easy B1
13 Eleonora B2
14 Livadhiotis City B4

15 Petrou Bros..B2
16 Sun Hall..C2

◈ Eating
17 Chris' Kebab C5
18 Flavours C3
19 Militzis..C5
20 Zephyros.....................................C5

◉ Drinking
21 Brewery.......................................C3
22 Savino's Rock Bar C4
23 Times C3

◎ Entertainment
24 Club Deep C3
25 Geometry....................................B3
  Savino Live................................ (see 22)

◉ Shopping
26 Academic & General B2
27 Emira Pottery B5
28 Fotinis Pottery....................................C4
29 Handworks Handmade......................C4
30 Stavros Pottery.................................C6
31 Studio Ceramics................................C6

hippopotamuses and elephants that inhabited Cyprus in 10,000 BC.

Municipal Historical Archives
(admission €1.70; ⊙9am-2pm Tue-Fri, to noon Sat & Sun) Next door to the Palaeontology Museum, the restored residence of the first colonial port master of Larnaka is now home to the city's archives. On the ground floor, the museum has a collection of ancient coins from Kition dating to the 6th century. It also has an interesting exhibit of photographs of old Larnaka going back as far as 1850.

Natural History Museum   MUSEUM
(Leoforos Grigoriou Afxentiou; admission €0.85; ⊙10am-1pm & 4-6pm Tue-Sun Jun-Sep, 10am-1pm & 3-5pm Tue-Sun Oct-May) The museum presents an excellent introduction to the natural history of the island, with exhibits dedicated to fauna, flora, geology, insects and marine life. Situated in the Municipal Gardens, it is regularly visited by school groups and is a fun place for children, who can see pelicans, flamingos, peacocks and macaws in cages outside the museum. There is also a little playground in the gardens.

Grand Mosque   MOSQUE
(Büyük Camii; Agias Faneromenis) Located at the beginning of Larnaka's **Turkish quarter**, with its maze of sleepy whitewashed streets, the Grand Mosque is the spiritual home of Larnaka's Muslim community. Left untouched when the Turkish community dispersed in 1974, it now predominantly serves Muslims from North Africa.

Originally built in the 16th century as the Latin Holy Cross Church, it was converted into a mosque. The current construction is the result of 19th-century restoration. More interesting is the small graveyard in front, with gothic-looking tombstones.

Mousio Theasis   EXHIBITION HOUSE
(⌨2465 8752; www.mousiotheasis.com; Louki Akrita 8; museums €3; ⊙10am-5pm) Larnaka's swish new exhibition venue holds events like open-air concerts and cinema. There is a gallery dedicated to the arts and two museums to take in. One offers a snapshot of the Byzantine period through iconography and the other is an interesting display of over 5000 owl effigies. Check the website for the latest exhibitions and cultural events.

LARNAKA & THE EAST LARNAKA

TOO HOT TO WALK?

Try the new **Larnaka City Cruisers** (☎7000 5960; Leoforos Athinon). These modern tricycles are powered by a friendly guide offering city-centre, arts-and-handicrafts and historical-themed **bicycle tours** (the latter is possibly the best). Each tour takes in 20 to 30 stops, giving you the opportunity to get out for a further look if you wish, and guides do their utmost to fill you with information. Tours cost €12 and go for about an hour each. It's a fun way to get to know the city. Cruisers depart from Plateia Evropis on the Finikoudes.

Yoga Room   YOGA
(☎9764 8173; Ermou 169; classes €10-30) This little studio sells yoga mats and has small intimate classes of no more than four students. Or try out private tuition and find your centre, in the centre of town.

☞ Tours

The **Cyprus Tourism Organisation** (CTO; ☎2465 4322; Plateia Vasileos Pavlou; ⊗8.15am-2.30pm & 3-6.15pm Mon, Tue, Thu & Fri, 8.15am-1.30pm Sat) runs free guided walks that are a great introduction to the layout of Larnaka and its rich history. The 'Larnaka – Its Past & Present' walk starts at 10am every Wednesday at the CTO, and takes in the Finikoudes promenade, Agios Lazaros and the Pierides museum.

The second walk, 'Skala – Its Craftsmen', leaves at 10am every Friday from the fort. It tours the old town with its traditional white-washed houses, balconies and arches. There are also stops at the pottery and handicraft workshops in its backstreets. Walks take around two hours, with breaks to rest and refresh.

✬ Festivals & Events

Kataklysmos Festival   RELIGIOUS FESTIVAL
Held in June each year, 50 days after Orthodox Easter, this festival has special significance for Larnaka as a coastal town. Kataklysmos, meaning deluge or cataclysm in Greek, is a traditional celebration of Noah and his salvation from the Flood.

Today, it is the perfect excuse for friendly water fights. During the day on the Finikoudes there are all kinds of fun water-based activities like windsurfing, kayak races and swimming competitions. At night the promenade hosts open-air concerts and bazaar stalls selling everything from corn on a stick to tacky trinkets.

Green Monday   RELIGIOUS HOLIDAY
This public holiday and celebration 50 days before Orthodox Easter is the beginning of fasting and penitence. The custom involves heading into the countryside for the day and picnicking with vegetables, seafood and wine.

Musical Sundays   MUSIC FESTIVAL
(⊗from 11am Sun Jan-May & Nov-Dec) On the seafront stage at the Finikoudes, Musical Sundays feature a variety of rock, jazz, traditional music and dancing events. Line-ups are listed in the free brochure *Larnaka this month* available at all bookshops.

✗ Eating

Larnaka has a variety of eateries, ranging from souvlaki bars to gourmet restaurants. Most places can be found on or just off the promenade, with one or two hidden gems in the backstreets. Dinners are usually available after 7pm, in keeping with Cypriots' big-lunch, late-siesta lifestyle. Often, good restaurants won't be full until 10pm.

┌TOP┐ Voreas   CYPRIOT €€€
└CHOICE┘
(☎2464 7177; Agiou Demetriou 3, Oroklini; mains €9-17; ⊗dinner Mon-Sat, lunch & dinner Sun) Ten minutes outside Larnaka, in the village of Oroklini, this traditional house and courtyard offers a taste of traditional foods, surrounds and hospitality. The aroma of herbs, the succulent variety of meat and the wild vegetable meze dishes leave you scrambling for space on the table and wondering if your stomach can take any more.

Zephyros   SEAFOOD TAVERN €€€
(Piyale Pasha 37; mains €9-18) Near the harbour, this contemporary tavern's service is only bettered by its high-quality fish meze. Calamari and silver sardines are an excellent choice. Dine here once and it's a safe bet you'll return.

Militzis   CYPRIOT €€
(Piyale Pasha 42; mains €9-12) This tavern by the sea has a traditional indoor-outdoor courtyard backing onto the domed *fourno* (traditional ovens) that 'all-day' bake incredibly soft lamb and chicken. Simple Cypriot meze is served with haloumi, giant beans and *bourgouri* (cracked wheat).

Flavours
GRILLED MEAT €€€

(25 Kosma Lysioti; www.stonegrillflavors.com; mains €18) At the end of Ermou is the unique 'stone-grill' dining experience, well and truly aimed at meat lovers. The cut of your choice is served raw on heated volcanic stone, and you get to cook your fillet to suit your taste.

La Spagetteria
ITALIAN €€

(Stylianou 1; mains €7-12; ✎) This intimate venue has an extensive menu of well-priced, flavoursome dishes. Everything from the traditional spaghetti Bolognese to the thin-crusted gourmet pizzas is perfectly presented and delicious. It also has imported Italian beers (Peroni) from €3 and an excellent wine list.

Nuevo Mexico
MEXICAN €€€

(Leoforos Artemidos 10; www.nuevomexico.com.cy; mains €8-15) Located on the 1st floor, this new urban restaurant has flavour-filled Mexican food like quesadillas and enchiladas cooked by Mexican chefs. Bright colours, comfy chairs and friendly staff ensure great dining for families. Be ready for the musical interludes, as bar staff and waitresses love to burst into impromptu salsa shows.

Zakos Beach
SEAFOOD €€€

(Makenzy Beach; www.zakosbeach.com; mains €8-18; ⊙9am-11.30pm) On Makenzy beachfront, with bright views of Larnaka town's best beach, fresh fish meze is served on traditional long tables. Try the succulent lemon-and-herb octopus with a glass of Aphrodite wine.

Chris' Kebab
FAST FOOD €

(Piyale Pasha; mains €6; ⊙noon-10pm) This tiny souvlaki bar has just a handful of outdoor tables. Try the soft chicken pita with home-made tahina sauce for extra tang. Watch out for the sea spray on windy days.

🍷 Drinking

Larnaka's drinking scene centres on the Finikoudes, offering bars and cafes of every style. More intimate pubs and *kafeneia* (cafes) can be found in the side streets leading away from the coast and tend to have more reasonable prices. Most places don't close until after midnight.

TOP CHOICE Ammos
BAR

(www.ammos.eu; Makenzy Beach; ⊙9am-late) Ammos (Greek for 'sand') is a splendidly bright white venue, perfectly located on the beach and open all day till late. You can eat in the classy kitchen bar or drink, chill and dance on the open rooftop to a mix of urban house and lazy funk. Don't be scared to kick off your shoes and enjoy the soft white sand featured in-house.

Savino's Rock Bar
BAR

(9 Ouotkins, Laiki Geitonia; ⊙7pm-late) With a hardwood bar and pictures of rock gods on the wall, this diminutive place is hidden just off the main promenade. It plays classic rock, jazz and blues and is a welcoming place to pull up a stool and enjoy a drink. It gets packed quickly, but fortunately Savino Live, its sister venue, is opposite for when the crowds expand and need to dance.

Times
BAR

(Leoforos Athinon 73; ⊙10am-1am) This swish cafe-bar on the seafront has a modern feel set off by cool white sofas stretched along the wall, perfect for lounging and sipping cocktails all night. There's live jazz on Sunday, Funky House Friday, and a rock night on Wednesday. Patrons dress smart and move on to Club Deep next door.

Brewery
BREWERY

(Leoforos Athinon 77; ⊙10am-1am) Pull your own pint from the micro-brew pumps brought to your table. There's a great selection of exclusive lagers, ales and well-hopped brews and a mix of fruity beers like cherry, lime and passionfruit. The burger menu is great for snacks but can be a bit pricey.

☆ Entertainment

While most tourists and party-goers head to Agia Napa for its world-class club and bar scene, there are some easy-going spots to enjoy in Larnaka. Once more, the seafront and surrounding streets provide some good clubs, but in Larnaka the hottest spot is the up-and-coming area of Makenzy Beach.

In summer, regular beach parties are held with guest DJs from around the globe and you can drink and dance all day at the beach bars on the sand. Watch out for the leaflets posted around town advertising musical acts.

Savino Live
LIVE MUSIC

(9 Ouotkins, Laiki Geitonia; ⊙Wed-Fri & Sat) This live-rock venue fits up to 300 people and it needs to. With its well-amplified stage and open dance floor, it's a great night of vivacious dancing. Bands from all over Cyprus come to play classic blues, jazz and rock till late.

Geometry
NIGHTCLUB

(Karaoli & Demetriou 8; ⊘Fri-Sun) The entrance is a floor-lit mirrored ramp which looks like a cross between a retro spaceship and the 'Billy Jean' film clip. Inside is a decadent club kitted out with geometric light patterns and prisms. Aimed at a posh crowd, it plays a good selection of dance, club and Greek tracks. Dress well, so you feel at home with locals who pack the place on weekends.

Club Deep
NIGHTCLUB

(Leoforos Athinon 76; ⊘Mon-Sun) Two floors of all-night clubbing right on the seafront. The lower club plays mostly chilled trance and progressive house. The main club (Deep) houses a huge dance floor melting with old school, R and B, and mainstream dance. It gets busy after midnight with a young, easy-going crowd.

K Cineplex
CINEMA

(⌀box office 2436 2167; www.kcineplex.com; Peloponisou 1; ⊘box office 5-10.30pm Mon-Fri) A cineplex with six screens, stereo surround sound, wide reclining seats and all the usual Hollywood blockbusters on show. All films are subtitled in Greek except animated features, which have Greek or English alternatives. The site also houses the 20-lane **Kmax bowling alley** (⌀7777 8373), a billiards venue and Finnegan's Irish pub-restaurant. The complex is 10 minutes' drive west of the city centre, near the Kamares Aqueduct.

🔒 Shopping

Larnaka's signature collectable is pottery. The old Turkish quarter features a number of high-quality ceramics workshops.

Stavros Pottery
CERAMICS

(www.stavrosceramics.com; Ak Deniz 8) The dynamic pieces here encompass the raku technique blended with artist Stavros' creative vision.

Studio Ceramics
CERAMICS, HANDICRAFTS

(www.studioceramicscyprus.com; Ak Deniz 18) Medieval pottery inspired by ancient Cypriot art. The Pierides-museum replicas are a standout.

Fotinis Pottery
CERAMICS

(Bozkourt 28) Beautiful everyday bowls and plates embellished with pomegranates (symbol of fertility during the island's pagan times).

Emira Pottery
CERAMICS

(www.emirapottery.com; Mehmet Ali 13) Unique, delicately patterned plates and traditional Cypriot cooking pots are some of the many pieces on offer. You can even try your hand at your own creation.

Handworks Handmade
JEWELLERY, ACCESSORIES

(www.handworkshandmade.com; Pavlou Valsamaki 22) Just 50m from Agios Lazaros towards the sea is this eclectic store featuring myriad pendants, stones, anklets, rings and necklaces in everything from wood to silver. This is a really well-priced shop for gifts and keepsakes.

TOP CHOICE Academic & General
BOOKS

(⌀2462 8401; Ermou 41) You could spend all day in here. The shop has thousands of English books, including the classics, history, philosophy and books on Cyprus. There's also a huge secondhand fiction section, ideal for beach reads. Cultural events are held here in summer and the friendly staff specialise in hard-to-find and rare books. Feel free to make a coffee and lounge upstairs on the couches.

ℹ️ Information

INTERNET ACCESS Wi-fi is available all along the Finikoudes.

Amalfi Café (Lord Byron 35; per hr €1.90; ⊘10am-1am) Centre of town, with billiards and gaming.

Replay (Leoforos Athinon; per hr €2.50; ⊘10am-1am) On the main promenade.

MEDICAL SERVICES Larnaka Hospital (⌀2480 0500; Leoforos Grigoriou Afxentiou)

Night pharmacy assistance (⌀1414)

MONEY Bank of Cyprus (⌀2414 4141; Zinonos Kitieos) Opposite the CTO.

Marfin Laiki Bank (⌀2481 4422; Lord Byron 33)

POLICE Police station (⌀2480 4040; cnr Leoforos Grigoriou Afxentiou & Leoforos Archiepiskopou Makariou III) At the main entrance to the Finikoudes promenade.

POST There's a **post office** (Plateia Vasileos Pavlou) close to the CTO office and another smaller branch close to Agios Lazaros.

TOURIST INFORMATION CTO airport (⌀2464 3576; ⊘8.15am-11pm); Larnaka (⌀2465 4322; Plateia Vasileos Pavlou; ⊘8.15am-2.30pm & 3-6.15pm Mon, Tue, Thu & Fri, 8.15am-1.30pm Sat)

ℹ️ Getting There & Away

AIR The new Larnaka international **airport** (⌀flight information 2464 3000) is 7km southwest of the city centre. Direct flights come from all major European cities and northern Africa.

BOAT Larnaka Marina (☎2465 3110; larnaca .marina@cytanet.com.cy) is an official port of entry into Cyprus. Offering a complete range of berthing facilities, it is full of activity and requires advance reservations.

BUS InterCity (☎2464 3492; www.intercity -buses.com; 1 way/all day & return €3/5) buses leave from Finikoudes bus stop, on the beach side in the middle of the main promenade.

Destinations:

Agia Napa and Paralimni At least hourly 6am to 7.30pm weekdays, 8am to 4.30pm weekends.

Lefkosia At least hourly 6am to 7.30pm weekdays, 6.30am to 4pm weekends.

Lemesos At least hourly 6am to 7pm weekdays, 8.30am to 5.30pm weekends.

SERVICE TAXI Travel & Express (☎2466 1010; www.travelexpress.com.cy; Kimonos 2) operates service (shared) taxis to all key destinations except Larnaka airport:

Agia Napa–Paralimni–Protaras €9 for the trip to these three destinations.

Lefkosia €9, 40 minutes.

Lemesos €11, one hour.

Pafos €21, one hour 40 minutes.

TAXI Sample journey fares and times:

Agia Napa €35 to €43, 30 minutes.

Lefkosia €42 to €50, 35 minutes.

Lemesos €50 to €60, one hour.

Pafos €105, one hour 40 minutes.

Troödos €80 to €90, one hour.

🛈 Getting Around

TO/FROM THE AIRPORT Buses 417 and 431 from the central police station and Finikoudes go to the airport (€1, 30 minutes). The first bus is at 6.20am and the last is a 431 at 9pm (5.45pm in winter).

Stavrakis Taxi Office (☎2465 5988; Ermou 64) is in the centre of town.

BUS Blue regional **buses** (☎2466 5531; www .zinonasbuses.com) arrive and depart at the stop opposite the police station. All districts are provided for five to six times daily. All-day tickets are €2; for timetables visit the website.

BICYCLE Bicycles can be hired at **Anemayia** (☎2465 8333; 19 Leoforos Archiepiskopou Makariou III; per day €10), which offers free delivery.

CAR & MOTORCYCLE There are many car-rental companies at the airport.

Andreas Petsas Rent-a-car (☎2464 3350; airport)

Anemayia Car, Motorbike & Bicycle Rentals (☎9962 4726) Also hires out cruisers, mopeds and buggies.

Thames Car Rentals Larnaka (☎2465 6333; Vasileos Pavlou 13); airport (☎2400 8700).

AROUND LARNAKA

🛈 Getting Around

It's no secret that the best way to see greater Larnaka (and the rest of Cyprus, for that matter) is with your own transport. A great alternative, though, is a **Love Buses** (☎9776 1761; Leoforos Athinon, Larnaka; per person €10; ⊙11am-5.30pm, night tours 8.30pm & 10pm summer) sightseeing tour aboard a bright red open-air bus that would look more at home in central London.

Tours include stops at Larnaka Salt Lake, Hala Sultan Tekke and the Kamares Aqueduct. On Saturday there's a route to Panagia Angeloktisti in Kiti, and kid-friendly Mazotos Camel Park. It does get hot on the top level of the bus, so bring water and a hat.

⛱ Beaches

Larnaka's beaches can be bland compared to those in Agia Napa and the east coast. Most have hard-packed, greyish sand and occasional pebbles. The waters, though, are generally very shallow and great for kids.

Makenzy   BEACH
Probably the best beach in town. It's about 2km south of Larnaka past Piyale Pasha.

Finikoudes   BEACH
Clean, shallow seafront beach that's packed with sunbeds and amenities.

CTO Municipal Beach   BEACH
On Dekelia road, east of Larnaka; popular with locals and backed by dozens of taverns, restaurants and hotels.

Cape Kiti and Perivolia   BEACH
Southwest of Larnaka, these secluded, narrow beaches have large, white stones and shallow waters. The Perivolia side of the cape is often exposed to tremendous winds, ideal for kite and windsurfing. You'll need to have your own equipment, though.

Kamares Aqueduct

Sanctioned in 1746 by Ottoman governor Bekir Pasha, and built in classical Roman style – some historians believe it is actually

LARNAKA & THE EAST KAMARES AQUEDUCT

a Roman creation that was simply refurbished by the Ottomans – the aqueduct was constructed to solve Larnaka's freshwater problems. It originally ferried water from a source 10km south using underground tunnels, hundreds of air wells and a series of overland arches, remnants of which can be glimpsed from the freeway to Lemesos. The aqueduct remained in use until the 1950s. Today it is known as 'the Kamares' or 'the Arches'. The Larnaka municipality holds open-air concerts on the lawns in front of the aqueduct, which is wonderfully illuminated by night. It can be found close to the K Cineplex on the old road to Lemesos.

Hala Sultan Tekke (Tekkesi)

Surrounded by date palms, cypresses and olive trees, the mosque and **tekke** (shrine; admission free, donation expected; ☺9am-7.30pm May-Sep, 9am-5pm Oct-Apr) sit wistfully on the edge of Larnaka's salt lake. Considered by some as the third holiest place in the world for Muslims, the shrine was founded in 674 during Arab raids on Cyprus. Apparently Umm Haram, the revered wet nurse (aunt) of the Prophet Mohammed, fell from her mule and died at this exact spot. The site comprises her tomb, mausoleum and shrine (1760), a mosque, a minaret and a convent (all from the late-18th century). The excavated tomb and sarcophagus of Hala Sultan (Umm Haram), meaning 'Great Mother' in Turkish, is found left of the entrance, in what feels like a cave.

The mosque itself is still used. The floor is layered with prayer mats, so you must remove your shoes if you wish to enter.

The *tekke* is 1km from the main road between Larnaka and the airport.

Larnaka Salt Lake

During winter this protected reserve fills with rainwater, creating an important migratory habitat for flamingos, wild ducks and water fowl. As summer approaches the waters slowly dry up and the birds leave. They are replaced by a crusty layer of salt amid heat waves that bounce and shimmer off its white surface.

Archaeologists have determined that in prehistoric times the central lake (known to locals as Aliki) was a natural port that facilitated important trade to the island. It

serviced a sizeable late–Bronze Age town that stood near where the Hala Sultan Tekke is now. In 1050 BC the town's population abandoned the site and shortly after the waterway dried up, thus creating the salt lake. For centuries afterwards salt was harvested from the lake and became a valuable export for Cyprus. Temporary harvest houses were set up and donkeys were used to cart salt in large woven baskets. By the 1980s rising costs and slowed production halted salt harvesting altogether.

Do not try four-wheel driving on the salt lake, as you will get bogged. Although travellers are not encouraged to walk on the lake itself, there are fantastic nature trails along its banks.

Kiti & Around

POP 3140

This village 9km southwest of Larnaka is home to the 11th-century domed cruciform church of **Panagia Angeloktisti** (admission free, donations welcome; ☺9.30am-noon & 2-4pm Mon-Sat Jun-Sep). The church, literally meaning 'built by angels', houses an extraordinary 6th-century **Mosaic of the Virgin Mary**. It was only discovered in 1952 amid the remains of the original 5th-century apse, which has been incorporated into the current building. Wonderfully preserved, the mosaic portrays Mary standing on a jewelled pedestal with baby Jesus in her arms, bordered by the archangels Gabriel and Michael. The church is still a place of worship with regular services.

Further along the coastline you will find the village of **Perivolia** and **Cape Kiti**. The cape, complete with cliffs and lighthouse, has some wonderful getaway hotels and simple ice-cream parlours.

Stavrovouni Monastery

This **monastery** (☺8am-noon & 3-6pm Apr-Aug, 8am-noon & 2-5pm Sep-Mar) is perched 668m high at the peak of Stavrovouni, which literally translates as 'Mountain of the Cross'. Revered as the oldest monastery on the island, it is perfectly isolated from the districts below and said to hold a piece of the Holy Cross, brought here by St Helena, mother of Emperor Constantine the Great, upon her return from Jerusalem in AD 327. St Helena gave the relic to the monks for protection and the monastery was founded.

START **KITI**
FINISH **LARNAKA**
DISTANCE **96KM**
DURATION **FIVE TO SEVEN HOURS**

Driving Tour
Craftwork of Traditional Villages

❯ From the church of ❶ **Panagia Angelok-tisti** in Kiti take the 403 road west towards the agricultural village of ❷ **Mazotos**. Kids will love its camel park. From here take the old coastal road west through fields and sparse terrain. You'll travel about 17km, with a view of the sea on your left, before reaching attractive ❸ **Maroni** village, where you can buy some local cucumbers and have a Greek coffee. Then take the short road southwest to ❹ **Zygi**, a diminutive fishing village known for some of the island's best fish taverns. After you've had a bite to eat, it's back on track westward for 1km. Head inland and turn right onto the B1 underpass (crossing the A1 motorway) for about 6km, then head left towards the valley and the scenic village of ❺ **Tochni**. The north road out of the village takes you 4km to the impressive prehistoric settlement of ❻ **Choirokoitia**. From this Neolithic site take a long stretch of climbing road inland northwest to ❼ **Vavla**, with its wonderfully restored homes. Next is the pretty, well-signposted stone village of

❽ **Kato Drys**, with its quaint balconies. A mere 4km more of winding road brings you to the lace- and silverwork village of ❾ **Pano and Kato Lefkara**, where you can wander the precipitous old town and barter for wares. From Pano Lefkara travel north for 7km on a good stretch of road until you see Lefkara dam on your left. Follow the road right over an incline for 16km to the pottery village of ❿ **Kornos**. After some clay hunting, follow the signs and road east, through the underpass (recrossing the motorway), to the town of ⓫ **Pyrga**, home of the 14th-century Lusignan **Chapelle Royale** (signposted as 'Medieval Chapel'). This church is dedicated to St Catherine and houses some fine frescos. About 4km north of the village you can turn right (east) onto the 104 road, stop in ⓬ **Agia Anna** for meze, then ease back into Larnaka.

Today this fragment from the Holy Land is preserved in an ornate 1.2m solid silver cross inside the church.

Ironically, nowadays St Helena herself could not view it, as the monastery grounds are closed to women. The site is still well worth the trip, though, for its uninterrupted views of the Mesaoria plain. On a clear day you can see Famagusta to the east, Troödos Massif to the northwest, all the way around to Larnaka and the salt lake, and as far as the clear blue Mediterranean.

Once inside the monastery you can take a seat in the sun-filled courtyard entrance to the church, admire the bell tower and ponder monastic life. While male visitors are freely exploring the many icons and arched hallways, female travellers can spend their time at the smaller Church of All Saints just outside the monastery. All can meet in the souvenir and bookshop, with a grand array of Bibles, hymnbooks and icons for sale. There are also handmade prayer bracelets, which are wonderful souvenirs at €4.

Stavrovouni is still a working religious community with a score of monks dedicated to lifelong ascetic principles. Pilgrims and visitors are welcome and can take confession by request but should arrive during visiting hours only. Photos are prohibited inside the monastery, so leave your camera behind. If you are a dedicated pilgrim (and male) you may be invited, by the monks, to sleep the night, meditate and dine with them on their organically grown produce.

The monastery is located 17km from Larnaka off the Lefkosia–Lemesos motorway (A1).

Choirokoitia

This well-preserved **Neolithic site** (admission €1.70; ☺9am-7.30pm Mon-Fri, to 5pm Sat & Sun May-Sep, to 5pm daily Oct-Apr) dates back to 7000 BC. Added to the World Heritage list in 1998, it is the earliest permanent human settlement found in Cyprus.

Believed to have been established by peoples from Anatolia and Asia Minor, the settlement occupies a well-defended hillside and has a large perimeter wall. The remains of over 50 cylindrical stone and mud dwellings have been discovered, along with prehistoric utensils, indicating that the Choirokoitians practised a sophisticated lifestyle that included well-developed hunting and farming. They also

appear to have buried their dead under the floors of their dwellings, as indicated by the remains of over 20 skeletons including those of infants.

There is a series of walkways around the settlement; the best remains are found at the top of the hill. At the foot of the original site visitors can see reconstructions of the original huts, to help visualise how they would have appeared long ago.

Choirokoitia is located 32km from Larnaka just off the main Larnaka–Lemesos highway. If you continue a further 10km towards Lemesos you can see the Neolithic site at **Tenta (Kalavasos)**, easily recognisable by the huge cone-shaped tent shielding it from the elements. It is a simpler version of Choirokoitia but just as important archaeologically.

Lefkara

POP 1100

During the Renaissance, with an affluent population of nearly 5000, this mountain village combining Pano and Kato Lefkara was one of the island's largest and most influential towns. It was already famous for its exquisite lace, handcrafted by the village women since medieval times, and for the men's fine silverwork, incorporating lacing techniques with silver smithing.

The area was a favoured destination for wealthy settlers and travellers, and it was poised to become a fully fledged city. Although it didn't quite make it, the village is still in a beautiful setting, surrounded by a steep valley of pines and wild carob trees. Its narrow cobbled streets and traditional houses charmingly show an obvious Venetian influence.

In 1481 Leonardo da Vinci is said to have visited Lefkara and obtained a fine piece of lace for the altar of Milan's cathedral. Lace and silver lovers the world over still come just for these crafts and are not disappointed. Shop owners sit outside in the streets, weaving lace and calling you to come and watch their work or look inside their stores with 'no obligation'. They can be overzealous but are genuinely pleasant about it. The lace is of exceptional quality, but it can be very pricey, so it's best to pick your favourite from the hundreds on offer and bargain about the cost. You will find the best quality and variety in the village itself. Keep in mind that the finest pieces are always found inside the stores and not displayed outside.

After souvenir shopping, it's fun to buy a bag of local, in-season fruit, walk around and check out the wonderful array of traditional doors, doorways and hidden courtyards. Follow the signs through the backstreets to find the **Museum of Traditional Embroidery & Silver-Smithing** (admission €1.70; ☉9.30am-4pm Mon-Thu, 10am-4pm Fri & Sat), formerly the home of one of Lefkara's wealthiest families. The building is set around a large courtyard complete with restored outdoor oven and pomegranate and citrus trees. The ground floor consists of a cold room, a living room and a dining area. It is dressed with giant clay pots, traditional utensils, tools, furnishings and examples of original lace and silverwork. Upstairs are the grandiose hall, workshop and bedrooms, complete with antique dressers, mirrors and beds.

In nearby Skarinou is the weird and wonderful **Fatsa Wax Museum** (Georgiou Papandreou; adult/child €5/3.50; ☉9am-5.30pm Oct-Mar, to 6.30pm Apr-Sep), inspired by Madame Tussauds. It houses over 120 waxworks that show Cypriot historical ages, events and culture, and such prominent citizens as presidents, war heroes and religious leaders. There's a cafe-restaurant for snacks.

The best lunch in town is at the **Lefkara Hotel & Restaurant** (www.lefkarahotels.com; 42 Timiou Stavrou Pano Lefkara; mains €12), whose ancient walls encircle the diminutive church of **St Mamas** (c 974). Sit at a low-lit table and enjoy fresh organic vegetables grown on site, blended with delights like soft smoked pork fillet stuffed with haloumi and served with sun-dried tomatoes and warm *bourgouri*.

You can get to Lefkara from the Lefkosia–Lemesos motorway (A1) or by the scenic road from Choirokoitia via Vavla. A daily bus (€1, Monday to Saturday) runs between Lefkara and Larnaka, leaving Lefkara at 7am and returning from Larnaka at 1pm.

AGIA NAPA

POP 2680

Phenomenal weather and perfect beaches have transformed this unassuming fishing village into the best party-holiday destination in Europe. Gorgeous white sandy beaches and literally hundreds of clubs and bars have made it a Disneyland for clubbers and partygoers the world over.

Its revamped square is surrounded with every incarnation of themed club you can imagine, with places dedicated to the Flintstones, Arthurian legend and '70s cop shows, to name a few, and world-famous DJs play headline acts here every summer.

High season is June to August, when it can be difficult to find a spot on the beach, let alone accommodation. Even amid the chaos, though, this is still a fantastic place to visit. The municipality has made a push towards more family tourism, which has increased dramatically, but Napa (as it's simply called) is still where the party is at its hardest.

Napa's central point is Plateia Seferi, known universally as 'the Square'. Most streets around the Square are pedestrianised. Buses arrive at the southern end of Leoforos Archiepiskopou Makariou III; service taxis arrive and depart near the Square.

◎ Sights

FREE **Agia Napa Monastery**   HISTORICAL SITE
(Plateia Seferi; ☉9am-6pm) Resembling a medieval castle, this beautiful monastery is a strong contrast to the pubs and clubs that populate the adjoining square. Best visited in the morning, it is the perfect example of the great history Agia Napa has to offer over and above its leisure scene.

Built in 1500 by the Venetians, it protects a cave in which an icon of the Virgin Mary was hidden during the iconoclasm of the 7th and 8th centuries. Surviving Ottoman rule undamaged, the remarkably well-preserved structure served as both a convent and a monastery during different periods until it was abandoned in 1758.

Inside its stout protective wall, designed initially to keep marauding pirates at bay, visitors can admire its large courtyard and humble cave-like church. The courtyard's best feature is the marble fountain, dating from 1530, covered by a domed stone spectator area. Also of interest is the enormous 600-year-old sycamore tree just outside the southern gate, complete with modern steel props designed to help hold its giant branches.

Thalassa Municipal Museum of the Sea   MUSEUM
(Leoforos Kryou Nerou 14; adult/child €3/1; ☉9am-1pm & 6-10pm Wed-Sun, 6-10pm Tue, closed Mon

Agia Napa

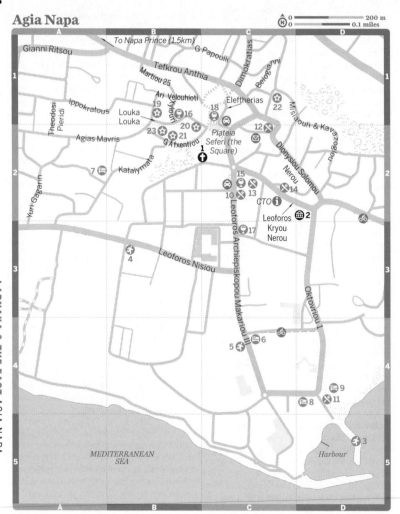

May-Oct, 9am-5pm Wed-Sun, 1-5pm Tue, closed Mon Nov-Apr) This contemporary museum opened in 2005. Dedicated to all things relating to the sea – *thalassa* means 'sea' in Greek – it shows the enormous impact the ocean has had on Cypriot life and culture. Exhibits include fossilised fish, corals, shells and all manner of sea urchins and sea plants.

The museum also houses an exact replica of an ancient vessel that was shipwrecked off the coast of Kyrenia in the 3rd century BC. Dubbed *Kyrenia II*, it was reconstructed by scientists using traditional methods and materials. The remains of the original shipwreck, discovered in 1967, are displayed at Kyrenia Castle in the North.

The museum covers over 700 years of sealife history and displays are accompanied by educational programmes. On the lower floor is the **Marine Life Museum**, with exhibits that include shells, Mediterranean fish, sharks, turtles and sea birds.

Makronissos Tombs   ARCHAEOLOGICAL SITE
Overlooking the sea, this ancient necropolis of 19 tombs cut into the rock is attributed to the Hellenistic and Roman periods. The chambers are practically identical, with

Agia Napa

⊚ Sights
1 Agia Napa Monastery C2
   Marine Life Museum .... (see 2)
2 Thalassa Municipal Museum of
   the Sea D2

✦ Activities, Courses & Tours
3 Black Pearl Pirate Boat D5
   Fantasy Boat Party .... (see 3)
4 Parko Paliasto B3
5 Sunfish C4

⊟ Sleeping
6 Diomylos C4
7 Green Bungalows A2
8 Limanaki Beach D4
9 Okeanos Beach D4

⊗ Eating
10 Fiji C2
11 Karousos Beach D4
12 Limelight C2
13 Quadro C2
14 Sage C2

◎ Drinking
15 Golden Arrow C2
16 Havana B1
17 Jello Bar C3
18 Marinella C1

⊛ Entertainment
19 Bedrock Inn B1
20 Black & White B2
21 Castle B2
22 River Reggae Club C1
23 Starsky's B2

wide steps leading down into the simple tombs, which have stone benches originally designed to hold sarcophagi. The site was heavily looted during the 1870s. Further excavations have found remnants of a quarry, pyres on the surface close to the road, and evidence of ancient Greek interments. The site is west of Napa.

🏊 Beaches

Nissi
BEACH
The main attraction, it boasts crystal-clear, shallow water, soft white sand and a picturesque rock island about 60m from its shore. In summer it gets extremely crowded with sunbathers, umbrellas, music and beach loungers, but it all seems to work. Well stocked with bars, water sports and shower amenities, it's 3km from the centre square, so most arrive by scooter or bicycle.

Kermia
BEACH
Ideal for those who prefer a quieter spot where it's easier to find a sun bed. About 2km east of Napa towards Cape Greco, this is a wonderfully secluded beach with golden sands and a rock break. A great choice for families.

Konnos
BEACH
A further 2km past Kermia, bordering Paralimni, is this lovely long stretch of white sand, sheltered by the bay and hills behind it. All kinds of water sports are on offer here, perfect with the placid waves.

🏃 Activities

A variety of big boats, glass-bottom boats and speedboats operate out of Agia Napa's remodelled harbour. Most do round trips to Cape Greco, Konnos Bay, Protaras or Pernera.

The waters from Nissi Bay to Cape Greco and Konnos Bay up to Protaras are exceptional for diving, with calm seas that are both warm and clear. There are a multitude of inlets and natural caves to explore.

Water World
WATER PARK
(www.waterworldwaterpark.com; Agias Theklis 18; adult/child €33/19; ⊙10am-5pm Apr-Oct) With a Greek-mythology theme, this water park west of Napa is easily the best in Cyprus. Yes, it can be rather expensive, particularly the snack bars inside, but for an all-day outing it's worth it. There are more than 18 rides, including all the usual suspects: the lazy river, whirlpools, wave pools and Kamikaze slides with 75m vertical drops. The Atlantis activity pool and the Trojan Adventure are perfect for young children and families. This is a safe and fun place for kids of all ages.

Parko Paliasto
AMUSEMENT PARK
(www.parkopaliatsocy.com; Leoforos Nisiou; ⊙4pm-midnight Apr-Oct; 👪) The highlight here is the Slingshot, and that's where the crowds gather. Supposedly the highest and fastest in the Med, it shoots you 100m skyward in a caged ball in one and a half

seconds. It's all caught on camera, too, so you'll have a keepsake of your contorted, petrified face. The park also offers less intense rides, like bumper cars, carousels and a ghost train.

Napa Bungee
BUNGEE JUMPING

(jump incl photo, DVD & free drink €70-80; ☺10am-6pm May-Sep) Situated on the rocky cape at Nissi Beach, west of Napa, the jump is over 60m high and sends you hurtling towards the clear blue sea. There are solo jumps, and tandems for those in need of moral support. Wedding jumps and naked jumps have also been performed. These guys are well prepared and have definitely seen it all. Perfect for adrenaline junkies.

Black Pearl Pirate Boat
BOAT TRIPS

(☑9940 8132; blackpearlayianapa.com; Napa Harbour; adult/child €35/15; ☺departs 11.30am-3.30pm May-Sep) This pirate-themed cruise on a large buccaneer ship is great fun for kids, with live pirates and treasure hunts. It stops at two picturesque swimming spots in the bays around Cape Greco. A full roast lunch, including Greek salad, is served afterwards on deck. There is also a bar on board (with rum, of course!), but drinks are additional.

Fantasy Boat Party
BOAT TRIPS

(☑9940 8132; www.fantasyboatparty.com; Napa Harbour; adult €20, drinks extra; ☺departs 5.30-9pm Tue & Sat Apr-Jun, Sep & Oct, daily Jul & Aug) DJs pump music while the crowd dances and drinks away some time on the sea. It's basically a floating nightclub, and there are some great swimming stops where diving games and screaming are encouraged. There are also day and night **Booze Cruises** which, as the name suggests, are not for the faint hearted. Women are generally not charged, and hardcore revellers are always expected.

Sunfish
DIVING

(☑2372 1300; www.sunfishdivers.com; Leoforos Archiepiskopou Makariou III 26) This trusted operator caters for both novices and professionals and covers more than 10 diving spots, including reefs, caves, canyons and the famous **Zenobia Wreck**. Certification programmes are offered, ranging from 'discover scuba diving' all the way through to 'master scuba diver'. Snorkelling to a depth of 2m is available and suitable for kids as young as eight. Ask for Dena when you get there. (For more on diving in Cyprus, see p25.)

Eating

While most eating in Agia Napa is generic and uncultured, there are some decent places among the plethora of fast-food chains and burger joints. Prices, although not exorbitant, tend to reflect the high tourism in the area.

TOP CHOICE Sage
INTERNATIONAL €€€

(www.sagerest.com; Leoforos Kryou Nerou 10; mains €25) With modern decor like slated walls and concatenate doors, this place has an elegant feel about it. The menu features fillet steaks with a range of accompanying sauces. The food is expensive, but deservedly so. The umbrella courtyard is a very relaxing spot in summer and not posh at all.

Karousos Beach
SEAFOOD €€€

(www.karousosbeach.com; Oktovriou 1; mains €22) Beautiful fresh-fish meze (try the ouzo mussels) and local wines are served on intimate tables right on the sea's edge. The service is impeccable and personal. This is also an ideal wedding venue.

Fiji
POLYNESIAN €€€

(www.polynesian-ayianapa.com; Leoforos Archiepiskopou Makariou III 23; mains €17; ☺5.30-11pm; ☑) There's a delightful Pacific-island atmosphere here with banana trees, oversized flowers and comfortable wicker furnishings. Dishes are lavishly served in white shells and aromatic petals. Try the mango beef or salmon teriyaki.

Quadro
ITALIAN €€

(Leoforos Kryou Nerou 7; mains €16; ☺10am-midnight) This modern Italian restaurant has an open dining terrace, comfortable seating, and affordable, great-flavoured food. The menu includes a grand array of pizzas and pastas, and takeaway is also available.

Limelight
CYPRIOT €€€

(www.limelighttaverna.com; D Liperti; mains €17) This traditional and well-established place excels at what it does best: chargrilled dishes. It serves steak, lobster and fish dishes, but it's the yielding beef, lamb and *stifado* (beef or rabbit stew) that burst with flavour.

Drinking

It all begins in 'the Square' with pubs and bars abounding in every direction. The sight of thousands upon thousands of tourists heaving together in this locale in the heat of a July night is mind-boggling. So enjoy the show!

Marinella BAR
(Plateia Seferi; ⊙9pm-2am) This designer bar is right in the heart of the Square and the action. It's a perfect pre-club venue with its indoor and outdoor bar, and the house DJ plays smooth R and B tracks, so you can hit the dance floor or chill on the stools.

Golden Arrow PUB
(Leoforos Archiepiskopou Makariou III 21; ⊙9am-2.30am) A stone's throw from the Square, this wonderful family bar is super friendly and full of entertainment. You can sit outdoors and watch the human traffic, pull up a spot at the bar, or watch football on the big screens.

Jello Bar BAR
(Leoforos Archiepiskopou Makariou III 43; cocktails €3-6; ⊙9am-2am) This trendy bar with hip pink and white ergonomic features serves everything from beers to cocktails, a good mix of burgers, super-sweet desserts and wild milkshakes like galaxy chocolate. The LED display in the toilets upstairs is impressive. Happy hour starts at 8pm.

Havana BAR
(Xylouri; ⊙7pm-2am summer) Styled like an open-air hacienda, Havana is very popular for its relaxed dance atmosphere. Straying from the Cuban theme with funk and garage, it compensates with cool style and setting. Entertainment includes penalty-shootout competitions.

☆ Entertainment

Revellers drink and dance in the Square and surrounding pubs between 10pm and 2am. Then it's time to hit the clubs, with a whole host to choose from. Most venues open after 1am and don't get full until 3am. A cover charge of €10 to €15 is normal – the best deals are found from ticket sellers in the Square.

Castle NIGHTCLUB
(www.thecastleclub.com; Grigoriou Afxentiou) The citadel is hard to miss. It holds over 2000 people, in three separate music rooms, and plays host to some of the world's best DJs during summer. Lovers of dance, house and garage will not be disappointed.

Black & White NIGHTCLUB
(Louka Louka 6) A staple of the hip hop, swing and soul scene since the 1990s, this dark little venue has multiple bars and an intimate dance floor. It gets full quickly and draws a big crowd from the pre-party at Havana bar.

Starsky's NIGHTCLUB
(www.starskysayianapa.com; Grigoriou Afxentiou) Specialising in commercial dance and house, it features an octagonal bar with dancing poles and retro disco balls. As the sign says 'All roads lead to Starsky's'.

Bedrock Inn KARAOKE BAR
(www.bedrockinn.com; Louka Louka) Bulbous stones, snaggleteeth and staff in leopard-skin togas – Bedrock offers hundreds of karaoke songs and drinking games to entertain the animated crowds.

River Reggae Club NIGHTCLUB
(Misiaouli & Kavazoglou; admission free) An outdoor club with palm trees, a wooded dance floor, winding pool and reggae music. It's usually best after 4am, when things can get crazy as revellers skinny dip and dance. So, if you're up for it...

❶ Information

INTERNET ACCESS **3W Internet Café**
(☎2372 3032; Leoforos Nisiou 27; per hr €3; ⊙10am-midnight) Internet, printing, photo downloads.
Backstage Internet Centre (☎2381 6097; Ari Velouchioti 7; per hr €3; ⊙10am-midnight) Internet access with games and pool table.
MEDICAL SERVICES **After-hours pharmacy assistance** (☎192)
Napa Olympic Polyclinic (☎2372 3222; Chavares 24) Private hospital.
Paralimni Hospital (☎2382 1211; Paralimni) Located 15 minutes' drive away in Paralimni.
MONEY ATMs are available on most streets.
Alpha Bank (☎2372 2353; Leoforos Nisiou 34) Main branch.
Hellenic Bank (☎2372 1588; Leoforos Archiepiskopou Makariou III 18) Just south of the Square.
POLICE **Police station** (☎2472 1553; cnr Ayia Napa Junction & Kavo Greko) North of central Agia Napa, at the big roundabout.
POST **Post office** (☎2472 2141; D Liperti 3) Just east of the Square.
TOURIST INFORMATION **CTO** (☎2372 1796; Leoforos Kryou Nerou 12; ⊙8.15am-2.30pm & 3-6.30pm Mon, Tue, Thu & Fri, 8.15am-2.30pm Wed & Sat) Southeast of the Square.

❶ Getting There & Away

AIR **Larnaka airport** (☎flight information 2464 3000), 48km away, is the closest airport.
BUS **InterCity** (☎2381 9090; www.intercity-buses.com; 1 way/all day & return €3/5) buses leave from Leoforos Kryou Nerou (Marina Hotel), Parko Paliasto and Water World. Destinations:

Larnaka Hourly 6am to 6.30pm weekdays, 8am to 4.30pm weekends.

Lefkosia At least hourly 6am to 3.30pm weekdays, 6.30am and 3pm weekends.

SERVICE TAXI **Travel & Express** (☑2382 6061; www.travelexpress.com.cy; Paralimni) operates shared taxis to all key destinations except Larnaka airport:

Larnaka €9, 45 minutes.

Lefkosia €18, one hour.

Lemesos €20, one hour.

Pafos €30, two hours.

TAXI Standard **taxis** (☑2372 1111) can be found on the edge of the Square. Journey fares and times:

Larnaka €35 to €43, 30 minutes.

Lefkosia €45 to €52, 35 minutes.

Lemesos €60 to €70, one hour.

Pafos €120, one hour 40 minutes.

Troödos €90 to €100, one hour.

❶ Getting Around

Catch a taxi or join the masses and hire a scooter, motorbike or buggy.

Easyriders (☑2372 2438; www.easyriders .com.cy; Gianni Ritsou 1) Rents 50cc scooters (from €20 per day), quads, and Kawasaki or Suzuki 800cc heavies (from €55 per day). There's a second outlet at Dimokratias 17.

V&L Tsokkos (☑9968 4785; Leoforos Nisiou 58) Has cars, quads, buggies and scooters for hire at competitive prices.

AROUND AGIA NAPA

❶ Getting Around

Other than InterCity buses (Paralimni–Agia Napa–Larnaka), the best option is to hire a scooter or buggy in Agia Napa or Protaras, where you can find reasonable rates.

Riding around the Paralimni region is wonderful, but you'll need a vehicle high in ccs. For beach-hopping along the Pernera–Protaras coastal strip, scooters, buggies or quad bikes will do nicely. The area is ideal for cycling enthusiasts, with designated paths between Agia Napa and Cape Greco.

If you want to explore the greater region, a car or small 4WD is more suitable.

Palaces & Sea Caves

Located at the inlet between Limnara Beach and Cape Greco are the unique rock formations known as the **palaces**. Carved into the cliff face by centuries of waves buffering the coast, they look like spy holes, framing the clear blue sea. The natural architecture plays host to divers, who can approach the rocks here only by boat.

Further east are the spectacular **sea caves** cut into the face of the rocky coastline. From lookout seats above you can hear the dynamic echoes created by the sea funnelling back and forth. When the sea is calm you can access some caves on foot, but on rough and windy days the spray reaches your face some 10m above, leaving you with tight cheeks and the taste of salt in your mouth. Again, the best views are from the sea, so consider one of the many charters that run from Napa's harbour.

Cape Greco

This national park has sweeping views of the sea and coast and is excellent for hiking and riding. A coastal track starting from Kryou Nerou in Agia Napa winds all the way to the lighthouse at the edge of the cape, approximately 3½ hours' walk. The region is unsheltered, so bring hats, water and sunscreen. There are some great picnic spots along the way. The track can get bumpy, so if you ride, mountain-bike tyres are more appropriate. The region has 15km of walking tracks with interesting local flora, such as sea squill, wild orchids and sand lilies, which have managed to prosper in high-salinity soil. Once you reach Cape Greco itself, you can walk north towards the little bay and scamper down to the rock platforms, where swimmers jump and dive into the idyllic waters.

Paralimni

POP 11,100 (INCLUDING PROTARAS & PERNERA)

Paralimni is located inland near the seasonal lake from which it derives its name. The unofficial capital of the Famagusta district, it has grown due to migration from the occupied North and the success of nearby resort towns Agia Napa and Protaras. Many of its inhabitants work and own businesses in these areas.

The town itself has few sights. It has a simple paved square, a church (Agios Georgios) and a growing strip of restaurants and shops.

Deryneia

POP 7500

Deryneia is primarily known for its location at the eastern rise of the closed 'border' that separates the occupied North from the

Republic of Cyprus. Here you can peer into the no-man's-land of Famagusta and see the ghost town of Varosia. It was once a thriving resort town and economic port, but its inhabitants were forced to flee the invading Turkish troops in August 1974. It is now entirely fenced off by the Turkish military.

There are viewing platforms at the **Cultural Centre of Occupied Ammochostos (Famagusta)** (Evagorou 35; admission free; ☺7.30am-4.30pm Mon-Fri, 9.30am-4.30pm Sat) and at **Annita's** (admission €1), which is the better of the two. Both provide binoculars and views of the UN buffer zone, military posts and abandoned Varosia. It can be a harrowing and politically charged experience, as the shock still lingers in the collective memory of resident Greek Cypriots.

Deryneia itself is a warm, traditional village with Byzantine churches dating from the 12th century and a **Folk Art Museum** (Demetris Lipertis 2; admission €1.70; ☺9am-1pm & 4-6pm Mon-Sat) worth visiting.

Dekelia Sovereign Base Area

In 1960, during independence negotiations between the nascent Republic of Cyprus and the British administration, the rights to two major sovereign base areas (SBAs) were brokered. Dekelia SBA is the second of these. The area comprises a large part of eastern Cyprus running from Larnaka Bay to the border with the North. You can pass through the base and even stop and enjoy fish and chips in the civilian area. It has a small beach populated with a few British-styled shops and a playground for kids.

The military site itself is off-limits. The base is still a critical centre for intelligence gathering and monitoring of the Middle East. The British government has stated that it is prepared to cede back some of the area if Cyprus becomes reunified.

The Kokkinohoria

POP 16,300

The Kokkinohoria ('The Red Villages') are so named because of the deep-red, mineral-rich earth found in the area. It comprises the inland rural villages of **Xylofagou**, **Avgorou**, **Frenaros**, **Liopetri** and **Sotira**. Most of these villages rely heavily on agriculture and are famous for their potato and *kolokasi* (a root vegetable similar to taro)

produce. Wind-powered water pumps dot the landscape and prosperous crops are cultivated three to four times annually.

The region is indicative of rural Cyprus, where you can find some excellent country taverns with simple dishes and fresh produce. Take a good map, as signposting is limited.

Pyla

POP 1370

Pyla (Pıle) is the only village where Greek and Turkish Cypriots still live together. There's a token UN peacekeeping contingent in the village, but it's the inhabitants who have made it work. The village itself is located in the UN buffer zone. In the village square, a red-and-white Turkish Cypriot coffee shop stands opposite a blue-and-white Greek Cypriot *kafeneio* in peaceful harmony. The neighbourhood is a mix of Cypriots simply going about their daily lives.

The only differences that arise relate to local taxes and utility costs. These are paid by the Greeks only; as the Turks are citizens of the North, they pay nothing. The politics, though, come second, as it is understood here that they are all Cypriots.

There are nearby vehicle crossings to Northern Cyprus at the town of Pergamos.

Protaras

POP 11,100 (INCLUDING PARALIMNI & PERNERA)

Protaras is the Med's hot-ticket resort town. Its growing stature includes refurbished hotels with sprawling lawns, swimming pools, and a modernised beachfront complete with walking path and bike track. Its safe beaches, good-quality taverns and generally slower pace make it ideal for couples and families. Protaras is centred on the main paved avenue with its concentration of shops, restaurants, bars and hotels.

◎ Sights & Activities

Magic Dancing Water   WATER SHOW
(Protaras Ave; adult/child €15/8; ☺9pm)
Young kids will love this show where water seems to dance and spin, accompanied by music, laser lights and holograms.

Ayios Elias   CHURCH
Rebuilt in 1980, this church is situated on a rocky peak just off the Protaras–Pernera road. A long set of stairs leads to the top,

CHILDREN'S CYPRUS: UNDERWATER WORLDS

At **Under Sea Adventures** (☎9956 3506; www.underseawalkers.com; De Costa Bay, Protaras) kids eight years and up with a sense of adventure can choose between 'shallow-water helmet diving' (adults €45, children eight to 16 €35) or 'riding on a BOB' (Breathing Observation Bubble; 13 years and up €55). Both are a fun and safe way to experience underwater life. The undersea walks go down to 3m, where you can see rock formations and sea life while your face remains completely dry inside your helmet. Air flows freely into the helmet and no other breathing equipment is required. The 30-minute BOB tour is led by a professional instructor. Comfortably inside an air-bubble helmet, you glide around on an underwater scooter observing the amazing aquatic habitat.

where you can enjoy magnificent views of Protaras and the bay. Follow the signs to get here.

Moonshine Ranch HORSE RIDING
(☎9960 5042; Cape Greco; rides €40; ☉8am-7pm) This 'Tex-Mex' looking ranch with sweeping views of Cape Greco offers accompanied rides taking in Konnos Bay, the cape and the surrounding mountainous valley. All skill levels are happily catered for. The ranch is just off the coastal road between Agia Napa and Protaras.

Beaches

Protaras BEACH
The main beach has soft golden sand, a series of shallow rocky coves and a walkway backed by the green lawns of the resort hotels. Fully equipped, it's perfect for sunbathing and swimming, and a multitude of water sports are available.

Fig Tree Bay BEACH
At the southern end of the main beach, Fig Tree Bay is very popular. It has a small sand island just off the coast, which is great for snorkelling with lots of fish to be seen. There are hotels and restaurants aplenty, so it's a great spot to eat, swim, drink and relax.

Eating

Most restaurants are on the main strip.

Kyklos Restaurant CYPRIOT €€
(Protaras Ave; mains from €12) Offers well-cooked, authentic food, like slow-baked meze (a standout item is lamb *souvla* tenderised with garlic and lemon). It's located at the southern end of Protaras' main street.

Nikolas Tavern CYPRIOT €€
(Fig Tree Bay, Protaras; mains from €11) Well-priced, excellent food and friendly service. Try the *stifado* or *kleftiko* (oven-baked lamb) with one of the local wines.

Pernera

Pernera is the coastal resort just north of Protaras, and is so close that the two have almost merged into one. This hidden gem has beautiful beaches and pocket-sized bays, perfect for a peaceful getaway. The town itself has a couple of really good restaurants, and shops dedicated to water sports.

Beaches

Louma BEACH
A small, curving strip of beach which drops away gently, protected by an artificial bay. The sand is fine and the water is clear. Trees at the northern end provide shade.

Pernera BEACH
This miniature version of Louma is a curvy sliver of good, soft sand with shallow waters and a beach restaurant.

Agia Triada BEACH
This cute little beach with low water levels and coarser sand is an excellent boat-launching site.

Skoutari BEACH
An isolated cove encircled by a cliff with hard-packed sand and rocks. Ideal for snorkelling.

Eating

TOP CHOICE **La Cultura Del Gusto** MEDITERRANEAN €€€
(Ifaistou Skarou Markou 9; mains from €18) This fashionable restaurant offers an innovative menu of mainly Italian-style cuisine. With courteous staff and specialities like lamb shank and succulent chicken, it makes for excellent dining.

Lefkosia (Nicosia)

POP 213,500

Includes »

Lefkosia (Nicosia).......... 126

Ancient Tamassos.......... 144

Monastery of Agios
Irakleidios 145

Agios Mamas
Church at Agios
Sozomenos 146

Maheras
Monastery...................... 146

Mesaoria Villages........... 147

Best Places to Eat

» Mattheos (p137)

» Christakis (p137)

» Syrian Arab Friendship
Club (p139)

» Zanettos Taverna (p137)

Best Places to Stay

» Classic Hotel (p208)

» Royiatiko (p208)

» Sky Hotel (p209)

» Centrum (p209)

Why Go?

If you grow weary of the coast's sea and sunbed scene, and even if you don't, make sure you spend some time in the country's capital, Lefkosia (Nicosia), as it's known officially and to Greek speakers. It is an enticing city and is ideal for experiencing what modern Cyprus is all about. The ancient walls, traditional restaurants and a growing multicultural core effectively showcase the city's basic make-up. Almost everything of interest lies within the historic walls, where a labyrinth of narrow streets reveals churches, mosques and evocative, often crumbling, colonial-style buildings. The country's best museum is also here, housing an extensive archaeological collection.

The city has been labelled 'the last divided capital', a reality that, although still present, is slowly changing thanks to 24-hour checkpoint crossings into its Turkish northern half – Lefkoşa (North Nicosia).

When to Go

The best time of year to visit is during spring and autumn, when the weather is pleasantly warm, interrupted by only an occasional outbreak of rain. Easter can be an extra-special time here, with traditional parades and a generally festive atmosphere.

Avoid mid-summer when the capital is one of the hottest places on the island, albeit a dry heat, with temperatures generally hovering around the 36°C mark. Many restaurants and hotels also close their shutters in August to allow employees to substitute the relative cool of the coastal resorts for the hot, dusty capital.

LEFKOSIA (NICOSIA)

History

Lefkosia has always been the country's capital, mainly because the defences of the coastal cities were so weak and prone to attack. The city's position in the centre of a plain provided at least some protection against marauding invaders. Lefkosia

flourished during the Byzantine period. The Byzantines were followed by the Venetians who took command of the city in 1489 but failed dismally in repelling the Ottomans who took control in 1570. The city stagnated until the British arrived in 1878, which also marked the time that development started to spread beyond the city walls.

Lefkosia (Nicosia) Highlights

1 Exploring the emblematic and superbly preserved **Venetian walls** (p130) snaking around the Old City

2 Seeing both sides of Europe's last divided capital by striding out north at the **Ledra St pedestrian crossing** (p130)

3 Enjoying a barbecue at one of the shady **picnic grounds** (p147) around Kapoura

4 Spending a day of blissful self-pampering at the stylish **Omeriye Hammam** (p134)

5 People-watching, accompanied by an ice-cold

frothy frappé, at one of the terrace cafes on **Ledra St**

6 Joining one of the excellent **free guided walks** of the Old City organised by the tourist office (p135)

7 Exploring the cobbled backstreets of Mesaoria villages such as **Pera** (p147)

In the 1950s violence against the British instigated by the Ethniki Organosi tou Kypriakou Agona (EOKA; National Organisation for the Cypriot Struggle) saw considerable carnage on the streets of the capital.

Further violence in the form of intercommunal disturbances between Greek and Turkish Cypriots in 1963 brought a de facto partition of the city. The so-called 'Green Line' came into being at this time, when the British army defined the Greek and Turkish areas by using a simple green pen on a military map. The name has stuck to this day.

The Turkish invasion of 1974 cemented the division of the city, which has remained bisected ever since, chaperoned by the watchful, but increasingly weary, eyes of UN peacekeeping forces. In 2003 crossing the Green Line was made possible for ordinary citizens, resulting in a number of Turkish Cypriots going to work on the southern side of the capital. The Greek Cypriots, in turn, frequent the North's numerous casinos and head to the northeast's wild coastline. The opening of the Ledra St pedestrian-only crossing in April 2008 has facilitated easier access in both directions.

For more information on the division of the city, see p224.

⊙ Sights & Activities

The most interesting part of the city for visitors is the Old City, lying within the 16th-century Venetian walls. Note that a massive redesign project has currently cordoned off much of Lefkosia's Plateia Eleftherias by the southern wall. When completed, the area will encompass a park and a pedestrian walkway flanked by palm trees and the existing ancient Venetian walls, at the base of which are car parks and municipal gardens.

The New City sprawls southwards, and its main artery is the modern Leoforos

ROAD DISTANCES (KM)

	Lefkosia	Fikardou	Tamassos	Pera
Fikardou	37			
Tamassos	21	34		
Pera	79	51	62	
Kato Pafos	76	80	75	95

Archiepiskopou Makariou III (Makarios Ave), where there are dozens of cafes, bars, restaurants and shops.

In addition to the crossover point at Ledra St, there is another at Ledra Palace Hotel, at the far west of the Old City; both are pedestrian only. Agios Dometios, northwest of the New City, is the car-only crossing point. See p2 for more information on crossing the border.

Cyprus Museum　　　　　　　　MUSEUM
(Map p128; Leoforos Mouseiou 1; admission €4; ⊙8am-4pm Tue, Thu & Fri, 8am-5pm Wed, 9am-4pm Sat, 10am-1pm Sun) This excellent museum houses the best collection of archaeological finds in Cyprus. The original museum, erected in 1883, is opposite the municipal gardens, a 10-minute walk west of Plateia Eleftherias.

Highlights include the remarkable display of **terracotta votive statues and figurines** in Room 4, discovered in 1929 by a Swedish-Cypriot archaeological team at Agia Irini, north of Morfou (Güzelyurt) in Northern Cyprus. The 2000 figures, dating back to the 7th to 6th centuries BC, are displayed as they were found, in a semicircular order. Apart from two female representations, the figures are male and many are warriors. Another highlight is the collection of three **limestone lions** and two **sphinxes** found in the Tamassos necropolis south of Lefkosia. The statues, which show an Egyptian influence, were only discovered in 1997. They date from the Cypro-Archaic II period (475–400 BC).

Also look out for the famous **Aphrodite of Soli** statue in Room 5, widely marketed as the 'goddess of Cyprus' on tourist posters. An enormous bronze statue of **Emperor Septimus Severus**, found at Değirmenlik (Kythrea) in 1928, is the main exhibit in Room 6 and is magnificent.

WHICH WAY NOW...?

The Cyprus Tourism Organisation (CTO) has a good map of the Lefkosia city centre and, on the reverse side, greater Lefkosia. This map is available free from all CTO offices. However, the *Street & Tourist Map of Nicosia* has better coverage of the outer suburbs, plus a street index. It is available from most bookshops and stationery stores in Lefkosia.

LEFKOSIA (NICOSIA)

Lefkosia (Old City)

LEFKOSIA (NICOSIA)

NORTH NICOSIA (LEFKOŞA)

LAIKI YITONIA

LEFKOSIA

Petieos River

400 m
0.2 miles

Leoforos Athinas
Leoforos Salamiss
Larnakas
Digeni Akrita

FLATRO (SIBELI) BASTION
CARAFA BASTION
DODGATARO BASTION
CONSTANZA BASTION
D'AVILA BASTION
TRIPOLI BASTION
ROCCAS (KAYTAZAĞA) BASTION
MULA (ZAHRA) BASTION

Agiou Georgiou
Leoforos Athinas
Minoos
Ermou
Dimonaktos
Othello
Thiseos
Plateia
Archiepiskopou Kyprianou
Patriachou Grigoriou
Korai
Leoforos N Foka
Leoforos Evgenias & Antoniou Theodotou
Stasinou
Apostolou Varnava
Ermou Cad
Dionsou
Soutsou Pendadak
Trikoupi
Areos
Aristokyprou
Aristidou
Eshyiou
Solonos
Onasagorou
Ledra St
Arsinois
Apollonos
Perikleous
Megalou Alexandrou
Vasiliou Voulgaroktonou
Vassili Patron Germanou
Palaion Patron Germanou
Fanoromenis
Liperti
Evripidou
Kuyumcular Sk
Arasta Sk
Leoforos Kykkou
Girne Cad
Bat Cad
Granikou
Pafou
Salahi Şevket Sk
Müftü Ziyai Efendi Sk
Saravonu Sk
Tanzimat Sk
Leoforos Markou Drakou
Leoforos Kostaki Pantelidi
Leoforos Aigyptou
Navarinou
Leoforos Mouseiou
Cyprus Museum
Leoforos Nechrou
Metohiou Hilonos
Leoforos Lordou Vyronos
Kostaki Pantelidi
Kostaki Mia
Sofouli
Diagorou
Omirou
Plateia Eleftherias
Plateia Solomou
Plateia Tyilirás
Plateia Tyilirás

Nicosia Municipal Arts Centre
House of Hatzigeorgakis Kornesios
Leventis City Museum

Municipal Tourist Office
CTO

CONSTANTINOU PALEOLOGOU
Leoforos Konstantinou Paleologou

Lefkosia (Old City)

◎ **Top Sights**

Cyprus Museum.....................................B3
House of Hatzigeorgakis
  Kornesios...E3
Leventis City Museum...........................D4
Nicosia Municipal Arts Centre...............E2

◎ **Sights**

1 Agios Ioannis Church..........................E3
2 Ahilleios Library.................................E4
3 Archbishop's Palace...........................E3
4 Bayraktar Mosque..............................E4
5 British Council....................................B3
6 Chrysaliniotissa Crafts Centre.............F2
7 Cyprus Classic Motorcycle
  Museum...C2
8 Ethnographic Museum........................E2
9 Famagusta Gate.................................F2
10 Faneromeni Church...........................D2
11 Holy Cross Catholic Church...............B2
12 Ledra Palace Hotel Crossing..............B1
13 Ledra St Crossing.............................C2
14 Liberty Monument.............................F3
15 Makarios Cultural Foundation.............E3
16 Master Plan Office............................B1
17 Ministry of Education Library..............D4
18 Municipal Gardens............................A3
19 National Struggle Museum.................E2
20 Omeriye Hammam.............................E3
21 Omeriye Mosque...............................D3
22 Pafos Gate.......................................B2
23 Panagia Chrysaliniotissa....................F1
24 Pancyprian Gymnasium
  Museums...E2
25 Shacolas Tower Observatory..............C3
26 State Gallery of Cypriot
  Contemporary Art...............................E4
27 Venetian Walls..................................F2

◎ **Sleeping**

28 Centrum...C4

29 Classic Hotel....................................B3
30 Royiatiko..C3
31 Sky Hotel..D4

◎ **Eating**

32 Christakis...C3
33 Da Paolo...E3
34 Egeon...F2
35 Habana...D3
Inga's Veggie Heaven....................(see 6)
36 Mattheos..D2
37 Pago Pago...C3
38 Power House......................................E2
39 Shiantris...C3
40 Zanettos Taverna..............................D3

◎ **Drinking**

41 Academy 32......................................E4
42 Brew...D4
43 Hammam...E3
44 Ithaki...F2
45 Oktana..D3
46 Plato's..D3
Uqbar...(see 45)

◎ **Entertainment**

47 La Casa de Cuba...............................F2
48 Lefkosia Municipal Theatre................B3
49 Weaving Mill.....................................D2

◎ **Shopping**

50 Andreas Papaeracleous
  Photostore...C3
51 Antiques...C2
52 Cyprus Handicrafts Centre.................D4
Debenhams...................................(see 25)
53 Messa...D3
54 Moufflon...B4
55 Utopia..E4

LEFKOSIA (NICOSIA)

A couple of lovely mosaics, such as **Leda & the Swan** from Palea Pafos, are exhibited in Room 7B, alongside various displays of gold objects excavated from tombs.

FREE **Nicosia Municipal Arts Centre** MUSEUM
(Map p128; Pierides Foundation; www.nimac.org.cy; Apostolou Varnava 19; admission free; ☉10am-3pm & 5-11pm Tue-Sat, 10am-4pm Sun) For something a little less cerebral than the historical museums, duck into the small arcade to the right of the National Struggle Museum and head along Apostolou Varnava for one block. Housed in a former power station, this contemporary-art museum is the city's equivalent to London's Tate Modern. The former industrial setting is suitably dramatic, with looming pitched ceilings and some original equipment (pulleys etc) that blend well with the cutting-edge installations. The permanent collection includes paintings, photography, videos, sculpture, and other works

from the Dimitris Pierides Museum of Contemporary Art in Greece.

Since 1968 the centre has organised the inclusion of pioneering Cypriot artists in the prestigious Venice Biennale. Exhibitions vary monthly; a recent highlight was a Juan Miró exhibition; the opening was attended by Queen Sofia of Spain. The centre also has a sophisticated restaurant, a gift shop and a comprehensive art library for visitors.

FREE **Leventis City Museum** MUSEUM
(Map p128; Ippokratous 17; ⊙10am-4.30pm Tue-Sat) Re-opened in 2010 after an extensive renovation, this museum concentrates on the history of Cyprus – in particular, Lefkosia – and, as a past winner of the European Museum of the Year, has plenty to feel smug about. The permanent collection includes traditional costumes, paintings, archaeological exhibits, and a historic and fascinating postcard collection; all are fittingly housed in a handsome historical mansion.

House of Hatzigeorgakis Kornesios
MUSEUM
(Map p128; Patriarchou Grigoriou 20; admission €1.70; ⊙8am-2pm Mon-Fri, 9am-1pm Sat) The well-preserved House of Hatzigeorgakis Kornesios belonged to Kornesios, the Great Dragoman of Cyprus from 1779 to 1809. A dragoman (*tercüman* in Turkish) was an interpreter or liaison officer between the Ottoman and Orthodox authorities. Kornesios, originally from Kritou Terra village, accumulated his vast wealth through various estates and tax exemptions, and became the most powerful man in Cyprus at the time. But, as you may guess, his extravagance was his undoing. A peasant revolt in 1804, aimed at the ruling classes in general, forced him out of Cyprus and to Istanbul. When he returned from exile five years later, he was accused of treason, his property was confiscated and he was unceremoniously beheaded. The house itself is more beautiful and interesting than the exhibits within. Only one room is set up as mock living quarters, with plush floor cushions and nargileh (water pipes) for smoking. The rest of the mansion is given over to displays of antiques and Ottoman memorabilia.

Venetian Walls
HISTORICAL SITE
(Map p128) The Venetian walls form a border around the Old City so unusual that, once seen on a map, you'll never forget it. And that's partly to do with its odd shape: is it

like a snowflake? A star? A hand grenade? Or a horizontally sliced artichoke?

Despite its memorable appearance, this circular defence wall, which surrounds both the northern and southern halves of the Old City, failed to fulfil the purpose for which it was built. The Venetian rulers erected the walls from 1567 to 1570 with the express aim of keeping the feared Ottoman invaders out of Lefkosia. The 11 fortifying bastions were spaced equally around the ramparts for added protection, and a moat was also dug, although it was never intended to contain water. In July 1570 the Ottomans landed in Larnaka and three months later attacked Lefkosia, storming the fortifications and killing some 50,000 inhabitants.

The walls have remained in place more or less unchanged ever since. Five of the bastions, **Tripoli**, **D'Avila**, **Constanza**, **Podocataro** and **Caraffa**, are in the southern sector of Lefkosia. The **Flatro** (Sibeli) Bastion on the eastern side of the Old City is occupied by Turkish, Greek Cypriot and UN military forces. The remaining bastions, **Loredano** (Cevizli), **Barbaro** (Musalla), **Quirini** (Cephane), **Mula** (Zahra) and **Roccas** (Kaytazağa), are in North Nicosia (Lefkoşa).

The city's walls were originally punctured by three gates: the Famagusta Gate in the east, the Pafos Gate in the west, and the Kyrenia (Girne) Gate in the north.

The Venetian walls and moat around Lefkosia (South Nicosia) are in excellent condition. They are used to provide car-parking spaces and venues for outdoor concerts, as well as for strolling and relaxing. In North Nicosia, the walls are in poorer shape and have become overgrown and dilapidated in parts.

There are vehicle access points around the walls, which allow regular traffic access to the Old City.

Ledra St & Ledra Palace Hotel Crossings
BORDER CROSSING
(Map p128) These two checkpoints are the only places on the island reserved exclusively for pedestrian and bicycle crossings between the North and the South. Masses of tourists and locals now cross from one side to the other, and many cross in the middle of the night, too, after a late night out. Don't forget to take your passport or you will not be allowed through the border.

At the Ledra St crossing, you will pass a small office with army and police officials from the Republic of Cyprus, who will only

YIANNIS TOUMAZIS: DIRECTOR, NICOSIA MUNICIPAL ARTS CENTRE (PIERIDES FOUNDATION)

Over the last 30 years the island's significant artists have created a multi-faceted mosaic, which I feel constitutes our contemporary artistic identity. Many young artists have studied abroad, which, combined with the political situation, has clearly profoundly affected their work.

Best for Cypriot Art

In Lefkosia, aside from the Nicosia Municipal Arts Centre (p129), there is the State Gallery of Cypriot Contemporary Art (p132), the Artos Foundation (www.artos foundation.org), the Pharos Trust (www.thepharostrust.org) and several private art galleries. In Lemesos there is the Lanitis Art Foundation (p51), housed in the Old Carob Mill near the castle.

Best Way to Appreciate Cypriot Culture

Travel off the beaten track and head for the mountains. Try the traditional cuisine at small restaurants in remote villages and visit the beautiful Byzantine churches to discover some fascinating frescos.

Best secret spot

Drive from Lefkosia to Polis through the mountains and make a stop at the Cedar Valley (p103). It's a whole different world.

check you on your return from the North and may well search your bags. They are generally friendly, though you should be careful not to exceed the amount of cigarettes and alcohol that you are permitted to bring from the North.

You'll then come to the Turkish Republic of Northern Cyprus' kiosks, where you will be asked to fill out a white 'visa form' with your name and passport number. You can keep one visa form for numerous entries into the North. After that, you're free to roam.

The process is the same at the Ledra Palace Hotel crossing. To the left, as you head north, is the former Ledra Palace Hotel, now renovated and occupied by the UN. The renovation is part of the EU-sponsored 'Nicosia Master Plan' project (see boxed text p133). Abandoned shops lie to the right of the hotel. A white iron gate marks the entry to Turkish Cypriot–controlled territory, after which lies the fairly innocuous Turkish Cypriot checkpoint building.

Shacolas Tower Observatory OBSERVATORY
(Map p128; 11th fl, Shacolas Tower, cnr Ledra & Arsinois; admission €0.90; ⊙10am-6.30pm; 🚺) Shacolas Tower Observatory sits, rather bi-

zarrely, above Debenhams department store and provides a superb vantage point across the city. You can use telescopes to gaze at the whole of Lefkosia, and trace the Green Line and the distant mountain beyond; the mountainside bears a vast (and controversial) painted Turkish flag. Explanations of various buildings and neighbourhoods are written in English, French and German.

Pancyprian Gymnasium Museums FREE MUSEUMS
(Map p128; www.pancypriangymnasium.ac.cy; Agiou Ioannou & Thiseos; ⊙9am-3.30pm Mon, Tue, Thu, Fri, 9am-5pm Wed, 9am-1pm Sat) Dating back to 1812, and the oldest school still operating in Cyprus, there are several museums here spread throughout a fascinating 12-room space. Highlights include an extensive natural-history collection, an exhibit of gothic sculptures and an art gallery with works by local painters, including former professors and students. Lawrence Durrell, author of *Bitter Lemons,* taught English at the school for several years in the 1950s.

Famagusta Gate HISTORICAL SITE
(Map p128; Caraffa Bastion; ⊙10am-1pm & 5-8pm Mon-Fri) Famagusta, the easternmost gate, is the most photographed and best-preserved

LEFKOSIA (NICOSIA)

PREPARING A NEW SQUARE

A massive reconstruction project has been obstructing much of Lefkosia's **Plateia Eleftherias** (Map p128). The architect is Zaha Hadid, one of the world's best. Renowned for her socially aware projects, Hadid's impressive CV includes the Strasbourg tram station, a housing project for IBA-Block 2 in Berlin, and the Mind Zone in London's Millennium Dome. Together with her Cypriot associate, Christos Passos, Hadid plans to construct a green belt along the moat that currently surrounds the Venetian walls, turning the area within into Lefkosia's central park, encircled by a palm-tree-lined pedestrian walkway. There will be a (concrete) square in the midst of the green belt, where pedestrians can stroll and congregate, giving the area a new town centre. Hadid calls the design an 'urban intervention'.

There has been some controversy – and what's a grand architectural work without controversy? – with local opponents complaining of too little public consultation on the project, concerns about the impact a large concrete structure will have on the ancient walls, and the reduction of access to the Old City. Work started in 2008, and the estimated completion time is late 2013.

of the three original gates that led into the Old City of Lefkosia. Following more than a century of neglect, the whole structure was renovated in 1981 and now serves as a concert venue and cultural centre used for regular local-themed exhibitions. The gate's impressive wooden door and sloping facade open out onto a tunnel that leads through the rampart wall. Beyond the tunnel to the right is a small open-air arena, where concerts are held during the summer months. The surrounding area has some popular restaurants and bars.

Liberty Monument   MONUMENT
(Map p128) Near the mosque on the Podocataro Bastion is this thought-provoking monument. It represents the Greek Cypriots' liberation from the British colonial powers, with the figures of 14 EOKA fighters being released from prison in 1959, alongside peasants and priests, representing the various strata of Greek Cypriot society. Presiding over it is the Statue of Liberty. The monument, erected in 1973, does not include any figures of Turkish Cypriots, reflecting the divisions between the two communities.

FREE **State Gallery of Cypriot Contemporary Art**   MUSEUM
(Map p128; cnr Stasinou & Kritis; ⊙10am-4.45pm Mon-Fri, 10am-12.45pm Sat) This superb museum seems to be omitted from the standard tourist trail, which is a shame, as it comprises a vast collection of quality Cypriot art, ranging from the mid-19th century to the late 1900s, and including

some fine sculptures. Housed in a historic colonial-style building, the galleries cover three well-laid-out floors. Highlights include a post-Impressionist painting of peasant life by famous Cypriot artist Adamantios Diamantis (1900–1994), who was heavily influenced by Cubism and Byzantine art.

Pafos Gate   HISTORICAL SITE
(Map p128) This westernmost gate, known by the Venetians as Porta San Domenico, is one of the three traditional entrances to Old Lefkosia. It has been the site of a kind of flag stand-off since 1963, with the flags of the Republic of Cyprus, Northern Cyprus, Greece and Turkey fluttering defiantly at each other. The gate served as an arsenal warehouse for the Ottomans and as a police headquarters for the British. The Pafos Gate, left firmly open, guards a narrow pedestrian passage

ⓘ DRESS CODE FOR VISITING MOSQUES

If you are planning to visit a mosque or monastery anywhere on the island, be aware that modest dress is obligatory. Neither men nor women should wear shorts or short-sleeved shirts and women, in particular, should cover up as much as possible. The good news is that, increasingly, mosques and monasteries are supplying expansive capes, or similar, for visitors to borrow free of charge – a veritable godsend if it's a hot sightseeing day.

under the wall. The adjoining breach in the wall, which allows traffic into the Old City, is a much later addition.

Holy Cross Catholic Church CHURCH

(Map p128) Across the road, east of the Pafos Gate on Pafou, this church is in the uncomfortable position of backing onto the Turkish sector while resting within the UN buffer zone. Despite this, the church still functions as a place of worship on the proviso that the back door leading onto the Turkish-controlled sector remains firmly closed. Mass times are posted inside the front-door vestibule.

Roccas (Kaytazağa) Bastion HISTORICAL SITE

(Map p128) The Roccas Bastion was unique throughout Cyprus as being, before 2003, the only place where Greek and Turkish Cypriots could face each other at close quarters. Now it's hardly an attraction, since it's so easy to actually cross over to the opposite side. It is interesting, however, as a reminder of the around 30-year lack of contact between the two communities.

It is situated about 200m south of the Ledra Palace Hotel crossing and is easily identifiable by the no-parking signs along the bastion walls. The UN buffer zone separating the two sides by a normally comfortable margin virtually disappears here for a stretch of about 200m, while the border of Turkish-controlled Northern Cyprus ends at the very edge of this bastion.

The Turkish-held side of the Roccas Bastion is accessible from North Nicosia.

Faneromeni Church CHURCH

(Map p128; Plateia Faneromenis) The centre of the city before Plateia Eleftherias took over in 1974, Plateia Faneromenis is a quiet square, so silent that birdsong can be heard only metres away from the bustle of Ledra St. In the centre is the impressive Faneromeni Church, built in 1872 on the site of an ancient Orthodox nunnery. It is the largest church within the city walls and is a mixture of neoclassical, Byzantine and Latin styles. The **Marble Mausoleum** on the eastern side of the church was built in memory of four clerics executed by the Ottoman governor in 1821, during the newly declared Greek War of Independence.

Laïki Yitonia NEIGHBOURHOOD

(Map p128) Laïki Yitonia, meaning 'popular neighbourhood', was restored after

CITY WITH A PLAN

In an effort to bring North Cyprus and the Republic closer together, close to 100 Ottoman, Frankish and Byzantine buildings on both sides of the border have been faithfully restored with funding from the UN and EU. Founded in 1979, the **Nicosia Master Plan** covers churches and mosques, *hammams* (Turkish baths) and tombs, mansions and monuments, museums and cultural centres – the aim being to promote understanding of the history shared by the two sides. Just by the Ledra Palace Hotel checkpoint, the **Master Plan Office** (Map p128; www.lefkosia.org.cy; ⊙8am-6pm Mon-Fri, 9am-5pm Sat & Sun) has displays of all the work completed and planned, and can provide information sheets on each project, as well as a free booklet *Walled Nicosia: A Guide to Its Historical and Cultural Sites,* which is well worth picking up.

it served for many years as an area for painted ladies and dodgy merchants. This tiny southern part of the Old City is Lefkosia's only tourist area. This means it's full of bad restaurants with tacky water features, where waiters try to lure you in with cheesy greetings and the food is often overpriced. However, it's still pretty and pleasant enough for a short stroll, although with so many good restaurants and taverns in the city, try to avoid eating in this area.

The Cyprus Tourism Organisation (CTO) has an office here, and you can stock up on most maps and other tourist brochures free of charge.

Omeriye Mosque MOSQUE

(Map p128; cnr Trikoupi & Plateia Tyllirias; ⊙outside prayer times) Originally the Augustinian Church of St Mary, the Omeriye Mosque dates from the 14th century. The church was destroyed by the Ottomans as they entered Lefkosia in 1570. It was subsequently restored as a mosque, based on a belief that this was the spot where the Muslim prophet Omer was buried in the 7th century. The tall minaret can easily be spotted some distance away; the entrance to the mosque is about halfway along Trikoupi. Today the mosque is used primarily as a

LEFKOSIA (NICOSIA)

DON'T MISS

OMERIYE HAMMAM

(☏2275 0550; www.hammambaths.com; Plateia Tyllirias 8; 2hr admission & Turkish bath €20, 20min body scrub €20, massage €40-50; ☺9am-9pm, men only Tue, Thu & Sat, women only Wed, Fri & Sun, couples Mon) Switch off your mobile, put on your shower cap and strip down to your birthday suit for a lovely relaxing Turkish bath at Omeriye Hammam. This tastefully restored building sports a luxurious, stylish design. The domed reception has an enormous chandelier hanging over the circular bar area, while candles, mirrors and a refreshing minty scent accompany the baths themselves. The 16th-century Omeriye Hammam is a safe, popular and relaxing spot, with separate days for men and women, and same-sex masseurs. As you enter, you get a complimentary bottle of water, towels (one large, one small) and a cup of herbal tea to relax with after the bath. Apart from the basic steam bath, you can indulge in a body scrub or have a Chinese or aromatherapy massage. If you don't fancy the bath experience, you can take a tour on a Monday.

place of worship by visiting Muslims from neighbouring Arab countries. Non-Muslims may visit as long as they observe the general etiquette required – dress conservatively, leave shoes at the door and avoid official prayer times.

Makarios Cultural Foundation   MUSEUM
(Map p128; Plateia Archiepiskopou Kyprianou; admission €1.70; ☺9am-4.30pm Mon-Fri, to 1pm Sat) The highlight of the foundation is the magnificent **Byzantine Art Museum**, which has the island's largest collection of icons relating to Cyprus. There are some 220 pieces in the museum, dating from the 5th to the 19th centuries. Among the more interesting are the icons of **Christ & the Virgin Mary** (12th century) from the Church of the Virgin Mary of Arakas at Lagoudera, and the **Resurrection** (13th century) from the Church of St John Lambadistis Monastery at Kalopanayiotis. Not to be missed, however, are the six examples of the magnificent **Kanakaria Mosaics**, which were stolen from the Panagia Kanakaria (Kanakaria Church) in Northern Cyprus after the 1974 Turkish invasion and finally returned in 1991 after a lengthy court battle.

Ethnographic Museum   MUSEUM
(Map p128; Plateia Archiepiskopou Kyprianou; admission €2; ☺9am-5pm Mon-Fri, 10am-1pm Sat) Located close to the Makarios Cultural Foundation, the Ethnographic Museum houses the largest collection of folk art and ethnography on the island. The building dates back to the 15th century, although some later additions have been made. Here you will see exquisite examples of embroidery, lace, costumes, pottery, metalwork, basketry, folk painting, engraved gourds, leatherwork and

woodcarving, the latter including beautiful, intricately carved chests.

National Struggle Museum   MUSEUM
(Map p128; Agiou Ioannou; admission €0.80; ☺8am-2pm Mon-Wed & Fri, 8am-2pm & 3-7pm Thu) This display is really for die-hard history buffs and bloodthirsty children. The National Struggle Museum exhibits documents, photos and other memorabilia from the often bloody 1955–59 National Liberation Struggle against the British. Exhibits include a harrowing copy of the gallows.

Panagia Chrysaliniotissa   CHURCH
(Map p128; Archiepiskopou Filotheou; ☺outside mass times) The church of Panagia Chrysaliniotissa is dedicated to the Virgin Mary and its name means 'Our Lady of the Golden Flax' in Greek. It's considered to be the oldest Byzantine church in Lefkosia and was built in 1450 by Queen Helena Paleologos. It is renowned for its rich collection of old and rare icons.

 AUDIO GUIDES

The Cyprus Tourism Organisation (CTO) has introduced a series of audio guides, which you can download in mp3 or mobile-phone format with a choice of six languages. Sights covered are the Cyprus Museum (Lefkosia); 10 Byzantine churches in the Troödos area; the archaeological site of Kourion (Lemesos); the Archaeological Park (Pafos) and the Tombs of the Kings (Pafos). For more information, check the website: www.visitcyprus.com.

Bayraktar Mosque
MOSQUE

(Map p128) Southwest of Famagusta Gate on the Constanza Bastion, this small mosque marks the spot where the Venetian walls were successfully breached by the Ottomans in 1570. The Ottoman *bayraktar* (standard bearer; after whom the mosque is named in Turkish) was promptly murdered by the defending forces but his body was later recovered and buried here. The mosque has historically been the target of terrorist activity; in the early 1960s, EOKA-inspired attacks damaged the building, as well as the nearby tomb of the standard bearer. After being repaired, the mosque was closed to the general public.

Chrysaliniotissa Crafts Centre
CRAFTS

(Map p128; Dimonaktos 2; ⊙10am-1pm & 3-6pm Mon-Fri, 10am-1pm Sat) This small arts centre is worth dropping into for its display of Cypriot arts and crafts. Eight workshops and a vegetarian restaurant surround a central courtyard in a building designed along the lines of a traditional inn.

Tours

The **Cyprus Tourist Organisation** (CTO; Map p128; ☑2244 4264; Aristokyprou 11; ⊙8.30am-4pm Mon-Fri, to 2pm Sat) runs free guided walks on Monday and Thursday, starting at 10am, from the CTO office in the Old City.

'Chrysaliniotissa & Kaimakli: the Past Restored' is a bus and walking guided tour that runs on Monday; Thursday is a walk through Old Lefkosia. The walks last two hours and 45 minutes, and include a 30-minute half-time break.

Alternatively, pick up a CTO walking-tour brochure or follow our walking tour around the Old City.

Eating

Lefkosia offers three basic locations for eating: the Old City, the New City and the burgeoning suburbs to the west and south. While this guide concentrates mainly on the Old and New Cities, suburbs such as Engomi to the west and Strovolos to the south have their own culinary enclaves, and a drive to either may turn up some surprising finds.

Dining in Lefkosia can be a real treat. Because the city is not a prime tourist target, it is thankfully bereft of low-quality, high-cost tourist traps. There are some excellent, simple local diners serving traditional Cypriot food, such as pulses, seasonal vegetables and stewed meat dishes. The growing internationalism of Cyprus has also equated to a rise in more sophisticated and ethnic cuisine.

Note that many restaurants in Lefkosia close for a couple of weeks in August for the annual holidays.

OLD CITY

Dining in the Old City is centred on two main areas, with a sprinkling of cheap, low-frills restaurants scattered in between. Laïki Yitonia is mainly popular with the lunchtime crowd of day-trippers, while the Famagusta Gate strip has several reliably good bars and restaurants that are frequented mainly at night by locals in the know.

LEFKOSIA (NICOSIA)

CULTURAL CENTRES

Want to wise up on Cyprus' extraordinary history and culture? You're in luck...there are several cultural centres with libraries that offer a wide range of periodicals and books for reference.

British Council (Map p128; ☑2266 5152; www.britishcouncil.org/Cyprus.htm; Leoforos Mouseiou 3)

Makarios Cultural Foundation (Map p128; ☑2243 0008; Plateia Archiepiskopou Kyprianou)

Ahilleios Library (Map p128; ☑2276 3033; Leoforos Konstantinou Paleologou 30)

Nicosia Municipal Arts Centre (Map p128; ☑2243 2577; www.nimac.com.cy; Apostolou Varnava 19)

Ministry of Education Library (Map p128; ☑2230 3180; www.moec.gov.cy (in Greek); Leoforos Konstantinou Paleologou)

START **PLATEIA ELEFTHERIAS**
FINISH **FLATRO (SIBELI) BASTION**
DISTANCE **2KM**
DURATION **TWO HOURS**

Walking Tour
Stepping Back in Time

❯ This tour goes along the Old City's main streets and past many of its museums. Starting from Plateia Eleftherias, follow Ledra St and turn right onto Ippokratous. At No 17 is the ① **Leventis City Museum**, which traces the city's development from prehistoric times to the present.

Continue along Ippokratous (which becomes Aristokyprou), turn left onto Thrakis and take the dog-leg onto Trikoupi. Soon you'll see the ② **Omeriye Mosque** on your right. Make a note to return to the nearby ③ **Omeriye Hammam** for a soothing self-pampering massage. Turn right onto Plateia Tyllirias and shortly after you will reach Patriarchou Grigoriou. About 125m along this street on the right is the ④ **House of Hatzigeorgakis Kornesios**, an 18th-century house that is now a museum.

The next left leads you to Plateia Archiepiskopou Kyprianou, dominated by the ⑤ **Archbishop's Palace**. Here you'll find the ⑥ **Makarios Cultural Foundation**, with its not-to-be-missed Byzantine Art Museum. In the grounds of the Foundation is the ⑦ **Agios Ioannis Church**, which was built in 1662 and has frescos dating from 1736. Next door is the ⑧ **Ethnographic Museum** and also nearby are the ⑨ **National Struggle Museum** and the ⑩ **Nicosia Municipal Arts Centre**.

Continue north before turning right onto Thiseos. A left and then another right leads onto Leoforos N Foka. Turn left and you'll see the imposing ⑪ **Famagusta Gate**, which was once the main entrance to the city and now hosts exhibitions and cultural events. From here it's a 400m walk past Lefkosia's trendy night-time dining area along Leoforos Athinas to where the street abruptly ends at the barbed wire and UN watchtowers of the ⑫ **Flatro (Sibeli) Bastion**. The most direct way back to Laïki Yitonia is to take Leoforos N Foka, following the signposts to the Cyprus Tourism Organisation (CTO). Check out the Venetian walls along the way.

TOP CHOICE Mattheos
CYPRIOT €

(Map p128; Plateia 28 Oktovriou 6; mains from €6; ☺lunch) A simple, atmospheric place next to the Faneromeni Church, with a clutch of outside tables set with colourful chequered tablecloths. Attracting lunching nine-to-fivers, the food is home-style Cypriot, with gutsy *kleftiko* (oven-baked lamb), *stifado* (beef or rabbit stew) and stuffed vegetables on the menu. It's one of the most popular places in town, and an empty seat is as rare as a mediocre meal.

Zanettos Taverna
CYPRIOT €€

(Map p128; Trikoupi 65; mains from €8) This place has a great reputation in the city, as it's allegedly one of the city's oldest traditional taverns, dating back to 1938. Locals flock here in their dozens for the succulent Greek-Cypriot meze, and it's definitely worth joining them – once you find the place, that is. (It's hidden away in the back streets.)

Christakis
CYPRIOT €

(Map p128; Leoforos Kostaki Pantelidi 28; mains €6) Locals rate this rough-and-ready restaurant across from the bus station the best place in town for *souvlaki*. Market-fresh salads, superb vegetable side dishes, traditional bean courses and a jovial family atmosphere complete the picture. Get here early to grab a table; there is only a handful.

Da Paolo
ITALIAN €€

(Map p128; Leoforos Konstantinou Paleologou 52; pizza from €11, pasta from €9) This small Italian restaurant has a terrace setting,

TAKE HEED

Lefkosia is a remarkably safe city to walk around. However, the Old City streets, particularly near the Green Line, can appear dingy and threatening at night, and solo women should avoid them. Crossing into the North is allowed only at official checkpoints; you'd be ill-advised to try to cross at any other place. This illegal move would lead to serious trouble. Also, be sure that you don't inadvertently take any photographs of the Green Line or the so-called no man's zone, as this will surely lead to your camera being confiscated and possibly some tough questioning.

beside the Venetian walls. It has a proper wood-fired pizza oven, traditional strings-of-garlic-style decor and a wide choice of pizza and pasta dishes, as well as some Middle East-inspired favourites, such as mussels in ouzo and garlic (the owner is Lebanese).

Inga's Veggie Heaven
VEGETARIAN €€

(Map p128; Chrysaliniotissa Crafts Centre, Dimonaktos 2; mains €10; ☺lunch; ✷) Inga is a friendly Icelandic chef who prepares several homely vegetarian dishes of the day, such as stuffed peppers or lentil burgers, always served with a salad and homemade bread. The lovingly created cakes are a calorific high point. Afterwards, check out the surrounding arts-and-crafts studios.

LEFKOSIA (NICOSIA)

WALKING THE GREEN LINE

Despite the fact that crossing into North Nicosia is now straightforward, the Green Line and the evocative buffer zone, with its abandoned, crumbling houses, are still fascinating. While there's not a lot to see once you are there (save for some creative graffiti work), its mere presence gives Lefkosia a bizarre edge. You'll see the double minarets of the Selimiye mosque, North Nicosia's most remarkable landmark, with the Turkish and Turkish Cypriot flags that hang between them like washing. The Green Line embodies the eeriness of the capital's and the country's division, especially when coupled with all those harrowing 1974 Cypriot stories.

UN and Greek Cypriot **bunkers** punctuate the line across the city, and you are not allowed to approach them too closely. The CTO-signposted walking tour takes you hard up to the line at the far eastern side of the city, close to the military-controlled **Flatro (Sibeli) Bastion**. Take the last turn left off Leoforos Athinas along Agiou Georgiou and look for the little street on the right named Axiothea. Walk to the end of this street and squeeze through the gap into the next street, following the walking-tour sign. There is an area of particular desolation and destruction towards the end of **Pendadaktylou** where it meets **Ermou**, the street that originally bisected the Old City.

Lefkosia (New City)

LEFKOSIA (NICOSIA)

Leoforos Kallipoleos

Leoforos Salaminos

Leoforos Stasinou

To Cyprus
Hilton (100m)

Strandriou Pindarou

Klimentos

Orfeos

Naxon

Kalavryton

Digeni Akrita

Voulgari

Androkleus

Kypranoros

Annis Komninis

Iras

Afroditis

Bouboulinas

Leoforos Archiepiskopou Makariou III

Leoforos Santaroza

Agapinoros

Zinonos Sozou

Avlonos

Hytron

Armalias

Mnasiadou

Foti Pitta

Mykalis

Leonidou

Theodotou

Theofanous

Themistokli Dervi

Tefkrou

Nikokreontos

Nikis

Sypros Kyprianou

Aiantas

Diagorou

Sofouli

Kosta Pella Ma

Hristodoulou
Sozou

Stasikratous

Leoforos Evagorou

G. Hatzidaki

Kosta
Hatzopoulou

Iasonos

Leoforos Demosthenis Severis

Leoforos Lordou Vyronos

Leoforos Georgiou Griva Digeni

Prodromou

Kitieos

Sosomou

Prodromos

Alkeou

Vyzantiou

Leoforos Lordou Vyronos

Metohiou Hilonos

Pedieos River

To Averof
(750m)

Illoupoleos

Evanthous

Vassilisa
Amalia

Aheon

Navarinou

Vasili Mihailidi

400 m
0.2 miles

Lefkosia (New City)

🔵 Activities, Courses & Tours
1 Eleon Swimming Pool...........................A3

⬛ Eating
2 Akakiko...E2
3 Mediterranean....................................F2
4 Mondo..E2
5 Sawa..F3
6 Syrian Arab Friendship Club A1
Zebra's ....(see 3)

🟢 Drinking
7 Finbarr's...F3
8 Sfinakia..D4

⚙ Entertainment
Sfinakia...(see 8)
9 Zoo..E2

Shiantris CYPRIOT €€

(Map p128; Pericleous 21; mains from €7; ⊘lunch) One of Lefkosia's hidden delights, Shiantris is named after its ebullient owner, who cooks up a fantastic array of seasonal beans with lemon, parsley and olive oil and, for carnivores, some meat dishes such as *afelia* (pork stewed in wine) or baked lamb.

Egeon CYPRIOT €€

(Map p128; Ektoros 40; meze from €17; ⊘dinner) The ever-so-discreet yet very popular Egeon draws a faithful following of mainly local devotees. The food, basically meze, is superb. You dine in the courtyard of an atmospheric old house in the summer and inside the house in winter. Reservations essential.

Pago Pago POLYNESIAN €€

(Map p128; Ouzounian 38; mains from €12) Located within the Castelli Hotel, the Tahitian duck is recommended, as is the skirt-swirling to live Cuban music.

Power House INTERNATIONAL €€

(Map p128; Apostolou Varnava 19; mains from €10; ⊘closed Sun & Mon) Part of the Nicosia Municipal Arts Centre, this sophisticated restaurant is suitably decorated with striking paintings and sculptures.

Habana CUBAN €€

(Map p128; Lykourgou 1; mains from €8; ⊘11am-1am) Cuban-themed with a warm exposed-brick interior and an extensive menu, including *fajitas* and spicy burgers.

NEW CITY

Leoforos Archiepiskopou Makariou III is packed with cafes and bars, while several of the surrounding residential streets are also home to some of the city's better dining spots, including leafy and affluent Klimentos.

TOP
CHOICE **Syrian Arab Friendship Club** MIDDLE EASTERN €€

(SAFC; Map p138; Vassilisa Amalia 17; meze from €15; 🖋) Apart from being one of the best places to eat in Lefkosia, this is the ideal place for vegetarians and families (it has a large garden in which children can play). The meze is vast and varied, with lots of tasty dips like beetroot and aubergine, plus delicious falafel, juicy parsley-and-tomato-laden tabouli, and plenty of meat dishes.

Zebra's INTERNATIONAL €€

(Map p138; Klimentos Towers, Klimentos 43; mains from €10) Run by a South African, Zebra's is famed for its superb steaks and seafood platters. Hearty appetites can go for the King's Platter (eight king prawns, mussels, calamari and fillet fish) or the only marginally more modest Queen's Platter. Mondays are set aside for spare-ribs aficionados, with a gut-busting all-you-can-eat special deal.

Sawa MIDDLE EASTERN €€

(Map p138; ☎2276 6777; www.abbarahbrothers .com; Klimentos 31; meze from €12) Known throughout the town for its superb Syrian dishes and fabulous sultan's-palace-style setting, with an elaborate carved-stone exterior, bubbling fountains and an elegant dining room. The mezes are recommended, ideally accompanied by a bottle of Lebanese Ksara riesling. Reservations essential.

Mediterranean SEAFOOD €€

(Map p138; www.mediterraneancy.com; Klimentos Towers, Klimentos 43; mains from €10) Seafood lovers should head here to enjoy well-priced fish dishes. Opened in 2011, a seafood platter for one costs a reasonable €10; or push the boat out with the lobster spaghetti with a whole lobster for just €18.

Akakiko JAPANESE €€

(Map p138; Leoforos Archiepiskopou Makariou III 9b; mains from €12) Japanese cuisine served in suitably minimalist surroundings with fine views of this bustling shopping street. All the favourites are here, including miso soups, tempuras, stuffed dumplings and sushi.

CHILDREN'S CYPRUS: LEFKOSIA

Unlike the seaside towns and resorts, Lefkosia is not immediately appealing to children, although Lefkosians are child-friendly, as are most Cypriots. There are no professional baby-sitting services in the city, as so many families seem to have their own live-in nannies.

The Cyprus Tourism Organisation (CTO) has a list of child-friendly events taking place throughout the year. If you're lucky your visit may coincide with a traditional Cypriot shadow-puppet theatre show; don't forget to ask at the tourist office.

When it gets too hot to traipse around the streets of Lefkosia, head to Engomi for the large **Eleon swimming pool** (Map p138; ☑2266 7833; www.eleonpark.com; Ploutarhou 3; adult/child €9.50/6; ☺8am-9pm), fringed by olive trees and with an elaborate children's play area.

The **Ostrich Wonderland Theme Park** (☑2299 1008/9; Agios Ioannis Maloundas; admission €1.70; ☺9am-7pm May-Oct, to 5pm Nov-Apr) might tickle your fancy. It's reputedly the biggest ostrich park (and farm) in Europe and is 25 minutes outside Lefkosia. Your kids can learn everything there is to know about the powerful flightless birds and their eggs, and use the park's, admittedly modest, playground. To get here, follow the Troödos highway, take the Palehori exit and follow the signs to Agios Ioannis Maloundas.

One really great place for the kids, where they get to wear uncomfortable shoes and share in Homer Simpson's great passion, is **Kykko Bowling Centre** (☑2235 0085; Archimidous 15-19, Engomi; ☺2pm-1am Mon-Fri, 1pm-1am Sat & Sun), a 16-lane bowling centre sitting right behind the Hilton Park. The cafe, which has snacks and drinks, will allow kids to share in his other passion (the fast food one).

Although the **Cyprus Classic Motorcycle Museum** (Map p128; ☑2268 0222; www.agrino.org/motormuseum; Granikou 44; admission €1.70; ☺9am-1pm & 3.30-7pm Mon-Fri, 9am-1pm Sat) attracts kids of all ages, it's a great stop to make with young ones, obsessed as they probably are with vehicles of all kinds. This is a private museum whose owner is more than happy to chat extensively about his 150-plus bike collection. It may just bring out the parents' inner Hell's Angel (bring a bandanna, just in case).

For a walk and a rest in the Old City on a hot summer's day, make for the **Municipal Gardens** (Map p128; Leoforos Mouseiou), which has a children's playground. For more dedicated big-time playground entertainment, consider heading to the appropriately named **Extreme Park** (☑2242 4681; www.extremepark.com.cy; 149 Strovolos Ave) south-west of the centre. The park has vast indoor/outdoor playgrounds complete with climbing wall, inflatable slides, bungee trampolines, rope obstacle course, minigolf, soccer, bowling, kiddie cinema and three cafeterias for essential downtime.

Mondo CYPRIOT €€

(Map p138; Leoforos Archiepiskopou Makariou III 9a; menu €12; 🛜) A spacious cafe and bar with an upstairs terrace and an inexpensive daily menu. Sweet treats include a delectable hazelnut-and-chocolate muffin.

 Drinking

From the Famagusta Gate area in the Old City to bars along Leoforos Archiepiskopou Makariou III, there are plenty of atmospheric and welcoming night-owl places to enjoy a drink or three.

OLD CITY

You'll find more atmospheric choices within the Old City walls, and a more boho crowd, than in the New City.

TOP CHOICE Oktana BAR

(Map p128; Aristidou 6) Rub shoulders with artists, actors and academics at this soulful place decorated with edgy art deco posters. There's a delightful sunken patio out back, and the rambling interior encompasses a bookshop and various rooms, including a basement space favoured by nargileh smokers. There are regular art exhibitions and poetry readings.

Hammam BAR

(Map p128; Soutsou Pendadaktylou 9) Right behind Omeriye Hammam, this handsome old colonial house, with a grand arched door, ceiling frieze and original tiled floors, is perfect for sipping a long, leisurely cocktail. In short, the music is good, the courtyard leafy and the atmosphere relaxed.

Brew
BAR

(Map p128; Ippokratous 30) Set in an old mansion, Brew is airy and spacious, with good music, painted white-wood furniture, and lots of tea, cocktails and light healthy eats.

Academy 32
BAR

(Map p128; Leoforos Konstantino Paleologou 32; ⊘closed Mon) The owner is a musician and it shows, with the intimate arty vibe, regular exhibitions, live jazz and plenty of romantic corners.

Plato's
BAR

(Map p128; Platonas 8) This Montmartre-style jazz cafe has a delightful outside terrace.

Ithaki
BAR

(Map p128; Leoforos N Foka 33) This popular street bar has occasional live music.

Uqbar
BAR

(Map p128; Aristidou 6) Across from Oktana, this bar has the same owners and a similar atmosphere.

NEW CITY

If you're about to hit the streets of the New City for a night out, be aware that jeans and trainers just won't cut it; Lefkosians like to seriously dress up.

Sfinakia
BAR

(Map p138; cnr Sypros Kyprianou & Themistokli Dervi) This is a buzzing pre-club bar that really packs in a crowd of people-watchers and posers. Part of the Sfinakia club.

Finbarr's
BAR

(Map p138; Leoforos Archiepiskopou Makariou III 52b) Popular with Lefkosians and expats for its Guinness on tap and suitably blarney atmosphere. Happy hour is from 4.30pm to 8pm.

☆ Entertainment

For entertainment listings, particularly classical-music concerts and the theatre, pick up the *Nicosia This Month* and *Diary of Events* pamphlets, available from the CTO.

TOP CHOICE Weaving Mill
CULTURAL CENTRE

(Map p128; ☑2276 2275; www.ifantourgio.org.cy; Lefkonos 69; ☏) Owner Leontios started this nonprofit educational and cultural association as a teaching base for the children of immigrants. These days the Mill

has a multicultural purpose, showing films, staging the occasional concert and providing a large comfortable space for wi-fi use, board games, reading (there is an extensive library) or just socialising. There is a modest bar for light snacks and drinks.

Zoo
NIGHTCLUB

(Map p138; Leoforos Stasinou 15) Zoo is the embodiment of style and sophistication on Lefkosia's club scene, with music that ranges from international to Greek pop.

Sfinakia
NIGHTCLUB

(Map p138; cnr Sypros Kyprianou & Themistokli Dervi) On super-trendy Themistokli Dervi, this place attracts girls in ankle-cracking high heels and boys shimmering with both brilliantine and expectation.

La Casa de Cuba
NIGHTCLUB

(Map p128; www.shakallis.com; Leoforos Athinas 7; admission €12) Latin music, including salsa and tango. The entrance price covers a drink.

K-Cineplex
CINEMA

(www.kcineplex.com; Makedonitissis 8; ⊘5-10.30pm; ⊕) This is the best cinema experience to hit Lefkosia, located 2.5km out of the city in Strovolos. Sporting six screens, K-Cineplex runs all the latest movie releases and offers ample parking, a cafeteria and high-tech sight-and-sound systems.

There are a number of other cinemas scattered around Lefkosia that show varying permutations of the latest films and occasional re-runs of English-language movies.

Theatre & Live Music

There is a thriving local theatre scene. However, plays performed in Lefkosia are almost always in Greek. The best way to get to see and hear some traditional music is to head for any of the restaurants offering live music in Laïki Yitonia. Otherwise keep your eyes peeled for posters over the summer advertising visiting musicians from Greece.

Lefkosia Municipal Theatre
THEATRE

(Map p128; ☑2246 3028; Leoforos Mouseiou 4) Opposite the Cyprus Museum, the theatre was recently aesthetically renovated, only to have the roof fall in after completion (fortunately no production was being staged at the time). At the time of writing, the replacement was underway – along with the legal suits. When it re-opens, the theatre will once again stage both musical (including classical) and theatrical events.

LEFKOSIA (NICOSIA)

Concerts are also held at the **Skali Aglantzias** (www.aglantzia.org.cy; Agiou Georgiou 15) outdoor venue in Aglantzia and the Scholi Tyflon (School for the Blind) outdoor theatre near the southern suburb of Dasoupolis.

Sport

Football (soccer) is the main spectator sport in Lefkosia. The football season is from September to May. Check out **Takis-on-Line** (http://takisonline.com) for the low-down on the nation's teams. The 16-times champion, APOEL Nicosia, held the top spot for many years. The city is also home to clubs Omonia and Olympiakos.

 Shopping

With its army of designer babes, it's no wonder that Lefkosia rules when it comes to clothes shopping. The so-called 'discount stores' offer clothes and shoes at 30% to 80% off their original price, and many Lefkosians can be found elbowing their way to the best bargain.

There are two main shopping areas. Ledra St in the Old City has lots of old-style, as well as high-fashion, boutiques and shops, and is home to Debenhams department store. Leoforos Archiepiskopou Makariou III in the New City is a mecca for well-known international chain stores, like Mango and Zara. Head for Arnaldas if you are a Gucci guy (or gal); there's a smattering of designer stores along this street. Tourist shops are centred on Laïki Yitonia in the Old City and sell items like backgammon boards and lacework; don't forget to barter.

Cyprus Handicrafts Centre   CRAFTS
(Map p128; Leoforos Athalassis 186; ☉7.30am-2.30pm Mon-Wed & Fri, 7.30am-2.30pm & 3-6pm Thu) Get your Cypriot lace and embroidery here at decent prices, as well as leatherwear, mosaics, ceramics and pottery. Even better, watch these products being made in various workshops at this government-sponsored foundation committed to preserving Cypriot handicrafts.

Antiques   ANTIQUES
(Map p128; ☑9966 4722; Vasiliou Voulgaroktonou 5 & 6) These two very dusty and intriguing antique shops are located on opposite sides of the street. You may have to ring the owner to come down for you to browse, but you'll find lots of great stuff, from retro bits and

pieces to attractive ceramics, paintings, ornaments and so on.

✐Utopia   FOOD & DRINK
(Map p128; www.utopia-cyp.com; Areos 48) The owner is an organic farmer, so this is the place to come for the ecological self-caterer. It also serves lunches on Fridays, as well as teas and drinks the rest of the week.

Andreas Papaeracleous Photostore   PHOTOGRAPHY
(Map p128; ☑2266 6101; Rigenis 48) In the Old City; this is a well-stocked shop catering to all your photography needs.

Messa   BAKLAVA
(Map p128; Aischylou 73) Sticky and delicious Syrian baklava exquisitely boxed-up for gifts or serious self-indulgence.

Moufflon   BOOKS
(Map p128; Sofouli 1) English-language books.

ⓘ Information

Emergency

The general emergency numbers for police and ambulance are ☑199 or ☑112.

Police station (☑2247 7434) Located in the Old City, at the northern end of Ledra St, by the barrier.

Internet Access

Most midrange and top-end hotels provide wi-fi access, as do many cafes if you purchase a drink. There are a few internet cafes in town. The tourist office can provide you with a list.

Medical Services

If you need a private doctor or pharmacy, ring ☑9090 1432. Visiting hours for doctors are normally from 9am to 1pm and 4pm to 7pm. Local newspapers list pharmacies that are open during the night, and on weekends and holidays, as well as the names of doctors who are on call out of normal hours. You can also check www.cytayellowpages.com.cy for details of doctors and dentists.

Lefkosia General Hospital (☑2280 1400; Leoforos Nechrou) West of the Old City.

Tourist Information

Cyprus Tourism Organisation (CTO; www.visitcyprus.org.cy; ☉8.30am-4pm Mon-Fri, to 2pm Sat) New City (☑2233 7715; Leoforos Lemesou 19); Old City (Map p128; ☑2244 4264; Aristokyprou 11) The CTO's head office is in the New City, although it's not really

NEW BUS SYSTEM

In mid-2010 there was a major shake-up of the former, reputedly unreliable, bus system in the Republic of Cyprus. Simply put, each of the five districts now operates its own bus company. Fares are government subsidised and have been pegged at €1 per ride, €2 per day, €10 per week and €30 for a month of unlimited journeys within the respective districts, which includes rural villages. All five companies have comprehensive websites: Lefkosia district, **Osel Buses** (www.osel.com.cy); Lemesos district, **Emel** (www.limassol buses.com); Pafos district, **Pafos Buses** (www.pafosbuses.com); Famagusta district, **Zinonas Buses** (www.zinonasbuses.com); and Larnaca district, **Osea Buses** (www .oseabuses.com). In addition, buses that connect the cities are run by the appropriately named **InterCity Bus Company** (www.intercity-buses.com), which is also government subsidised and, therefore, very reasonable, given the distances involved. Each route also offers discounted fares on multiple journeys over a day/week/month or year. You can buy your tickets on the bus.

geared to handling over-the-counter queries from the public.

Municipal Tourist Office (Map p128; Ledra St; ☺7.30am-2.30pm daily & 3-6pm Wed) At the Ledra St crossing, this new municipal office has multilingual leaflets about the city. Look for the large Peace sign on your left just before the border. There are also regular photographic exhibitions and similar, generally with an evocative, thought-provoking theme.

Getting There & Away

Air

Lefkosia's international airport is in the UN buffer zone and is no longer a functioning airport. All air passengers for Lefkosia arrive at the smart new Larnaka airport in the South.

Most airlines that serve the Republic of Cyprus have offices or representatives in Lefkosia:

Alitalia (☑2267 4500; www.alitalia.com; Leoforos Evagorou I 54-8)

British Airways (☑2276 1166; www.british airways.com; Leoforos Archiepiskopou Makariou III 52a)

Cyprus Airways (☑2275 1996; www.cyprus airways.com; Leoforos Archiepiskopou Makariou III 50)

KLM (☑2267 1616; www.klm.com; Zings Anther 12)

Lufthansa (☑2287 3330; www.lufthansa.com; cnr Leoforos Archiepiskopou Makariou III & Leoforos Evagorou I)

Olympic Air (☑2267 2101; www.olympic.com; Leoforos Omirou 17)

Bus

Local buses primarily leave from the Urban Bus Station on Plateia Solomou, abutting the Tripoli Bastion.

InterCity Buses Co (www.intercity-buses.com; Plateia Solomou) runs regular buses to the main cities and resorts, including the following:

TO AGIA NAPA & PARALIMNI Six buses run daily Monday to Friday and three on Saturday (€4, one hour).

TO LARNAKA Twelve buses run daily Monday to Friday and six on Saturday (€3, 45 minutes).

TO LEMESOS Four buses run daily Monday to Friday and two on Saturday (€5, one hour).

TO PAFOS Four buses run daily Monday to Friday and two on Saturday (€5, 1¾ hours).

Car & Motorcycle

Traffic approaching Lefkosia tends to come from either the Troödos Massif to the west, or Larnaka and Lemesos in the South. The Larnaka–Lemesos motorway ends fairly abruptly on the outskirts of Lefkosia, about 6km south of the Old City. By following the extension of the motorway into the city centre, you will eventually reach Leoforos Archiepiskopou Makariou III, the main thoroughfare in the New City. Traffic from Troödos will enter the city along Leoforos Georgiou Griva Digeni.

Parking is most easily found at the large car parks abutting the city bastions, to the right of Leoforos Archiepiskopou Makariou III, or to your left if you approach from Troödos. The most convenient one for new arrivals is the large lot between the D'Avila and Constanza Bastions on Leoforos Stasinou. Parking for a day should cost no more than €10.

Getting out of Lefkosia is made easy by the prominent signs all along Leoforos Stasinou. Be wary, however, of the many one-way streets and the numerous on-street parking restrictions. Avoid the peak period of 11am to 1pm on weekdays when traffic can be very slow.

LEFKOSIA (NICOSIA)

Service Taxi

Travel & Express (Map p128; ☎7777 7474; www.travelexpress.com.cy; Municipal Parking Place, Leoforos Salaminos) has several popular routes, including Lemesos (€11, 1½ hours), Pafos (change at Lemesos, €22, 1½ hours), Larnaka (€9, one hour) and Agia Napa (€18, one hour).

Although Travel & Express will pick you up at an appointed time from anywhere in urban Lefkosia, delays of up to 30 minutes are the norm; similarly, passengers boarding at the Podocataro Bastion will usually spend up to 30 minutes picking up other passengers before actually departing Lefkosia. Be prepared and allow for at least an extra hour.

Taxi to Northern Cyprus

Things have changed significantly when it comes to crossing into the North, though you're not advised to take a rented car into the North – see the box, p260. The easiest thing to do if you have luggage and don't want to walk is to get a taxi to take you anywhere in the North. Most drivers should be happy to do this, but if one refuses, try another. Most taxi drivers who go to the North will generally have the visa leaflet you'll need to fill out. A journey from Lefkosia to Northern Cyprus should cost anywhere between €25 and €40, though you'd be best advised to cross to North Nicosia on foot and rent a car there – it'll be cheaper and more flexible.

For more info on crossing the Green Line, see the boxed text, p257.

⊙ Getting Around

To/From the Airport

There is no public or airline transport between Lefkosia and Larnaka or Pafos airports. You can, however, take a service taxi to either airport, but make sure you leave at least an extra hour for your journey, as picking up and dropping off other passengers can take a long time. This particularly applies to those flying from Pafos airport, because passengers travelling from Lefkosia to Pafos with a service taxi have to change in Lemesos, which can sometimes include a wait of around 30 minutes.

A service taxi to Larnaka airport will cost around €12, and it's around €25 to Pafos airport. Service taxis will drop you off at the airports, but won't pick you up. The only way to get into Lefkosia from either of these airports is by renting a car or hiring a taxi (which may turn out to be quite expensive). Check whether your hotel organises airport pick-ups.

Bus

Osel Buses (www.osel.com.cy) Lefkosia's urban bus company has a network of routes covering the city and suburbs. Check the website for more information.

Car & Motorcycle

The car-rental agency **A Petsas & Sons** (☎2246 2650; www.petsas.com.cy) is located at Plateia Solomou. You can also opt for **Hertz** (☎2220 8888; www.hertz.com.cy; 16 Aikaterinis Kornaro, off Leoforos Athalassis) in Strovolos; it has some good online rates. Beware that the drop-off charge is €35 if you rent a car in Lefkosia and leave it in another city.

There are no motorbikes for rent in or around the Old City.

At the base of the walls there are car parks.

Taxi

There is a large taxi stand on Plateia Eleftherias. Some local taxi companies:

Apostrati (☎2266 3358; Plateia Eleftherias)

Elpis (☎2276 4966; Leoforos Archiepiskopou Makariou III 63c)

Ethniko (☎2266 0880; Plateia Solomou)

AROUND LEFKOSIA

The plain of the Mesaoria (which means 'between two mountains') is a sprawling, parched landscape during the summer months, when the land is totally exposed to the relentless sun. But come spring and winter, the Mesaoria, like most of Cyprus, transforms into a green, fertile plain. The two mountain ranges bordering the plain are the Kyrenia (Girne) Range to the north and the Troödos Massif to the west and southwest. For the visitor wanting to explore the Mesaoria, there are a couple of ancient archaeological sites and a sprinkling of churches and monasteries. Note that for some of the churches and monasteries, you need to be in a group to any of interest to those with the keys to unlock the buildings.

⊙ Getting There & Around

A car will be necessary to see some of the sites listed in this section. While public buses (often colourful and old-fashioned) connect most of the Mesaoria villages with Lefkosia, they're basically scheduled to service workers and schoolchildren, not curious travellers, and so will be of limited use.

Cycling in the area is easy because of the mostly gentle gradients, but bear in mind that the weather gets very hot in summer and the traffic on the main highways can be heavy and dangerous.

Ancient Tamassos

Homer apparently mentioned **Ancient Tamassos** (admission €1.70; ⊙9am-3pm Tue-Fri, 10am-3pm Sat & Sun) in *The Odyssey,*

where it is referred to as Temese. The goddess Athena says to Odysseus' son, Telemachus: 'We are bound for the foreign port of Temese with a cargo of gleaming iron, which we intend to trade for copper.' The site of this otherwise obscure and little-known city kingdom is on a small hillside about 17km southwest of Lefkosia next to the village of Politiko.

Tamassos' main claim to fame was its seemingly endless supply of copper – the mineral from which the name of Cyprus (Kypros in Greek; Kıbrıs in Turkish) is derived. A copper-producing settlement here dates from at least the 7th century BC, and production of copper ran well into the Hellenistic period. Excavations of the remains of the citadel began in 1889 and, around this time, two tombs dating back to the 6th century BC were discovered. Today these two tombs constitute the site's major attraction, as the citadel itself is

little more than a scattering of nondescript foundations.

It is thought that the tombs probably contained the remains of the citadel's kings. Looters have long since spirited away the rich burial treasures that may once have been buried here. You can even see a hole in the roof of the larger tomb showing where grave robbers broke in. The walls are unusually carved in such a way as to imitate wood – a feature that some archaeologists have linked to a possible Anatolian influence at the time of the citadel's zenith. Some theorists suggest that Tamassos was even part of the Hittite Empire.

Monastery of Agios Irakleidios

Easily combined with an excursion to Tamassos is a visit to this nearby **monastery** (⊘groups 9am-noon Mon, Tue & Thu). St

AUTHENTIC CYPRIOT CUISINE

If you want to dine on authentic Cypriot cuisine, seek a *taverna* that displays a Vakhis sign (although, at the time of writing, there are only around 10 in the whole Republic). The Vakhis scheme was established by the Cyprus Tourism Organisation in association with the Eurotoques International, a European chefs' association, among others, as part of an EU-funded island-wide drive to promote rural tourism. Vakhis is named after Cyprus' original Jamie Oliver–style celebrity chef, who lived and, more famously, cooked in the ancient city of Kition around 300 AD.

Typical dishes you can expect today include ingredients like wild asparagus, artichokes, various leafy greens, extra-virgin olive oil and fresh herbs. At **Kiniras Garden** restaurant (p88), part of the Vakhis scheme, owner Georgios uses at least 10 different herbs in the marinade for his slow-cooked lamb.

Aside from Kiniras, several other member restaurants of the Vakhis scheme are clustered together in the picturesque villages of the wine-growing area in the Troödos foothills southwest of Lefkosia, including **Loufou-Agrovino** (☏2547 0202; www.lofou -agrovino.com), **Kamares** (☏2547 0719) and **Kazani** (☏2547 0243), all located in the pretty village of Lofou, and **Takis** (☏2594 3631) in nearby Vouni. In general, Vakhis restaurants sport pretty traditional décor, with chequered tablecloths, wooden tables, wicker chairs and similar.

Irakleidios was born in Tamassos and guided St Paul and St Barnabas around Cyprus. He was later made one of the first bishops in Cyprus by Barnabas. The bishop has been subsequently credited with the performance of a number of miracles, including exorcisms.

The original church was built in the 5th century AD, but the current monastic buildings date from the late 18th century. The church today boasts the usual panoply of frescos and icons. On a table to the eastern side of the church you can spot a reliquary containing one of the bones and the skull of St Irakleidios.

Agios Mamas Church at Agios Sozomenos

This is the somewhat forgotten site of the 16th-century Gothic church of Agios Mamas, whose arches were never finished in the first place; it's like an exercise in non-starters. Perhaps that's why the beautiful arches have a sense of nostalgia about them. The church was built in retrograde Lusignan style, and although the site is locked and cannot be entered, the arches, the nave and two aisles can be easily seen and admired. The isolated ruins are in the deserted mud village of Agios Sozomenos, an area that has been abandoned since some intercommunal incidents in 1964.

The church and village can be reached from Lefkosia on the A1, taking exit 6 (for Potamia) and going on to a minor, paved road about 2km before Potamia, following a sign for Agios Sozomenos.

Maheras Monastery

It's a fair hike out to this sprawling **monastery** (⊙9am-noon Mon, Tue & Thu) perched in the foothills of the eastern spur of the Troödos Massif and under the all-seeing radar installation on Mt Kionia (1423m) to the south. The Maheras Monastery was founded in a similar way to the Kykkos Monastery. In 1148 a hermit named Neophytos found an icon guarded by a sword (*maheras* means knife or sword in Greek) in a cave near the site of the present monastery. The monastery developed around the icon and flourished over time. Nothing remains of the original structures; the current building dates from around 1900.

The monastery has become a popular outing for Cypriots, who possibly come as much for the cooler climate as for spiritual enlightenment. There is a small cafeteria in the grounds and pilgrims may stay overnight. One less spiritually inspired visitor was Grigoris Afxentios during the EOKA uprising of 1955–59. The fearsome EOKA leader hid out in a cave just below the monastery but was eventually tracked down and killed by British soldiers in 1957. A huge black statue of the hero now looms over a commemorative shrine.

The monastery is open for visits by groups of parishioners only at certain times. Ask locally or perhaps at the CTO in Lefkosia about how you might join one of these groups, which will mostly consist of Cypriot pilgrims. Visits should be conducted with reverence and solemnity. Maheras Monastery is best approached via Klirou and Fikardou, since the alternate route via Pera and the E902, while very pretty, is winding and very slow.

Mesaoria Villages

Renting a car and driving around the Mesaoria is a good way to see the area's villages, but keep in mind that roads tend to fan out haphazardly along roughly defined valleys and ravines, and cross from one valley to another. The journey can therefore be slow as the roads are narrow and winding. Jeep tours often take travellers to see some of the villages of the Mesaoria as part of a wider tour around Cyprus.

One of the more popular villages in the area is **Pera** (population 1020), situated a couple of kilometres from Tamassos. While there are no specific sights here, Pera is nonetheless pretty. Head for the signposted Arghaggelou Michail church, where you can park and wander around the surrounding cobbled backstreets. Photographers will find some particularly evocative scenes: old houses covered in bougainvillea, ancient stone jars, pretty doors and cats on walls. Visitors stop for refreshments at the *kafeneio* (coffee shop), where the locals, and often the village priest, enjoy coffee and gossip in a world where time means little.

The villages of **Orounda** (population 660) and **Peristerona** (population 2100), west of Lefkosia, have interesting and photogenic churches. The village of **Lythrodontas** (population 2620), 25km south of Lefkosia, has a lovely large central square with a couple of atmospheric traditional cafes.

The postcard-pretty village of **Fikardou** (population 16) is close to the Maheras Monastery; visits to both are easily combined. Fikardou is the 'official' village in a clutch of well-preserved villages in the eastern Troödos Massif. Its Ottoman-period houses with wooden balconies are gradually being restored and are a visual relief after the cement structures of many modern Troödos mountain villages. That said, there's not a lot to Fikardou, and only a handful of people live here permanently.

The main street is no more than a few hundred metres long, dominated by the Church of Apostles St Peter & Paul. Opposite, there are some harrowing photos of four young local soldiers (aged 22 to 24 years) who were killed during the Turkish invasion in 1974. With little else to do, most visitors content themselves with a visit to the village's cafe-cum-restaurant before moving on. Still, if you are in the region, a visit is recommended since there are few places left in Cyprus that are as representative of the culture and archaeology of the recent past.

Just to the south, in pretty **Lazanias**, stop in at the **Magic Lazania** (☎9653 0129) with its terrace overlooking the mountains and monastery. Owner Luis is a trained chef, and it shows in the excellently prepared local dishes, such as *kleftiko*, courgettes with eggs, and juicy chicken kebabs. Call ahead if you are a large group.

From these villages, roads lead by various routes to the higher reaches of the Troödos, via the Pitsylia region, offering a slow but scenic journey into the mountains. This option is particularly useful on weekends when Lefkosians in their hundreds storm the Troödos via the main B9 road (through Astromeritis and Kakopetria) for picnics and a day out in order to escape the city heat.

You will find a tavern or restaurant in most villages and even in out-of-the-way places along the road. Many Lefkosians come to the country to eat on weekends and usually have their favourite haunts.

Advertised widely around **Agia Marina** (population 630) is **Katoï** (☎2285 2576; Agia Marina Xyliatou; mains from €8), overlooking the village itself. Its lights are visible from some distance away at night, and it commands a great view over the Troödos foothills and the Mesaoria. The restaurant serves solid Cypriot staples and an imaginative selection of mezes.

There are, in the area, a number of pleasant picnic grounds, usually situated in cool and leafy spots. Try the **Xyliatos Dam** near the village of the same name, or **Kapoura**, on a picturesque back road (F929) linking Vyzakia with the B9; or, alternatively, higher up in the Maheras Forest south of Pera at **Skordokefalos**, along the E902 leading to the Maheras Monastery. All picnic grounds in this region have barbecue areas, tables, chairs and, most importantly, shade.

North Nicosia (Lefkoşa)

POP 39,000

Includes »

Sights & Activities 149

Walking Tour 154

Eating 155

Drinking &
Entertainment 156

Shopping.........................157

Information....................157

Getting There &
Away.............................. 158

Getting Around 158

Best Places to Eat

» Bay Kahkaha (p155)

» Boghjalian (p155)

» Passport Cadde (p156)

» Califorian Gold (p156)

Best Places to Stay

» City Royal (p209)

» Golden Tulip (p209)

» Saray (p210)

Why Go?

Home to roughly a third of the population of North Cyprus, the northern half of Lefkosia is another world. Approached from the smart boutiques in Ledra St, North Nicosia sees the avenue fracture into a medina-style market of stalls and kebab houses. Thanks to the Nicosia Master Plan, many of the historic buildings are being restored and the area around the Selimiye Mosque has a real sense of heritage. Overall, though, life moves slowly and the dusty streets are lined with ancient mosques and Frankish ruins.

This is essentially a daytime city where the appeal lies in observing daily life and exploring the historic centre's streets. Now, with the relaxing of border restrictions, many people take a day trip from the Republic (and vice versa) via the Ledra Palace or Ledra St checkpoints. Make sure you stay until dusk, when the minarets light up and release their evening call to prayer and the air is scented with smoke from the kebab houses' grills.

When to Go

North Nicosia can be an uncomfortably hot and dusty city in July and August, which is also when many inhabitants leave for cooler coastal climes. Take note of when Ramadan falls, as well, although it's not as strictly observed here as on the Turkish mainland. In September the temperature cools but the action heats up, with the town taking centre stage for the International Cyprus Theatre Festival. The spring and autumn months are pleasantly warm, while December and January see the most rainfall and the temperature at its coolest, hovering around the 15°C mark.

History

Up until 1963, North Nicosia, not surprisingly, shared much of the same history as its dismembered southern sector. For details of this period, see p126.

The capital was effectively divided into Greek and Turkish sectors in 1963, when violence against Turkish Cypriots by insurgents from the Ethniki Organosi tou Kypriakou Agona (EOKA; National Organisation for the Cypriot Struggle) forced them to retreat into safe enclaves or ghettos. The Green Line, as it has become known, was established when a British military commander divided up the city on a map with a green pen. The name has remained ever since.

The Turkish military invasion of 1974, which most Turkish Cypriots saw as a rescue operation, formalised the division between the two halves of the city. A wary truce was brokered by the blue-bereted members of the UN peacekeeping forces, who had been guarding the Green Line since sectarian troubles broke out in 1963. It is now easy for visitors (and Cypriots) to cross over the border but, despite this, the city is still divided and its reunification looks far off.

◎ Sights & Activities

To visit and appreciate the historic renovation that is taking place here, pick up a copy of the *Nicosia Trail* brochure from the tourist office or visit the Nicosia Master Plan headquarters at the Ledra Palace Hotel. The main sights are marked on the North Nicosia map. If you get lost, head for the Venetian walls, which you can easily follow in order to reach a main point of reference. Running south from the Kyrenia Gate is Girne Caddesi, which leads onto Atatürk Meydanı, the main square, surrounded by banks and shops.

FREE **Büyük Han**
& Kumarcılar Han   HISTORICAL BUILDINGS
(Great Inn; Araşta Sokak) The **Büyük Han** is both a wonderful example of Ottoman architecture and a rare surviving example of a medieval caravanserai. During the medieval Ottoman period, travellers and traders could find accommodation at these *hans* (inns), as well as a place to stable their horses, trade their goods and socialise with fellow travellers.

The Büyük Han was built in 1572 by the first Ottoman governor of Cyprus, Musafer Pasha. Renovated in the early '90s, it has once again become the centre of the Old City's bustle, with cafes, shops and traditional craft workshops housed in the small cells that originally served as the inn's sleeping areas. The central courtyard has a *mescit* (Islamic 'chapel') in the centre, which is balanced on six pillars over a *şadrvan* (ablutions fountain). This design is found only in this inn and two others in Turkey.

To the north, on Agah Efendi Sokak, is the **Kumarcılar Han** (Gambler's Inn), a late-17th-century caravanserai, which worked in a similar way to the Büyük Han. It was closed for reconstruction at the time of research, and looks like it might remain closed for some time yet. Rumour has it that once it's been renovated, the building might once again become a place for gamblers. This would be no surprise considering the passion for gambling that grips the North.

FREE **Selimiye Mosque**   MOSQUE
(Selimiye Camii; Selimiye Meydanı) North Nicosia's most prominent landmark, which is also clearly visible from the southern half of the city, is the Selimiye Mosque. This strange-looking building, a cross between a French Gothic church and a mosque, has an interesting history. Work started on the church in 1209 and progressed slowly. Louis IX of France, on his way to the Crusades, stopped by in 1248 and gave the building process a much-needed shot in the arm by offering the services of his retinue of

CROSSING THE LINE

Border restrictions in Cyprus were relaxed in December 2003, allowing overnight trips across the Green Line. Pedestrian crossings are at Ledra St and Ledra Palace Hotel in Lefkosia; from the latter it's a 10-minute walk to the Kyrenia Gate. There are seven access points linking the Greek Cypriot and Turkish Cypriot sides of Cyprus; the latest is the Limnitis-Yeşilirmak crossing in the northwest of the island, which opened in October 2010. See p2 for more information on crossing the border.

Hire cars can only be taken from South to North, not the other way. See p260, for car-insurance options and advice.

North Nicosia (Lefkoşa) Highlights

❶ Visiting **Büyük Han** (Great Inn; p149), a grand Ottoman structure full of intriguing craft shops

❷ Strolling through the streets of the **Old City** (p154), an ancient and colourful maze

❸ Tasting a fantastic kebab, *pide* or *lahmacun* (Turkish pizza) at one of the traditional restaurants or kiosks (p155)

❹ Entering the sparseness and silence of the magnificent **Selimiye Mosque** (p149)

❺ Walking between watermelon mountains at the **Belediye Pazarı** (Municipal Market; p155)

❻ Picking up the **Nicosia Trail** brochure and seeing first-hand the renovations of historical buildings taking place throughout the Old City (p149)

❼ Taking a twirl at the **Mevlevi Shrine Museum** (p153), a former shrine of the fascinating and mystic whirling dervishes artisans and builders. However, the church took another 78 years to complete and was finally consecrated in 1326 as the **Church of Agia Sofia**.

Up until 1570, the church suffered depredation at the hands of the Genoese and the Mamelukes, and severe shakings from two earthquakes in 1491 and 1547. When the Ottomans arrived in 1571, they stripped the building of its Christian contents and added two minarets, between which the Turkish Cypriot and Turkish flags now flutter.

The Gothic structure of the interior is still apparent despite Islamic overlays, such as the whitewashed walls and columns, and the reorientation of the layout to align it with Mecca. Note the ornate west front with the three decorated doorways, each in a different style. Also look out for four **marble columns** relocated from Ancient Salamis and now placed in the apse off the main aisles.

Today the Selimiye Mosque is a working place of worship and you are able to go inside. Try to time your visit either just before or just after one of the five Muslim prayer sessions.

FREE **Bedesten**   CHURCH

(Arasta Sk; www.undp-pff.org; ⊘10am-1pm daily, 2-5pm Wed) Recently renovated as part of the Nicosia Master Plan (see p133), the imposing Bedesten (St Nicholas of the English) dates from the 6th century, when it was built as a small Byzantine church. It was grandly embellished in the 14th century and reborn as a Catholic church. After the Ottomans' arrival in 1571, the church was used as a grain store and general market but was basically left to disintegrate.

More recently, at a cost of some two million EU-funded euros, this magnificent building has been restored to its former glory and was recognised, in 2009, with the prestigious Europa Nostra Award for cultural heritage.

The north doorway has some splendid-looking **coats of arms** originally belonging to noble Venetian families. These families may have been supporters of the Orthodox Church, which was nonetheless allowed to continue with its business, despite the Catholic dominance of religious life in Cyprus.

Explanatory panels outline the restoration works and the history of the building. Currently, the Bedesten is used primarily as a cultural centre.

NORTH NICOSIA (LEFKOŞA) SIGHTS & ACTIVITIES

THE WHIRLING DERVISHES OF THE MEVLEVI ORDER

The founder of the Mevlevi Order was the poet Jelaluddin Mevlana, known in the West as Rumi, who was born in the 13th century. His most famous work is *Mathnawi,* a long poem that details Mevlana's teachings and understanding of the world, and emphasises the belief that an individual's soul is separated from the divine during one's earthly life; only God's love has the power to draw it back to its source. Rumi's teachings were also based on the belief that everything was created by God, so every creature was to be loved and respected. The order paid special attention to patience, modesty, unlimited tolerance, charity and positive reasoning. It forbade any expression or nurturing of anger, hypocrisy and lies.

But most importantly, and shockingly to orthodox Muslims at that time, Rumi claimed that music was the way to transcend the mundane worries of life, and that one could connect with the divine through dancing, or indeed whirling.

The slow, whirling, trancelike dance of the dervishes is called *sema,* and it is accompanied by the sound of the *ney* (reed flute), an instrument central to Rumi's idea of yearning for the divine. The sound of the *ney,* whose tonal range is equal to that of a human voice, is supposed to symbolise the soul's cry for God. The *oud* (Levantine lute) and *kudum* (paired drums) are the other instruments that accompany *sema.* During their dance, the dervishes hold one palm upwards and the other downwards to symbolise humanity's position as a bridge between heaven and earth. The *sema* was performed exclusively as a spiritual exercise, and it was considered blasphemy to perform for money or show.

The Mevlevi order flourished for 700 years in Turkish life and spread from Konya in Turkey to the Balkans and southeastern Europe, until they were banned in Turkey by Atatürk in 1925. Today the dervishes perform in theatres all over the world, and it's possible to see their beautiful dance in most Western countries.

North Nicosia (Lefkoşa)

Ⓝ 0 ——— 200 m
0 ——— 0.1 miles

FLATRO (SIBELI)

CARAFFA

Leoforos Athinas

Yüksel Sk

Defne Sk

Necmi Ayktıran Sk

Şafak Sk

İzmir Sk

Hüseyin Paşo Sk

Yenice Sk

Reşadiye Sk

Albay Karaoylan Cad

LOREDANO (CEVIZLI)

Saraçoylu Meydanı

Agiou Georgiou

Patroklou

KORHUT EFENDI

Minoos

Ermou

Dimonaktos

Thiseos

LEFKOSIA

Kütüphane Sk

Pendaktylou

Haydarpaşa Sk

Zühdüzade Sk

Uray Sk

Ermou Cad

Kırhizade Sk

● 3

⊞ 5

Selimiye Mosque

Selimiye ● Bedesten

● 1

Kuyumcular Sk

To Long Distance
Bus Station (750m)

To Main NCTO Office (400m);
Golden Tulip (500m)

İstanbul Cad

BARBARO (MUSALLA)

NCTO ⓘ

Kyrenia (Girne) Gate

Cemal Gürsel Cad

⊞ 6

⊗ 8

NORTH NICOSIA (LEFKOŞA)

SELIMIYE

Agah Efendi Sk

Cumhuriyet Sk

Haci Sk

Selimiye Sk

Arasta Sk

13

18

Büyük Han ⊙ 4

Büyük Hammam

Yeşil Gazino

14 12

10

Liperti

E Çetin Sk

Mecidiye Sk

Tabak Sk

Adana Sk

Asmaaltı Sk

İran Bey Sk

16

Girne Cad

Kurtbaba Sk

Belig Paşa Sk

LAIKI YITONIA

Artemidos

Atatürk Meydanı

Kyrenia (Girne) Gate

QUIRINI (CEPHANE)

Mahmut Paşa Sk

19

7

Ankara Sk

Po Sta Sk

A'Yavuz Sk

Müftü Ziyai Efendi Sk

Koruhu Sk

Müftü Ziyai Efendi Sk

⊞ 2

Ledra Street Crossing

Ledra Sk

Patou

⊗ 9

Sarayönü Sk

İkinci Selim Cad

To Passport Cadde
(300m); Mahzen
Wine & Gourmet (300m);
Califorian Gold (400m);
Museum of Barbarism (2km)

⊗ 17

Osman Paşa Cad

Sommuncuoylu Sk

Şehit Aziz Sk

Su Sk

Server Sk

İkinci Selim Cad

Ledra Palace
Hotel Crossing

MULA (ZAHRA)

ARABAHMET

11

Salahi Şevket Sk

Tanzimat Sk

ROCCAS (KAYTAZAĞA)

Yiğitler Park

15

NCTO ⓘ ⊗

Muzaffer

Leoforos Markou Drakou

North Nicosia (Lefkoşa)

◎ **Top Sights**
Bedesten D3
Büyük Hammam D3
Büyük Han D3
Selimiye Mosque E3

◎ **Sights**
1 Belediye Pazarî D4
2 Dervish Pasha Museum C3
3 Haydarpasha Mosque E3
4 Kumarcîlar Han D3
5 Lapidary Museum E3
6 Mevlevi Shrine Museum D2

◎ **Sleeping**
7 Saray C3

◎ **Eating**
8 Amasyali D2
9 Bay Kahkaha C2
10 Bereket D3

11 Boghjalian B3
12 Özerlat D4
13 Sabor D3
Saray Roof .... (see 7)
Sedirhan Cafe .... (see 18)
14 Yumurtacioglu D4

◎ **Drinking**
15 Atoyle Cadi Kazani Cafe B4
16 St George's Cafe & Bar C3
17 Street Corner Pub A1

◎ **Entertainment**
18 Cyprus Turkish Shadow
Theatre D3

◎ **Shopping**
Koza .... (see 18)
Mosaic Art Gallery .... (see 18)
19 Rüstem Kitabevi C3
Shiffa Home .... (see 18)

Mevlevi Shrine Museum　　MUSEUM
(Mevlevi Tekke Müzesi; Girne Caddesi; adult/child 5/3YTL; ⊙9am-12.30pm & 1.30-4.45pm Jun–mid-Sep, 9am-2pm mid-Sep–May) The Mevlevi Shrine Museum is a former 17th-century *tekke* (Muslim shrine) of the mystic Islamic sect known as the Mevlevi order or, more famously, the whirling dervishes. Their spiritual philosophy, which started in the Turkish town of Konya, is based on the mystical branch of Islam called Sufism.

Among the displays of the dervishes are interesting photographs of their dances in Nicosia in 1954. The most fascinating part of the museum is the former kitchen of the *tekke*, the centre of the hierarchical order in which the dervishes lived and moved from 'interns' to achieving dervish status. Each new intern would have to prove himself worthy by taking on the role of a kitchen servant for several years; at meal times, he would stand in the corner silently, watching out for subtle signals indicating the dervishes' needs. Lifting a piece of bread indicated that the dervish was thirsty and more water was needed.

The museum also houses a room with the coffins of the 16 Mevleri sheiks. Outside in the courtyard is a collection of Muslim tombstones.

Dervish Pasha Museum　　MUSEUM
(Derviş Paşa Konaği; Beliğ Paşa Sokak; adult/child 5/3YTL; ⊙9am-12.30pm & 1.30-4.45pm Jun–mid-Sep, 9am-2pm mid-Sep–May) This small ethnographic museum is housed in a 19th-century mansion. Built in 1807, it belonged to a wealthy Turkish Cypriot, Derviş Paşa, who published Cyprus' first Turkish-language newspaper. The house became an ethnographic museum in 1988. Household goods, including an old loom, glassware and ceramics, are displayed in former servants' quarters on the ground floor. Upstairs is a rich display of embroidered Turkish costumes and, in the far corner, a sumptuous *selamlık* (a retiring room for the owner of the mansion and his guests), replete with sofas and nargileh (Middle Eastern water pipes), and even some guests, in the form of eerie mannequins dressed up in suits.

Büyük Hammam　　STEAM BATHS
(www.grandhamam.com; Tarihi Büyük Hamam, Great Baths; Irfan Bey Sokak 9; treatments 60-100YTL; ⊙9am-9pm) Reopened after years of closure and restoration, the Büyük Hammam baths are entered via a low ornate door, sunk 2m below street level. The door was originally part of the 14th-century Church of St George of the Latins. Inside is a nail that marks the height reached by the waters of the Pedieos River (Kanlı Dere), drowning about 3000 Lefkosians in 1330.

START **HAYDARPASHA MOSQUE**
FINISH **LEDRA ST CROSSING**
DISTANCE **4KM**
DURATION **APPROX. TWO HOURS**

Walking Tour
Stepping Back in Time

❯ Our self-paced walking tour starts at **①** **Haydarpasha Mosque**, originally the 14th-century Church of St Catherine. Next, head down to the **②** **Lapidary Museum**. Close by you'll find the former Lusignan Church of Agia Sofia, now the **③** **Selimiye Mosque**, incongruous with its soaring minarets added after the Ottoman conquest.

Continue by walking along Araşta Sokak towards superbly renovated former church the **④** **Bedesten**, across the street from all the banter and barter of the municipal market, the **⑤** **Belediye Pazarı**. Carry on down Araşta Sokak to the **⑥** **Büyük Hammam** and then head north to see magnificent Turkish caravanserai the **⑦** **Büyük Han** and the **⑧** **Kumarcılar Han**, still under reconstruction.

Head west along Idadi and Mecidiye Sokak, and make for the main square of **⑨** **Atatürk Meydanı**, from where it's a short stroll north along Girne Caddesi to the Mevlevi Tekke, originally home of the whirling dervishes but now the **⑩** **Mevlevi Shrine Museum**. At the northern end of Girne Caddesi, you'll see **⑪** **Kyrenia (Girne) Gate**, which was cut off from its protective walls when the British created a thoroughfare for traffic.

Walk back down Girne Caddesi and turn right into Beliğ Paşa Sokak, in the lovely Arabahmet neighbourhood, where you can visit the **⑫** **Dervish Pasha Museum**, a small ethnographical collection housed in an old Turkish mansion. Follow Beliğ Paşa Sokak and turn left into Salahi Şevket Sokak, checking out the street life and the renovated or dilapidated old houses.

At the end of Salahi Şevket Sokak, you'll spot the small Yiğitler Park that sits atop the **⑬** **Roccas (Kaytazağa) Bastion**. While crossing is easy now and there's little mystery about the 'other' side, for around 30 years this was the only point along the whole of the Green Line where Turkish and Greek Cypriots could see each other at close quarters.

From here, trace your way along the Green Line on Baf Caddesi, noting the empty barrels and eerie atmosphere of the frontier, to surface at the **⑭** **Ledra St crossing**.

These days you can, more happily, choose from a choice of treatments, including mud baths, coffee-peeling and aromatherapy massage. Friday is for women only.

FREE **Belediye Pazarı**
(Municipal Market)   MARKET
(◷6am-3pm Mon-Sat) Reopened in early 2011 after extensive restoration, this is a fantastic place to check out local produce and local characters; the market bustles with action. Bargaining is rife and sellers either shout out their offers to shoppers or sleep on the counters amid piles of vegetables and fruit. There's also an area with souvenirs; don't forget to bargain.

FREE **Haydarpasha Mosque**   MOSQUE
(Camii Haydarpaşa; Kirlizade Sokak; ◷9am-1pm & 2.30-5pm Mon-Fri, 9am-1pm Sat) This mosque was originally built as the 14th-century Church of St Catherine but now functions as an art gallery. It's the second most important Gothic structure in North Nicosia after the Selimiye Mosque. The ornate sculptures, both inside and out, sprout gargoyles, dragons, shields and human heads.

FREE **Museum of Barbarism**   MUSEUM
(Barbarlık Müzesi; Irhan Sokak 2; ◷9am-12.30pm & 1.30-4.45pm Jun-Sep) Although the gruesome posters and photographs that used to greet arrivals at the Ledra Palace Hotel crossing have been removed, this museum has some similarly harrowing exhibits, including photo-documentary displays, particularly of Turkish Cypriots murdered in the villages of Agios Sozomenos and Agios Vasilios.

The Museum of Barbarism is in a quiet suburb around 3km to the west of the Old City and takes a bit of seeking out.

FREE **Lapidary Museum**   MUSEUM
(Taş Eserler Müzesi; Kirlizade Sokak; ◷9am-3.30pm Mon-Wed & Fri, 9am-5pm Thu) Housed in a lovely 15th-century building, exhibits here include a varied collection of sarcophagi, shields, steles and columns, and a Gothic window rescued from a Lusignan palace that once stood near Atatürk Meydanı.

✕ Eating

North Nicosia's eating scene is varied, with small kebab houses, *meyhane* (taverns), traditional restaurants, and chic, modern eateries. Lunchtime eating is better than dinner, since there are more small kebab houses

open, offering a choice. At dinnertime the Old City gets very quiet and a little dark, so apart from the places we recommend there aren't that many options. To the northwest of the Old City there's a scattering of restaurants open in the evenings; these are usually hard to find and best reached by taxi.

OLD CITY

TOP
CHOICE **Bay Kahkaha**   TURKISH €€
(Tanzimat Sk 166; mains 18YTL) Turkish Cypriot owner Mehmet recently returned from several years in Australia to open up this exceptional place. The evocative setting is a 1928 building with original tiles, several intimate dining rooms and a garden dining space with palms and olive trees. The cuisine is traditional, with *kahkah tavuk dolma* (traditional stuffed chicken with mushrooms) a speciality. When it opened in May 2011, the prime minister showed up to the launch; it's that kind of place. There's regular live music.

Boghjalian   TURKISH €
(☎228 0700; Salahi Şevket Sokak; meze around 10YTL; ◷closed Sun) Housed in the former mansion of a wealthy Armenian, Boghjalian is a quality, popular restaurant. The set menu consists of either meze or mixed kebab, and food is served in a leafy courtyard or a choice of two elegant dining rooms. Try the sublime *ceviz macunu* (green walnuts and almonds with lemon, sugar and cloves). Reservations recommended.

Sabor   MEDITERRANEAN €€
(Selimiye Meydanı 29; mains around 15YTL) Right next to Selimiye Mosque, this is North Nicosia's best choice for those who can't take another kebab. The menu specialises in Italian and Spanish food, with some Asian noodle dishes. The portions are generous, the prices are low and the staff (and resident cat population) are friendly.

Sedirhan Cafe   TURKISH €
(Büyük Han; mains 7YTL; ◷9am-5pm Mon, Wed & Fri, to 1am Tue & Thu, to 1pm Sat) This cafe is the best place to eat Turkish ravioli, while you admire the beauty of the Büyük Han; the Sedirhan is in its courtyard. You can also have a coffee or a beer, and eat some *börek* (meat or cheese rolled in thin pastry).

Bereket   FAST FOOD €
(Irfan Bey Sokak; pide & lahmacun 7-10YTL; ◷4am-1.30pm) A rough-and-ready kiosk a few metres away from the grand Büyük Han,

Bereket is run by Ilker, who makes the best *pide* and *lahmacun* (Turkish-style pizza, topped with minced lamb and parsley) in town in his stone oven. There are a couple of chairs outside or you can munch on the go.

Saray Roof TURKISH €
(Atatürk Meydanı; fixed-menu meals 12YTL) On top of the Saray hotel, and commanding the best views of the city, this place is great for an evening cocktail. Unfortunately, the Turkish and 'European' food is unremarkable. The view is what you pay for, when you get to watch the city lights twinkle in the night.

Amasyali KEBABS €
(Girne Caddesi 186; kebabs 1.50YTL; ☺9am-11pm) Open all day; does simple, tasty doner kebabs to eat in or take away.

Yumurtacioglu SWEETS €
(Araşta Sokak) Come here for diet-defying Turkish delight and halva made on the premises.

Özerlat CAFE €
(Araşta Sokak 73; coffees 2.50YTL) Sells any kind of tea or coffee you can think of. The friendly owner makes her own cakes.

NEW CITY
The main restaurant (and shopping) street in the new part of town is Mehmet Akif Caddesi, home to the city's most sophisticated eating places, with at least a dozen options and an emphasis on modern Cypriot and international cuisine. There are laid-back bars here, as well, with attractive outside terraces and at least one with Irish beer on tap. For parking, head for the residential side streets. Califorian Gold has its own car park.

TOP CHOICE **Passport Cadde** INTERNATIONAL €€
(www.caddepassport.com; Mehmet Akif Caddesi 88; mains 16YTL) One of the most packed out and justifiably fashionable restaurants on this foodie street. It has a round-the-clock DJ, a vast interior and terrace seating space, a menu that includes Asian-inspired cuisine, Italian choices, curries, fajitas and some good salads.

Califorian Gold INTERNATIONAL €€
(www.califoriangold.com; Mehmet Akif Caddesi 74; mains 14YTL; ℗♪) This is one of the most popular restaurants among this energetic stretch of eateries. The sprawling terrace and two floors of tables are generally packed with a youthful, well-heeled crowd, here for the tasty international cuisine, including fajitas, pasta, steaks, kebabs and interesting salads, like a tasty vegetarian choice with lentils, red peppers and goats cheese.

Mahzen Wine & Gourmet INTERNATIONAL €€
(Mehmet Akif Caddesi 75; mains 14YTL) In a historic building backing onto the old railway station, which dates to 1905 (it ceased operation in 1951). The menu includes pasta and chicken dishes with various sauces, and the excellent wine list offers vintages from South Africa, France and Italy.

☆ Drinking & Entertainment

Turkish Cypriots will themselves admit that nightlife in their capital is not all that hot, at least in the Old City. In the New City, Mehmet Akif Caddesi is reasonably animated, but if you're looking for more vigour and choice, head to Kyrenia, 25km away.

A popular drinking area in the Old City is behind the Belediye Pazarı within the

---

CHILDREN'S CYPRUS: SHADOW THEATRE & GO-KARTS

Considering the illustrious place of shadow theatre in the history of Cyprus, it's a surprise that the **Cyprus Turkish Shadow Theatre** (☎0542 850 3514; Büyük Han, Araşta Sokak) is the only place of its kind on the entire island. Shadow-puppet plays take place in the Büyük Han, but you'll have to go there or call to enquire about details with Mehmet Ertuğ, the puppeteer.

If you fancy yourself as a bit of a Formula 1 whiz, seek out **Zet Karting** (☎0533 866 6173; www.zetkarting.com; Lefkoşa-Güzelyurt Anayolu; per 10min 20-40YTL; ☺4pm-midnight Tue-Sun Jun–mid-Sep, noon-8pm Tue-Sun mid-Sep–May), which has a large and very professional-looking series of circuits. You can rent carts from 20YTL for 10 minutes on the junior 300m course, 30YTL for the medium 900m course, or 40YTL on the 1200m professional circuit. Unwind in the Z1 Bar or Z1 Cafeteria. Zet Karting is just off the main roundabout on the road going north out of North Nicosia. At the roundabout, take the turn-off to Morfou (Güzelyurt); it's on the left, after the Alaykoy turn-off.

restored old market building. Although it resembles a kind of warehouse, with tall ceilings and low-hanging lamps, the space has an upbeat, modern look. There are several bars inside and plenty of places to puff on a nargileh.

The Büyük Han has live music on Tuesday and Thursday evenings in its central courtyard.

Nostalgia Music Bar NIGHTCLUB
(227 7901; Kurtuluş Meydanı; ⊙10pm-late) On the northern side of town, this is a popular venue for those who like a little skirt-swirling salsa, starting with a 90-minute warm-up class, followed by a live band playing Latin, reggae and pop.

St George's Cafe & Bar BAR
(Iplik Pazari 2B) Enjoy a warm-wood interior and outside tables on this quiet corner, with live traditional music at weekends.

Street Corner Pub BAR
(Osman Paşa Cad; ⊙10pm-late) Popular Irish pub.

Atolye Cadi Kazani Cafe CAFE
(Tanzimat Sokak 77) Artist-run and popular small cafe and bar tucked down a side street. The owner's artwork is on the walls.

🛍 Shopping
The Büyük Han is the best place for tourists to pick up some memorable souvenirs, with some genuine arts and crafts on display and for sale. The following three places are particularly worth seeking out.

Koza SILK DECORATIONS
(⊙9am-6pm) Cyprus' heritage of producing silk from silkworms and the once ubiquitous mulberry tree comes alive in this shop where the owner, Munise, and her elderly mother hand weave the silk patterns. The patterns were traditionally used for picture frames, or simply as framed wall decorations themselves.

Mosaic Art Gallery CRAFTS
(www.buyukhan-art.com; ⊙9am-6pm) Inexpensive but exquisite handmade jewellery with a floral theme is on sale here, as well as colourful mosaic art pieces.

Shiffa Home ORGANIC PRODUCTS
Shiffa's owner makes handmade soaps, jams and preserves. She also sells and advises on local herbal and aromatherapy remedies.

ⓘ SHOPPERS BEWARE
A word of warning: if you're visiting from the South and decide to go on a shopping spree in the North or vice versa, beware the Greek Cypriot customs regulations: you can't take more than 200 cigarettes and 1L of alcohol or wine, plus €100 worth of other goods across the North–South border. So don't go indulging in expensive carpets!

Rüstem Kitabevi BOOKS
(228 3506; Girne Caddesi 22) Once almost legendary for its organised chaos, this place has taken control of its stock and all is now neatly arranged on shelves. It is still, however, a well-supplied store, with old and new books, and many English-language reads, plus a rack of all kinds of magazines. Also has a branch of Gloria Jeans Coffee with 14 caffeine fixes to choose from, and an outside patio with fruit trees and umbrellas.

ⓘ Information
EMERGENCY Call 155.
Police station (228 3311; Atatürk Meydanı)
INTERNET ACCESS Wi-fi is almost nonexistent in cafes in the North, so you'll be bound to use the internet cafes, which are, more often than not, swarming with men but with few women. But that shouldn't be a problem.
Orbit Internet Cafe (Girne Caddesi 180; per hr 2YTL; ⊙24hr) Busy and central.
MEDICAL SERVICES **Burhan Nalbatanoğlu Devlet Hastanesi** (228 5441) North Nicosia's main hospital.
Poliklinik (227 3996; Gazeteci Kemal Aşik Caddesi) Where foreigners can seek medical treatment.
MONEY You can change your money into Turkish lira (YTL) at any of the money-changing facilities just past the passport-control booth at both the Ledra Palace Hotel and Ledra St crossings. ATMs can be found at **TC Ziraat Bankası** (Girne Caddesi) at the northern end of the road, or at **Kıbrıs Vakıflar Bankası** (Atatürk Meydanı). Both change foreign currency, as do private exchange offices nearby.
TOURIST INFORMATION **North Cyprus Tourism Organisation** (NCTO; 227 2994; www.tourism.trnc.net) Kyrenia Gate (⊙9am-5pm Mon-Fri, to 2pm Sat & Sun); Ledra Palace Hotel crossing (⊙9am-5pm Mon-Sat, to 2pm Sun); main office (Bedrettin Demirel Caddesi; ⊙9am-5pm Mon-Fri, to 2pm Sat) Has two convenient offices in the city centre with maps

STREET WISE

North Nicosia is a safe city at any time of the day, and you should feel no concern about walking the streets.

At night, the Old City can seem uncomfortably quiet, especially for urban folk, and visitors may feel intimidated walking alone along dimly lit and often narrow streets. It's best to avoid them if you feel uncomfortable. The areas abutting the Green Line look threatening, with large black-and-red signs that clearly forbid photography or trespassing in the buffer zone.

Do not take photographs on the Roccas (Kaytazağa) Bastion, at the western end of the Old City limits, where you can still look over into Greek Lefkosia. Despite the loosening of the border-crossing laws, the buffer zone is still a military area. Watchful soldiers stationed not so obviously on the bastion may confront you and confiscate your camera.

and brochures for Northern Cyprus. If you don't find the information you want here, you can always make the 2km trek out to the main office. It's a long walk, so take a taxi from Kyrenia Gate (2YTL).

TRAVEL AGENCIES Birinci Turizm (☏228 3200; Girne Caddesi 158a) Issues ferry tickets to Turkey and airline tickets, and offers a range of other travel-related services.

ⓘ Getting There & Away
Air

Ercan airport (Tymvou; ☏231 4703) is about 14km northeast of North Nicosia and is linked to the city by an expressway. Many visitors to the North now fly to Larnaka airport, as the flights are direct and less subject to delays. There are scheduled flights to London and several destinations in Turkey from Ercan airport. All charter flights operate from Ercan, although occasional flights are diverted to the military airport at **Geçitkale** (Lefkoniko; ☏227 9420), closer to Famagusta, when Ercan is being serviced.

The two airlines serving Northern Cyprus are based in North Nicosia:

Cyprus Turkish Airlines (Kıbrıs Türk Hava Yolları, KTHY; ☏227 0084; www.kthy.net /kthyen/index.html; Bedrettin Demirel Caddesi)

Turkish Airlines (Türk Hava Yolları, THY; ☏227 1061; www.turkishairlines.com; Mehmet Akif Caddesi 32)

Bus

The long-distance bus station is on the corner of Atatürk Caddesi and Gazeteci Kemal Aşik Caddesi in the New City. Buses to major towns leave from here. You may prefer the bus to the sometimes hair-raising rides in service taxis or *dolmuş* (minibuses).

Car & Motorcycle

Drivers and riders will enter North Nicosia via one of two main roads that lead directly to the Old City. If you come from Famagusta or Ercan airport, you will enter North Nicosia via Mustafa Ahmet Ruso Caddesi and then Gazeteci Kemal Aşik Caddesi. This road leads directly to Kyrenia Gate. Arriving from Kyrenia, you will enter North Nicosia via Tekin Yurdabay Caddesi and eventually Bedrettin Demirel Caddesi, which also leads towards Kyrenia Gate.

If you are entering North Nicosia from the Republic of Cyprus, the car crossing point is at Agios Dometios, west of the city. The easiest way into the Old City is to turn immediately right after passing the Ledra Palace Hotel crossing and enter via Memduh Asar Sokak. Turn left onto Tanzimat Sokak as soon as you cross the moat and you will reach Kyrenia Gate after about 200m.

Parking is usually not a problem, though finding a place in the Old City may get tricky if you arrive late in the morning on a working day. If you arrive early, you can easily park on Girne Caddesi.

Service Taxi & Minibus

Minibuses to local destinations and further afield start from various stations outside the Venetian walls and from the Itimat bus station, just outside the Kyrenia Gate. The most convenient stop for service taxis to Kyrenia is just southeast of the Mevlevi Shrine Museum. City destinations include Famagusta (8YTL, one hour) and Kyrenia (5YTL, 30 minutes). Service taxis also leave from the Itimat bus station.

ⓘ Getting Around
To/From the Airport

Buses to Ercan airport leave from the office of **Cyprus Turkish Airlines** (☏227 0084; Bedrettin Demirel Caddesi). They depart two hours before any flight and cost 2YTL. A taxi from Kyrenia Gate to the airport will cost around 20YTL.

Bus

While there are public buses in North Nicosia, they tend to mainly service the suburbs outside the Old City. They're only really useful if you need to get to the Cyprus Turkish Airlines office or the main NCTO office (both on Bedrettin Demirel Caddesi). Buses leave from near Kyrenia Gate.

Car

For car hire, **Bicen Rent a Car** (☎227 1680; Bedreddin Demirel Caddesi 61) and **Sun Rent a Car** (☎227 2303; www.sunrentacar.com; Abdi Ipekçi Caddesi 10) are good choices. If you're coming from the South, you can call ahead and see if they'll pick you up from Kyrenia Gate. Rates start at around 65YTL per day. In high season there may be a minimum hire period of three days.

Taxi

There are plenty of taxi ranks in North Nicosia, though the most convenient and easiest to find are at Atatürk Meydanı and Kyrenia Gate. A ride to anywhere in town should cost no more than 2YTL, and the drivers are usually good about turning on the meter.

Among the more reliable taxi companies in North Nicosia are **Ankara Taxi** (☎227 1788), **Özner Taxi** (☎227 4012), **Terminal Taxi** (☎228 4909) and **Yılmaz Taxi** (☎227 3036).

Kyrenia (Girne) & the Northern Coast

Includes »

Kyrenia (Girne) 161
Around Kyrenia & the
Ranges 167
St Hilarion Castle..........169
Bellapais
(Beylerbeyi) 170
Lapta (Lapithos)............174
The Northwest...............174
Koruçam (Kormakitis)
Peninsula 175
Morfou (Güzelyurt)........176
Lefke (Lefka)..................176
Ancient Soloi..................177
Ancient Vouni................178

Why Go?

Centred on the beautiful vista of its old-world harbour, its wild-flowered slopes and imposing mountain range, Kyrenia is one of the island's most intriguing towns.

The ruins of its 12th-century abbey and surrounding gothic castles have even, according to legend, been the inspiration for fairytales.

The area's enchanting effect on visitors is well known. It was a favourite haunt of colonial civil servants, who flocked here after retiring from service to the British Empire. Lawrence Durrell, who made his home here, turned the region into a literary starlet when he wrote about it in *Bitter Lemons of Cyprus*.

Kyrenia's north coast is now fast changing. Vast olive fields, old village houses and natural habitats are making way for new developments and infrastructure such as tourist towns and roadways. Although this has taken a toll on some of the region's natural beauty, there is still plenty to enjoy along its coast.

Best Places to Eat

» Kyrenia Tavern (p165)

» Anı (p166)

» Kybele (p171)

» Stone Arch (p165)

» No.14 (p165)

Best Places to Stay

» White Pearl Hotel (p210)

» Club Z (p210)

» Lapida (p210)

» Sempati (p211)

» Bellapais Monastery Village (p211)

When to Go

From February to March vibrant wildflowers and rare orchids bloom across Kyrenia's mountain range, contrasting with its Gothic ruins. May takes on a musical flavour with the Bellapais Music Festival, set against the backdrop of the abbey and its stunning arches.

During June and July, discover the historic castles of the North, before heading to the coast and cooling off at Kyrenia's sandy beaches. In September and October strong winds send you skyward as you paraglide from the heights of the Pentadaktylos mountains, with their unforgettable views of the coast.

KYRENIA (GIRNE)

POP 22,000

With its impressive Byzantine castle and horseshoe-shaped Old Harbour, gentle waters, fishing boats and high buildings (formerly carob warehouses), it's easy to understand why this picturesque town is the centre of tourism in the North.

The harbour now bustles with bars, restaurants, cafes, boat-excursion touters, and waiters speaking in broken English and beckoning you into their restaurants. It's a far cry from the expectations of barefoot fishermen joyfully pulling nets onto wooden boats with the old castle as a backdrop. Only a 30-minute drive from the capital Lefkosia/North Nicosia, this is where North Nicosians come for good restaurants and nightlife. It is also home to one of the largest British expat settlements on the island, complete with church and community centre. Kyrenia is lively, and its busy coast has more hotels, restaurants and bars (in one spot) than anywhere else in the North.

History

Once one of the ancient city-kingdoms of Cyprus, Kyrenia was founded by Mycenaean Greeks around 1200 BC. From this point Kyrenia's history is, in essence, the history of its castle. Little more is known about the town until the castle's construction by the Byzantines in the 7th century to ward off continuing Arab raids.

In 1191 the castle was captured by Richard the Lionheart of England, on his way to Jerusalem and a third crusade. The castle was then used as both a residence and prison. It was sold to the Knights Templar and then gifted to Guy de Lusignan when he became king of Cyprus.

In the 14th century the Venetians extended the castle and built the bulbous seafacing fortifications still seen today. During Ottoman rule, changes to the castle were again made, while Kyrenia itself functioned primarily as the island's only northern port.

Kyrenia has long since given up this role, as the Old Harbour's size and depth only allow it to service tourist crafts, fishing boats and the small yachts commonly found in its cluttered quays. Two kilometres to the east of Kyrenia, there is now a large purpose-built harbour created to receive commercial and passenger ships from Turkey.

During British rule, the town became a favourite with retiring (ex-colonial) British

ROAD DISTANCES (KM)

	Morfou (Güzelyurt)	Bellapais (Beylerbeyi)	Lapta (Lapithos)	Koruçam (Kormakitis)
Bellapais (Beylerbeyi)	83			
Lapta (Lapithos)	51	32		
Koruçam (Kormakitis)	77	6	26	
Lefke (Lefka)	26	109	77	103

civil servants. When Turkey invaded Cyprus in 1974, it used the beaches to the west of Kyrenia as the prime location for landing its army. Almost all Greek Cypriots and many British retirees fled.

Now, 37 years later, Kyrenia supports a growing tourist industry, mainly from Britain, Germany and Turkey.

⊙ Sights

While Kyrenia is spread out over a wide area, the central Old Town (tourist area) is fairly compact. Taxis and minibuses arrive at and depart from Ecevit Caddesi and stop near the main square, **Belediye Meydanı**, which is 200m south of the Old Harbour. To the west of Belediye Meydanı runs Ziya Rızkı Caddesi, where you will find shops and banks. Mustafa Çağatay Caddesi runs southeast from Belediye Meydanı to the New Harbour, at which ferries to and from Turkey dock.

Kyrenia Castle　　　　HISTORICAL SITE, MUSEUM
(Girne Kalesi; adult/child 12/3YTL; ⊙9am-7pm Jun–mid-Sep, 9am-4pm mid-Sep–May) The shielding Kyrenia Castle is the dominant feature of the charming Old Harbour. Its convoluted history has made it an interesting architectural and cultural mix.

Built by the Byzantines, possibly over the remains of an earlier Roman fort, the castle staved off many attacks, including the Ottoman invasion of 1570 – at least until the Venetian occupants surrendered it in the wake of Nicosia (Lefksia) being overrun.

A large rectangular structure, it includes a cistern, dungeon, chapel, gallery and museum, guarded by four fortified bastions, one on each corner.

You can enter the castle via the stone bridge over the former moat, which leads to the small 12th-century Byzantine **Chapel of St George**. Its broken mosaics and Corinthian columns, originally outside the walls,

Kyrenia (Girne) & the Northern Coast Highlights

1 Enjoying the cafes, restaurants and bars of Kyrenia's charming **Old Harbour** (p161)

2 Discovering Kyrenia's **Byzantine castle** and its **Shipwreck Museum**, which boasts the oldest recovered shipwreck in Cyprus (p161)

3 Rambling across mountains and coasts on the expansive **northern hiking trails** (p168)

4 Seeing the sights at **Bellapais** (p170), exploring its abbey and taking in its spectacular views

5 Climbing the steps of the fairytale ruins at **St Hilarion Castle** (p169)

6 Going **wild orchid hunting** (p164) round the southern slopes of the Kyrenia range

7 Getting a bird's-eye view of the coast from the heights of **Buffavento Castle** (p172)

8 Exploring the sites of **Ancient Vouni** (p178) and **Ancient Soloi** (p177) on the northwest coast

MEDITERRANEAN SEA

To Kaplıca (Davlos, 44km); Kantara Castle (50km); Karpas (Kırpaşa) Peninsula (52km)

To Famagusta (Mağusa; 38km)

KYRENIA RANGE

BESPARMAK (PENTADACTYLOS) RANGE

REPUBLIC OF CYPRUS

Morfou Bay

KORUÇAM (KORMAKITIS) PENINSULA

UN Buffer Zone

NORTH NICOSIA (LEFKOŞA)

Map labels:
- Korucam Burnu (Cape Kormakitis)
- Sadrazamköy (Liveras)
- Church of Agios Georgios
- Koruçam (Kormakitis)
- Horse Shoe Beach
- Gecitköy (Panagra)
- Hisarköy (Kampyli)
- Güzelyalı (Vavlas)
- Karşıyaka (Vasileia)
- Lapta (Lapithos)
- Alsancak Beach
- Alsancak (Karavas)
- Yavuz Çıkarma (Five Mile) Beach
- Karaman (Karmi)
- Karaoğlanoğlu (Agios Georgios)
- Profitis Ilias (888m)
- Pinarbaşı (Krini)
- Kyparissovouno (1024m)
- Akçiçek (Sysklipos)
- Kılıçaslan (Kontemenos)
- Kozan
- Çamlibel (Myrtou)
- Ozhan (Asomatos)
- Tepebaşı (Diorios)
- Agios Vasileios (Türkeli)
- Yılmazköy (Skylloura)
- İkidere (Duo Potami)
- Kalkanli (Kalo Horio)
- Olive Tree Orchard
- Agia Mamas Church
- Kato Kopia (Zümrütköy)
- Argaki (Akçay)
- Kato Zodeia (Yu Bostanci)
- Avlona (Gaytetköv)
- Kokkinotrimithia
- Zodhia Crossing
- Astromentis
- Toumba tou Skourou
- Morfou (Güzelyurt)
- Nikitas (Güneşköy)
- Pano Zodeia (Aş Bostanci)
- Prastio (Aydınköy)
- Pentageia
- Angolemi
- Syrianochori (Yayla)
- Yedidalga Belediyesi Plaji
- Ancient Vouni
- Soloi
- Gemikonaği (Karavostasi)
- Pirj Osman Pasha Mosque
- Lefke
- Petra
- Paliocastro
- Oxgos River
- Aloupos River
- Elaia River
- Karaağaç (Harkia)
- Yialias (935m)
- Afanteia (Gazıköy)
- Troulli
- Sourp Magar Monastery
- Alevkaya Herbarium Forest Station
- Değirmenlik (Kythrea)
- Demirhan (Trahoni)
- Vakıflar Alagadi (Turtle) Beach
- Vrysi (Acapulco) Beach
- Vrysi (Lara) Beach
- Karakoumi (Karakum)
- Çatalköy
- Çatalköy (Agios Epiktitos)
- Beşparmak (Pentadaktylos; 740m)
- Buffavento Castle
- Beşparmak Pass
- Minareliköy (Neo Horio)
- Balikesir (Palaikythro)
- Ercan Airport
- Haspolat (Mia Milia)
- Trachonas
- Ozanköy (Kazafani)
- Bellapais (Beylerbeyi)
- Panagia Absinthiotissa Monastery
- Yu Dikmen (Pano Dikomo)
- Aşağı Dikmen (Kato Dikomo)
- Taşkent (Vouno)
- Güngör (Koutsoventis)
- KYRENIA (Girne)
- St Hilarion Castle
- Ağırdağ Castle
- Ağırdağ (Agirda)
- Agios Dometios Crossing
- Nicosia International Airport
- Kioneli (Gönyeli)
- Gerolakkos (Alaykóy)
- Egkomi
- Agianga (Aglantzia)
- Kato Lakatameia
- Pano Lakatameia
- Geri
- Agioi Trimithias
- Tymvou

were incorporated into the larger structure by the Venetians.

In the northeast bastion, the Venetian tower has mock displays of battle scenes. Dressed in armour and military uniforms, the models show the castle's history, ranging from the Byzantine period to the British.

In the north room is the infamous **torture chamber**, where King Peter I's (pregnant) mistress, Joanna L'Aleman, was tortured by order of the king's jealous wife, Queen Eleanor.

You can walk between the four towers via the handrailed ramparts, but follow the marked routes as some sections can be quite dangerous. Keep younger children close by at all times. Views of the Old Harbour are fantastic from here, especially in the morning light.

Admission to the castle includes entrance to the Gallery of Tomb-Finds and the Shipwreck Museum within the castle walls.

Gallery of Tomb-Finds

With exhibits from the Neolithic and Bronze ages, and the Hellenistic and Byzantine periods, the gallery has some of the best displays within the castle complex. They include amphorae, gold jewellery and ancient coins. Another display shows a reconstruction of the Neolithic II Period houses (4500–3900 BC) made from mud and stone, found at the archaeological site of **Ayios Epiktitos – Vrysi**, just outside Çatalköy.

Shipwreck Museum

A highlight of the castle is the **Kyrenia Shipwreck** chamber, which contains the oldest shipwreck ever recovered from Cypriot waters. A wooden-hulled (Aleppo pine) Greek merchant ship, it sank just off the Kyrenia coast around 300 BC, and was discovered by a local diver in 1967. Its cargo consisted of amphorae, almonds, grain, wine and millstones from the Greek islands of Samos, Rhodes and Kos. Its crew most likely traded along the coast of Anatolia and as far as the islands of the Dodecanese in Greece.

New evidence suggests that the boat, 80 years old at the time, sank because of piracy and not its age. Much of its cargo seems to have been plundered, and it has what appear to be spear marks in its hull. A curse tablet was also found with the wreck. At the time, pirates believed that placing these tablets on a sinking ship would conceal its fate, by keeping the wreck forever at the bottom of the sea.

WHAT'S IN A NAME?

Since 1974, all the original Greek place names have been replaced by Turkish names, so those only familiar with the pre-partition names may find it difficult to navigate without a Turkish-language map. Greek road signs and wall signs of any description have completely disappeared, and many of the touring roads do not have highway numbers or names. Most simply state the name of the village you're heading toward. As such, being in the North can feel a lot like being in some distant region of Turkey.

An excellent modern reconstruction of the ship (using the same materials) can be viewed in Agia Napa's Thalassa Municipal Museum of the Sea (p117).

Folk Art Museum　　　　MUSEUM
(Halk Sanatları Müzesi; admission 3YTL; ☉9am-6pm Jun–mid-Sep, 9am-12.30pm & 1.30-4.45pm mid-Sep–May) Located in a Venetian-influenced building along the harbour-front, this museum holds a small but interesting collection of traditional furniture, fabrics and utensils. You can also see a traditional wooden olive-press on the ground floor.

Archangelos Icon　　　　MUSEUM
(Canbulat; admission 4YTL; ☉9am-2pm daily & Mon 3.30-6pm Jun–mid-Sep, 9am-1pm & 2-4.45pm mid-Sep–May) Situated to the west of the Old Harbour, at the church of the Archangel Michael, easily distinguished by its prominent belltower, this exhibit holds icons from the 17th and 18th centuries. The collection, spread over three floors, is made up of icons salvaged from the looting of Orthodox churches in the region. Notable depictions include Saint George and the Dragon, the beheading of John the Baptist, and Virgin and child.

Old Town　　　　HISTORICAL SITE
Situated south of the Old Harbour between Canbulat Sokak and Kale Sokak, inside the remnants of the ancient city walls, is the diminutive old town, well worth a wander. It's very striking, with abandoned (Greek) buildings in disrepair mixed with those with obvious Ottoman influences. Within the twisting and turning alleyways, you'll find concealed staircases and ruined walls, along

Kyrenia (Girne)

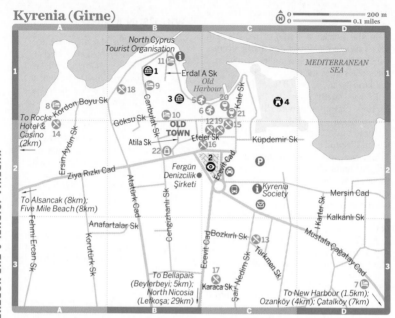

with an ancient Greco-Roman tomb and the rundown church of Khryssopolítissa, built in the 14th century.

🏃 Activities

Scuba diving is really well organised in Kyrenia. Diving is also very popular in the south of the island. For information, see p25.

Scuba Cyprus   DIVING
(☑865 2317; www.scubacyprus.com; Karaoğlanoğlu; ☺9am-5pm) Has regular PADI and BSAC diving courses and operates out of Camelot Beach in Alsancak, about 8km west of Kyrenia. The boat is often moored in the Old Harbour, and the operators offer try-drives from €30.

Blue Dolphin Scuba   DIVING
(☑0542 851 5113; www.bluedolphincyprus.com; ☺9am-5pm) Based in the Jasmine Court Hotel on Naci Talat Caddesi, it also has a contact stand on the Old Harbour. It operates two boats from Escape Beach in Alsancak, and has PADI open-water courses available, starting at around €150.

Boat Cruises   BOAT TRIPS
Kyrenia's Old Harbour boat-cruise scene is like a market where everyone is selling the same thing. For 50YTL to 60YTL you can

expect to get a day cruise on a Turkish gulet (traditional wooden ship with raised bow) with two swimming stops and snorkelling, usually finishing with an on-board barbecue lunch (drinks are extra). The boat typically leaves at 10.30am and returns at 5pm. It takes up to 20 passengers.

Aphrodite Boat Fishing   BOAT TRIPS
(☑0533 868 0943; musaaksoy@superonline.com; Girne Limanı; cruises €25) This gulet offers cruises around the bay, fishing trips and deep-sea fishing excursions. Captain Musa Aksoy will even grill up your catch, after swimming and leisure stops at Escape Beach and a few other beautiful inlets.

Highline Tandem   PARAGLIDING
(☑0542 855 5672; www.highlineparagliding.com; adult incl transport, flight & insurance €70) This is situated at the Old Harbour and run by a New Zealander-Cypriot couple. The company helped a 100-year-old Scottish woman paraglide her way into the *Guinness Book of Records* as the oldest woman ever to take up the adventure sport. Flights run four times a day from an altitude of 750m.

Walks and Wild Orchids   WALKING TOUR
(☑0542 854 4329; www.walksnorchidsnorthcyprus .com; mid-Feb–May incl lunch €18) Rambles start

Kyrenia (Girne)

◎ Sights
1 Archangelos Icon...................................B1
2 Belediye Meydanı...............................C2
3 Folk Art Museum (Halk Sanatları
   Müzesi)..B1
   Gallery of Tomb-Finds...................(see 4)
4 Kyrenia Castle....................................C1
   Shipwreck Museum.......................(see 4)

◑ Activities, Courses & Tours
5 Aphrodite Boat Tours & Fishing............B1
   Blue Dolphin Scuba (contact
   stand)..(see 5)
6 Highline Tandem Paragliding.................C1

◉ Sleeping
7 Club Z...D3
8 Dome Hotel...A1
9 Harbour Scene......................................B1
10 Nostalgia..B1

11 White Pearl Hotel..................................B1

◉ Eating
12 Baragadi Bar & Restaurant...................C2
13 Kyrenia Tavern......................................C3
14 Niazi's Restaurant & Bar.......................A2
15 No.14..C2
16 Öz-Vip..C2
17 Padişah...C3
18 Six Brothers Restaurant.........................B1
19 Stone Arch..C2

◉ Drinking
20 Café 34...C1
21 Ego Bar...C1
   White Pearl Hotel Bar...................(see 11)

◉ Shopping
22 Round Tower...B2

in **Hisarköy**, a traditional village on the southern slopes of the Kyrenia Range. The area is ideal for wildflower and orchid enthusiasts and birdwatchers alike. Walks usually last around two hours, over easy terrain, and take in orchid glades and black tulips. Enjoy identifying over 20 species of orchids, including the extremely rare *Orchis punctulata,* aka punctate orchid. This flower is only found in parts of Cyprus, Crimea, Turkey and Iran. There are also many other excellent examples of endemic wildflowers to be seen.

✕ Eating

Kyrenia offers a string of restaurants along the Old Harbour; however, the area is best utilised for a coffee or an evening drink. Most of the eateries rely on their stunning locations and views, as opposed to good gastronomy.

There are some excellent restaurants further inland, in the old Turkish Quarter and Kyrenia town.

OLD HARBOUR & TURKISH QUARTER

TOP CHOICE **Kyrenia Tavern**   TURKISH €€€
(Bag Sokak; mains 30-40YTL; ☺dinner) Situated in the back streets, near the small fire station, this humble garden venue is well worth the effort it takes to find. Serving simple, well-cooked Turkish Cypriot food, it has no menu as such, but meze, moussaka and soft

lamb are usually prepared daily, with the freshest ingredients. If you like it authentic and rustic, this is the spot for you.

Stone Arch   INTERNATIONAL €€€
(Efeler Sokak 13; mains 30-40YTL; ☺dinner; ☑) Barely five minutes' walk from the Old Harbour, this restaurant offers a pretty courtyard and delightful atmosphere. The well-flavoured food, such as king prawns and steaks, is pricey, but deservedly so. Excellent service and a good range of well-priced wines makes this an ideal venue.

No.14   INTERNATIONAL €€€
(Yazıcızade Sokak; mains 18-28YTL; ☺dinner) Found behind the door of 'Yazade House' in the old Turkish Quarter, this elegant poolside garden restaurant offers home-cooked delights like cheeky pork with peppercorn, fillet steaks and stuffed calamari. Its simple menu is accompanied with excellent service. Try the delicious sticky toffee pudding.

Niazi's Restaurant & Bar   GRILLED MEAT €€
(www.niazis.com; Kordon Boyu Sokak; full kebab 25YTL; ☺11am-midnight) On offer is a variety of charcoal-grilled kebabs and, of course, traditional *meze*. It's very popular with the locals, who come here for the 'full kebab', a mixture of Turkish and Cypriot tastes with *sheftelia, köfte* and *shish* variations.

Six Brothers Restaurant
TURKISH €€€

(Kordon Boyu Sokak; mains 35YTL) Just outside the Old Harbour, this restaurant serves well-priced meze, kebabs and fish. The best tables and seating are located outside, across from the restaurant, overlooking the bay.

Baragadi Bar & Restaurant
TURKISH €€

(Doğan Türk; mains 20-25YTL; ◷dinner;) With its old colonial interior, this place specialises in Turkish food, and fresh fish caught daily and delivered to the Old Harbour. Also has a cool, breezy garden and bar, which is great during the hot summer evenings.

Padişah
CYPRIOT €

(Ecevit Caddesi; kleftiko 11YTL) The decor is simple, with a walled and shaded courtyard for alfresco dining. It serves traditional food like *kleftiko* (oven-baked lamb) and meze. It's in the nook, opposite the Colony Hotel.

Öz-Vip
SUPERMARKET

(Efeler Sokak; ◷9am-6pm) Ideal for anyone self-catering or those planning a picnic or a mountain walk. It has all the essentials plus a few non-essentials, all reasonably priced.

OUT OF TOWN

Anı
SEAFOOD €€

(Zeka Adil Caddesi, Çatalköy; fish dishes 10-20YTL; ◷dinner) This is an excellent and affordable fish tavern, with garden seating. Try the 'salted fish' with home-grown vegetables. Located 2.5km east of Ozanköy, it's considered one of the best fish taverns in Cyprus.

Erol's Bar & Restaurant
CYPRIOT €€

(Ozanköy; kleftiko 12YTL; ◷dinner) To the east, on the way to Bellapais, this place has good grills, meze and fish dishes. With great views over the village of Ozanköy, it also serves hearty homemade soups in winter.

Address Restaurant & Brasserie
MEDITERRANEAN €€

(Ali Aktaş Sokak 13; mains 11-16YTL; ◷dinner) Towards Karaoğlanoğlu, this restaurant is situated on the main road west. It sits on a small point overlooking the sea. The menu includes fish, pastas and steaks. Try the splendid orange-tarragon chicken.

Ambiance
INTERNATIONAL €€€

(www.ambiancecyprus.com; Parasut Sokak 20, Karaoğlanoğlu; mains 35-45YTL;) This swish new restaurant and beach club, just west of Kyrenia on the seafront, has an extensive menu, including chicken, fish and steak dishes. It also has some delectable sweets and wines that can all be enjoyed poolside.

Altınkaya I
TURKISH €

(Yavuz Çıkarma Plaj; mains 10YTL; ◷dinner) Named after the nearby beach, and on the way to Lapta (Lapithos), this restaurant is around 10km west of town. The food here is great value for money, with good meze and fresh-fish main courses to choose from.

Drinking & Entertainment

The bars and cafes on the waterfront don't offer much variety, but try some of the following.

Ego Bar
BAR

(Doğan Türk; ◷9pm-2am summer) With its chilled-out atmosphere, this is a great spot for an evening drink within the stone walls of an open-air courtyard. In summer it showcases live bands, playing a mix of jazz, rock, blues and soul.

Café 34
BAR, CAFE

(Girne Limanı; ◷4pm-2am) Situated on the edge of the Old Harbour walkway, Café 34 is ideal for a cold beer or coffee and cake by day. At night things liven up with music and local youngsters hitting the scene.

Five Mile
BAR, RESTAURANT

(Yavuz Cikarma Plaji, Alsancak; mains 10-30YTL; ◷dinner) After 10pm the restaurant, with its wooden deck terrace, transforms into a party bar. Now incorporating Escape Beach, it's an open-air all-round drinking, dancing and chill-out zone, with circular leather sofas.

Escape Beach
CLUB

(www.escapebeachclub.com; Yavuz Cikarma Plaji, Alsancak) Now located at Five Mile, this gets packed with clubbers enjoying the rich mix of R&B, hip-hop and Turkish music. Overlooking the sea, it is 20 minutes' drive from Kyrenia on the western coastal road, just out of Alsancak.

Ice Lounge
BAR

(www.icecyprus.com; Yavuz Cikartma Plaji, Alsancak; ◷9pm-2am) Found above Cikarma Plaji beach, in the Alsancak quarter, this club is one of the most popular spots for night life. Iridescent lights glow on its outdoor bars and stage. Also plays host to international DJs during the summer.

🛍 Shopping

There is a small shopping mall with boutiques and brand-name imported goods off Ziya Rızkı Caddesi. There's also a wide range of tourist shops that sell everything from snorkelling gear to leather goods.

Round Tower CRAFTS

(Ziya Rızkı Caddesi; ⊙10am-5.30pm) In the centre of Kyrenia, inside the restored Lusignan-era Round Tower, is this small art-and-crafts shop with a selection of interesting goods such as pottery, rugs and paintings.

Green Jacket BOOKS

(Temmuz Caddesi 20) West of the town centre near the Astro supermarket, this is the place to go for foreign-language books.

ℹ Information

INTERNET ACCESS Cafe Net (Efeler Sokak; per hr 3YTL; ⊙10am-midnight) This is the best place for checking your email, with 12 terminals. English-speaking owner Mehmet Çavuş serves hot and cold drinks and jacket potatoes. It also runs a small book exchange.

Bati Net Cafe (Ziya Rızkı Caddesi; per hr 3YTL; ⊙10am-11pm) West of Belediye Meydanı; has 14 terminals.

MEDICAL SERVICES Akçiçek Hastahanesi (☎815 2254; Mustafa Çağatay Caddesi) Kyrenia's hospital is 300m southeast of the post office.

MONEY There are a number of **ATMs** along Ziya Rızkı Caddesi.

Türk Bankası (Ziya Rızkı Caddesi) Near Belediye Meydanı.

İş Bankası (cnr Ziya Rızkı Caddesi & Atatürk Caddesi)

MONEY-EXCHANGE OFFICES Yazgın Döviz (☎228 6673; Ziya Rızkı Caddesi)

Gesfi Exchange (Kordon Boyu Sokak 40) Opposite the Dome Hotel.

POST Post office (Mustafa Çağatay Caddesi) Southeast 150m from Belediye Meydanı.

TELEPHONE The telecommunications office is directly opposite the post office.

TOILETS Public toilets are on the breakwater, on the western side of the Old Harbour.

TOURIST INFORMATION North Cyprus Tourism Organisation (NCTO; Girne Limanı; ⊙8am-6pm) Found at the western end of the Old Harbour; publishes a free city map in English.

Kyrenia Society (Mersin Caddesi; ⊙10am-noon) Behind the post office. It advertises upcoming events and excursions (particularly in summer). Check the noticeboard for more information.

MOVING ON?

For tips, recommendations and reviews, head to shop.lonelyplanet.com to purchase a downloadable PDF of the Eastern Mediterranean chapter from Lonely Planet's *Turkey* guide.

TRAVEL AGENCIES Ferries to Turkey leave from the **New Harbour** (2.5km east). Tickets are available from the following:

Fergün Denizcilik Şirketi (☎815 3866; Mustafa Çağatay Caddesi 6/2c)

Ertürk Turizm (☎815 2308; fax 815 1808; İskenderum Caddesi) Near the New Harbour.

ℹ Getting There & Away

BUSES & MINIBUSES The long-distance bus station is on Bedrettin Demirel, in the New Town. Minibuses (*dolmuş*) depart from Belediye Meydanı and go to Famagusta (Mağusa, 5YTL, 1¼ hours, every 30 minutes from 7am to 6.30pm) and North Nicosia (Lefkoşa, 3YTL, 20 minutes, every 30 minutes from 7am to 6.30pm).

BOATS Express boats to Taşucu in Turkey leave 9.30am daily (55YTL, three hours) from the New Harbour, east of town. A slow ferry runs daily (40YTL, seven hours). Tickets available at Fergün Denizcilik Şirketi passenger lounge at the port. During summer, twice-weekly express ferry runs to Alanya in Turkey (35 €, 4½ hours).

AIR Cyprus Turkish Airlines (Kıbrıs Türk Hava Yolları, KTHY; ☎815 2513; www.kthy.net /kthyen/html; Philecia Ct, Suite 3, Kordon Boyu Sokak) Has an office west of the Old Harbour.

ℹ Getting Around

CAR HIRE Kyrenia is ideal for walking, but should you need to travel further afield, there are many car-hire outlets.

Prices are similar all over the island; €40-50 per day is average. **Oscar Car Rentals** (☎815 2272; Kordon Boyu Sokak) is opposite the Dome Hotel.

TAXIS Service taxis run from Kyrenia to many destinations, including Ercan airport (30YTL, one hour), Bellapais (12YTL, 20 minutes) and St Hilarion (7YTL, 25 minutes).

AROUND KYRENIA & THE RANGES

Kyrenia is perfectly placed for excursions to other parts of the North, which offers beaches, trekking, mountains and natural wilderness. There are also some incredible medieval castles and ancient sites. The whole area is quite condensed, with short driving distances. Most roads are easily accessible by regular-drive cars.

Hiking

The **Kyrenia Mountain Trail** is an excellent hiking option. It is 240km in total, traversing Northern Cyprus east to west, from **Koruçam Burnu** (Cape Kormakitis) to **Zafer Burnu** (Cape Apostolos Andreas). You can choose a section that appeals to you, or for serious ramblers, it can constitute one long amazing trek, where you'll experience varied environments.

Spring is the best season, as you'll get to see a large number of the impressive 1600 plant, 350 bird and 26 reptile species that live on the Karpas (Kırpaşa) Peninsula. It's also ideal for admiring the wild orchids (p164) that bloom along the ranges, alongside the wild donkeys, ancient churches and deserted ridges.

The NCTO produces a *Mountain Trails* brochure with a map, available from their office in Kyrenia. It covers two main sections in the Kyrenia Range that are ideal starters; all hikers are advised to obtain more complete maps of the area from Green Jacket bookshop in Kyrenia before heading off.

The hike from **Ağırdağ** (Agirda) to **Geçitköy** (Panagra) is a good trek for experienced walkers. Best tackled in sections over a few days, it runs west along the southern flank of the Kyrenia Range. It starts at the village of Ağırdağ on the Kyrenia–North Nicosia road and finishes at Geçitköy on the Kyrenia–Morfou (Güzelyurt) road. The trail passes through **Lapta** (Lapithos; p174), an ideal stop, and most sections take two to three hours.

The hike from Alevkaya to Kantara is a long easterly trail, with over 40km of hiking, connecting the Alevkaya Herbarium Forest Station (p172) to Kantara Castle.

The hike along the spine of the **Beşparmak (Pentadaktylos) Range** takes in forest trails and several villages along the way. Again, this is best walked in sections, staying in one of these villages. Check out www.kyreniamountaintrail.org to help plan your route.

🦎 Beaches

Northern Cyprus has separated many of its beaches into paid and public beaches, called *halk plajlari*. To benefit from the best amenities available, visit the paid beaches surrounding Kyrenia; they are designed to be tourist friendly and will cost you a nominal amount of around 6YTL to 10YTL. The public beaches are now mostly frequented by locals, who generally want to bathe and picnic, and while some are wonderful, they're generally underdeveloped, with few or no facilities.

Yavuz Çıkarma (Five Mile) is by far one of Kyrenia's best swimming beaches. Situated west of the town, it is also the location of the Five Mile bar and restaurant (p166). The sandy cove goes by three names: Altınkaya, after the rock next to it; Beşinci Mil, meaning five mile; and Yavuz Çıkarma, meaning the resolute outbreak. This was one of the beaches used by the Turkish Army to launch the 1974 invasion. On the road overlooking the beach you'll notice a phallic-looking **monument**, a salute to the event. The monument is known locally as 'the Turkish erection'.

Today the beach is very popular, and during summer you need to get there early to find a space to sit. Hire a sun lounger and an umbrella to counter the lack of shade. There are also a multitude of water sports available around the rocky islet that protects the beach from the open sea. Swimmers should be mindful of the strong wind that can come in off the open water, which is great for waterskiing, kiteboarding and jet-skiing.

Çatalköy Beach, 7km east of Kyrenia, is a quieter, less developed beach. The beach here is narrow with soft sand, in a protected and attractive little bay. You can rent sunbeds here and dive from the pontoon. The beach is 1.5km to the right, off the main road.

A private beach further east, **Vrysi (Acapulco) Beach** is managed by the **Acapulco Holiday Village** (☑824 4110), which caters mainly to package tourists. It does accept casual guests as well, and admission to the complex is 5YTL with access to all the facilities.

Another 3km along, **Lara (Vakıflar) Beach** is particularly popular with expats. The beach has grey compact sand and clean water. It also has good toilet and changing-room facilities, near the small snack bar.

Alagadı (Turtle) Beach, approximately 19km east of Kyrenia, is where the Society for the Protection of Turtles (SPOT) has its small monitoring station, called the 'Goat

THE TALE OF TWO TURTLES

Turtles have been living on earth for over 200 million years, which is far longer than humans. There are eight species of turtles in the world, and two of these species live in the eastern Mediterranean.

The green turtle (*Chelonia mydas*) and the loggerhead turtle (*Caretta caretta*) have long lived in the Mediterranean basin and in particular on the island of Cyprus. It is estimated that the biggest population of the now-endangered green turtle lives in Cyprus, with many making the beaches of the north coast and the Karpas (Kırpaşa) Peninsula their favoured nesting grounds. The loggerhead turtle, now classified 'vulnerable' by conservationists, also nests on these pristine coastlines.

Gradual human encroachment into turtle territory has lessened the survival rate of these wonderful marine animals, and their numbers have decreased significantly over the years.

One of the turtles' prime breeding grounds in Northern Cyprus is Alagadı Beach, 19km east of Kyrenia (Girne). Golden Beach (Nangomi Bay) and large sections of Famagusta Bay are also popular breeding grounds, as is the largely untouched northern tract of the Karpas (Kırpaşa) Peninsula.

So visitors to Cypriot beaches should be aware that their presence during nesting season (particularly at night) disrupts the breeding cycle.

When visiting a turtle beach, do so with caution and care. Some beaches (Alagadı Beach) are closed between dusk and dawn, and have the breeding areas marked with protective cages. On others, simple ideas like planting umbrellas close to the water's edge, helps immensely in not disturbing the eggs nestled in the soft sand.

If you are particularly keen to see some turtles, go with a professional volunteer group such as the **Cyprus Turtle Project** (www.seaturtle.org).

Shed'. This is not really used as a swimming beach, but you are able to enjoy the habitat. Its twin sandy beaches are intentionally undeveloped, as they are considered turtle territory, although weekend revellers sometimes aren't considerate enough of the area, leaving rubbish and holding barbecues. The beach is closed from 8pm to 8am from May to October. If you get hungry, **St Kathleen's Restaurant** (☏0533 861 7640) is on the nearby main road. The meze, grills and fish dishes, such as *tsipura* (bream), are excellent and good value.

Golf

Korineum   GOLF
(☏6001500; www.korineumgolf.com; Mersin 10 Esentepe) Situated 10 minutes east of Alagadı (Turtle) Beach, in the Esentepe region, this course offers 18 holes for you to tee-off at. There is also a pro shop, driving range, restaurant, hotel and clubhouse. You can pay your daily green fees at the club; during the summer high season, 18 holes costs €68 and nine holes €35. Golf carts start at €25 a day.

ⓘ Getting Around

BUSES & MINIBUSES Kyrenia's public transport consists of buses and minibuses that run during the day between the major towns and larger villages. Fares are cheap (around 3YTL), but the buses can be late and infrequent.

SERVICE TAXIS Known as *dolmuş*, these taxis also travel between local towns and villages. They are well priced (4YTL to 6YTL) and do go to some rural destinations. Taxi drivers tend to be rather aggressive on the roads, so if you are a nervous passenger, you may want to hire your own car.

PRIVATE TAXIS Hired from near the Old Harbour and will take you anywhere.

CYCLING A good-weather alternative, as the region provides for some of the best cycling in Northern Cyprus. East–west routes are mostly flat and well serviced with places to stay, eateries and beaches.

St Hilarion Castle

The outline of the **castle** (☏0533 161 276; adult/child 7/3YTL; ☉9am-6.30pm Jun–mid-Sep, 9am-12.30pm & 1.30-4.45pm mid-Sep–May) and its fairytale-like remains become fully apparent once you're beneath it. The stone walls and ruined buildings blend seamlessly into the rocky landscape. The castle (*kalesi* in Turkish), with its hidden rooms, tunnels, overgrown gardens, steep staircases and paths, will leave you gasping for breath and children asking for more.

Rumour has it that Walt Disney drew inspiration from the jagged contours of St Hilarion when he created the animated film *Snow White*. And a local legend tells that the castle once had 101 rooms, the last of which was a secret internal garden belonging to a fairy 'queen'. The enchantress, who seduced hunters, shepherds and travellers, would rob them, placing them into a deep slumber.

The castle's real history is a bit less fantastic. The lofty fort is named after the monk Hilarion, who fled persecution in the Holy Land. He lived (and died) in a mountain cave that overlooked the Kyrenia plain, protecting the pass between the coast and Nicosia (Lefkosia).

In the 10th century, the Byzantines built a church and monastery over Hilarion's tomb. Due to the site's strategic position, it was used as a watchtower and beacon during the Arab raids of the 7th and 8th centuries. It was an important link in the communication chain between Buffavento and Kantara castles further east.

In 1191 Guy de Lusignan seized control of St Hilarion, defeating the self-proclaimed (Byzantine) emperor of Cyprus, Isaak Komninos. The castle was then extensively expanded and used as both a military outpost and a summer residence of the Lusignan court. Later, during Venetian rule, the castle was neglected and fell into disrepair.

In 1964 the (TMT) Turk Müdafaa Teskilati, an underground Turkish Nationalist group, took control of the castle again for its strategic position. It has been in Turkish Cypriot hands ever since, with a sheltered Turkish military base located on the ridge below.

The site consists of three main parts that are not immediately obvious. You enter the barbican main gate into the **lower enceinte**, once used as the main garrison and stabling area. Then follow the meandering path up to the **middle enceinte**, originally protected and sealed by a drawbridge. Here, remains of the church, barrack rooms, four-level royal apartments and a large cistern, vital to the storage of water, are found.

Access to the **upper enceinte** is via a steep, winding track (now paved), which leads to the Lusignan Gate. Guarded by the Byzantine tower it opens on to the central courtyard, adorned with more royal apartments, kitchens and ancillary chambers.

Finally one last climb takes you to **Prince John's Tower**. Legend has it that Prince John of Antioch became convinced his two Bulgarian bodyguards were plotting to assassinate him. He had them thrown from the cliff, to their deaths.

The arduous climb to the tower is well worth the stunning views, and on clear days you can even see the Taurus Mountains, 100km away in Turkey. In summer it's best to arrive early and avoid climbing in the heat of the day.

Bellapais (Beylerbeyi)

The vertiginous road to this high mountain village leads you to the spectacular **Bellapais Abbey**, and its impressive and endless views of the horizon. Bellapais itself is a wonderfully verdant village that makes a perfect day trip from Kyrenia. Just past the monastery there is a large car park on the left, so you can avoid stopping in the main street.

The village, immortalised by the British writer Lawrence Durrell, who lived here during the Ethniki Organosi tou Kypriakou Agona (EOKA; National Organisation for the Cypriot Struggle) uprising against British rule, showed his lasting love for the village (and for Cyprus) in his entertaining memoir *Bitter Lemons of Cyprus*.

◉ Sights

Bellapais Abbey   HISTORICAL SITE
(adult/child at ticket booth 9/3YTL; ☺9am-8pm Jun–mid-Sep, 9am-12.30pm & 1.30-4.45pm mid-Sep–May) The exquisite ruins of this Augustinian monastery are reason enough to drive up the mountain. It was built in the 12th century by Augustinian monks fleeing Palestine after the fall of Jerusalem to the Saracen leader, Saladin (Selahaddin Eyyubi) in 1187. The monks established the monastery and called it Abbaye de la Paix (Abbey of Peace), from which the corrupted version of the name, Bellapais, evolved.

The original structure, built between 1198 and 1205, was augmented between 1267 and 1284, during the reign of Hugh III. The cloisters and large refectory were added after that by Hugh IV (1324–59), and these embellishments are most of what remains today.

Now an interesting mixture of well-preserved parts and ruins cover the area. The **refectory** on the north side of the cloister is frequently used for gatherings, events and wedding photos. From here you can savour incredible views of the sea and plains below. On the western side is the **kitchen court**, which has all but a few walls remaining. Those who are more daring scramble onto a particularly precarious section of wall for even better views.

The dim **church** is in decent condition, and remains much as it was in 1976, when the last of the stoic Orthodox faithful had to leave.

The 14th-century **cloister**, lined with cypress trees, is the monastery's most poignant section. It is almost intact, apart from its western side, where the walls have fallen or been destroyed. It now overlooks **Kybele** restaurant, where you can appreciate the ambience from the open courtyard, while you dine on meze.

Home of Lawrence Durrell   NOTABLE BUILDING
(admission 13YTL; ◎11.30am-1pm Sep) Bellapais' resident literary genius, Durrell, lived here in the early 1950s, when he described the near-idyllic, mixed-community life in his *Bitter Lemons of Cyprus* memoir. With those days now gone, the book is still considered by many to be compulsory reading for visitors to Cyprus.

The **Tree of Idleness**, under which Durrell's characters spent many an indolent hour, still remains. However, Durrell's house (marked by a yellow plaque over the main door) is now a private residence and is only open during September. To reach the house,

head inland along the street to the right of the Huzur Ağaç Restaurant. You'll find it 200m further along on the left, in the narrow alleyway.

⭐ Festivals & Events

Bellapais Music Festival   MUSIC
(www.bellapaisfestival.com) Held annually during May and June, the festival takes place in and around the abbey. It consists of concerts, recitals and brass-band performances in the refectory. Look out for event details in Kyrenia and around town.

✗ Eating

TOP
CHOICE **Kybele**   CYPRIOT €€
(abbey grounds; mains 30YTL; ◎dinner) Surrounded by lush foliage, this place has fantastic views of the abbey, as it's right next door. With well-priced, traditional food and excellent service, it's perfect in summer and has cool welcoming gardens.

Guthrie's Bistro Bar   INTERNATIONAL €€€
(✆815 2820; mains 45YTL; ◎dinner, drinks all day) This small restaurant in a gorgeous garden serves freshly prepared food. The menu includes starters such as gazpacho (cold tomato soup), or *haloumi* (*helimi*) and tomatoes; mains of *kleftiko,* garlic chicken or sweet-and-sour pork; and desserts of ice creams and fruit compote. Reservations are usually required.

Huzur Ağaç (Tree of Idleness) Restaurant   MEDITERRANEAN €€€
(✆815 3380; mains 35YTL) A contender for the title of Durrell's famed 'Tree of Idleness', a

KYRENIA (GIRNE) & THE NORTHERN COAST BELLAPAIS (BEYLERBEYI)

TWO TREE HILL

When writer Lawrence Durrell took up residence in Bellapais (Beylerbeyi) between 1953 and 1956, he little realised the minor controversy he would leave behind, almost 50 years later. His famous book *Bitter Lemons of Cyprus* described life in the then blissfully bucolic mixed community and his trials and tribulations while purchasing and renovating a house in the village, along with the intrigues and gossip of village life.

Among the villagers' favourite activities was spending many hours in idle conversation under the so-called 'Tree of Idleness', which dominated the main square. However, throughout the book, Durrell never once mentioned what kind of tree it was. Maybe it was a plane, or a mulberry, or perhaps an oak?

Today there are two trees that vie for the title. One is a leafy mulberry tree, overshadowing the coffee shop next to the monastery ticket office. The other contender, hardly 20m away, is a Robinia casting shade over the Huzur Ağaç (Tree of Idleness) Restaurant. In fairness, both trees qualify for the role pretty well: both have their supporters and draw idle crowds of onlookers who like to sit and drink coffee or a cold beer, just as the villagers did in Durrell's day. So pick your tree, sit idly by, and ponder.

200-year-old Robinia, is here, which makes for atmospheric dining. The fixed menu in the evening has an abundance of starters, appetisers and a main. The restaurant also has a decent snack menu during the day.

Paşa   TURKISH €
(meals 12YTL) A basic eatery at the end of the main street, Paşa offers *lahmacun* (Turkish pizza) and Turkish ravioli, served with a good portion of salad. This is a simple and humble venue, with good homemade food.

Buffavento Castle

Situated between the Kantara and St Hilarion castles, **Buffavento** (Buffavento Kalesi; admission free; ☉dawn-dusk) perches precariously at 940m, overlooking the Mesaoria (Mesarya) plain. The constant pummelling it endures from high winds is how it derived its name, 'challenger of the winds' in Italian.

Little is known about its early history. In medieval times, it was known as the Castle of the Lion, when Richard the Lionheart took it from the daughter of Byzantine emperor Isaak Komninos in 1191. The Lusignans later used it as a prison and beacon tower, connecting both Kantara to the east and St Hilarion to the west.

Now the attraction of the castle lies in its remoteness and the breath-taking views from its ruins. It has deteriorated more than the other castles, but its protected walkways and the views from the top are truly incredible.

The castle is divided into two main sections, the lower enceinte and the upper enceinte, which occupies a smaller area on the rocky peak. The castle was built in such a way that no fortifications other than its outer walls were needed. Its naturally guarded location provides for only one approach, through the main entrance.

Certainly getting there is half the fun. Prominently signposted (as Buffavento Kalesi) off the Beşparmak (Pentadaktylos) Pass, it's a 15-minute drive along the track to the parking area below the castle. From here it's a steep but gradual walk that takes about 40 minutes. Closed footwear is definitely advised.

Panagia Absinthiotissa Monastery

Located on the flank of the Beşparmak Range, this monastery sits idyllically among juniper trees, taking in the views over the Mesaoria (Mesarya) plain.

The late-Byzantine-era monastery, with its colossal 12-windowed drum and dome, was inhabited by Latin monks during the 15th century. They added gothic vaulting and an unusual narthex with double apses at its end. Across the courtyard, to the north, is the refectory with its shallow ceiling, vaulting and distinctive lancet windows.

Fastidiously restored during the 1960s, the monastery was unfortunately badly vandalised after 1974, with its many frescos either stolen or defaced.

The monastery is approximately 15 minutes from Buffavento Castle. To make this your next stop, simply exit the car park and follow the tarmac road.

Alevkaya Herbarium

On the back road in the Beşparmak (Pentadaktylos) Range, you'll find the forest station between Esentepe (Agios Amvrosios) and Değirmenlik (Kythrea). The **herbarium** (admission free; ☉8am-4pm) here is home to endemic Cypriot flora, including some 1250 native plant species. It displays a range of preserved and live specimens, developed from a collection created by English botanist Deryck Viney, whose book *Illustrated Flora of North Cyprus* documents the country's diverse botanical treasures.

To get to the herbarium, take the signposted forest road, off the southern side

---

CHILDREN'S CYPRUS: OCTOPUS AQUA PARK

The nonstop summer fun of water parks are all the rage in Cyprus and junior travellers love them. The **Octopus Aqua Park** (☑853 9674; Beşparmak Caddesi, Çatalköy; ☉8am-5pm summer), 8km east of Kyrenia, is a haven of water, where the little ones can climb, swing, slide and bounce on watery and dry spaces, while their parents relax at the pool bar and restaurant.

START **OZANKÖY (KAZAFANI)**
FINISH **KAPLICA (DAVLOS)**
DISTANCE **115KM**
DURATION **SIX TO EIGHT HOURS**

MEDITERRANEAN SEA

Driving Tour
Combing the North Eastern Ridge & Coast

Barely 4km east of Kyrenia, pretty **1 Ozanköy** is noted for its olive oil and carob syrups. After picking up a bottle and taking a look at the medieval church, head east to **2 Çatalköy** (via the road of the same name). Its caves provided sanctuary to the hermit Epiktitos in the 13th century. Take the northeast road (signed as 'Uğur Mumcu Bulvan') to the fork, staying left and hugging the coastal road. Here you'll stop at the remains of the Neolithic site of **3 Vrysi** and its eroding headland. Getting back to the coastal road, head east for 10km to **4 Alagadı (Turtle) Beach** (turn left at the 'Alagadı Beach' sign), great for a dip or some in-season turtle-watching. Continue along the coast, then take the hard right signed as 'Karaağaç'. The mountain scenery here is outstanding. Turn right for the forestry station (signed) and picnic area at **5 Alevkaya** (Halevga), where nature lovers can check out the herbarium. Continuing 2.5km to the west (on the main road), you'll see the battered ruins of the 11th-

century Coptic Armenian **6 Sourp Magar monastery** on your right, nestled in pine trees below. To get there, turn right at the picnic site and follow the forestry track that winds down to the church. Double back east for 17km, parallel to the mountains, following the scenic ridge road (past the outskirts of Esentepe) to the Byzantine **7 Antifonitis monastery**.

At the nearby mountain junction, take the main (paved) road southeast, passing the modest village of Bahceli (Kalogaia), before views of the sea prompt you to turn right and rejoin the coastal trek. After you pass the proposed marina town of Küçük Erenköy (Kapsalos), 40km of naked coastline follows, with fleeting glimpses of abandoned carob warehouses. The road gently follows the shoreline until you reach the resettled town of **8 Kaplıca** (Davlos), where you can watch the sunset on the small beach and finish with a giant shish kebab at 'Kaplica', the town's best restaurant.

BUYER BEWARE

Over 4000 Britons live in Northern Cyprus. Its picturesque location and relatively low property and land prices make this an enticing location for a Mediterranean summer home. However, overseas buyers need to be wary of unauthorised selling and the legalities involved. Cases have been heard in the European Court of Human Rights where Turkish land-occupiers have sold Greek-owned land, belonging to those displaced after the 1974 division. Buyers have had to demolish the houses they built on such land after the court ruled in favour of the legal, Greek owners. So, if you're tempted to buy in the North, check that all papers are valid and legal and that land is being sold by the correct owners.

of Pentadaktylos Pass. Alternatively, from the northern coastal road, take the road signposted as Karaağaç (Harkia) or Esentepe.

KYRENIA WEST

Lapta (Lapithos)

Lapta was one of the original city-kingdoms of Cyprus and a regional capital under Roman rule. Its abundant water supply and protected position have made it a favourite choice of foreign rulers and settlers for centuries.

A mixed village pre-1974, Lapta accommodated Greek and Turkish Cypriots in harmony, until the skirmishes of the 1960s saw a mosque's bell tower spoiled in the wake of local differences. In the mid-1990s, forest fires devastated much of the region but fortunately missed this town.

Popular for day trips, with its proximity to Kyrenia, the sprawling village is best enjoyed on foot, with its green leafy lanes and traditional charm. Today the village is populated by a blend of expats, mainland Turks and Turkish Cypriot villagers.

The best place to eat in town is **Başpınar restaurant** (☑821 8661; mains 20YTL), located above the village at the top of the hill. It sits around an old Roman aqueduct

with fantastic views. It serves rabbit stews and the usual meze. Call in advance for a booking.

If you need more action, head to the coastline of Lapta, where you'll find five-star resort hotels and casinos, like the huge **Lapethos Resort Hotel Casino & Spa** (☑821 8669), which has pools, waterslides and an aqua park. The casinos themselves are often frequented by mainlanders coming over on weekend ferries from Turkey and Greek Cypriots arriving from the South, where gambling is still technically illegal.

THE NORTHWEST

The northwest region of the Kyrenia Range includes the Koruçam (Kormakitis) Peninsula. To the south are the agricultural town of Morfou and its bay (Güzelyurt Körfezi). The pretty hilled village of Lefke (Lefka) and one-time mining port of Gemikonağı (Karavostasi) are to the west. Further still are the important archaeological sites of Ancient Soloi and Ancient Vouni.

Distances here are relatively short, with the journey best seen in a circular route, returning to North Nicosia (Lefkoşa) via the peninsula and Kyrenia, or vice versa. There is also a border crossing (at the Green Line) to the Republic of Cyprus, at Zodhia, near Morfou.

🏊 Beaches

The 12km stretch west of Gemikonağı has a mixture of sand and pebbly beaches, ending at the border with the South.

A pebbled beach with stretches of imported sand, **Yedidalga Belediyesi Plajı** has a wooden pier for diving and swimming, a small bar and restaurant, a changing room and toilet facilities. It is well signposted and easily found.

Asmalı Beach is the next best spot, in front of the border village Yeşilirmak (Limnitis). It's a clean pebbled beach, with a few restaurants surrounding it, catering to those who travel this far. While here check out the huge grapevine, planted in 1947, that completely covers the outside dining area of the Asmalı Beach Restaurant to the west.

ℹ Getting Around

BUSES Regular daily buses run from North Nicosia (Lefkoşa) to the following:

Morfou (3YTL, every 30 minutes)
Gemikonağı (5YTL, every 30 minutes via Morfou)

Lefke (5YTL, every 30 minutes via Morfou)

SERVICE TAXIS Vehicles from North Nicosia (Lefkoşa) or Kyrenia do service the area in round trips. However, getting around is far easier with your own transport, especially if you want to see Ancient Soloi and Ancient Vouni.

Koruçam (Kormakitis) Peninsula

A trip to the exposed northwestern tip of Northern Cyprus, known as **Koruçam Burnu** (Cape Kormakitis), is a fantastic day excursion, with a number of deserted beaches on the way. Pack a picnic lunch, and enjoy the solitude at the cape and its surrounds. Apart from being the 'land's end', it is also home to one of Cyprus' least-known religious communities, the Maronites.

Getting there is pretty simple, with a mostly paved road taking you almost all the way. It's best tackled as a loop starting from the northern end of the Kyrenia–Morfou road, at the junction after the village of **Karşıyaka** (Vasileia). Follow signs to the mainland-Turk settlement of **Sadrazamköy** (Livera).

From the junction follow the signs to Sadrazamköy (Livera). On your right you will see signs to the petite **Horse Shoe Beach** and **Horseshoe Beach Restaurant** (☏851 6664; grills & fish 8YTL), which are perfect spots for lunch and a swim.

To get to the cape, follow the winding road for 10km past Sadrazamköy; from here you find a 3.5km dirt track, which is easily driven with a conventional car. There are bare rocks, a solar-powered shipping beacon and a small rocky islet just offshore. This is the island's closest point to Turkey, which is a mere 60km across the sea.

For a different and interesting drive back, go via the picturesque inland loop road, through Koruçam village and past the massive Maronite **Church of Agios Georgios**, built in 1940 with funds raised by the villagers.

Koruçam's Maronites have kept their dialect of Aramaic (the forgotten language of Christ) for hundreds of years, interlacing it with Greek, Turkish, French and Italian words, creating a richer version of their own language. While most communicate in this dialect or Turkish, some locals at the small coffee shop in the village speak Greek. **Yorgo's Restaurant** (set menu 15YTL) in the square, opposite the church, is a fantastic place to have lunch. It serves succulent *kleftiko* and meze prepared daily in the outdoor ovens.

The final leg back to the Kyrenia–Morfou road is through a Turkish military area, with checkpoints at which you may be stopped. Once past, get on the main highway at Çamlibel (Myrtou) and head back to Kyrenia. From here you can also go south to Morfou or turn southeast toward North Nicosia (Lefkoşa).

THE MARONITES OF KORUÇAM (KORMAKITIS)

During the 4th century Maronites broke away from the prevailing Orthodox religious theory of Christianity, which said God was both man and god. In contrast, they followed the Monophysite religious line, which states that God could only be viewed as one spiritual persona.

Persecuted by Orthodox Christians for their beliefs, they first sought refuge in Lebanon and Syria, before coming to Cyprus in the 12th century in the wake of the crusaders, whom they had helped as auxiliaries in the Holy Land campaign.

Post-1974 the Cypriot Maronites have clung to a tenuous existence in Koruçam village, where they still maintain a church. Over the years, the once-vigorous congregation has gradually left, and now barely 100 remain to keep the old traditions and religion alive. The Maronites, like the Armenians and Latin religious communities, had to choose allegiance with either the Greek or Turkish communities in the 1960s. They chose the Greeks, and since '74 the youth from the village has gradually all but disappeared, crossing over into the South to study in Greek schools. Those who remained in the North have managed to tread the fine line between political and religious allegiances, with some degree of success. Pre-2003 their relatives from the South were even able to visit them on weekends. Since the borders have opened, the South's Maronites visit for longer periods. Many hope that some of the younger generations will return to live here, preserving the village and its people's traditions.

Morfou (Güzelyurt)

POP EST 15,000

The quiet town of Morfou (renamed Güzelyurt by Turkish Cypriots) was once the centre for Cyprus' lucrative citrus industry.

Turkish Cypriot businessman Asil Nadir owned the company Sunzest here and produced vast quantities of orange juice for the export market. Now the company languishes in receivership as Nadir awaits trial in the UK, and the potentially lucrative citrus industry has taken a severe downturn. The majority of the citrus groves here are still owned by Greek Cypriots, and the area has remained an important point of contention in all reunification talks since 1974.

The vast groves start shortly before the village of Şahinler (Masari), stretching all the way to the sea and watered by a series of underground aquifers. Unfortunately, the level of water reserves has fallen dramatically. This, combined with rising salinity levels in the underground water and a lack of cultivation and maintenance, means that the once magnificently fertile groves have suffered badly.

During better days, in the early 20th century, Morfou's vibrant oranges were transported by train across the Mesaoria (Mesarya) plain to Famagusta for overseas export. Although this old train route ceased passenger services in 1932, it continued to transport freight until 1951. The line has long since been abandoned and fallen into complete disrepair. You can, however, still see one of the two surviving locomotives, a 1924 Baldwin, out of Philadelphia, at the Belediye Parki, just outside Morfou.

Morfou now consists of a few narrow, winding streets, small shops and sputtering agriculture. In the town square an impressive mosque has been built, across from which you can see the Agios Mamas Orthodox Church, dedicated to the island's beloved tax-repelling patron saint. The church was formerly the site of a pagan temple. Before 1974, the faithful used to visit the ancient marble tomb of Saint Mamas, from which a mysterious liquid is said to have oozed when the Ottomans pierced it looking for treasure. The liquid, apparently flowing freely at irregular intervals, was supposed to have cured earaches; as such, ear-shaped offerings can be seen around the tomb. The church is usually locked, but you can gain access from the curator at the nearby Archaeological and Natural History Museum (admission 6YTL; ⊙9am-6pm). The museum itself is worth a quick look, although it doesn't house a great deal, with basic displays of odd taxidermy, artefacts and ancient pottery from Toumba tou Skourou and Soli.

Morfou also has one of the best meze houses in the North, Nayazi Şah (☏714 3064; meze 25YTL), located south of the northern roundabout. There is regular live music on weekends and constant platters of meats, including quail and lamb sausages.

Gemikonaği (Karavostasi)

From the calm and secluded rough-pebble beach, you can see the entire coast stretching northeast around Morfou Bay. Although the beaches here are not as visually appealing as the softer, sandy ones found on the north coast, there are far fewer swimmers.

Pre-1974, local villagers from Morfou and the Troödos foothills came to the bay to swim, and now with the border crossings open, some are again.

The once-flourishing port of Gemikonaği dominates the bay, with its abandoned jetty slowly sagging by the port itself.

East of town, you'll notice the scarred hinterland, heavily mined by a large conglomerate. It ceased mining after 1974 and has left the town with a decidedly backwater appearance.

Nonetheless, the town supports a small local tourist industry, thanks to a few good restaurants and its beaches. Visitors who prefer more rustic and less touristy swimming and dining options should stop here. The nearby Mardin Restaurant (☏727 7527; mains 35YTL) has a terrace that overlooks the sea, offering quality fish dishes, meze, and full Adana kebabs. There is also an artificial beach next door, to cool off in afterwards.

Lefke (Lefka)

POP EST 9000

A few kilometres from Gemikonaği, the road runs at a right angle to the hillside village of Lefke. Its position amid limitless greenery and rolling hills gives it a pleasant and fresh feel.

The town's name is derived from the Greek word *lefka* (meaning 'poplar'). Today, with more orange groves and palm trees than poplars, the village is known for its superb citrus fruits.

Home to a large community of British ex-pats, it is also regarded as a stronghold for the Islamic faith. It is the headquarters of the Naqshbandi order of Sufism and their charismatic leader, Şeyh Nazım Kıbrıslı, and his followers. This order follows the principles of Islam dutifully and urges less-strict Turkish Cypriots to do the same.

There is little to do in the village itself, save for taking in the **Piri Osman Pasha Mosque** and its courtyard, walking the windy streets, eating the delicious oranges and spotting pieces of broken aqueducts.

The border crossing at Zodhia is best reached by the main road south from Morfou. The crossing has opened up the region again to Tylliria and Pafos Forest, which are only 3km away. The roads through these mountains are buffeted by winds but are an enjoyable drive. There's also another (new) border crossing not far from Ancient Vouni, at Limnitis-Yeşilırmak, close to Kato Pyrgos, so now the region is even more accessible.

Ancient Soloi

Another of the ancient city kingdoms, **Soloi** (Soli Harabeleri; adult/child 7/3YTL; ⊙9am-7pm Jun–mid-Sep, 9am-12.30pm & 1.30-4.45pm mid-Sep–May) was originally referred to as Si-il-lu, on an Assyrian tribute list that dates from 700 BC.

In 580 BC, King Philokyprios moved his capital here, from Aepia, on the advice of his mentor, the Athenian philosopher Solon. Philokyprios promptly renamed the citadel Soloi in his honour.

In 498 BC, with the island under Persian rule, Soloi was part of the Ionian revolt, formed by Onesilous, king of Salamis. He had united all the city-kingdoms of Cyprus (except Amathous) in an attempt to overthrow the empire, but was ultimately defeated.

Soloi then languished until Roman times, when it flourished once again thanks to its rich copper mines. As was the case in many parts of Cyprus, Soloi and its wealth suffered sacking and looting by Arab raiders in the 7th century AD.

Today the site consists of two main parts: the (now covered) **basilica** near the entrance to the site, and the **theatre**, up the hill and south of the basilica. The remains of a royal palace can also be seen at the **acropolis** next to the theatre, though it is believed that this dates from a later period.

St Mark was baptised at this site by St Auxibius, and its first **church** is thought

---

KEEPING THE COAST

The stretch of coast from Kyrenia (Girne) to Yenierenköy (Yiallousa) was once one of the most untouched habitats in the region. Today it's seen many changes. New roadways have caused great swaths of coastline to be paved, and large stretches of undisturbed land have been heavily and quickly developed, with tourism complexes shooting up en masse.

This development began in earnest when the 2004 Annan Plan, which provided a framework for the island's reunification, stipulated that all undeveloped Greek land in the North would be returned to its pre-1974 owners, and that compensation would be awarded in cases where land had already been developed. Ultimately the South rejected the Annan Plan by majority referendum. However, Northern developers ploughed ahead in case an agreement eventuated.

Turkish Cypriot newspaper *Yeni Duzen* stated that, in 2000, new developments covered 607,000 sq metres. In 2005, this area had increased to over 4.4 sq km. Development has affected much natural habitat, regional wildlife and many ancient olive groves. Cultural heritage sites are also at risk. In 2004 the Turkish Cypriot Department of Antiquities and Museums was up in arms after the necropolis of Vounos, near Kyrenia, was damaged: 140 ancient tombs were 'bulldozed, damaged and completely flattened' by a private company building luxury-home complexes. Even after discovery, the company pushed ahead, citing its right to build with government permits. Politically, these incidents have only added to Greek Cypriot concerns over their rights and land ownership, further complicating the most difficult aspect of any resolution process between North and South. For now, environmentalists on both sides would settle for measured, sustainable and eco-friendly development that would keep certain areas safe while negotiations continue to secure the island's future.

to have been built in the 4th century. From what's left today, it is difficult to appreciate the size and extent of the church, which by all accounts, was impressive. Most notable are the surviving decorated floors, including the mosaic of a swan, with entwined floral patterns and small dolphins nearby.

The **Roman theatre** is somewhat restored, after much of its original stonework, taken by the British in the late 19th century, was used to rebuild the dockside at Port Said. The theatre is said to have been able to accommodate up to 4000 spectators in its day. The famous Roman statuette of Aphrodite of Soli was discovered nearby. It is now on display in the Cyprus Museum in Lefkosia (Nicosia; p127).

Ancient Vouni

With a superb hilltop location, this **ancient site** (Vouni Sarayı Kalıntıları; adult/child 6/3YTL; ☺9am-5pm Jun–mid-Sep, 9am-12.30pm & 1.30-4.45pm mid-Sep–May) originally housed a palace and an extensive complex of buildings, dating back to the 4th century BC.

Its origins and history are convoluted, but it's speculated that the palace was built by a Persian ruler from the nearby city-kingdom of Marion (today's Polis). The intent was to watch over the nearby Greek-aligned city of Soloi. However, this is unconfirmed at best, and based on scant entries by Herodotus, in Book V of his *Histories*. It is true, however, that the stronghold does exhibit Persian palace architecture, which was added to and embellished later under Hellenistic rulers.

The site consists of a discernible **megaron** (three-part rectangular room with central hearth and throne), private rooms and steps leading down to a courtyard under which is the **cistern**. Here there is a pear-shaped stone believed to have supported a windlass (a machine for raising weights).

The palace was burned down in 380 BC (it's not known why or by whom) and was never re-established. Today the site stands forlornly on its hill, commanding excellent views of the region. It is reached by following a narrow road, off the main highway (signposted as Vouni Sarayı) to the north, until you reach the car park. Entry is paid at the ticket office at the very top.

Famagusta (Mağusa) & the Karpas (Kırpaşa) Peninsula

Includes »

Famagusta (Mağusa) ... 182
Ancient Salamis............ 188
Ancient Enkomi
(Alasia)........................... 191
İskele (Trikomo)............. 191
Boğaz (Bogazi) 193
Karpas (Kırpaşa)
Peninsula 193
Kantara Castle 194
Yenierenköy
(Yiallousa).................... 195
Sipahi (Agia Triada)...... 195
Agios Filon
& Afendrika 196
Monastery of
Apostolos Andreas 196

Why Go?

Arguably the island's most captivating region, with a wealth of historical buildings, ancient ruins and archaeological gifts of incredible beauty, Famagusta and the peninsula offer vast potential and myriad discoveries for the independent traveller.

The ancient city of Salamis is one of the island's most impressive windows into the Hellenic world, and the coast of the Karpas (Kırpaşa) Peninsula, the long stretch of virginal land pointing towards the Asian mainland, is mesmerising. Even with renewed efforts to develop the area it remains one of the quietest and most serene parts of the country, with fantastic natural beaches and the wilderness of nature.

At the very tip of the peninsula is the revered Orthodox monastery of Apostolos Andreas, one of the few churches in the North to survive invasion and to which Greek Cypriots still make a twice-yearly pilgrimage.

Best Places to Eat

» Aspava Restaurant (p186)
» Ginkgo (p186)
» Cyprus House Restaurant (p186)
» Petek Confectioner (p186)

Best Places to Stay

» Crystal Rocks (p211)
» Salamis Bay Conti (p211)
» Nitovikla Garden (p212)
» Karpaz Arch Houses (p212)
» Club Malibu (p212)

When to Go

From March to May northern beaches are visited by a variety of bird life, such as hoopoes, rollers and golden orioles. In September and October the peninsula's wild beaches become home to rare species of Mediterranean turtles that nest and hatch their eggs in the soft sands.

Midsummer evenings in June and July are filled with music, dancing and theatre as Famagusta takes centre stage during the city's international art and culture festival, held in parts of the Old Town and at the ancient ruins of Salamis.

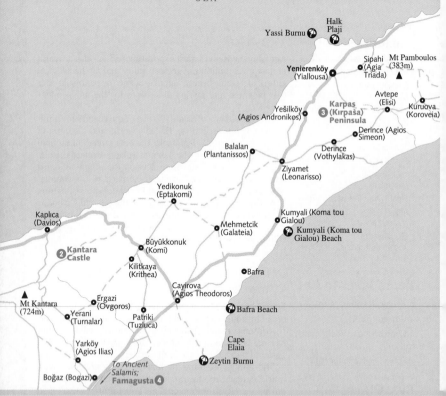

Famagusta (Mağusa) & the Karpas (Kırpaşa) Peninsula Highlights

1 Exploring one of the most important cities of Cypriot antiquity at **Ancient Salamis** (p188)

2 Climbing the ramparts of **Kantara Castle** (p194) and savouring its spectacular views of the coast and peninsula

3 Enjoying the silence and solitude offered by the wild landscapes of the **Karpas (Kırpaşa) Peninsula** (p193)

Zafer Burnu
(Cape Apostolos
Andreas)

Kleides

7 Monastery of
Apostolos Andreas

5 Golden Beach
(Nangomi Bay)

Agios Filon
Beach

6 Agios
Filon

Dipkarpaz
(Rizokarpaso)

Kaleburnu
(Galinoporni)
Skoutari (Üsküdar)

*MEDITERRANEAN
SEA*

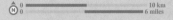

0   10 km
0   6 miles

4 Viewing the gated city
of **Famagusta** from its
imposing Venetian walls and
commanding bastions (p184)

5 Swimming on one of the
island's finest untouched

stretches of sand at **Golden
Beach** (Nangomi Bay; p193)

6 Discovering the mosaics,
archaeological site and
enchanting beaches of **Agios
Filon** (p196)

7 Visiting the **Monastery of
Apostolos Andreas** (p196),
one of the few remaining
Orthodox churches of the
Karpas, at the island's very tip

FAMAGUSTA (MAĞUSA)

POP 30,000

History

Famagusta and its surroundings have an affluent and complex history. The wide sweep of Famagusta Bay and the sprawling Mesaoria (Mesarya) plain was home to three major settlements over the ages: the Bronze Age city of Ancient Enkomi (Alasia), which existed during the 17th century BC; the Mycenaean settlement and tombs from the 9th century BC, described as a flourishing culture in Homer's *Iliad;*

and the illustrious kingdom of Salamis, which prospered through the 6th century BC.

Founded by Ptolemy Philadelphus of Egypt in the 3rd century BC, Famagusta was originally known by its Greek name, Ammochostos, meaning 'buried in the sand'. For many years it was considered the bridesmaid to the famous city kingdom of Salamis, just to its north.

After Salamis was abandoned in AD 648, Famagusta's population greatly increased, but the city didn't truly bloom until the fall of Acre in 1291.

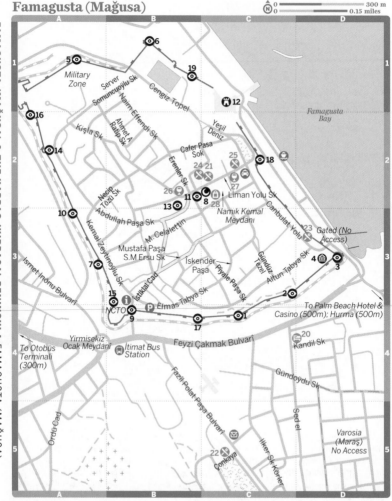

Famagusta (Mağusa)

0 — 300 m
0 — 0.15 miles

At this point, Christians fleeing the Holy Land took refuge in the city. In the late 13th century it became the region's main shipping stopover, gaining immense wealth almost overnight. A lavish and decadent lifestyle bloomed and more jewels and gold were said to be in Famagusta than in all of Europe's royal courts. This provoked scorn from the pious, who criticised what they felt were the loose morals of its citizens. To counteract this, a great number of churches were quickly built.

The great city's first decline began when the Genoese took control in the 14th century, prompting an exodus of its wealthiest and most illustrious citizens.

Although the town was recaptured by the Venetians 117 years later, its former

ROAD DISTANCES (KM)

	Maraş (Varosia)	İskele Trikomo	Boğaz (Bogazi)	Agios Filon & Afendrika
İskele Trikomo	25			
Boğaz (Bogazi)	28	9		
Agios Filon & Afendrika	69	47	38	
Yenierenköy (Yiallousa)	64	45	36	15

fortune and decadence never really returned. During this time the huge walls and bastions were constructed, but this belated measure did little to prevent its capture by the Ottomans in 1571. In the bloody 10-month siege that ensued, an estimated 100,000 cannonballs were fired.

Under the Ottomans, Famagusta rotted like a bad tooth. Its ruined buildings were never repaired, leaving it in an almost Gothic time warp. The Old Town, Kaleici, became a Turkish Cypriot stronghold.

The region flourished again in the early 1960s when the renowned, predominantly Greek resort town of Varosia (Maraş), to the south, annually pulled thousands of sun-seeking tourists to its stunning beaches.

However, communal conflicts in 1964 saw more skirmishes in the area, resulting in the Turks essentially barricading themselves within the Old Town's walls and exiling any Greeks left to the confines of Varosia.

The island's invasion by the Turkish army in 1974 forced Famagusta, and more particularly Varosia, into the restricted border zone. Deserted by its Greek population in anticipation of the fast-approaching Turkish military, Varosia remains part of the large, uninhabited buffer zone and is now a ghost town. Haunting, with its gaping dark windows and abandoned tower blocks, and barricaded by oil drums and barbed wire, it is as it was in 1974, save for a few military outposts and occasional UN patrols.

Orientation

Famagusta is easy to navigate, as the majority of your time will be spent within or near the Old Town.

The New Town's large square, Yirmisekiz Ocak Meydanı, is capped by an enormous black statue of Atatürk. It's the major landmark and impossible to miss. Across from the square is the Land Gate, which is the

Famagusta (Mağusa)

⊙ Sights
- **1** Andruzzi Bastion................................C4
- **2** Camposanto Bastion C3
- **3** Canbulat Bastion D3
- **4** Canbulat Museum D3
- **5** Del Mezzo Bastion A1
- **6** Diamante Bastion B1
- **7** Diocare Bastion...............................A3
- **8** Lala Mustafa Paša C2
- **9** Land Gate.......................................B4
- **10** Moratto Bastion A3
- **11** Namık Kemal Prison.........................B2
- **12** Othello's Tower C1
- **13** Palazzo del Provveditore B2
- **14** Pulacazara Bastion..........................A2
- **15** Ravelin (Rivettina) Bastion...............B3
- **16** San Luca Bastion............................A2
- **17** Santa Napa Bastion.........................B4
- **18** Sea Gate..C2
- **19** Signoria Bastion B1

⊜ Sleeping
- **20** Portofino D4

⊗ Eating
- **21** Aspava Restaurant..........................C2
- **22** Cyprus House Restaurant.................C5
- **23** Desdemona Bar & Restaurant..........D3
- **24** Ginkgo B2
- **25** Petek Confectioner..........................C2

⊙ Drinking
- **26** D&B...B2
- **27** Monks Inn C2

⊙ Shopping
- **28** Hoşgör...C2

FAMAGUSTA (MAĞUSA) & THE KARPAS (KIRPAŞA) PENINSULA FAMAGUSTA (MAĞUSA)

easiest way into the Old Town. There's also a handy car park just to the right as you enter.

İstiklal Caddesi is the main thoroughfare, running through the Old Town to Namık Kemal Meydanı, the square in front of Lala Mustafa Paşa mosque. East of the Old Town is the port, where ferries from Turkey arrive and dock.

To the south is the abandoned town of Varosia; you can approach the wire fences, but it is not accessible. Look out for the signs regarding restricted or limited roads.

Maps

The North Cyprus Tourism Organisation (NCTO) issues a free City Plan of Gazimağusa in English and Turkish. It lacks detail of the Old Town but gives a good overall view of the city, and most of the main regional destinations are included.

◉ Sights & Activities

From the top of Othello's Tower on the northeastern corner of the Venetian walls, Famagusta's shattered churches and Gothic buildings punctuate the skyline. Winding streets with low houses now make up the crumbling surroundings of what was once Cyprus' most lavish and important city. The eclectic mix of arched lanes, chapel ruins, Turkish baths, Byzantine churches and Knights Templar and medieval quarters are best appreciated on foot – allow the better part of a day to see the city properly.

Infrastructure here is still a little poor, and although tourism is solid due to the area's incredible history, most visitors choose to base themselves elsewhere.

Venetian Walls   HISTORICAL SITE

Once defending and now defining the Old Town, these imposing and sprawling ramparts have been compared to those of Jerusalem and Istanbul by Colin Thubron in his book Journey into Cyprus.

At over 15m high and up to 8m thick, the walls were constructed, with a now waterless moat, by the Venetians in the early 16th century. Despite their formidable appearance, the ramparts failed to keep the Ottomans at bay in 1571, though they did survive the following havoc within the city itself.

Like their counterpart in Lefkosia, the Old Town's walls comprised 14 bastions and five gates. You can walk almost the entire length of the roughly rectangular layout and enjoy the excellent views of the city below.

(Note that there are Turkish military posts at certain points.)

You can start at the southern end near the **Land Gate** on the **Ravelin (Rivettina) Bastion** (admission 5YTL; ⊘9am-6pm weekdays), known as the 'Akkule' or 'white tower'. It was here that the Ottomans first breached the fortifications, surrendered by the white-flag-waving Venetians.

From the Ravelin Bastion the walls head north, passing four minor bastions, **Diocare**, **Moratto**, **Pulacazara**, **San Luca** and the steeply pitched **Martinengo Bastion**. This in turn leads seaward, passing the **Del Mezzo**, **Diamante** and **Signoria Bastions**. Further on is the impressive citadel known as Othello's Tower.

The **Sea Gate** on the eastern side originally opened directly onto the sea. Today the wharfs of the modern port have extended the land bridge considerably.

At the southeastern extremity is the **Canbulat Bastion**, in which Ottoman hero General Canbulat Bey died valiantly whilst attacking the walls on horseback during the bloody siege. From here the walls loop back to the Land Gate via the **Camposanto**, **Andruzzi** and **Santa Napa Bastions**.

Othello's Tower (The Citadel)   HISTORICAL SITE

(Othello Kalesi; adult/child 7/3YTL; ⊘9am-8pm Jun–mid-Sep, 9am-12.30pm & 1.30-4.45pm mid-Sep–May) An extension of the Old Town's main walls, on the northeast seaward side, the tower was constructed in the 12th century during Lusignan rule in order to protect the harbour and the Sea Gate entrance, further south. In 1492, when the Venetians were in charge, the citadel was further fortified and transformed into an artillery stronghold.

The tower's name stems from a vague link to Shakespeare's play Othello, which has a modest stage note referring to 'a seaport in Cyprus'. Above the citadel's impressive entrance you'll see the **Venetian Lion** inscribed by its architect, Nicolò Foscarini. Famagusta's 'celebrity visitors list' is said to include Leonardo da Vinci, who apparently advised on the refurbishment of the tower during his visit to Cyprus in 1481.

The citadel itself consists of various towers and corridors leading to artillery chambers, a large courtyard bordered by a refectory, and living quarters; both the refectory and the living quarters above date to the Lusignans.

The courtyard, with stage (for folkloric performances), is bordered by the Great Hall, with beautiful vaults and corroded sandstone walls on its far side. Ventilation shafts look out to the border ramparts, leading to Lusignan corridors and sealed chambers. Legend has it that fortunes still lie hidden here, buried by Venetian merchants in the face of the advancing Ottomans.

The ramparts offer the best views over the town, perfect in the early morning or evening.

Lala Mustafa Paşa   MOSQUE
(Erenler Sokak; adult/child 7/3YTL; ☉outside prayer times) The finest example of Lusignan Gothic architecture in Cyprus, the mosque was built between 1298 and 1326.

During the Lusignan reign it was Famagusta's centrepiece and originally known as the Cathedral of Agios Nikolaos. As such, the last Lusignan king of Cyprus, Jacques II, and his infant son (Jacques III) were buried here.

Modelled on the Cathedral of Reims in France, it outshines its sister church, the Church of Agia Sofia (now Selimiye Mosque) in North Nicosia (Lefkoşa). Converted into a mosque or *camii* (in Turkish) after the Ottoman invasion in 1571, it dominates the skyline of the Old Town.

The church was damaged considerably during the Ottoman siege of Famagusta and its twin towers were destroyed. The Ottomans added the minaret, stripped the church's interior of its Christian accoutrements and emptied the floor tombs.

The west-facing facade, now a pedestrian zone, is the most impressive part, with three gracious portals pointing towards a six-paned window, decorated with a circular rose.

The walls inside have been whitewashed in Islamic fashion, but the soaring Gothic architectural lines are still easy to follow. Visits can only be conducted around prayer times and you will need to be conservatively dressed.

Namık Kemal Prison   MUSEUM
(palace precinct; adult/child 5/3YTL; ☉9am-2pm Jun–mid-Sep, 9am-12.30pm & 1.30-4.45pm mid-Sep–May) This former prison housed Turkish poet, playwright and dissident Namık Kemal (1840–88) for nearly four years after

---

VAROSIA (MARAŞ)

Before 1974, the Varosia (Maraş in Turkish) district was a thriving community of Greek Cypriots. Many owned and ran the large resort hotels in what was considered Famagusta's riviera, overlooking perhaps the island's most amazing beaches.

In August of that year, with air raids and Turkish military advances in the North, Varosia's residents fled, leaving uncleared breakfast dishes and taking with them little more than the clothes they wore. Many left on the assumption that they would return within a few days, once the emergency was over and a semblance of normality was restored. That didn't happen. The Turkish army marched on the town unimpeded, and to this day Varosia has remained empty.

Now the barricades at Varosia are one of the island's most haunting sights, a lingering reminder of the dark days of 1974. Apartment blocks, shops and houses have remained untouched for 37 years, and are covered in dust and sediment. A looted car dealership still stocks a single 1974 model, entombed in its showroom, frozen in time. The grand hotels of this once booming resort town now have bare windows and shell-fire deposits, and have been left to slowly decay like giant hollow sentinels on the coast.

The city also held Varosia's wealthy Archaeological Museum. No one knows what happened to its vast collection after the initial lootings. This is impossible to verify due to the town's isolation. Historians fear important pieces have been relocated or sold on the black market.

Varosia and the rest of the 'dead zone' are surrounded by barbed-wire fences, and metal drums block the streets, preventing passage within. Visitors cannot enter the area, except for visits to the Agios Ioannis Church (admission 4YTL; ☉9am-1pm Mon-Fri), 120m into the restricted area. You will need to pass a checkpoint before you approach – don't be surprised if you're simply turned away.

A very small part of the town is still inhabited, 200m off the main strip of Polat Paşa, where you can drive alongside the fence and peer in. Photography is forbidden.

his writings offended the sultan. The square between the prison and the Lala Mustafa Paşa mosque is named in his honour.

Immediately west of this was the original Venetian **Palazzo del Provveditore**, of which little is left, except some haphazard cannonballs, decaying arches and supporting columns taken from Salamis.

Canbulat Museum   MUSEUM
(Canbulat Yolu; adult/child 5/3YTL; ☉9am-7pm Jun–mid-Sep, 9am-12.30pm & 1.30-4.45pm mid-Sep–May) During the siege of Famagusta, Ottoman hero Canbulat Bey reportedly charged his horse at a gruesome medieval siege device consisting of a spiked wheel. He destroyed the device, himself and his horse in the process but inspired the Ottomans to conquer the Venetian-held city.

His tomb, at the southeastern corner of the Venetian walls, contains a small museum with a fairly simple collection of pottery and portraits featuring the sultan Suleyman and Lala Mustafa Paşa. There's also a historical display detailing the Turkish take on the events of 1974, and the enclaves of the Old Town.

🏖 Beaches

Palm Beach   BEACH
The best beach in Famagusta, this strip is located in front of the Palm Beach Hotel & Casino, which is accessible to non-guests. Its amenities are decent but costly. Follow the 'To the Beach Club' signs south of the hotel.

Glapsides   BEACH
This sandy public beach is 4km north of Famagusta. Shallow and sheltered by its position in the bay, it's popular with locals and great for kids.

There's a beach bar and restaurant, and you can hire sun loungers and umbrellas and use the shower and toilet facilities. Jet-skis, pedal-bikes and canoes are available for hire, and the conditions are great for snorkelling. The beach is also an avid birdwatching location during migratory seasons.

Glapsides is accessed via the path beside Golden Terrace restaurant, on the main road from Famagusta.

✨ Festivals & Events

International Famagusta Art & Culture Festival   CULTURAL FESTIVAL
(www.magusa.org/festival) Taking place annually between 20 June and 12 July, the festival has a wide range of music including classical, jazz, hip hop and reggae, performed by international and local artists. Theatrical performances are also staged at Namık Kemal Meydanı, Othello's Tower and the Salamis amphitheatre.

🍴 Eating

Famagusta offers a few good restaurants and eateries in and around the Old Town.

TOP CHOICE Ginkgo   FUSION €€€
(Liman Yolu Sokak 1; mains 15-25YTL; ☉10.30am-11.30pm Mon-Sat) This trendy cafe-restaurant right next door to the Lala Mustafa Paşa mosque occupies an old *madrasa* (Islamic religious school) and arched Christian building. Its great atmosphere accompanies a wide-ranging menu, from massive homemade burgers and salads to classic pastas, grilled fish and meat.

TOP CHOICE Petek Confectioner   BAKERY €
(☑366 7104; Yeşil Deniz Sokak 1; sweets from 4YTL; ☉10am-11pm) This perfect coffee and cake stop is a temple to all things sugary. *Lokum* (Turkish delight) stands in multicoloured spirals, circles and geometric patterns, and there are homemade honey cakes, nut cakes, chocolate cakes, *simit* (circular bread with sesame seeds) and *baklava*, to name just a few. Can be pricey, but the sweet-toothed won't mind.

Aspava Restaurant   TURKISH €€
(Liman Yolu Sokak 19; kebabs 11YTL; ☉lunch & dinner) Succulent grilled shish kebabs, mixed grills (15YTL) and meze. Food is served in a vine-covered garden that looks onto the square and mosque.

Desdemona Bar & Restaurant   TURKISH €€
(Canbulat Yolu Sokak 3; mains 17YTL) Located in a windowless tower, the bar-restaurant has generous, well-priced meze and an old-world atmosphere. In winter its almost exclusively a hip music bar for locals.

Hurma   MEDITERRANEAN €€€
(Kemal Server Sokak 17; mains 25YTL; ☉dinner) Practically next door to the Palm Beach Hotel, this stylish hacienda-styled restaurant with palm trees and tranquil terrace overlooking the sea serves swank international cuisine like escargot and fresh fish with lemon-garlic herbs.

Cyprus House Restaurant   TURKISH €€
(Fazıl Polat Paşa Bulvarı; mains 15YTL; ☉dinner) Housed in an old mansion in the New Town,

Cyprus House has a cool, shady dining area in which you can enjoy its full kebab dishes and grills. Belly-dancers often entertain the tables on weekends. It's around 400m southeast of Yirmisekiz Ocak Meydanı.

Eyva Restaurant CYPRIOT €€
(Salamis Yolu; mains 15YTL; ⊙dinner) An all-evening affair with freshly cooked *kleftiko* (oven-baked lamb) and traditional Greek or Turkish live music (and dancing) on the weekends. The food and music spectacle costs 25YTL. Eyva is on the left of the Salamis junction along the main road to the ancient city.

 Drinking

Famagusta is pretty light on drinking and entertainment. The road heading past the university towards Salamis is usually your best bet, with a string of clone-like bars and cafes.

D&B CAFE
(Namik Kemal Meydanı; ⊙10am-11.30pm Mon-Sat) This place is great for a drink amid the ruins, directly opposite the main mosque. It's predominantly filled with locals and students.

Monks Inn BAR, BISTRO
(Namik Kemal Meydanı; ⊙6-11.30pm Mon-Thu, noon-11.30pm Fri & Sat) Inside a medieval house, this bar is all about chilling out and sampling the cocktails. It's just outside the square and is an ambient spot for a cold drink or a snack.

 Shopping

Famagusta is very limited when it comes to shopping. Be aware that certain products are most likely counterfeits from Turkey, including items like brand-name watches, sneakers and apparel.

TOP CHOICE Hoşgör ANTIQUES
(Mahmut Celalettin Sokak 24/1; ⊙10am-2pm Mon-Sat) In this interesting antiques trove you can find traditional Cypriot ceramics, engravings, embroidery and gifts.

❶ Information

There's an ATM on the main square opposite Lala Mustafa Paşa. Phonecard telephones are on Liman Yolu Sokak, adjacent to the mosque.
Hospital (☑366 2876; Fazıl Polat Paşa Bulvarı) Five minutes south of the Old Town.

Money-exchange office (İstiklal Caddesi; ⊙8am-5.30pm Mon-Fri, to 6.30pm Jun & Jul)
North Cyprus Tourism Organisation (NCTO; ☑366 2864; İstiklal Caddesi; ⊙8am-5pm Mon-Sat) At the Land Gate; English-speaking staff.
Police station (☑366 5310; İlker Sokak Körler)
Post office (☑366 2250; Fazıl Polat Paşa Bulvarı)
Telephone centre (☑366 5332; İlker Sokak Körler)

❶ Getting There & Away

BOAT Ferries to Mersin (Turkey) leave from the port east of the Old Town on Tuesday, Thursday and Sunday (80YTL/50YTL one way per adult/student including tax, 10 hours, 9pm). Tickets are available from the passenger terminal and **Cyprus Turkish Shipping** (☑366 4557; cypship@superonline.com; Bulent Ecevit Bulvarı).
BUS Otobüs Terminali (☑366 6347; www.gocmentransport.com; Gazi Mustafa Kemal Bulvarı), the city's main bus station, is on the west side of the Old Town; services:
North Nicosia 5YTL, 45 minutes, every 15 to 30 minutes 6am to 7pm.
Kyrenia (Girne) 6YTL, 1¼ hours, hourly 7am to 6.30pm.
Yenierenköy 5YTL, 1¼ hours; via **Kyrenia**.
MINIBUS There are frequent minibuses from **İtimat bus station** (☑366 6666; Yirmisekiz Ocak) to the following:
North Nicosia 6YTL, 45 minutes.
Kyrenia 5YTL, one hour; via **North Nicosia**.

❶ Getting Around

There's a taxi stand in the Old Town, near the Sea Gate. **Ulaş Taksi** (☑366 8988/1276) operates in and around Famagusta and further afield. Tariffs are generally fixed, but check before accepting a ride.

There are no public buses within the city, as most major sights and services are within walking distance.

AROUND FAMAGUSTA

The main sites and beaches of the region are 9km to 10km north of Famagusta and around its bay.

You can base yourself at one of the hotels on the coast, or at the low-key resort of Boğaz (Bogazi). If you're driving you can check out some of the less-frequented inland villages like Geçitkale (Lefkoniko) and İskele (Trikomo) of the Mesaoria (Mesarya).

Around Famagusta (Mağusa)

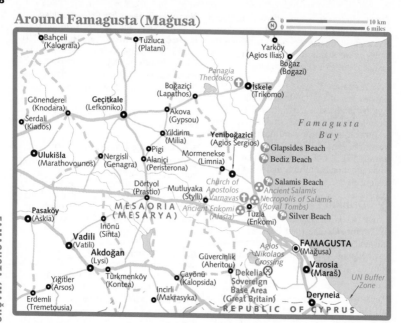

🏖 Beaches

Great stretches of beach can be found from Ancient Salamis, north of Famagusta, right around Famagusta Bay. The sea is knee deep to about 70m out and can be quite choppy on windy days.

Silver beach   BEACH
North of Famagusta before Salamis, this shallow sandy beach is perfect for swimming and snorkelling, whereby you can explore the submerged harbour of the ancient city.

Bediz beach   BEACH
Just past Salamis, this soft sand beach offers all amenities, including sun beds, umbrellas, showers and a restaurant bar. If it's hot and you plan to see the ruins, take a swim here afterwards.

Bafra beach   BEACH
This signposted public beach is 10km beyond Boğaz; turn right towards Bafra Bay. The beach is sandy with clear water and basic facilities.

ℹ Getting Around
The area is best seen with your own car, but most sites are close enough together for taxis to be affordable. (A return taxi from Famagusta to Ancient Salamis will cost around €14.)

Cycling is another good option, but you will need your own bike – there aren't any good bike-hire places in Famagusta.

Town buses between Famagusta and Yenierenköy stop at Boğaz and pass near Salamis, but they run infrequently and the last bus goes at 5.30pm.

Ancient Salamis

Salamis is the most significant of the 10 ancient city kingdoms of Cyprus.

According to legend, the city (Salamis Harabeleri; adult/child 9/5YTL; ⊙9am-8pm Jun–mid-Sep, 9am-12.30pm & 1.30-4.45pm mid-Sep–May) was founded around 1180 BC by Teucer (Teukros), the son of Telamon, King of Salamina, on the Greek mainland. Brother to the Greek hero Ajax, he was unable to return home from the Trojan War after failing to avenge his brother's death.

Salamis later came under Assyrian rule; the first recorded mention of it is on an Assyrian stele dated to 709 BC.

After a land and sea battle between the Greeks and the Persians in 450 BC the city (and island) submitted. The city remained under Persian control until the great patriot king Evagoras fought for and obtained independence. During his reign Salamis

Ancient Salamis

Cold Rooms (Frigidaria)
Columned Courtyard
Swimming Pools
GYMNASIUM
Stoa
Latrines
Stoking Rooms (Praefurnium)
Latrines
Stoa
Stoa
Sweating Room (Sudatorium)
Cold Rooms (Frigidaria)
AMPHITHEATRE
Swimming Pools
Hot Water Baths (Caldarium)
Sweating Room (Sudatorium)
Aqueduct
THEATRE

Famagusta Bay

To İskele (Trikomo; 14km); Boğaz (Bogazi; 16km)
Entrance
See Enlargement

To Ancient Enkomi (Alasia; 3km)
To Famagusta (Mağusa; 9km)

Ancient Salamis

⊚ Sights

1 Agora		C4
2 Basilica of Agios Epifanios		C3
3 Baths		C3
4 Cellarka Tombs		B4
5 Church of Apostolos Varnavas		A4
6 Gymnasium		C3
7 Kambanopetra Basilica		C3
8 Necropolis of Salamis (Royal Tombs)		B4
9 Reservoir		C4
10 Roman Villa		C3
11 Temple of Zeus		C4
12 Theatre		C3

flourished. It issued its own money and nurtured a thriving philosophical and literary scene, receiving noted Greek thinkers and poets.

Later, after Alexander the Great put an end to Persian domination across the island, the city saw a short period of peace. After Alexander's death it was under Ptolemaic rule from 294 BC to 58 BC. Ptolemy appointed the military ruler Nicocreon (the last King of Salamis) to govern the city and island. For reasons that are unclear, he committed suicide and the city floundered. Pafos then superseded Salamis as the island's chief city.

It wasn't until Cyprus became a Roman colony that the city prospered again, through rebuilding and public works. It went on to suffer two earthquakes and a tidal wave, requiring rebuilding once more, courtesy of Emperor Constantine II. In AD 350 the city was renamed Constantia and declared Episcopal.

Constantia suffered similar problems to its predecessor and in the 7th and 8th centuries it suffered Saracen Arab raids.

Its silted-over harbour became unusable and the city was essentially forgotten. Many of its stones were later used to build Famagusta.

Today Salamis is one of the island's premier archaeological sites, with explorations still ongoing.

◉ Sights

Allow half a day for your visit, with about 7km of rambling to see it all. Once you pass the main entrance, stick to the site map so that you don't retrace your steps too much.

On hot days take a hat and bottles of water with you, as there's no shade. Also be wary of snakes, especially in the more overgrown parts of the site. The adjacent beach is perfect for a swim after a day's exploring, and there's also a handy restaurant at the entrance for lunch.

Salamis is situated 9km north of Famagusta on the seaward side of the Famagusta–Boğaz highway.

Gymnasium   HISTORICAL SITE
The remains of the city's gymnasium, with columned courtyard and adjacent pools, used for exercise and pampering, allude to Salamis' original grandeur. Its northerly portico is surrounded by headless statues despoiled by Christian zealots as symbols of pagan worship. Many that had survived numerous raids have disappeared since 1974. Fortunately, some made it to Lefkosia's Cyprus Museum and are now prized exhibits.

Baths   HISTORICAL SITE
East of the portico are the Hellenistic and Roman baths, where you can see the exposed under-floor heating system. The southern entrance has a fresco of two faces, and two of the site's finest mosaics – dating from the 3rd and 4th centuries AD – can be seen in the south hall. One mosaic depicts Leda and the swan, the other Apollo and Artemis combating the Niobids. Some believe that the latter is a scene of a battle between warriors and Amazons.

Theatre   HISTORICAL SITE
Dating from the time of Augustus (31 BC to AD 14), the theatre once held 15,000 spectators. Much of it was destroyed by earthquakes, leaving stone raiders to seize its blocks for building projects elsewhere. Since then, it has been partially restored and occasionally hosts outdoor events (look out for advertisements in Famagusta).

Roman Villa   HISTORICAL SITE
South of the theatre, the villa was originally a two-storey structure made up of a reception hall and an inner courtyard with columned portico.

Kambanopetra Basilica   HISTORICAL SITE
This 4th-century basilica has an intricate mosaic floor and a columned courtyard.

Basilica of Agios Epifanios   HISTORICAL SITE
Central to the site, this structure was built during the episcopacy of Epifanios (AD 386–403) and was once the largest basilica in Cyprus.

Reservoir   HISTORICAL SITE
Further south you'll see what is left of the reservoir.

Agora   HISTORICAL SITE
The remains of the city's place of assembly.

Temple of Zeus   HISTORICAL SITE
Also south of Agios Epifanios.

Necropolis of Salamis   HISTORICAL SITE
(Royal Tombs, Salamis Mezarlık Alanı; ☑378 8331; adult/child 7/3YTL; ☺9am-8pm Jun–mid-Sep, 9am-12.30pm & 1.30-4.45pm mid-Sep–May) A scattering of 150 graves spread out over a wide area, this ancient cemetery dates back to the 7th and 8th centuries BC. The arrangement of the burial chambers closely matches descriptions of Mycenaean tombs in Homer's *Iliad*. Kings and nobles were buried here with their favoured worldly possessions, food, drink, and even their sacrificed slaves. Particularly gruesome reminders of this practice are the skeletons of two hapless horses, sacrificed after transporting one king to his tomb (No 79). Most tombs have been looted over the years, though at least three have yielded treasure and antiquities that are now in Lefkosia's Cyprus Museum.

Further south on the site, marked by a lone eucalyptus tree, are the **Cellarka tombs**. These smaller rock-cut tombs were used for less important members of the royal community. The tombs have steep steps leading to the underground chambers where stone urns were placed pending the decomposition of their contents. Thereafter the bones were removed and the chambers reused.

The tombs are prominently signposted south of Salamis along the road to Apostolos Varnavas church.

Church of Apostolos Varnavas CHURCH
(☎378 8331; adult/child 7/3YTL; ⊙9am-8pm
Jun–mid-Sep, 9am-12.30pm & 1.30-4.45pm mid-
Sep–May) This important Orthodox church
was spared from the destruction and looting that befell many churches in the North
when Turkish authorities turned it into a
museum. Although many Greek Cypriots
have objected to the site's use for monetary
gain and not for worship, they are pleased
the church has survived.

Three monks (who were also brothers)
called Barnabas, Stefanos and Khariton
governed the monastery from 1917. They attempted to remain after 1974 but ultimately
left in 1976, following constant searches of
the premises and travel restrictions imposed
by the Turkish authorities. They lived out
their days at Stavrovouni Monastery.

The church is dedicated to St Paul's good
friend Varnavas (Barnabas), who was born
in Cyprus and carried out his missionary
work here. Although his name and work are
listed in the Bible's 'Acts of the Apostles', he
was never officially one of them.

The original church was built in AD 477,
over the site of Varnavas' tomb. It was discovered by Anthemios, the bishop of Constantia (Salamis), following a revelation in a
dream. The current structure was built by
Archbishop Philotheos in 1756 and incor-
porates much of the original church. Today
the church is an **icon museum** with a wide
selection of Orthodox icons.

In the courtyard there is also a small
archaeological museum, which contains
finds from Salamis and nearby Enkomi.
Some of its contents may have been moved
from Varosia's now defunct Archaeological
Museum.

The artefacts and the rooms are not well
signed. Clockwise from the entrance, the first
room houses Bronze Age objects, the next has
exhibits from the Venetian period, and there's
a mixture of Ottoman and Classical periods
in the final room. The most interesting exhibit is the statue of a woman holding a poppy,
believed to be the goddess Demeter.

The church is 9km northwest of Famagusta,
near Salamis. Take the turn-off opposite Ancient
Salamis. It's well signposted from there.

Ancient Enkomi (Alasia)

This **Bronze Age city** (Enkomi Ören Yeni; adult/
child 5/3YTL; ⊙9am-7pm Jun–mid-Sep, 9am-
12.30pm & 1.30-4.45pm mid-Sep–May) dates
back as far as 1800 BC. It rose to prominence
when it became a large copper-producing
centre during the late Bronze Age (1650–
1050 BC).

Akkadian cuneiform slabs found in Tel
el-Amarna, Egypt, contain promises of copper to the pharaoh from the king of Alasia,
in return for silver and luxury items. It's still
unclear whether the name Alasia referred to
Cyprus as a whole or just Enkomi itself.

What remains of the present site dates
from around 1200 BC. The rectangular grid
layout was established then, and its fine
public buildings were erected. The city was
once known for its high standard of living
and its wealthy merchants who conducted
trade as agents of the Mycenaeans.

A fire and at least two earthquakes led to
Enkomi's decline, and then its inland harbour silted up. Some speculate that its last
residents headed to the coast and founded
Salamis. Much of the site has been looted,
but many of its tombs were said to have
held gold, ivory and exquisite Mycenaean
pottery.

The site is widespread and requires a lot
of walking to get around. Go to the ticket
office to pick up a leaflet with a map.

Highlights include the **House of Bronzes**,
where bronze accoutrements were unearthed in 1934, the **House of Pillar**, a public building, the **Sanctuary of the Horned
God**, where a 60cm-tall bronze statue (now
in the Cyprus Museum) was found, and
Tomb 18, where most of the site's treasure
was recovered.

Other important sights are the **wall forti-
fication** and the **Cenotaph mound**, built
on a rocky outpost. Its funeral pyre and its
construction concealed much of its contents
from looters; limestone statues, amphorae
from Rhodes, an archaic bronze shield
and clay effigies have been recovered from
the site. Archaeologists now contend that
this probable tomb may have belonged to
Nicocreon and that the plain between
Enkomi and Salamis was once a significant
connection between the two cities.

The ancient city is situated west of the
Necropolis of Salamis.

İskele (Trikomo)

The crossroads village of İskele, birthplace
of Ethniki Organosi tou Kypriakou Agona
(EOKA; National Organisation for the
Cypriot Struggle) leader Georgios Grivas,

START İSKELE
(TRIKOMO)
FINISH KALEBURNU
GALINOPORNI
DISTANCE 85KM
DURATION FIVE TO SIX
HOURS

Driving Tour
Remote Rural Villages of the Karpas

❯ After perusing the church and museum
at ① **İskele**, head north past Ardahan
(Ardana), swinging east along 12km of pined,
zigzagging road past cliffs, hills and the
hidden medieval ② **Kantara Orthodox
monastery**. Take the main road leading
south to the village of ③ **Yerani** (Turnalar),
where you can check out the church of
Panagia Evangelistria, 1km to the town's
west. From here go east (via Kutulus
Turnalar Yolu) through the traditional
village of ④ **Ergazi** (Ovgoros), then a
further 9km northeast, grading downward, to
⑤ **Kilitkaya** (Krithea). Another 2.5km along
this road is the settlement of ⑥ **Büyükkonuk**
(Komi), Cyprus' first eco village, with
restored traditional buildings and an old
olive mill. After you've tried some local
almonds and figs, take the old road east
to the village of ⑦ **Sazlikoy** (Livadia) and
the 6th-century ruins of Panagias tis Kryas
church. The road northeast takes you to the
vineyards of ⑧ **Mehmetcik** (Galateia)
village and its 95-proof *zivania*. Leave via the

main northeasterly road (not the stadium
road) through the centre of the Karpas, and
travel 16km through fields and groves to
reach ⑨ **Balalan** (Plantanissos). Continue
southwest another 3km to ⑩ **Ziyamet**
(Leonarisso), where the scenery becomes
notably hilly. Carry on past the crossroads
in Karpas Anayolu and past Gelincik (Vasili)
to the village of ⑪ **Boltasli** (Lythrangomi).
Here you'll find the 6th-century church
of Panagia Kanakaria (now locked). From
here a good (slender) road joins a string of
small villages, Derince, Avtepe and Kuruova,
with a series of unmarked tracks that lead
to ancient cliff-tombs and the Bronze Age
stronghold of ⑫ **Nitovikla** (3km away) on
the southern coast. Ask at the villages for the
best paths to hike. Once you've covered this
small area, hop back in the car and go east
to ⑬ **Kaleburnu** (Galinoporni), the most
substantial of these small peninsula towns.
Grab a bite and take the beach track to
Skoutari (Üsküdar) for a refreshing swim.

is noteworthy for its 12th-century church **Panagia Theotokos** (Church of the Blessed Virgin Mary). The domed building, with arched recesses in its side walls, has fine paintings of the Virgin Mary of the Annunciation and the Prayer of Joachim and Anna, in which the couple are seen embracing while a young girl peers from behind a window. The marble inlay from the church's original iconostasis is in the belfry.

The church is now an **icon museum** (İskele İkon Müzesi; adult/child 5/3YTL; ☺9am-12.30pm & 1.30-4.45pm Jun–mid-Sep, 9am-2pm mid-Sep–May) with a small collection of 12th- to 15th-century wall paintings and more recent icons from the 1950s and '60s.

Panagia Theotokos is easy to spot on the western edge of the village.

Boğaz (Bogazi)

A small fishing village about 24km north of Famagusta, Boğaz is the last beach stop before the road takes you inland to the Karpas Peninsula proper. There's a small harbour, south of which is a stretch of developed beach with straw umbrellas and sun loungers. Many tourists on package holidays base themselves in the village's low-key hotels (see p212). The area is particularly popular with Russian and German tourists and the seafront is now filled with pricier fish taverns. Located on the sea walk, with great views, reasonably priced **Kiyi** (mains 25-30YTL) serves fresh fish (caught daily) with large portions of chips.

KARPAS (KIRPAŞA) PENINSULA

A far cry from urban activity, the Karpas Peninsula (also known as Karpasia and Kırpaşa in Turkish) offers miles of rolling fields, wildlife, olive groves, carob trees, endless beaches with fantastic swimming, forgotten archaeological sites and the remains of broken Christian churches. The area is bliss for cyclists and ramblers, with mesmerising wildflowers that burst into colour every spring (see p233).

The peninsula has remained virtually untouched by development, its smattering of villages almost lost in time. The region somewhat sidestepped the events of 1974 as its isolated Turks and Greeks ignored the call to segregate themselves and continued to live alongside each other.

The village of Dipkarpaz (Rizokarpaso) remains home to some elderly Greek Cypriots, but most villages are now populated by mainland Turkish settlers, which is more apparent the further north you go.

The most sizeable village is Yenierenköy (Yiallousa), with its small square and village centre. It has a good tourist office, set up with the intention of increasing interest in the region. With access from the Republic of Cyprus now essentially a non-issue, more travellers are beginning to visit the Karpas, and prices are beginning to reflect this.

Many Greek Cypriots make the twice-yearly pilgrimage from the south to the very tip of the island to visit the revered Monastery of Apostolos Andreas.

Developers are starting to encroach further up the peninsula, and you may notice some gaudy out-of-place concrete stuccoes cropping up (see the box, p196). Thankfully, the entire cape from Dipkarpaz upwards has been declared a national park, and it's hoped that this will preserve the area's wildlife and ecology for years to come.

🐾 Beaches

Kumyali (Koma Tou Gialou) Beach   BEACH
This little beach–fishing harbour, just outside the village of Kumyali, is ideal for a last stop and swim as you drive up the western flank of the peninsula to the more exquisite beaches.

Golden Beach (Nangomi Bay)   BEACH
Possibly the best on the island, Golden Beach is worth the trip to the Karpas in itself. Its white sand dunes and gentle curves meet the calm, clear sea, and wild donkeys graze nonchalantly on the hills while you soak up the tranquillity. It's truly enchanting, with little development.

Now part of the national park, the beach is also prime turtle-nesting ground (see the box, p169). If you're visiting in September, contact the certified volunteers who monitor the progress of the turtles and you may even be lucky enough to witness baby turtles hatching.

The beach is 5km before Zafer Burnu (Cape Apostolos Andreas). Situated between scrubby headlands and stretching for several kilometres, it's reached by sand and dirt roads. There are basic beach huts (see p212) and a couple of restaurants.

Karpas (Kırpaşa) Peninsula

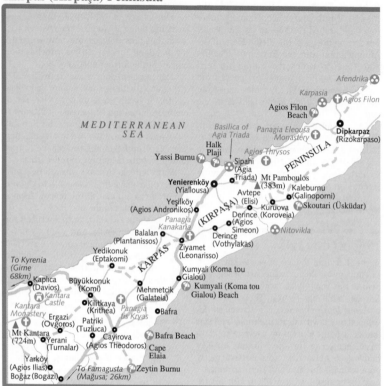

MEDITERRANEAN SEA

Afendrika

Karpasia

Agios Filon

Agios Filon Beach

Dipkarpaz (Rizokarpaso)

Basilica of Agia Triada

Panagia Eleousa Monastery

Halk Plaji

Agios Thrysos

Yassi Burnu

Sipahi (Agia Triada)

Mt Pamboulos (383m)

PENINSULA

Yenierenköy (Yialousa)

Avtepe (Elisi)

Kaleburnu (Galinoporni)

Yeşilköy (Agios Andronikos)

Kuruova (Koroveia)

Skoutari (Üsküdar)

Panagia Kanakaria

(KIRPAŞA)

Derince (Agios Simeon)

Balalan (Plantanissos)

Ziyamet (Leonarisso)

Derince (Vothylakas)

Nitovikla

Yedikonuk (Eptakomi)

KARPAS

To Kyrenia (Girne 68km)

Kumyali (Koma tou Gialou)

Kaplica (Davios)

Büyükkonuk (Komi)

Mehmetcik (Galatea)

Kumyali (Koma tou Gialou) Beach

Kantara Castle

Kilitkaya (Krithea)

Panagia tis Kryas

Bafra

Kantara Monastery

Ergazi (Ovgoros)

Patriki (Tuzluca)

Mt Kantara (724m)

Yerani (Turnalar)

Cayirova (Agios Theodoros)

Bafra Beach

Cape Elaia

Yarköy (Agios Ilias)

To Famagusta (Mağusa; 26km)

Zeytin Burnu

Boğaz (Bogazi)

Agios Filon Beach   BEACH
With its soft sand and big, flat sea rocks, this is another fantastic beach, near the Oasis at Ayfilon hotel and restaurant (p212). It's also another turtle-hatching beach and a great place to watch the sunset.

❶ Getting Around

The only public transport in the area is the bus from Famagusta to Yenierenköy (6YTL, 1¼ hours). Thus your own transport is necessary to explore this region properly. Taxis can be arranged locally.

The main road to the peninsula is first-rate, though signs to some of the sites lack clarity and prominence, so bring your own map.

Kantara Castle

The easternmost of the three Lusignan Gothic castles, **Kantara** (Kantara Kalesi; adult/child 6/3YTL; ☺9am-5pm Jun–mid-Sep, 9am-12.30pm & 1.30-4.45pm mid-Sep–May) is also the lowest in

elevation at 690m. It has a 360-degree view of the region, taking in the seas on both sides of the peninsula. On a clear day you can see the coast of Turkey and even Syria.

In 1191 Richard the Lionheart seized the castle from Isaak Komninos, the Byzantine emperor of Cyprus. Kantara was considered a crucial mountain fortress and was used as a beacon station to communicate with Buffavento Castle to the west.

In the 16th century Venetian military strategists relied more on firepower than elevation for protection, and the ports of Famagusta, Larnaka and Kyrenia overtook the castle in importance. The Venetian garrison relocated in 1525 and the castle was left open to raiders searching for the treasures told of in legends about Kantara.

Today you can see the castle's well-preserved northern section, its towers and walls still resolutely standing. The outer entrance leads into the now somewhat

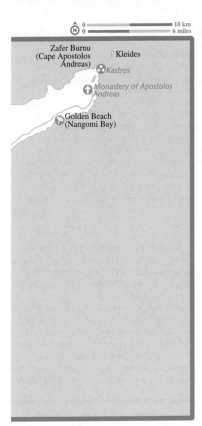

Zafer Burnu
(Cape Apostolos
Andreas) Kleides

Kastros

Monastery of Apostolos
Andreas

Golden Beach
(Nangomi Bay)

0 ── 10 km
0 ── 6 miles

Yenierenköy (Yiallousa)

Formerly a predominantly Greek village, Yenierenköy was resettled by Turkish Cypriot residents of Erenköy (Kokkina) in the South. It's the peninsula's second-largest village, with a new €15-million, 500-plus-berth marina in the works. Once completed, the marina's impact on the village and wider peninsula is expected to be significant.

At the **tourist information office** (☎374 4984; ☺10am-6pm Jun–mid-Sep, 9am-1pm & 2-5pm mid-Sep–May) the staff speak English and have lots of information on the peninsula. Sites in the region include the colossal **cave tombs** at Derince (Vothylakas) and some smaller versions between Avtepe (Elisi) and Kuruova (Koroveia). This area is largely unexplored. The many rough tracks here head south, toward the sea, leading you to the ruins of the ancient Bronze Age fort of **Nitovikla**.

Further east along the coast are some **sandstone caves** near Kaleburnu (Galinoporni). If you intend to drive these tracks, a 4WD is recommended. Take a good map with you, and ask at the information office (or in the local village) about how to best go about finding these unmarked sites before setting out.

Sipahi (Agia Triada)

The small village of Sipahi is home to many mainland Bulgarian Turkish settlers and a tiny community of Karpas Greeks. Like the equally small group in Dipkarpaz, they refused to leave their homes in the North and have continued to live on the peninsula despite the political situation.

The village has some superb mosaics in the now-ruined **Basilica of Agia Triada** (adult/child 5/3YTL; ☺9am-5pm), dating from the 5th century.

While little is left of the main structure, the basilica has extensive flooring, intricately patterned with geometric and abstract mosaics. Greek inscriptions at both the northern and southern ends of the former nave reveal that the church's construction was partly financed by Deacon Iraklios on a personal vow of dedication.

The site is at the eastern end of the village and is best approached from the Dipkarpaz end of Sipahi. Tickets for the site can be obtained from the small kiosk opposite.

overgrown barbican. The north and south towers guard the inner entrance, where you enter the castle proper. Inside you'll find the garrison, latrines and a cistern.

The highest point of the complex is the lookout tower, from where flares were lit to warn of impending danger. At the castle's southwestern end are further garrisons and the postern gate, used to unleash troops and catch would-be attackers off-guard. The roof of the north tower is narrow, unfenced and vertiginous, but the views are incredible.

A free map is provided; you'll need about an hour to see everything. Children should be accompanied by an adult at all times, as there are some unfenced drops, rough tracks and uncapped holes on the site.

Kantara is best reached from Boğaz, a 45-minute drive away. From Kaplıca the route is narrow but easily driveable. It takes around two hours to reach the castle from Kyrenia. There is no public transport.

FAMAGUSTA (MAĞUSA) & THE KARPAS (KIRPAŞA) PENINSULA YENIERENKÖY (YIALLOUSA)

PROTECTING THE WILDERNESS

In 1983, 150 sq km of the Karpas region, from the municipality of Dipkarpaz to Cape Apostolos Andreas, was declared a national park by Turkish Cypriot authorities. Since then, encroaching development and the building boom of 2004, in anticipation of the island's unification, saw nearby places like Bafra and Yenierenköy (Yiallousa) build new hotels and resort complexes. This rapid development has conservationists deeply concerned about the sustainability of the region's greater environment, particularly its unique wildlife, plant life, undiscovered archaeological sites and rugged beaches. Now lobby groups, biologists and environmentalists are banding together and pushing for an extension to the park's boundaries to include Ronas Bay (north of Dipkarpaz). They want a commitment to adhere to stricter guidelines regarding the peninsula's use and further development. Most pressing are concerns over the building of new roadways and the scope of electrification plans for remote areas of the cape. It's clear that declaring the area a national park is a step in the right direction, but more needs to be done to protect one of the island's last unspoilt habitats.

Dipkarpaz (Rizokarpaso)

POP 3500

This is the peninsula's largest and most remote village, where a large contemporary mosque sits next to an old Orthodox church. The church is a silent companion, as its bell is no longer tolled, although a small number of Greek Cypriots still live in the village. The once thriving town is now mostly populated by mainland Turks and Kurds, who work the land and live in difficult rural conditions.

A small ring of shops and a petrol station are the only real facilities and the last chance to fill up. The best restaurant is right next to the Karpaz Arch Houses (p212), 500m from the village centre. Manolyam Restaurant (mains 20-30YTL) serves traditional Turkish-style food in a small but filling array of mixed meze.

Agios Filon & Afendrika

The 12th-century Agios Filon Church stands silently on the sparse coastline some 5km north of Dipkarpaz. Right next to the Oasis at Ayfilon hotel (p212), its well-preserved outside walls were built over an earlier 5th-century Christian basilica. The conceptual mosaics from the basilica can be seen outside the walls of the later church. This area was once the ancient site of Karpasia, prominent during the Hellenistic period and the Middle Ages. A Roman harbour was also situated here, and the remains of the breakwater can still be seen in the sea.

Bordering is the idyllic Agios Filon Beach (p194) and the Oasis Restaurant (Oasis at Ayfilon; mains 20-30YTL; ✍), serving char-grills and the peninsula's best freshly caught fish, marinated in olive oil.

A further 7km east is Afendrika, a major city in the 2nd century BC. What remains is a set of contiguous ruins comprising three churches: 6th-century Agios Georgios, Panagia Khrysiotissa and 10th-century Panagia Asomatos. Nearby are the necropolis and what remains of the citadel.

Monastery of Apostolos Andreas

On 15 August and 30 November every year, scores of Greek Cypriot pilgrims make the trek north to this monastery (donations accepted) near the tip of the Karpas Peninsula. From 1996 Turkish Cypriot authorities allowed some pilgrims to enter the North, in organised visits only, on these two dates.

Today, with certain border crossings opened, the pilgrimage is far simpler and the faithful can visit this site of holy miracles unescorted.

The current church dates from 1740, though the whole monastery complex was expanded in later years. The monastery's reputation for miracles was obtained during the time of St Andrew (the patron saint of sailors), who reputedly restored the sight of a ship's captain when he arrived from Palestine.

Since then attested-to miracles range from curing blindness and epilepsy to healing the crippled and granting extraordinary wishes. Before 1974 the monastery was well supported by its devotees and pilgrims.

Today, isolated from its patrons and with only a few (Greek Cypriot) caretakers, the great monastery has deteriorated. It now awaits the start of a long-planned restoration programme, with funding of around €5 million to be provided by the UN and EU.

Visitors are welcome to see the monastery throughout the year. If you can find one of the caretakers, they will happily show you through. Contributions are always appreciated and go towards the upkeep of the church. There's also a small stall outside selling souvenirs such as prayer bracelets.

Zafer Burnu (Cape Apostolos Andreas)

A mere 3km from Apostolos Andreas monastery, along a dirt track, is the easternmost tip of Cyprus. From here you can see the cluster of rocky isles known collectively as the **Kleides** (The Keys).

The Neolithic site of **Kastros** was once located here. Later, the ancient Greeks built a temple to Aphrodite, of which nothing remains. If you happen to have a 4WD, you can take the rougher northern track back to Dipkarpaz, though it can be particularly difficult in wet weather.

Accommodation

Includes »

Lemesos & the South
Coast 200
Troödos Massif 202
Pafos & the West 204
Larnaka & the East 206
Lefkosia (Nicosia) 208
North Nicosia
(Lefkoşa) 209
Kyrenia (Girne) &
the Northern Coast 210
Famagusta (Mağusa)
& the Karpas (Kırpaşa)
Peninsula 211

Best Places to Stay

» Lapida (p210)
» Aeneas (p208)
» Elyssia (p203)

Best Budget Hotels

» Crystallo Apartments
(p204)
» Petrou Bros (p207)
» Luxor Guest House (p200)

Best Agrotourism Options

» Amarakos Inn (p205)
» Apokryfo (p201)
» Archontiko Rousias (p204)

Where to Stay

Part of the charm of Cyprus is that each region has a distinctive character, so deciding on *what* you want from your holiday experience is the first priority. In the south, Larnaka is at the centre of the most tourist-driven part of the island, with nearby Agia Napa still the clubbing capital. To the west, sophisticated Lemesos is the restaurant hot spot and is an ideal central base for exploring inland and further afield. Still due west, Pafos is a favourite with families but also provides easy access to the unspoilt west-coast beaches and the Troödos mountains. The urban flip side is the capital, cultural Lefkosia/North Nicosia, with fantastic museums, galleries and historic sights. In North Cyprus, Kyrenia has some superb hotels overlooking the harbour while, to the west, the Karpas (Kırpaşa) Peninsula is perfect for those who want to get away from it all, surrounded by stunning scenery, pristine beaches and coves.

Pricing

The price indicators in this book refer to the cost of a double room, including private bathroom and excluding breakfast unless otherwise noted. Prices quoted are for the low (winter) and high (summer) seasons.

In the budget category you may have to share a bathroom and facilities will be limited. Midrange choices often include satellite TV, private balconies and wi-fi, while the top end offers all this and more, with the accommodation generally housed in a sumptuous historical (or cutting-edge contemporary) building.

CATEGORY	COST
€ Budget	<€60 (Republic of Cyprus)
	<€40 (Northern Cyprus)
€€ Midrange	€60-90 (Republic of Cyprus)
	€40-70 (Northern Cyprus)
€€€ Top end	>€90 (Republic of Cyprus)
	>€70 (Northern Cyprus)

Types of Accommodation

Cyprus runs the gamut of places to unpack your suitcase, ranging from huts on a beach to super-luxurious hotels. The rates listed in the *Cyprus Hotel Guide,* issued free by the Cyprus Tourism Organisation (CTO), are maximum allowable prices, and will normally only be applicable in mid-summer.

AGROTOURISM

There is a good range of agrotourism places to stay in the South. Some are self-contained houses with gardens that are ideal for large families or friends, while couples may prefer a self-contained apartment within a historic stone-clad complex. All are fully equipped, and many have extras like swimming pools and wi-fi.

This is a superb and often very economical way for independent travellers to see the country. Rates are about €35 for a single room, €50 to €70 for a double and €100 for a luxury studio.

Most properties are away from major centres, so you'll need your own transport to get around, or you'll have to rely on sometimes sketchy public transport.

CAMPING

In the South there are only four licensed camping grounds, all with seasonal opening times. All have hot showers, a mini market and a snack bar. The North has even fewer camping grounds, and facilities aren't as good as in the South. Costs are similar, however.

PRIVATE ROOMS

Domatia (private rooms for rent), advertised by the word *camere,* are not common in Cyprus; in fact, the practice is officially discouraged by the CTO. However, in Agia Napa you'll see signs advertising rooms, and occasionally come across them in the more popular mountain resorts such as the Troödos Massif and the Pafos district in the South. Unsurprisingly, the rooms are exceedingly cheap, generally hovering around €15 to €20,

and meals can often be provided. If you don't see any obvious signs, consider asking in the local taverna or bar.

HOTELS

In the main southern resorts, many hotels deal primarily with package-tour groups. However, individual travellers can usually still find a room even in 'resort' hotels. Quality varies markedly, though prices are strictly controlled by the CTO. In general, hotels will have good facilities, mainly geared for families; most offer breakfast included in the price.

The quality of hotels in the North is generally good at the top end of the scale. Package-tour visitors constitute the bulk of guests, but as in the South, there will usually be a room available for walk-ins. The *North Cyprus Hotel Guide* is available from the North Cyprus Tourism Organisation (NCTO), and from tourist offices in the main towns.

Throughout Cyprus you can often save money by booking hotels online.

APARTMENT HOTELS

Apartment hotels are becoming increasingly popular and are prevalent in the main southern resorts of Pafos, Lemesos and

ACCOMMODATION

VILLA RENTALS

Renting a villa is a very common practice in Cyprus, since it's cheaper for a week or 10-day stay than a hotel room. You'll be able to find good villas, with or without pools, in the tourist centres or in the middle of nowhere. Real estate agencies can often help. Alternatively, check the classified sections in the local English-language newspapers. Expect to pay from €40 per person per night. There's usually a minimum stay of at least two weeks.

Larnaka, as well as in and around Kyrenia in Northern Cyprus. Most have well-equipped kitchens.

Costs typically start at around €35 for a studio apartment and €40 for a double room (both including kitchenette).

LEMESOS & THE SOUTH COAST

Lemesos (Limassol)

The good news is that there are plenty of hotels in Lemesos. The bad news is that they are mostly along a 9km tourist strip to the northeast of the old city, and are often crowded and overpriced. The old city doesn't feature many high-quality establishments, but hotels in this area are more used to walk-in travellers and are likely to have rooms vacant.

The cheapest hotels are clustered to the east of the castle, while the more luxurious hotels are located at the far northeastern end of the tourist centre.

TOP CHOICE **Chrielka** APARTMENTS €€
(☑2535 8366; www.chrielka.com.cy; Olympion 7; low-high studios €60-70, 2-person apt €85-110; ❋☷) Staying at Chrielka is a bit like staying with a well-travelled great uncle; owner Mr Nikitas has collected some wonderful Asian ceramics and various artefacts from his travels, and developed a fine wine cellar (yes, there *is* a bar). The 33 apartments are tastefully decorated and include balcony, kitchenette and satellite TV; some overlook the Municipal Gardens. The small pool is an unexpected plus.

Curium Palace HOTEL €€€
(☑2536 3121; www.curiumpalace.com; Vyronos 2; s/d €90/115; P❋@☎☷) This longstanding hotel is a gleaming white-marble palace that may qualify as one of Lemesos' classiest and best choices. You can expect an extremely comfortable stay, with excellent restaurants, sophisticated bars, pools and a fitness centre, plus sauna and tennis court (with a resident coach to develop that killer serve). The hotel is conveniently located opposite the Municipal Gardens.

Luxor Guest House INN €
(☑2536 2265; www.luxorlimassol.com; Agiou Andreou 101; dm €12, d €35; @) The Luxor is the only place in the city, and possibly in the country, that has a real backpacking atmosphere – in a positive sense. The rooms are airy, with painted wood-board ceilings and small balconies overlooking this bustling pedestrian street – which can make it noisy if you fancy a lie-in. There's one en-suite double and free internet use for guests.

Londa BOUTIQUE HOTEL €€€
(☑2586 5555; www.londahotel.com; George A 72, Potamos Yermasoyias, Yermasoyia; low-high r incl breakfast €114-170; P❋☎☷) The island's first couture hotel, the Italian-owned Londa sports custom-made furnishings ranging from the hand-carved headboards to the Cavallino carpets. Rooms are spacious, with lashings of white linen and cool earth colours. Extensive facilities include spa, infinity pool and the Caprice Bar, which flips to a smoochy club in the evening when the

SEASONS

July and August is holiday time in Cyprus, so you can expect a marked increase in local tourism, particularly in the beach resorts, and a corresponding hike in hotel prices. This is also school-holiday time throughout Europe, which also equals a boost in tourist numbers. August is uncomfortably hot in Lefkosia and North Nicosia; many shops and restaurants close for a week or so. March to June and September to October are ideal times to visit: accommodation prices are reasonable and the weather is pleasantly warm. November to February is low season and there are generally good deals on hotel rooms.

resident DJ takes centre stage. Located 550m east of the historic centre.

Aquarius Hotel HOTEL €€
(☑2532 6666; www.aquarius-cy.com; Amathus 11; low-high s €40-50, d €50-70; P❋❄🎔) This is a sound choice, located a thong's throw from the beach and 5km from the historic centre. The Aquarius is great for those who want to do more swimming than sightseeing, and enjoy upmarket facilities at down-to-earth prices. The rooms are spacious and tastefully decorated and most have sea views. Welcome extras include heated indoor pool, sauna, and health and fitness centre offering a range of beauty treatments. There are also tango lessons and an aqua gym on offer for the seriously energetic, as well as free bike hire.

Lordos Hotel Apts APARTMENTS €
(☑2558 2850; www. lordoshotelapts.com; Andrea Zaimi 13; 2-person apt from €55; ❋🎔) This modern apartment hotel offers good-value, spacious apartments with separate sitting room and kitchen, plus satellite TV and small balcony. Conveniently situated for self-caterers, it's a block away from Debenhams (which is an excellent directional landmark). The historic centre is a 2km walk away, but there are plenty of restaurants and shops nearby.

Metropole HOTEL €
(☑2536 2330; www.metropolehotel.com.cy; Ifigenias 6; s/d €45/55; ❋) A sound budget option in the heart of the historic centre, this comfortable place sports soothing pale-peach-and-cream decor with pleasant prints of local scenes on the walls. Some rooms have refrigerators. The hotel also runs the popular adjacent weekends-only Retro Music Club (11pm to 4am) if you feel like revving up your energy levels on the dance floor to tunes from the '60s to the '80s.

Le Meridien Limassol HOTEL €€€
(☑2586 2000; www.lemeridien-cyprus.com; low-high s €101-170, d €120-292; P❋@🎔🎔) This is a luxury giant with grottoes and fountains spurting water in the large pools. There's a range of room choices, from standard to presidential suites offering masses of opulence, to two-bedroom 'citrus garden villas' housing up to seven people. Le Meridien also has special luxury rooms for travellers with disabilities, plus a dedicated restaurant for children and special family packages. The hotel is located around 13km north of the Municipal Gardens, following the coastal road.

Around Lemesos

TOP CHOICE **Apokryfo** AGROTOURISM €€€
(☑2581 3777; www.apokryfo.com; Lofou; r incl breakfast from €150; P❋❋🎔🎔) The name means 'hidden away' in Greek, and it's certainly appropriate for this charming secluded property located on the edge of picturesque Lofou village. Comprising several stone cottages renovated by a Greek Cypriot architect and his interior-designer wife, the result is exquisite. Finest-quality marble, limed wood, natural colours, local woven fabrics and a soothing colour scheme typify the interior. Baby baths, cots and highchairs can be arranged. The hotel's Agrino restaurant is also top notch.

Art by Praxis APARTMENTS €€
(☑9989 4737; www.praxis-designs.com; Governor's Beach; 4-/8-person apt per week €240; ❋🎔) These new ultra-modern apartments have striking contemporary artwork and a sleek minimalist look. Situated within walking distance of Governor's Beach and several good seafood restaurants, rentals are for a minimum of one week. Praxis is a Lemesos-based architectural and design company that focuses on bioclimatic design. Consequently, the apartments are built with recyclable materials, the energy is exclusively solar and irrigation is supplied by recycled water.

Bunch of Grapes Inn AGROTOURISM €
(☑2522 1275; Ioannou Erotokritou 9, Pissouri; s/d €30/50) Part of a popular restaurant (p60),

this atmospheric old mansion dates back some 200 years and was once the home of a wealthy Pissourian. Located in the centre of the village (and well signposted), it was rediscovered and renovated some 30 years ago, and has served as an inn ever since. Its nine basic rooms (all doubles; no air-conditioning, fans only) have stained-glass windows and look out onto a central courtyard perfumed by jasmine and honeysuckle.

Vouni Lodge AGROTOURISM €€
(☏9968 5395; www.agrotourism.cy.com; Vouni; 2-/4-person apt €65-85; P🛜🏊) Located on the main street in the village, this 200-year-old building has three apartments, decorated in rustic traditional style with beamed rooms, wrought-iron furniture, lacy bedcovers and outside tables under the olive trees. The top-storey apartment has distant sea views. There's a minimum three-night stay.

TROÖDOS MASSIF

Troödos

Troödos Forest Park has four camp sites. The Troödos camp site, listed below, is best for longer stays. The other three sites, Platania (see p68), Kampi tou Kalogyrou and Prodromos dam, are also good but are designed for shorter stays or weekenders and have more basic facilities.

TOP CHOICE Jubilee HOTEL €€
(☏2542 0107; jubilee@cytanet.com.cy; r €40-70, d €60-98; P❄@) This old and elegant hotel is 350m from the village on the Prodromos road. Decorated with dark wood and big armchairs, its rooms are cosy and comfortable, with central heating for winter. It's the best place to stay during the snow season for access to the slopes.

Troödos CAMPGROUND €
(☏2242 1624; camp sites per tent €6; ⊘May-Oct; P) Situated 500m east of Central Troödos, with cooking facilities, showers, toilets and water.

Platres

Colonial Britain still lingers in the mountain hotels: most have a very old-world feel to them and are full of character. Agrotourism is becoming more and more popular throughout the villages, with some great options now available.

TOP CHOICE Semiramis HOTEL €€
(☏2542 2777; www.semiramishotelcyprus.com; Spyrou Kyprianou 55; r €45-75; P❄) Great little family-run hotel amongst the pines, with cosy rooms and 1900s charm. Staying here feels a lot like your own private getaway, with catered brekkie, a relaxed atmosphere and personable staff.

Pendeli HOTEL €€
(☏2542 1736; www.pendelihotel.com; Makariou 12; r Apr, May & Sep €38, Jun-Aug €75; ⊘closed Oct-Mar; P❄@🏊🐕) This substantial hotel is modestly decorated, clean and neat. Nearly all the rooms have spectacular views of the valley below, and there's a fantastic pool on the mezzanine that's seldom busy. If you feel like being pampered, check out the health club, with gym, sauna, Jacuzzi and spa treatments, available at an extra charge.

Forest Park HOTEL €€€
(☏2542 1751; www.forestparkhotel.com.cy; Spyrou Kyprianou 62; r €90-150; P❄@🏊🐕) This big hotel is dripping with history, having played host to Greek, Egyptian and British royalty. Its appeal has faded somewhat over the years, although the old-world glamour still echoes in its sumptuous bar. There are two pools, a gym, a massage parlour and a sauna, and the rooms are fully equipped. It is frequented by wealthy Cypriots.

Minotel New Helvetia HOTEL €€€
(☏2542 1348; www.minotel.com; Elvetias 6; r per person low-high €75-90; P❄@🐕) In an isolated and peaceful location at the northeastern end of the village near the main highway. All rooms are double and have TV, phone and small balcony. Atmospheric, dark and broody, the bar has a wonderful terrace surrounded by pines. You can also hire cars and mountain bikes here.

Around Platres

TOP CHOICE To Spitiko tou Arhonta AGROTOURISM €€
(☏2546 2120; www.spitiko3elies.com; 2-/4-person apt €75/130; P❄🛜🐕) Perched almost on top of the village of Treis Elies, with a shady garden, the house has two one-bedroom apartments and one two-bedroom apartment, all self-catering and decorated like a rustic

paradise. Friendly owner Androulla may even give you a lesson in cooking *kleftiko* (oven-baked lamb), as she prepares meals on request. If you're exploring the E4 route, this is an ideal base.

To Spiti tou Xeni
AGROTOURISM €

(☑9941 9251; studios €40-50; P ❄) This well-maintained traditional house in the village of Galata is completely self-catering. It has good-size beds, a fireplace and clay ovens. The views of the surrounding hills and valley are wonderful, and there's a sense of serenity about the whole place. Call Mrs Vathoulla directly for access and group rates.

Marathasa Valley

The sleeping options in Pedoulas are respectable; you can expect the basics of simple decor and comfort.

TOP CHOICE Elyssia
HOTEL €

(☑9975 3573; Filoxenias 47, Pedoulas; r €40-60; P ❄) These spacious and pretty rooms all have balconies that overlook the valley. The hotel is obviously well cared for by the owner, who is charming and eager to please. The rooftop terrace is a wonderful alternative to the swimming pool, and the small restaurant downstairs offers breakfast and traditional Cypriot food later in the day.

Two Flowers
HOTEL €

(☑2295 2372; Filoxenias 26, Pedoulas; full board per person Sep-Jul €25, Aug €40; P) An attractive little B&B that offers individualised rooms – red curtains and a matching red quilt in one, a simple, white rustic look in another – some with a view of the valley. It's very family friendly and great value.

Health Habitat
HOTEL €€

(☑2295 2283; www.healthhabitat.com; Pedoulas; r €56-90; P ❄) Hidden away amongst the pines, this hotel offers healthy eating and relaxation programs. With a qualified dietician on hand, it's a great option if you want to slim down or de-stress. The quiet, simple rooms have private balconies with mountain or valley views. There are no TVs in the rooms, but sauna, gym and lots of exercise are available.

Olga's Katoï
AGROTOURISM €€

(☑2235 0283; Kalopanayiotis; d €70; P ❄ @ ❄) This two-storey traditional stone house has been meticulously maintained for over 300 years. It consists of a main house with sitting room, kitchen and two of the 12 bedrooms located upstairs; the 10 other bedrooms are built in a row separately, and all have fantastic views of the surrounding valley. Breakfast is served on the terrace.

To Spiti tis Polyxenis
AGROTOURISM €€

(☑2249 7509; 2-/4-person houses €100/175; P ❄) This two-bedroom house is on the Lefkosia side of Kalopanayiotis village. The house is decorated with traditional furniture, with large wooden doors opening onto a peaceful, sun-filled courtyard. There's also a kitchenette and a large bathroom.

Solea Valley

Kakopetria is the only place in the mountains with two excellent hotels right opposite each other.

TOP CHOICE Linos Inn
HOTEL €€€

(☑2292 3161; www.linos-inn.com.cy; Palea Kakopetria 34, Kakopetria; d €95-135; P ❄ @) The captivating original architecture has been retained here wherever possible. The inn is laden with antique furniture, rustic rooms, four-poster beds covered in woven white linen, and fireplaces. In the top-end suites and studios are plasma-screen TVs and Jacuzzis (there's a separate sauna). Book in advance if you're visiting on a weekend. The restaurant serves high-quality traditional food.

Mill
HOTEL €€

(☑2292 2536; www.cymillhotel.com; Mylou 8, Kakopetria; r €45-70; ⊙closed 20 Nov-20 Dec; P ❄) Situated at the old mill site, on the hill side of the river, this historic hotel offers a range of well-sized, comfortable rooms decorated in a plush neo-colonial style. Bright and airy, with big bathrooms (some with Jacuzzi), it's ideally located two minutes from the town square.

Ekali
HOTEL €

(☑2292 2501; www.ekali-hotel.com; Grigoriou Digeni 22, Kakopetria; r 40-55; P ❄) A straightforward, tidy and clean option, with decent rooms decorated in dark-red hues, and laminated-wood flooring. It's a good hotel for families with young children, as the rooms have baby-monitoring facilities. Can be overpriced without a booking.

Agros

Archontiko Rousias
AGROTOURISM €€

(☎2275 0605; 2-/4-person houses €100/175; P❋⛄) This replete old house offers agrotourism at its finest in the village of Palichori (past Agros). The house has deluxe rooms with modern facilities (dishwasher, air-con), but retains all its original characteristics. Great for self-catering families or romantics looking for a mountain escape. The balconies have unparalleled views over the village.

Rodon
HOTEL €€

(☎2552 1201; www.rodonhotel.com; Agros; s/d €65-95; P❋@⛄⛄) This gigantic hotel is smart and swish, catering to large groups and package tourists with excellent facilities like the restaurant, bar, two pools and tennis courts that are worth a visit on their own. Ideal base for the area's many walking paths.

PAFOS & THE WEST

Pafos

Accommodation in Pafos is mainly designed for package-tour groups, with only a handful of good budget places. Although most standard hotels aren't used to independent travellers, they will accommodate you if there is space, which outside July and August is generally not a problem. Consider an apartment hotel, which keeps the costs down and usually equals considerably more living space than a standard hotel. Most hotels are in Kato Pafos.

Kiniras
HOTEL €€

(Map p89; ☎2694 1604; www.kiniras.cy.net; Leoforos Archiepiskopou Makariou III 91; low-high s €40-60, d €65-80; ❋⛄) Bang in the centre of Ktima, Kiniras is passionately run by charismatic owner Georgios, who also painted the colourful frescos and paintings throughout the hotel and restaurant. The rooms have a homey, historic feel with high ceilings, muted colours and all the essentials, including telephone, radio, TV, fridge and safe box. The communal areas have the original 1920s tiles. The hotel's downstairs restaurant, Kiniras Garden, is a good place to eat.

Axiothea Hotel
HOTEL €€

(Map p89; ☎2693 2866; www.axiotheahotel .com; Ivis Malliotis 2; low-high s €40-60, d €52-75; P❋⛄) This dusky pink hotel, just southwest of the CTO office in Ktima, has a vast reception area and lounge with original stone floors and comfy sofas to enjoy the panoramic views of the town and sea. Family run with a congenial elderly owner, the rooms are carpeted and comfortable, but vary in size; those in the back are smaller.

Agapinor Hotel
HOTEL €€

(Map p89; ☎2693 3926; www.agapinorhotel.com .cy; Nikodimou Mylona 24-25; low-high s €45-65, d €65-90; P❋⛄) This Ktima hotel is popular with tour groups and has excellent facilities, with two pools, a sun terrace, airy rooms and a recently revamped evening restaurant which specialises in Cypriot cuisine, but gives in with a Brit-style roast beef and Yorkshire pud lunch on Sundays.

TOP CHOICE ⟩ Crystallo Apartments
APARTMENTS €

(Map p86; ☎2695 4233; crystallo@cytanet.com .cy; Ikarou 2; 2-person studios low-high €35-40; @⛄) These spacious studio apartments in Kato Pafos are well equipped with kitchenettes (including plenty of pots and plates), dining table and chairs, sofa, comfy chairs, TV and small terraces, most of which overlook the adjacent historic Ayia Marina church. The furniture and decor are fairly drab and worn but, given the location, this is a cheap sleep winner. There are a couple of internet terminals in the lobby and an adjacent bar-cafe. Owner George will give you a warm welcome.

Annabelle
HOTEL €€€

(Map p86; ☎2693 8333; www.annabelle.com.cy; Posidonos; low-high r incl breakfast €200-250; P❋⛄⛄⛄) A fabulous Kato Pafos hotel with luxurious rooms, some with private pools (oh, the decadence). The large hotel pool snakes through the site and the deck chairs that sit on the pool's edge are shaded by lofty palm trees. There are several restaurants and bars, plus a spa and yoga classes. Families can also enjoy excellent children's facilities, including a kids club, indoor and outdoor playgrounds, babysitting service and children's menus.

Dionysos
HOTEL €€

(Map p86; ☎2693 3414; www.dionysoshotel paphos.com; Dionysou 1; low-high s €55-60, d €60-70; ❋@⛄) Off the main Posidonos avenue in Kato Pafos, the Dionysos is a solid midrange choice with a shady courtyard, a small pool and solarium area and a warm colour scheme throughout with plenty of natural timber and limestone. The rooms are pleasant, if unexceptional, but have benefited from a recent revamp with a choice of tiled or carpeted rooms, plus private balconies and satellite TV. You pay a few euros extra for a pool view. Free wi-fi is available in reception.

Pyramos Hotel   HOTEL €

(Map p86; ☑2693 0222; www.pyramos-hotel .com; Agias Anastasias 4; low-high incl breakfast s €35-40, d 45-50; ✳) For something different, grab a room overlooking the fascinating adjacent archaeological site of Hrysopolitissa Basilica. Soothingly decked out with cream walls, orange throws and classy mosaic-tiled bathrooms, this is one of the better small hotels in Kato Pafos. The hotel is fronted by a classy small bar, which also offers complimentary wi-fi to guests.

Daphne   APARTMENTS €€

(Map p86; ☑2693 3500; www.daphne-hotel.com; Alkminis 3; low-high s €33-60, d €50-73; ✳≋👶) An apartment complex off the main tourist beat, Daphne is a good self-catering choice. The apartments are fully equipped and neat, and there is a slightly exposed (to the street) pool at the front. There's a children's area, free cots and good concessions for kids. The Kato Pafos location is very central and the service friendly.

Alexander the Great   HOTEL €€€

(Map p86; ☑2696 5000; www.kanikahotels.com; Posidonos; low-high r incl breakfast €105-150; P✳🛜≋👶) A stylish Kato Pafos place that caters mainly to a well-heeled package-tour crowd. The rooms are plush and carpeted with an elegant blue-and-gold colour scheme and tasteful artwork on the walls. It has everything you need if you don't want to leave the hotel: tennis, gymnasium, children's area, indoor and outdoor pools, restaurant and bar, and it's right on the beach. Discounts of 40% apply out of season.

Around Pafos

Camping Feggari   CAMPGROUND €

(☑2662 1534; camp sites per adult/child/tent €3/1/3; ⊙Apr-Oct) Surrounded by cypress trees, just a couple of minutes' stroll from Coral Bay beach and close to plenty of shops and restaurants, this is a pleasant campground with good facilities, including a snack bar.

Akamas Heights

🔝 Amarakos Inn   AGROTOURISM €€

(☑2663 3117; www.amarakos.com; Kato Akourdalia; low-high studios €60-68, 1-bedroom apt €77/94; ✳@🛜≋) This glorious place has spacious air-con apartments in a wood-and-stone complex of buildings surrounding a flower-filled central courtyard with fragrant honeysuckle and jasmine and an original grape press. Two of the apartments have fireplaces. The family owners (grandma is the cook) can organise cultural minibus excursions as well as horse riding. There is a pool, plus children's facilities and an excellent in-house restaurant.

Sapho Manor House   AGROTOURISM €€

(☑2633 2650; www.agrotourism.com.cy; Dhrousia; studios from €50, 2-bedroom apt €70; ⊙May-Oct; ≋) This aesthetically restored mansion dates back to 1912 and is located within confessional distance of the pretty village church. There are several studios and apartments, all decorated in the traditional style, with doors and windows made out of Cypriot pine. You can pay €10 more for a private studio terrace. There is a communal garden, a swimming pool and a laundry room (€5 per load).

Kostaris   AGROTOURISM €€

(☑2962 6672; www.agrino.org/eleonora; Goudi; 2-person houses €130; ≋) These five beautiful wood-and-stone houses are located at the top of the pretty village of Goudi. The two-person house is particularly lovely, with a fireplace, courtyards, palm trees, pots of brilliant-red geraniums and shady vines. There's a pool for the use of guests.

Ayii Anargyri Natural
Healing Spa Resort   HOTEL €€€

(☑2681 4000; www.aasparesort.com; Miliou; r from €150; ✳🛜≋) Situated just outside the unspoilt village of Miliou, in a valley surrounded by thickly wooded slopes, this gorgeous place is set in a former monastery (18 of the rooms are former monks' cells). There's little that's monastic about the adjacent luxurious spa, all glossy marble and traditional healing treatments like a sulphur-mud soak (€45) or the tempting 'Timeless Youth' face-firming treatment (€75), combined with the latest therapeutic techniques. The mineral-rich spa water gurgles forth from the 17th-century Ayi Anargyri springs.

Makriniari AGROTOURISM €
(☎2693 2931; www.agrotourism.com.cy; Kritou
Terra; 2-person apt from €40) This single-storey
stone-clad rural house is perfect for passing
a relaxing few days. The one-bedroom apartments surround a central courtyard and
garden, complete with traditional oven and
overlooking a green gorge.

Akamas Peninsula

TOP
CHOICE **Bougainvillea Hotel
Apartments** APARTMENTS €
(Map p98; ☎2681 2250; www.bougainvillea.com;
Verginas 13; studios/1-bedroom apt €50/65; ☺Apr-
Oct; ❀❀❀) Positively the best place to stay
in Polis. A flowery path runs alongside the
apartments, which have one bedroom, a
living room, and a balcony with views of
peaceful olive groves. The whole place has
an intimate, homey feel, with a swimming
pool, plus lawn and a small playground
for children.

Polis Camp Site CAMPGROUND €
(off Map p98; ☎2681 5080; camp sites per adult/
child/tent €2.50/1/3; ☺Apr-Oct) Surrounded
by fragrant eucalyptus trees that offer good,
thick shade, this lovely camp site has its own
quality beach. There's plenty of space, and
good facilities. Located about 2km north of
Polis, it's signposted from the town centre.
Concerts are regularly staged here during
the summer months.

Stephanos Hotel Apartments APARTMENTS €
(Map p98; ☎2632 2411; www.stephanos-hotel.com;
Leoforos Arsinois; 2-person apt €50; ❀❀❀❀)
Comprising two apartment blocks surrounding a central pool, this Polis option
is well maintained and sparkling with light
pine-and-cream decor, well-equipped kitchenettes and private balconies. It's popular
with walkers from the UK and Germany.
The sprawling downstairs restaurant serves
decent, if unexceptional, Cypriot food.

Nicki Holiday Resort APARTMENTS €€
(off Map p98; ☎2632 2226; www.nickiresort.com;
Polis; low-high studio apt €40-70; ❀❀❀❀) An
attractive family-run apartment hotel situated a little out of town on the way to Latsi.
The low-rise apartments are surrounded by
landscaped gardens and three swimming
pools, including a paddling pool for tots.
Additional facilities include restaurant, snack
bar, tennis courts and fitness centre. When
it's time to flop at the end of the day, you

won't be disappointed: the rooms are just
fine, with well-equipped kitchenettes and
satellite channels for that favourite soap.

Tylliria

Tylos Beach Hotel HOTEL €
(☎2652 2348; www.tyloshotel.com.cy; Nikolaou
Papageorgiou 40, Kato Pyrgos; r per person incl
breakfast €30; ❀❀) Decorated in modern
(rather than contemporary) style, Tylos
has tidy, small rooms with chipped marble
floors, pine-and-pale-blue decor and small
balconies, most overlooking the harbour.
The downstairs restaurant is vast both inside and out and seems more suited to huge
tour groups than the normal smattering of
diners.

Western Troödos

Stelios House AGROTOURISM €
(☎2672 2343; www.agrotourism.com.cy; Pano
Panagia; 2-person apt from €48) Stelios is one
of several traditional stone houses that have
been converted into apartments for tourists.
There is little to choose between them, with
their warm rustic colour scheme, wooden
shutters and private balconies. Stelios has
the advantage of a lovely large courtyard.

LARNAKA & THE EAST

Larnaka

The town offers excellent, small midrange
hotels, good-value self-catering apartments,
rooms in restored houses and new sleep-
only hotels. Many of these are ideal for independent travellers exploring the island
from a single base. There are, of course, still
the plush hotels that roll out along Dekelia
beach, east of town. Advance bookings are
generally a good idea during the summer
months.

TOP
CHOICE **E-Hotel** HOTEL €€€
(☎2474 7000; www.hotel-e.com; Faros dromo 1;
s/d €70/140; ❀❀@❀❀) Overlooking the
quiet cliffs of Faros Beach, this swish new
hotel and spa is located 20 minutes west of
town by car. Luxurious, modern rooms are
well-equipped with plasma TVs, sparkling
bathrooms and neutral colourings. It has
everything for those looking for high-end

treatment and the serenity of staying just outside town. No expense has been spared in the Eden spa, which has a traditional hammam, a sauna, a steam room, a hydra-oxygenated pool and a whole host of facial and body treatments to choose from.

Petrou Bros APARTMENTS €
(Map p108; ☑2465 0600; www.petrou.com.cy; Armenikis Eklisias; 2-bed apt €45-60; P❄@🛜) Good value and central, with sizeable, if dimly lit, kitchenettes equipped with a fridge, two hotplates and plenty of pots and pans. The bedrooms are small by comparison but pleasantly furnished, with private terraces.

Easy HOTEL €€
(Map p108; ☑2410 2703; www.easyhotel.com; Kimonos 1; r €60; P❄) In the heart of town, it has all the basics: comfort, location and, depending on your room, some good views. The diminutive, no-fuss plastic retro rooms are clean and purpose built, with no sharp edges.

Alkisti City HOTEL €
(Map p108; ☑2481 5140; www.cityalkisti.com; Agiou Lazarou; d €45; P❄) This traditional stone house was completely renovated in 2006 and converted into a charming eight-room hotel. The rooms are modern and compact, all with en suite. Downstairs there's a lovely little courtyard for sunbathing, the reception area and a restaurant. Situated just across from Agios Lazarus and only 100m from Finikoudes promenade, the location is perfect.

Livadhiotis City HOTEL €€
(Map p108; ☑2462 6222; www.livadhiotis.com; Nikolaou Rossou 50; r €60-115; P❄@🛜) Recently refurbished and in a central location (a stone's throw from Agios Lazarus and the beach), this hotel offers comfortable, clean, compact rooms with late-retro decor. Cool coffee shops in and around this place make it a summer hot spot.

Eleonora APARTMENTS €€
(Map p108; ☑2462 6222; www.eleonorahotelapts.com; Ermou 55; r €55-85; P❄🛜🍳) Ideally located right in the heart of the town, Eleonora has large, simply decorated rooms and studios with balconies overlooking busy little Ermou square. It's a great value-for-money option with extras like two-room apartments, ovens, ironing board (and iron) and discounts for sun beds on the seafront.

Sun Hall HOTEL €€€
(Map p108; ☑2465 3341; www.aquasolhotels.com; Leoforos Athinon 6; s €100-110, d €145-180; P❄@🛜🍳) Right on the seafront, this plush hotel has awesome views from the rooms and balconies that look over the main promenade and sea. Sun Hall has just reopened after extensive refurbishment, and everything is new, sparkling and waiting to be enjoyed by its guests. The full Finikoudes, coastal-town experience is worth the higher price bracket.

Golden Bay HOTEL €€€
(☑2464 5444; www.goldenbay.com.cy; s €135-175, d €195-240; P❄@🛜🏊) Larnaka's luxury giant leads the list of beachfront hotels on Dekelia road and has everything you would expect from a top-end establishment. Spacious and comfortable rooms head skyward from its open halls and elegant corridors. The large swimming pool, gym, beauty salon and stylish restaurant cap off the opulence.

Agia Napa

Between mid-June and mid-August you will need to have pre-booked. Being a resort town, Napa offers a plethora of accommodation, with everything from unlicensed rooms to top-end hotels. Rooms generally reflect the fact that many visitors only use them to sleep in (or sleep it off in). Most are clean but plain (sometimes dated), with prices somewhat inflated across the board. Independent travellers will be welcomed if there is space (or shuffled off to a buddy hotel), but expect another price hike for just rolling up. Many hotels along the coast only operate from March to October.

TOP CHOICE **Okeanos Beach** HOTEL €€
(Map p118; ☑2372 4440; www.okeanoshotel.com.cy; 1 Oktovriou; r €60-100; P❄@🏊🍳) Well-priced, tight rooms with double beds, basic holiday furnishings and nice little balconies overlooking the pool and beach. It has a great location that's walking distance to everything.

Limanaki Beach HOTEL €€
(Map p118; ☑2372 1600; 1 Oktovriou 18; r €70-120; P❄@🏊🍳) Situated near the port, this family-friendly hotel is within walking distance of the Square. The rooms are clean but on the small side, with balconies overlooking the pool and sea.

Diomylos
APARTMENTS €€

(Map p118; ☎2372 2219; Leoforos Archiepiskopou Makariou III 35; r €40-70; P✱✲) Funky block of apartments, with sun terraces and swimming pool. The friendly staff makes this an easy and comfortable place to stay. It's centrally located, and there's a bus stop right outside for venturing further afield. Air-con is charged an extra €7 per day, so go for a corner room with a breeze.

Napa Prince
APARTMENTS €€

(off Map p118; ☎2372 1483; www.napaprince.com; Tefkrou Anthiou 65; r €40-70; P✱✲) Recently refurbished, this family-owned and run hotel has a friendly atmosphere. The spacious, well-equipped rooms are clean and well maintained. Only three minutes' walk to the Square, it has an excellent pool with a refurbished bar, and staff who are happy to help with anything. Air-con is an extra €6 per day.

Aeneas
HOTEL €€€

(☎2372 4000; www.aeneas.com.cy; Leoforos Nisiou 100; s €220, d €450; P✱@☎✲) For those wanting something a little more up-market, the Aeneas is the way to go. It boasts contemporary 'inland' rooms, which open onto one of the biggest pools in the Med. This place is an opulent haven dedicated to water, with all the trimmings. It is also ideally situated opposite Nissi Beach.

Green Bungalows
APARTMENTS €

(Map p118; ☎2372 1511; www.greenbungalows.com; Katalymata 19; r €45-65; ◎Apr-Oct; P✱✲) Uncomplicated studios with tiled floors, basic furniture, open lounges, balconies and small kitchenettes. Can attract revellers and is a good place for groups to stay.

Around Agia Napa

The majority of hotel options are clustered along the Protaras–Pernera road, with most geared to package-holiday visitors. There is little in the way of budget accommodation but an array of choice otherwise. Bookings are recommended in high season.

Brilliant
APARTMENTS €€

(☎2383 2211; www.brillianthotelapts.com; Kavo Greco, Protaras; r €60-120; P✱@☎✲⛵) Clean and bright, open style apartments with kitchenettes and terraces. Great pool facilities, bar, and restaurant with good-quality food.

Cavo Maris Beach
HOTEL €€€

(☎2383 2043; www.cavomaris.com; Protaras; r €80-150; P✱@☎⛵) Good value and luxurious, this hotel is located on its own beach, with pools, restaurants, bars and night-time activities. The spacious rooms have balconies.

Seagull
APARTMENTS €€

(☎2383 1270; www.seagullhotelapts.com; Hifastios 2; r €55-110; P✱✲) Located close to the beach in Pernera, 2km further along the coast from Protaras, Seagull has very fresh, bright and spacious apartments with balconies. The pool is an excellent size, so it's great for families. Full breakfast is available from around €6.

LEFKOSIA (NICOSIA)

Budget accommodation is quite poor in Lefkosia. Most of what once existed has either closed down or been upgraded to a midrange category. Lefkosia's top-end hotels are all the usual suspects, with luxurious comfort and design, although, with a couple of exceptions, there's a lamentable lack of imaginative and original establishments here.

Lefkosia (Nicosia)

TOP CHOICE Royiatiko
HOTEL €€€

(Map p128; ☎2244 5445; www.royiatikohotel .com.cy; Apollonos 27; s/d incl breakfast €85/110; P✱☎✲) Opened in early 2010, this hotel is a welcome addition to the city's sleeping scene. The rooms are elegantly decorated in tones of brown and cream, with large marshmallow-soft cushions on the beds. There are fridges, kettles, fresh flowers and stylish bathrooms with steely-grey floor tiles, plus a well-equipped gym and heated pool (in winter). The location is perfect, in the heart of the historic centre.

Classic Hotel
HOTEL €€

(Map p128; ☎2266 4006; www.classic.com.cy; Rigenis 94; s/d €80/97; P✱☎) This hotel, close to Pafos Gate, is a member of the 'Small Luxury Hotels of the World' group, and you can see why. Fully renovated in October 2010, everywhere, from the reception to the rooms, is done up in relaxing colours of creams and woods; the design is minimalist and the rooms are smart and comfortable. The 59 Knives restaurant, part of the hotel, specialises in haute cuisine, adding its own contribution to the Classic's luxuries – together with the rooftop gym.

Centrum HOTEL €€
(Map p128; ☎2245 6444; www.centrumhotel.net; Pasikratous 15; low-high incl breakfast s €70-90, d €90-110; ❊@❧) A fairly stylish place that's a cross between a boutique and a business hotel, the Centrum offers spacious rooms, some with balconies, decked out in blush and salmon colours; some have baths, too, so state your preference when booking. The hotel is within seconds of Plateia Eleftherias. The business facilities are excellent, and a fitness centre opened in early 2012, as well as a new Byzantine wing with more traditionally furnished rooms. The restaurant is known for its Cypriot cuisine.

Sky Hotel HOTEL €
(Map p128; ☎2266 6880; www.skyhotel.ws; Solonos 7c; s/d €49/60; ❊) The best budget place in Lefkosia, Sky is bang in the middle of the historic centre, surrounded by souvenir shops and cafes. Rooms are carpeted and spacious, with pine furniture and pale paintwork; most have large balconies overlooking the rooftops.

Averof HOTEL €
(off Map p138; ☎2277 3447; www.averof.com.cy; Averof 19; s/d incl breakfast €50/65; ❊❧) Close to the historic centre, near the British High Commission and in a quiet residential part of Lefkosia, this place prides itself on its rather kitsch rustic decor and attentive service. The mock-traditional rooms are clean and bright. There are excellent cut-price deals for longer stays.

Cyprus Hilton HOTEL €€€
(off Map p138; ☎2237 7777; www.hilton.com; Leoforos Archiepiskopou Makariou III; low-high incl breakfast s €173-218, d €207-252; ❒❊❧❅) This premier hotel was apparently the gathering ground for Eastern and Western spies during the Cold War, when Cyprus' strategic position was invaluable. Who knows what political manoeuvring went on in its luxurious rooms, indoor and outdoor pool, tennis and squash courts, and in-house restaurants? Check the website for special cut-price deals.

Around Lefkosia

TOP CHOICE Avli House AGROTOURISM €
(☎2254 3236; www.agrotourism.com.cy; Markou Drakou 3; d low-high €45-52, family ste €60, house €268) Situated close to the Maheras Forest, this delightful rural accommodation is in the village of Lythrodontas. It can sleep up to 14 people in self-contained rooms and has a pretty plant-filled central courtyard surrounded by the apartments and house, all of which have benefited by the fact that the owner is an accomplished artist. There are paintings and (tasteful) etchings on the walls, plenty of warm woodwork, colourful fabrics and rugs and some eye-catching traditional architectural features. A two-night minimum stay is required.

NORTH NICOSIA (LEFKOŞA)

North Nicosia has a fairly bleak range of accommodation. The budget 'hotels' are around the Selimiye Mosque area and in the streets east of Girne Caddesi. They all have dorm-style rooms where a bed costs around €7, but we don't recommend any of them. Apart from that, there's a handful of mid-range to top-end hotels which, despite the presence of casinos, are reputable.

City Royal HOTEL €€
(☎228 7621; www.city-royal.com; Gazeteci Kemal Aşik Caddesi; s/d €50/70; ❊❧❅) A popular choice with travellers on business and with casino lovers. Rooms are carpeted and spacious with minibar, phone, satellite TV, and even a phone in the bathroom. There is also a swimming pool and a gym. To reach here, head northeast of the Kyrenia Gate for around 300m.

Golden Tulip HOTEL €€€
(off Map p152; ☎610 5050; www.goldentulipnicosia.com; Dereboyu 1; s/d €85/135; ❒❊❧❅) One of the latest hotels to open here, the Golden Tulip looks more like an upended glass canister than anything more floral. Within there's a glossy corporate look and a comprehensive list of facilities, including health club and spa, children's nursery and, yes, yet another casino if you fancy a flutter. The standard is high and the service is top notch, but the atmosphere is international – and anonymous.

Saray HOTEL €€
(Map p152; ☑228 3115; saray@northcyprus.net; Atatürk Meydanı; s/d €50/75; ❄) On the verge of reopening during research, after much-needed renovation, this hotel is located in the centre of the Old City on Atatürk Meydanı and is an unmissable landmark. Check out the rooftop bar with its sweeping cityscape views.

KYRENIA (GIRNE) & THE NORTHERN COAST

Kyrenia (Girne)

The town centre has small guesthouses and little, generally older, hotels, while the outskirts boast luxury giants with resorts and casinos. The following options are central.

TOP CHOICE **White Pearl Hotel** BOUTIQUE HOTEL €€
(Map p164; ☑815 4677; www.whitepearlhotel.com; Girne Limanı; r €40-60; ❄) This refurbished, good-value place has nine individually decorated rooms that are understated and clean. Some rooms have balcony, and there are pretty views of the harbour. The roofterrace bar is perfect for late-night cocktails and drinks, even if you're not staying in the hotel.

Club Z HOTEL €€
(Map p164; ☑815 1549; www.hotelclubz.com; Mustafa Çağatay Caddesi; r €45-60; P❄@🌐🛗) Close to town and the harbour, Club Z has straightforward, spacious self-catering apartment studios and villa rooms. The decor is basic, if not a little dated, but the hotel's good value for the locale. Ask for a spot overlooking the adjoining pool area in summer.

Nostalgia HOTEL €€
(Map p164; ☑815 3079; fax 815 1376; Cafer Paşa Sokak 7; r €35-55; ❄) A charming clutter of vintage radios, books and typewriters decorates the reception area of this lovely old townhouse-hotel. Superbly located two minutes' walk from the harbour, the rooms are rustic, old-fashioned and clean. More luxury can be found in the suite, with its gorgeous four-poster bed.

Dome Hotel HOTEL €€€
(Map p164; ☑815 2453; www.dome-cyprus.com; Kordon Boyu Sokak; s/d €80-110; P❄@🌐🛗🐾) Situated on the seafront, as mentioned in Durrell's *Bitter Lemons,* this stalwart of Kyrenia's hotel scene is still considered the town's best. The comfortable and cosy rooms have all modern facilities, and there is a large seawater swimming pool and a shallow children's pool.

Rocks Hotel & Casino HOTEL €€€
(off Map p164; ☑650 0400; www.rockshotel.com; Kordon Boyu Sokak; s/d €105-140; P❄@🌐🛗🐾) This hotel-casino giant offers stylish, modern rooms with views of the sea or the mountains. Packed with all the electronic amenities you need, rooms are complemented by the service. There are excellent and extravagant spas, saunas, massages and Turkish baths for when you're not poolside or up big on the tables.

Harbour Scene HOTEL €
(Map p164; ☑815 6855; Canbulat Sokak 32; r €35; ❄) This place offers clean, budget accommodation with comfortable rooms that look onto sea and mountains. It has the most wood seen in any bar on earth. Also has great proximity to restaurants and nightlife, if you don't mind their late-night ruckus.

Around Kyrenia & the Ranges

Bellapais has some excellent alternative places to stay. It's close enough to Kyrenia to be easily accessible, but far enough (and high enough) away to feel peacefully distant.

TOP CHOICE **Lapida** HOTEL €€
(☑862 1500; www.lapidahotel.com; Ibrahim Nidai Cad, Lapta; r from €40; P❄🛗🐾) A family-run hotel with wonderful lush gardens and pool. The bright, clean, spacious rooms make you feel right at home. The peaceful patios are ideal for taking in the serenity and scent of the surrounding citrus valley.

Hideaway Club HOTEL €€€
(☑822 2620; www.hideawayclub.com; r from €70; P❄@🌐🛗) Has a brilliant white theme, with decadent pools and patios, backed by the grandeur of the mountains. The spotless sea-view cottages are dressed with fresh flowers and lace. This is an ideal and serene getaway for couples and romantics, as the hotel has a child-free policy. It's about 4km west of Kyrenia toward Lapta, in the village of Karaoğlanoğlu (Agios Georgios).

Sempati
HOTEL €

(☎821 2770; www.hotelsempati.com; Ali Ocak Sokak 7; r from €30; P❄@🛜🅿🏃) Situated 100m inland from Lapta's coast (9km from Kyrenia harbour), this is an excellent value-for-money venue. Cosy rooms with simple decor and balconies, and spacious self-contained bungalows surround a large sun-lounged pool.

Dedeman Olive Tree
HOTEL €€

(☎824 4200; Onar, Çatalköy; r €60-80; P❄@🛜🅿🏃) Family-friendly bungalows and villas dot the well-kept gardens at this relaxing hotel. The very clean, cosy rooms are done up in cool reds or retro oranges. The pool has a brilliant bar, where you can slip off for an out-of-the-sun drink in the water.

Bellapais Monastery Village
HOTEL €€

(☎815 9171; www.bellapaismonasteryvillage.com; Bellapais; r €50-70; P❄@🅿) Located close to the monastery, the hotel has comfortable studio villas with bedrooms on the mezzanine level, and hotel rooms. There's a relaxing pool and deck with expansive views of Kyrenia town to the harbour. The restaurant offers an à la carte menu during the day and made-to-order breakfast. Children under 12 years old are not catered for.

Bellapais Gardens
HOTEL €€€

(☎815 6066; www.bellapaisgardens.com; Bellapais; r low-high €70-90; P❄@🛜🅿) This luxurious resort has self-contained studios and one- and two-bedroom apartments, all with expansive sea views. A lush, almost tropical garden is at the centre, with a swimming pool and a bar to relax in. Situated below the abbey, you can admire its architecture whilst sipping brandy sours poolside.

Gardens of Irini
HOTEL, COTTAGES €€

(☎815 2820; www.gardensofirini.com; Bellapais; s/d from €40, d per week €300) At the top of the village, amongst verdant shrubbery and adjacent to a traditional house, Gardens of Irini has self-catering cottages with private courtyards and kitchens decorated with rustic cookers (and one with a fireplace) and rugs. Owner Deirdre cooks up full breakfasts (and dinners by request), served in the leafy surrounds. You must love animals to stay here, as the gardens have become a sanctuary for cats and placid stray mutts.

The Northwest

Güzelyurt Otel
HOTEL €€

(☎714 3412; Bahçelievler Bulvarı; s/d €30-50; ❄🅿) Situated on the edge of Morfou, this basic hotel is the only decent accommodation around – a layover option should you need a break from the road. The rooms are simple and there's a swimming pool, bar and laundry service.

Soli Inn
HOTEL €€

(☎727 7575; soliinn@northcyprus.net; s/d €30-50; P🅿) West of Morfou at Gemikonaği, this former caravanserai is now a comfortable budget hotel. By the sea, it has simple doubles and (better-equipped) suites. There's a decent pool and golf course nearby. Rates include breakfast.

FAMAGUSTA (MAĞUSA) & THE KARPAS (KIRPAŞA) PENINSULA

Famagusta (Mağusa)

Famagusta's hotels are generally an either-or equation: either ultra-swanky or basic, with very little in between.

TOP CHOICE Crystal Rocks
BUNGALOWS €€

(☎378 9400; www.cypruscrystalrocks.com; Yolu Salamis; r €57-70; P❄@🛜🅿🏃) Over 60 awesome little bungalows close to the beach and not far from Salamis. Modern, bright and relaxing rooms are tastefully decorated and set amid scented gardens, with rainbow-shaped pool and kids' pool. A good choice for couples and families.

Salamis Bay Conti
HOTEL €€€

(☎378 8201; www.salamisbay-conti.com; Gazi; r €60-90; 🅿🏃) Located 8km north of Famagusta, in Salamis Bay, this good-value giant has a large outdoor and indoor pool, and its own expansive sandy beach. The bedrooms are suitably big and pompous to match the massage parlours, twinkling casinos and Turkish baths. It's perfect if you're looking for a long holiday in the sun. Rooms without sea view are more cost effective.

Portofino
HOTEL €

(Map p182; ☎366 4392; www.portofinohotel-cyprus.com; Feyzi Çakmak Bulvarı 9; r €25-40; P❄🅿) Well located at the ancient port of the Old Town, with spacious rooms that are a little dated. Clean and uncomplicated, this is a budget hotel in every sense. If you want somewhere to lay your head on the cheap, then stay here. It does have a decent pool.

Around Famagusta

Boğaz
HOTEL €€

(☎371 2559; www.bogazhotel.com; Gazi Mustafa Kemal Bulvarı, Boğaz; r €37-50; P ❄ ≋) A comfortable budget hotel with good-sized, neutral rooms and big sofas. It has a small indoor pool and Jacuzzi; the better outdoor pool is across the (somewhat busy) road. Rates include breakfast.

Exotic
HOTEL €€

(☎371 2885; www.cyprusexotic.com; Boğaz; r €35-50; P ❄ ≋ ⛟) Without a beachside location, but with neat, clean rooms at good prices. Outdoor activities are covered with pools for adults and kids, both equipped with water slides. Prices include breakfast.

Karpas (Kirpaşa) Peninsula

The peninsula offers some remarkable alternative accommodation not found elsewhere on the island.

TOP CHOICE Nitovikla Garden
AGROTOURISM €

(☎375 5980; www.nitovikla.com; Mehmetcik Kumyali; r €25-37; P ❄ ≋) A fantastic agrotourism venture in the seaside village of Kumyali. Owner Zekai has put all his efforts into imparting his expertise and general love of food and fine life into his hotel and restaurant. The hotel has 10 rooms, decorated in traditional Cypriot style (carved wooden furniture and silk embroidery), with balconies overlooking the sea. There's a good pool and a nearby beach.

Theresa
HOTEL €

(☎374 4266; www.theresahotel.com; Yenierenköy; r €25-37; P ❄) This small seaside place has simple, neat rooms with spacious bathrooms, and balconies overlooking the sea.

There's an in-house restaurant, and outside the hotel is a sandy beach with parasols and loungers. The hotel is 7km east of Yenierenköy.

Club Malibu
HOTEL, BUNGALOWS €€

(☎374 4264; www.clubmalibucy.com; Yenierenköy; r €45-65; P ❄ ⛟) Simple, smart, bright rooms here have balconies and open views to the beach. There's also a scattering of beachside bungalows. This hotel is ideal for families looking for an outdoor-fun, budget holiday.

Karpaz Arch Houses
AGROTOURISM €

(☎372 2009; www.karpazarchhouses.com; Dipkarpaz; r €30-40; P ❄) Approximately 500m from the centre of Dipkarpaz village, this hotel is one large arch-house with 12 traditional rooms. The self-catering accommodation is surrounded by green gardens with a courtyard. A community feel, with guests barbecuing outside their rooms, makes for a social atmosphere.

Oasis at Ayfilon
HOTEL €

(☎840 5082; www.oasishotelkarpas.com; Agio Filon Beach; r €30-45; P) Ideal for nature lovers, the seven clean, minimalist rooms here have comfortable double bed, mosquito net and oil lamp, and look out directly onto the small beach. Bathrooms are shared in four of the rooms; the other three have en suites. Rates include a whopping brekkie with fresh bread and vegetables.

Blue Sea
HOTEL €

(☎372 2393; www.blueseahotelkarpaz.com; Dipkarpaz; r from €25; P ❄) Family run, quiet and basic, Blue Sea is near Alagadı (Turtle) Beach. On the peninsula's south side, it's built on a rocky spur shaded by shoreline trees. Fresh fish is caught daily and served by the hotel's owner.

Seabird
BUNGALOWS €

(☎372 2012; r from €25; P) Barely 1km past the Monastery of Apostolos Andreas, this seasonal restaurant offers a handful of basic wooden and stone huts to rent, right on the beach. It's low-key island living with beds, mosquito nets and no hot water. Good for campers and divers.

Understand Cyprus

CYPRUS TODAY 214

Since the rejection of reunification via referendums, the island has moved forward, but is prosperity more important than partition?

HISTORY 216

From the development of ancient city kingdoms to modern times, the island has been a much-sought-after possession.

THE CYPRIOT WAY OF LIFE 229

The national identity, though complicated by history ancient and recent, nonetheless binds the people in their everyday lives.

CYPRUS' NATURAL ENVIRONMENT 232

Mountains, plains, sand and sea: Cyprus' unique flora, fauna, geography and geology is laid out before you.

THE ARTS 237

Artistic highs here include exquisite modern icons, entertaining puppet theatres and lacework as fine as a spider's web.

population per sq km

CYPRUS   UK   GREECE

≈ 86 people

Cyprus Today

Peace Talks, the Never-Ending Cycle?

Since its division in 1974, talks to reunite Cyprus have taken place sporadically with little success. They were revived in 2008, when the Republic's president Demetris Christofias promised to work with the then Turkish Cypriot leader Mehmet Ali Talat, generating over 100 meetings. Their attempts at camaraderie, aimed at creating a 'climate of peace', began to worry officials on the Turkish mainland. The situation was quickly blunted when the pro-Turkish Dervis Eroglu came to power in 2010.

Since then the usual rhetoric regarding talks with UN mediators has continued. It is unclear how long the current talks will last, as time limits are generously imposed and repeatedly disregarded. Often they merely lead to the agreement to agree on another round of talks.

Meanwhile, problems locally (particularly economic) are overlooked while the best minds concentrate on the more difficult, and perennial issues, of resolving power sharing and land ownership. With the current leaders at odds ideologically, the ability to devise a peace proposal that's acceptable to all is becoming increasingly difficult.

As such, most Cypriots are not very optimistic that there will be a solution anytime soon. Many had hoped Cyprus' EU membership would increase the chances of reunification, but, sadly, it seems to have only muddied the waters, with the bigger EU nations weighing in on the debate.

» Population: 1,120,489 (285,000 estimated Northern Cyprus)

» Area: 9251 sq km (3355 sq km Northern Cyprus)

» GDP: Republic of Cyprus US$22.18 billion; Northern Cyprus US$4.4 billion

The EU & the Economy

EU succession (2004) has changed the landscape in a variety of areas. The common practice of the relaxed application of laws and fines for things like parking on pavements, not wearing helmets on motorbikes, or seatbelts in cars, are now enforced, when they were once met with a simple *'dembirasi'* (doesn't matter).

Dos & Don'ts

» Cypriots love to talk on mobile phones and not use indicators while driving. Make eye contact at intersections before you pull out.

» Be tactful when discussing politics, division and the Green Line.

» If you're invited out for a meal, the bill is paid by the host and not split. Offer to contribute, knowing you'll most likely be scoffed at.

» Don't praise possessions or good fortune too much, as many Cypriots believe this attracts envy and the 'evil eye'.

Top Books

The Island that Everybody Wanted (Marina Christofides & Eleni Lambrou) A history.

A Traveller's History of Cyprus (Tim Boatswain) A concise history.

The Cyprus Conspiracy (Brendan O'Malley & Ian Craig) Events leading to the invasion.

belief systems
(% of population)

78

Greek Orthodox

18
Muslim

•
4
Others

if Cyprus were 100 people

71 would live in towns
29 would live in the country

Fees and charges have increased should you wish to buy a house, or build on a block of land. The cost of water and electricity has skyrocketed.

The price of food and local produce has also indirectly risen, slighting the traditional saying 'in Cyprus you'll never go hungry'.

There have been changes in demographics as well, with foreign workers from Eastern Europe, Asia, Africa and India filling the labour markets. This has created cheap labour and generated complaints of socially problematic behaviour, and rising crime. Now restaurants and shops are predominantly staffed by Eastern-bloc waiters and sales staff. Many families have Sri-Lankan or Philippine maids and nannies.

Not wanting to rely solely on tourism, the government is also focusing on the large quantities of crude oil and natural gas, believed to be located in the seabed between Lebanon, Israel and Cyprus. Negotiations for exploration are currently taking place.

Northern Numbers

The socio-political problem regarding the status and future of Turks or 'population boosters', who have settled on the island since 1974, is one of the most debated and politically manipulated issues in Cyprus. The Greek Cypriots claim there are over 150,000 'Türkiyeli' in the North. Independent researchers put the figure closer to 90,000, and some claim it's as high as 250,000.

The Turkish Troops themselves number around 40,000, and of the Turkish Cypriot population, at least 50% are agrarian immigrants from mainland Turkey.

The Turkish Cypriot side recently rejected requests for a population census (under the auspices of the UN) to determine the real number of settlers who have been given Turkish Cypriot 'citizenship'.

CURRENCY

The Republic of Cyprus adopted the euro as its national currency on 1 January 2008, replacing the consistently very strong Cypriot pound, which had been in circulation since the late 1800s.

Top Surfs

» **Talk Cyprus** (www.talkcyprus .org/forum) Where Cypriots meet to discuss politics.

» **Laika Music** (wn.com/laika _(music)) Cypriot folk music.

» **Cypriot Food** (www.flavoursof cyprus.com) Classic and modern recipes for authentic cuisine.

Kypriaka

» '*Kypriaka*' is Cypriots' very expressive spoken language.

» A derivative of ancient Greek, the dialect is infused with Old French, Italian, Provencal, Arabic and lexis unique to the island.

» Most other Greek speakers have trouble understanding *Kypriaka*.

Safe in Cyprus

» Cyprus' crime rate is only 17% of the European average.

» Its 6.4 crimes per 1000 inhabitants are predominantly minor offences.

» It's one of the safest countries, not only in Europe but in the whole world.

History

Situated at the nautical crossroads of the eastern Mediterranean basin, the island has a rich and varied history much like the intricate 6000-year-old mosaics found on its shores.

Over the centuries countless settlers, invaders, and immigrants have landed or attempted to possess the island. It has been a part of the Greek, Phoenician, Egyptian, Byzantine, Roman, Lusignan, Genoese, Venetian, Ottoman and British Empires, each one leaving an indelible mark on Cypriot history and culture. Remnants can be seen in the great many temples, tombs, ports, churches, basilicas, aqueducts and castles, as well as in the chapels, bastions, fortresses and ancient city walls that cover the island.

It is this combination of influences and contrasts that make Cyprus the incredible place it is today.

Ancient Cyprus

City Kingdoms of Cyprus

The Hellenic settlers established a series of city kingdoms at Kourion, Pafos, Marion (now Polis), Soloi, Lapithos, Tamassos and Salamis, and two more were later established at Kition and Amathous. The Phoenicians, great traders from across the sea, also settled here around this time, in Kition (Larnaka).

Between 1400 and 1200 BC, Mycenaean and Achaean Greek settlers began to arrive en masse, bringing with them language, culture, art and gods. The Cypriots found a particular affiliation with the fertility goddess, Aphrodite.

The city kingdoms oversaw a period of advancement and increasing prosperity from 750 BC to 475 BC, demonstrated by the spectacular Royal Tombs near Salamis (p190). The tombs contained extravagant examples of wealth, and closely match Homer's descriptions of Mycenaean burials in *The Iliad*.

TIMELINE	Millions of Years Ago	10,000–8000 BC	6000 BC
	The island is forced to the surface from the Mediterranean ocean floor, revealing the Troödos Massif, Kyrenia mountain ranges and Mesaoria plain. Scientists now study the sea bed here.	Hunter-gatherers develop the first settlements. The world's earliest water wells are made and domesticated animals are introduced.	Stone buildings, like those of Choirokoitia, are built in small enclosed villages. Inhabitants begin to form working societies with organised crops, stonework and domestic pets.

During this time, Greek influence spread throughout the island, and Cyprus attracted a string of foreign rulers including the Assyrians, the Egyptians and then the Persians. These powers sought control through tribute more than settlement, essentially leaving the city kingdoms to self-govern.

In 498 BC, under King Onesilos of Salamis, the city kingdoms joined in the Ionian revolt against Persian rule, with the exception of Amathous, which aligned itself with the Phoenicians. The Persians landed their army just off Salamis, and a ferocious battle raged. Ultimately the King of Kourion, Stesenor, betrayed the Greeks. Onesilos was killed and the revolt was crushed.

The island maintained its strong links with Hellenism, despite Persian hegemony. In 381 BC, King Evagoras of Salamis tried to unite the city kingdoms with the Greek states, and attempted to overcome the Persians once more. He was defeated and assassinated seven years later, effectively ending the classical age of Greek influence (the remains of which are prevalent on the island to this day).

Hellenistic Cyprus

Alexander the Great's victory over Persian ruler Darius III at Issus in 333 BC released the island from the Persian Empire. Alexander's control of Cyprus, as a part of the Greek Empire, was fleeting. He asserted his authority by giving the city kingdoms autonomy but refusing to allow them to make their own coins. After his death in 323 BC, the city kingdoms were subjugated by Ptolemy I of Egypt, who took over the island as a part of Hellenistic Egypt.

Cyprus is one of the five richest copper-deposit areas in the world. The island's name in Greek is 'Kypros', which some believe may be the reason behind the metal's Latin name, *cuprum*.

HOUSE OF STONE

Human habitation of the island began around 10,000 BC, when hunter-gatherers roamed the coastal caves of Akrotiri Aetokremnou (Vulture Cliff) and its peninsula in the South. Some of the world's oldest water wells have also been found in Cyprus' west.

Eventually in around 6000 BC these nomads built stone villages like the Aceramic Neolithic settlement of Choirokoitia. Built on the side of a hill, beside the banks of a river, its more than 300 inhabitants dwelled in round, flat-roofed *tholoi* (huts) made of stones and mud. They were similar to the contemporary buildings found in Crete and Mesopotamia. The huts were organised within a protective rock wall, around a central courtyard, with some chambers dedicated to cooking and eating, others to sleeping and storage.

Evidence shows the inhabitants produced stoneware tools, weapons, containers and jewellery. They picked fruit, fished and kept sheep and goats. They even kept pets. The oldest known feline-human connection – a domesticated cat buried with its owner – was unearthed here, far pre-dating similar ancient Egyptian finds.

2500 BC	2300–1950 BC	1950–1650 BC	1650–1050 BC
Levantine immigrants bring new technologies and styles. Artistic achievements include the production of cross-shaped human figurines made from picrolite, a local Cypriot stone.	The early Bronze Age; objects are cast using imported tin and imaginative pottery designs flourish, drawing noticeably on human and animal life in and around the villages.	Middle Bronze Age; sustained copper mining and the beginning of trading relationships with the Aegean. Settlements keep to the foothills and plains, in largely agrarian communities.	Writing in the form of a linear script known as Cypro-Minoan is adapted from Crete. Extensive foreign trade coincides with production of fine jewellery, carving and pottery.

COPPER ISLAND

Once copper was discovered in around 2600 BC, it progressively replaced the old stone repertory and led to the excavation of abundant copper deposits in the Troödos Massif.

The country's production and export of copper became highly organised, and trade with Mediterranean islands and Egypt began in earnest. This gave Cyprus great commercial importance in the civilised Mediterranean world.

During the island's transition to the Bronze Age, around 2000 BC, a wave of foreign influence, from immigrants like the Hittites, brought new technologies and styles.

This age also saw new towns established around the coast, with overseas trade of pottery containers and copper ingots (shaped like oxhide) expanded further.

Cyprus enjoyed an unprecedented level of prosperity, accompanied by the movement of foreign goods and people into the island. It became a meeting point of Western and Eastern civilisations thanks to its location and natural wealth.

The island's capital was moved from Salamis to Pafos, which is closer to Egypt. Nicocreon, the last king of Salamis, assisted Ptolemy in centralising power away from the city kingdoms to a single appointed governor general in Pafos. Later suspected of betrayal, he burnt Salamis to the ground before committing suicide.

A *demos* (house and senate) version of parliament was established on the island and it remained a Ptolemaic colony for a further 200 years.

Romans & Rising Christianity

Greek Cypriots are mainly the descendants of early Mycenaean and Achaean settlers, who intermingled with the indigenous population around 1100 BC, and subsequent settlers up to the 16th century.

Cyprus was annexed by the expanding Roman Empire in 58 BC, orator and writer Cicero becoming one of its first proconsuls. Then in 40 BC the island was given to Cleopatra VII of Egypt by Roman general Mark Antony (her lover). Their deaths handed control back to Rome 10 years later.

Cyprus enjoyed some 600 years of relative peace and prosperity under Roman rule, and many public buildings, aqueducts and roads date from this time.

Salamis became a centre of education, commerce and culture, until earthquakes in 15 BC destroyed much of the city. This prompted Emperor Augustus to have it rebuilt in grand Roman style. The buildings he commissioned include the theatre at Kourion, the colonnaded gymnasium at Salamis and the Sanctuary of Apollon Ylatis. Much of these ancient ruins can still be seen today, along with the many mosaic floors depicting scenes from Greek mythology.

1200 BC	1200–1100 BC	1200–1000 BC	11th Century BC
The island enjoys an unprecedented level of prosperity and immigration. The first Greeks settle on the island, introducing new language, art, gods and culture.	Cities are built (or rebuilt) in a rectangular grid plan. Town gates and important buildings correspond to street systems. Increased social hierarchy and order are introduced.	The great Greek city kingdoms of Salamis, Kourion, Pafos, Marion, Soloi, Lapithos and Tamassos flourish. And the island enjoys a period of rapidly increasing advancement and prosperity.	Classical authors credit Greek heroes returning from the Trojan War with founding influential towns: Salamis is said to have been established by Teucer, and Pafos by Agapenor (of Tegea).

Island of Saints

Christianity made its early appearance on the island in AD 45. It was during this period that the apostle Paul began spreading the new religion on the island, accompanied by Barnabas, a Greek Jewish native of Salamis. He was later canonised St Barnabas, or Agios Varnavas in Greek. The missionaries travelled across the island preaching the word of God and converting many locals. Once they reached Pafos, the Roman proconsul Sergius Paulus granted them an audience. A court magician mocked the Apostles upon their speech about Jesus, angering Paul, who is said to have temporarily blinded the sorcerer for his disbelief. The proconsul was so struck by this act that he was among the first to convert to Christianity. Cyprus became the first country in the world to be ruled by a Christian and Christianity flourished on the island.

The Apostles set up the Church of Cyprus, one of the oldest independent churches in the world, and the island quickly became known as 'The Island of Saints'.

A number of those involved in the early development of Christianity were sanctified, including Lazarus, raised from the dead by Jesus, who became the archbishop of Kition. St Helena also visited the island with pieces of the 'Holy Cross' that she left in the protection of Stavrovouni Monastery and at Tochni, where they can still be found today.

By the time of Constantine the Great, Christianity had almost completely supplanted paganism.

If you love ancient Cypriot pottery and sculpture, as displayed in museums and often emulated by local artists, get more information at www.thebritish museum.ac.uk.

Byzantine Cyprus

Constantinople Calling

The Roman Empire was divided in AD 395 and Cyprus fell under its eastern half, the Byzantine Empire, with its capital in Constantinople. Byzantine rulers were sent to Cyprus to govern the island.

The island was able to keep a considerable degree of ecclesiastical autonomy when the Archbishop of Cyprus convinced the Byzantine emperor that the Church of Cyprus had been founded by the Apostles.

In AD 488 the archbishop was granted the right to carry a sceptre instead of an archbishop's crosier. He was also given authority to write his signature in imperial purple ink, a practice which continues to this day.

During this period many of the stunning churches of the island were built, with frescoed walls, mosaics and domed roofs, including the church of St Barnabas, built over his grave in Famagusta (p191).

This relative stability would not last long, as the island would soon be at the forefront of clashes between the Byzantines and the growing Islamic empire.

The best site for dabbling in archaeology is www.ancient cyprus.ac.uk. Amateur or expert, you'll find plenty of resources here to aid your research of Cyprus' ancient history.

HISTORY BYZANTINE CYPRUS

8th–3rd Centuries BC	560–525 BC	499–450 BC
The Assyrians become the first of a series of conquerors to control Cyprus, followed by the Egyptians under emperor Amasis (568–525 BC), and the Persians, under King Cyrus (525–333 BC).	The first Cypriot coins appear under the auspices of the King of Salamis. They are created out of base metals, using the Persian weight system.	The city kingdoms of Cyprus join the Ionian revolt against the Persians. Salamis is punished for its role as the revolt is crushed. Kition becomes an important Phoenician trading post.

» Ancient statue, Salamis

BRONZE

Arab Raids

Islamic expansion in the 7th century had a profound effect on the island. The lands of the Byzantine Empire were attacked. Fleets of ships began a series of bloody raids starting in AD 647, killing many and destroying coastal cities. Salamis (Constantia) was ravaged and sacked heavily, never quite recovering. The city kingdom of Kourion declined dramatically, and coastal settlers moved inland.

In response, fortifications and castles were built, the three grandest being those of St Hilarion, Buffavento, and Kantara in the Kyrenia mountains, defending the north coast.

During one such raid in Kition, Umm Haram, the wife of an Arab commander and the aunt of the Prophet Mohammed, fell from her mule and died. The mosque at Hala Sultan Tekke was built at the site of her fall on the edge of Larnaka's salt lake. It is among the holiest places in the Muslim world.

In AD 688, a truce was called when Justinian II and the Arab caliph Abd-al-Malik signed an agreement for the joint rule of Cyprus. This agreement remained until AD 965, when Emperor Nikiforos Fokas sent an army of men to the island to regain complete control for the Byzantines.

New governors were sent to Cyprus as dukes. Due to the devastation of the coastal cities, the capital was moved inland to Lefkosia and built on the remains of the old city of Ledra.

The Crusades

Byzantine rule may well have continued had it not been for renegade governor Isaak Komninos, who proclaimed himself emperor of Cyprus in 1184.

On his way to the Holy Land as part of the Third Crusade, King Richard the Lionheart's fleet met with inclement weather and was forced to dock in Lemesos. The first ship to make port was that of the recently widowed Queen Joan of Sicily, Richard's sister, and his fiancée, Berengaria of Navarre.

Komninos attempted to capture the royal party and hold them to ransom. King Richard was outraged at this news and marched on Lemesos, overthrowing Komninos and seizing control of the island. This effectively brought an end to Byzantine rule.

Komninos fled to Kantara Castle in the north, and King Richard married his queen in Lemesos Castle's Agios Georgios chapel in 1191. To this day Cyprus is the only foreign country to have held an English royal wedding.

Richard fell ill and stayed in Cyprus, postponing his campaign to the Holy Land. He was joined by the French knight Guy de Lusignan, who assisted him in finishing off Komninos. Upon Komninos' capture, he was chained in silver, instead of iron, at his pleading.

In the 1st century BC, tin was imported to Cyprus and mixed with copper to make bronze. This composition was stronger and more durable, creating better tools and weapons.

411–325 BC	323 BC	323–58 BC	300 BC
The Classical Age; Alexander the Great releases Cyprus from the Persians (351 BC). Cypriot art develops under strong Attic influence. Zenon the philosopher is born in Cyprus (334 BC).	After the death of Alexander, Cypriot kings side with Ptolemy I against Antigonos. Ptolemy becomes ruler of Egypt, Syria, Pentapolis (Libya) and Cyprus (323–283 BC).	Strong commercial relationships with Athens and Alexandria maintain Hellenistic influence on the island. Carried out by administrators from Egypt, Ptolemaic rule continues until 58 BC.	Zenon's Stoic school of philosophy becomes dominant in Athens. Based on logic and formal ethics, it flourishes during the Hellenistic period through to the Roman era.

Richard went on to conquer the entire island and stayed for a year until he was well enough to travel. He then sold Cyprus to the Knights Templar, to boost his coffers. The Knights ultimately were unable to afford the upkeep and, in turn, sold it to the dispossessed king of Jerusalem, Guy de Lusignan, in 1192.

Lusignan Dynasties

The French-speaking lord of Cyprus, Guy de Lusignan, established a lengthy dynasty that brought mixed fortunes to the island. He died in 1194 and was buried at the Church of the Templars in Lefkosia and succeeded by his brother, Amalric.

Guy had invited Christian families who had lost property in the Holy Land to settle in Cyprus, many of whom were still concerned with the territorial affairs and disputes in Jerusalem. This proved to be a great economic strain on Cyprus, until the fall of Acre (Akko) in 1291.

For 100 years or so thereafter, Cyprus enjoyed a period of immense wealth and prosperity, with current-day Famagusta (Mağusa) the centre of unrivalled commercial activity and trade. Many of the Byzantine castles were added to in grandiose style, and fine buildings and churches were erected. The Church of Agia Sofia in North Nicosia (Lefkoşa), Bellapais Abbey in Kyrenia (Girne), and Kolossi Castle, near Lemesos, were completed during this period.

The Stones of Famagusta is a 2008 documentary that traces the historical remains of Famagusta's beautiful, ruined architecture. A labour-of-love project by two British expats, it's treasured by the local population.

Lusignan descendants continued to rule the Kingdom of Cyprus until 1474. The island's prosperity reached its zenith under King Peter I (r 1359–69), who spent much of his time overseas at war. He squashed many attempts at Turkish piracy raids, before mounting a counter attack in 1365. During this unsuccessful crusade, he only managed to sack the city of Alexandria. Upon his assassination at the hands of his nobles, the fortunes of the Lusignans took a turn for the worse.

Eyeing Cyprus' wealth and strategic position as an entrepôt, Genoa and Venice jostled for control. Genoa ultimately seized Famagusta and held it for 100 years; the fortunes of both Famagusta and the island declined as a result. The last Lusignan king was James II (r 1460–73), who managed to expel the Genoese from Famagusta. He married Caterina Cornaro, a Venetian noblewoman, who went on to succeed James. She was the last queen of Cyprus and the last royal personage from the Lusignan dynasty. Under pressure, she eventually ceded Cyprus to Venice.

Venetian Forts

The Venetians ruled Cyprus from 1489 to 1571 AD. Their control was characterised by indifference to the Greek population, who fared no better under their new overlords than they had under the Genoese.

289 BC	60 BC	58 BC–AD 395	45
Ptolemy II becomes co-regent of Egypt, Cyprus and the outlying areas. The important trade port of Famagusta (near Salamis) is founded during his reign (285–247 BC).	Noted Cypriot physician Apollonios of Kition is born. He would write several important medical books of antiquity. *Peri Arthron* (On Joints), with hand-painted sketches, is the only one to survive.	Romans take over from the Ptolemaic dynasty. Important public buildings are constructed, such as theatres and gymnasiums. Roads and vital aqueducts are built, bringing water to settlements.	Christianity is brought to the island by St Paul and St Barnabas. The Church of Cyprus is established. Cyprus is the first country to be ruled by a Christian.

As excellent traders, the Venetians' chief concern was the expansion of their maritime empire. They used the island for its position along the vital 'silk route' to China and as a defence against the growing Ottoman threat.

They built heavy fortifications around the cities of Lefkosia and Famagusta, believing the Ottomans would attempt to strike there.

The Ottomans first attacked Lefkosia, defeating it swiftly and slaughtering the garrison. They then turned their attentions to Famagusta. The severed head of Lefkosia's governor was sent as a grim message to Famagusta's Venetian captain-general Marcantonio Bragadino. He quickly prepared for the assault, with some 8000 men at the ready.

The Ottomans laid siege to the city with over 200,000 men and 2000 cannon. Bragadino held out for nearly a year, completely surrounded, with Famagusta bay filled with Ottoman ships.

Upon his capture, Bragadino was tortured horrifically for his defiance. His ears and nose were cut off before he was skinned alive.

The fall of Famagusta signalled the end of a Western presence and Christian outpost in the Levant for the next 300 years.

> The citizens of Famagusta (Mağusa) were so rich and so debauched that a merchant once ground a large diamond to season his food, in front of all his guests.

Ottoman Rule

Over 20,000 Turks settled in Cyprus following its capture from the Venetians in 1571, but the island was not a high priority for the Ottomans. The ruling sultan sent Turkish governors to rule the island, who quickly suppressed the Latin church. They abolished serfdom and restored the Orthodox hierarchy and Church of Cyprus, to better appease and control the population.

From then on, taxes were arbitrarily increased for the Greek Cypriot population, and the Orthodox archbishop (considered the leader) was made responsible for their collection. In the wake of huge taxes, some Greeks converted to Islam to avoid oppression.

The Ottomans appointed a Dragoman of the Serai (translator to the governor's palace) to each town. They resided in opulent stone houses and acted as arbitrators for all business with Greek Cypriots.

Ottoman rule was marked by indolence and corruption, and (frequent) dissent was put down by oppression. There were bloody uprisings in 1764 and 1833.

In 1821, Greeks from the mainland were fighting the great war of liberation against the Ottomans. Cypriot Orthodox Archbishop Kyprianos sent money and support to Greece, in the hope that it would help to free Cyprus also. When the *paşa* (lord), Mehmed Silashor, found out, he had the archbishop hanged in the public square in front of the *serai* (palace). Any support for the growing Greek revolution was quickly crushed. Another three bishops were beheaded on similar

> Turkish Cypriots are descendants of Ottoman settlers who arrived in Cyprus from 1570, following their conquest of the island over the ruling Venetians.

115–16	4th Century AD	350	395–647
A major Jewish revolt throughout Mesopotamia spreads to Cyprus and leaves thousands massacred. Roman emperor Trajan intervenes to restore peace and expels the Jews from Cyprus.	A series of powerful earthquakes rock the island and many coastal cities are badly damaged or destroyed, including the prized city of Salamis. Drought and famine also result.	Salamis is rebuilt by Constantius II, son of Constantine the Great. The site is lavishly decorated and renamed Constantia.	The island comes under Byzantine rule after the Roman Empire splits. The Church of Cyprus receives unprecedented ecclesiastical autonomy from Constantinople, a practice that continues today.

suspicions, and several priests, including the Abbot of Kykkos, were put to death.

The Ottomans remained in control of the island until 1878, when the British sought authority in the region.

Modern Cyprus

Civil Struggle

In 1878, Turkey and Britain signed an agreement whereby Turkey would retain sovereignty of the languishing colony, while Britain would shoulder the responsibility for administering the island. Britain's aim was to secure a strategic outpost in the Middle East, from where it could monitor military and commercial movements in the Levant and the Caucasus. As part of the agreement, Britain would protect the sultan's Asian territories from threat by Russia. In 1914 the start of WWI meant the parties were at war. Britain assumed outright sovereignty of the island, but Turkey would not recognise the annexation of its territory until the 1923 Treaty of Lausanne. This treaty also included territorial claims with the newly independent Greece.

British control of Cyprus was initially welcomed by its mostly Greek population, since it was assumed that Britain would ultimately work with the Greeks to achieve 'enosis' (union) with Greece. Turkish Cypriots, a 17% minority of the population, were less than enthusiastic at the prospect, fearing they would be ostracised.

Between 1955 and 1958 a Cypriot lieutenant colonel, Georgios 'Digenis' Grivas, founded the Ethniki Organosi tou Kypriakou Agona (EOKA; National Organisation for the Cypriot Struggle), and launched a series of covert attacks on the British military and administration. EOKA began these attacks to show their frustration with the British for not helping to further their ultimate goal of enosis.

The British came up with various proposals for limited home rule, but Turkish Cypriots began to demand *taksim* (partition), whereby the island would be divided between Greece and Turkey.

In 1959, Greek Cypriot ethnarch Archbishop Makarios III and Turkish Cypriot leader Faisal Küçük met in Zurich. They came to ratify a previously agreed plan whereby independence would be granted to Cyprus, under conditions that would satisfy all sides.

The British were to retain two military bases and a number of other sites as part of the agreement. Cyprus also agreed not to enter into any political or economic unions with Turkey or Greece, or to be partitioned. Political power was to be shared on a proportional basis of 70% Greek and 30% Turkish. Britain, Turkey and Greece were named as the 'guarantor powers' of the island.

Colin Thubron's *Journey into Cyprus* is a classic travel tale. In 1974, just before the Turkish invasion of the island, the author crossed almost 1000km on foot, weaving myth, history and personal stories.

Numerous mainland Turkish settlers have married Turkish Cypriots. These relationships are somewhat frowned upon by middle-class Turkish Cypriots, who see themselves as different from the mainlanders.

647

The first of the Arab raids causes great destruction and suffering. Salamis is destroyed and Kourion fades. Coastal inhabitants migrate inland to avoid constant pillaging and attacks.

» Byzantine frescos

688–965

Justinian II and the Arab Caliph Abd-al-Malik agree to jointly rule Cyprus. Their agreement is broken in 965 and the Byzantines once again take over the island.

1191

Richard the Lionheart is shipwrecked at Lemesos on his way to Acre; the English king conquers Cyprus and weds Princess Berengaria at Agios Georgios chapel, in the town.

PARTITION

New Republic

The independent Republic of Cyprus was realised on 16th August 1960. Transition from colony to independent nation was difficult, with sporadic violence and protest, as extremists from both sides pushed opposing agendas.

Serious sectarian violence broke out in 1963, further dividing the Greek and Turkish communities. Turkish Cypriots withdrew from government, claiming that President Archbishop Makarios (see the box, p74) was pro-enosis, and wasn't doing enough to control radicals.

In 1964 the UN sent a peacekeeping force to the island headed by Major General Peter Young. The general drew a green line on a map of Lefkosia separating the Greek and Turkish areas of the capital, thus forming the 'Green Line', which would go on to divide the entire island. Many Turkish Cypriots moved to enclaves around the island, separating themselves from the Greeks.

With the Cold War at its peak, Cyprus had strategic value for the British and the Americans in monitoring Soviet activity. Makarios sought a position of political nonalignment, and was suspected of being a communist. The Americans and their British allies feared another Cuban crisis – only in the Mediterranean – which added urgency to their interference.

Whilst the island was still politically unstable, the situation on the ground quietened between 1964 and 1967, as Turkish Cypriots withdrew to consolidated areas. This included setting up a provisional government in northern Lefkosia (North Nicosia).

Coup d'État & Invasion

Many Orthodox churches in the North were destroyed by the Turks after the 1974 partition. Those that survived have been converted to mosques, locked up or used as barns for storing animals, save for a precious few.

Discussion of segregating the Greek and Turkish Cypriot communities stepped up again in 1967. A coup in Greece installed a right-wing military junta, and Greece's relations with Cyprus cooled. Makarios had a number of diplomatic meetings with the Soviets, in keeping with his policy of nonalignment. Both the Greek junta and the Americans were suspicious of this, and were fearful that the island would lean towards communism.

In July 1974, the CIA sponsored a Greek junta–organised coup in Cyprus, with the intention of installing a more pro-Western government.

On 15 July, a renegade detachment of the National Guard (numbering a mere 180), led by officers from mainland Greece, launched an attempt to assassinate Makarios and establish enosis. Makarios narrowly escaped as the presidential palace was laid to waste. Cypriot Nikos Sampson, a former EOKA member with ties to the Greek junta, was proclaimed president of Cyprus.

Five days later, Turkish forces landed troops close to Kyrenia (Girne), using the right to restore a legal government as the pretext.

1191–92	1192	1194	1478
Richard falls ill amid concerns for his coffers. After finishing off Lemesos governor Isaak Komninos, he sells Cyprus to the Knights Templar to raise funds for a third Holy Crusade.	Guy de Lusignan takes Cyprus from the Knights Templar. Splendid churches and castles are built.	The feudal system is introduced to the island by Amalric Lusignan upon the death of his younger brother Guy. He becomes King of Cyprus as Amalric I.	The last Lusignan king, James II, weds Venetian noblewoman Caterina Cornaro, who becomes the last queen of Cyprus. In 1489 she cedes Cyprus to Venice.

The regular Greek Cypriot army tried to resist the Turkish advance. However, once the Turks established the bridgehead around Kyrenia, they quickly linked with the Turkish sector of North Nicosia. From this point the Greek Cypriot army was outnumbered and could not stop the crushing Turkish assault.

On 23 July 1974, Greece's junta on the mainland fell and was replaced by a democratic government under Konstantinos Karamanlis. At the same time, the Cypriots removed Sampson and replaced him with Glafkos Clerides, president of the House of Representatives and a member of the democratic government.

The three guarantor powers – Britain, Greece and Turkey – met for discussions in Geneva, as required by the treaty, but it proved impossible to make the Turkish halt their advance. They pressed on for over three weeks, until 16 August 1974. At that time Turkey controlled 37% of the northern part of the island. By the time Makarios returned to resume his presidency, having escaped the assassination attempt, Cyprus was divided.

A total of 190,000 Greek Cypriots who then lived in the northern third of Cyprus were displaced, losing their homes, land and businesses. Many were caught in the onslaught and killed; the rest fled south for safety. At the same time around 50,000 Turkish Cypriots moved from the South to the Turkish-controlled areas in the North.

The human and economic cost to the island was catastrophic. The now-truncated Republic of Cyprus was deprived of some of its best land, two major cities, its lucrative citrus industry and the bulk of its tourist infrastructure.

The invasion and forced division of Cyprus served convoluted political and military purposes. Reinstatement of the rightful government and dissipation of the military junta did not alter the Turkish government's stance. It forcibly continued its illegal occupation of the North and the Turkish troops remained.

The UN has maintained a peacekeeping force along the Green Line and the border that runs the length of the island ever since.

The declaration of a separate Turkish Republic of Northern Cyprus (TRNC), by President Rauf Denktaş, came in 1983. It is only officially recognised by Turkey.

Unification Attempts

In the years since division, talks to reunite the island have taken place sporadically and with little success, with both sides presenting entrenched and uncompromising points of view.

During the spring and summer of 2002, Cyprus and Turkey were seeking entry into the EU. The leaders of both the North and the South had

Cyprus: A Modern History by William Mallinson explores Cypriot history with a focus on the post-1974 period. It examines the great importance of EU membership for both Cyprus and Turkey.

While Turkish and Greek Cypriots may be separated by physical barriers, they share the notion of a single God – even though they worship two different religions, Sunni Islam and Eastern Orthodoxy.

HISTORY MODERN CYPRUS

1571	1625–1700	1821	1878–1923
The Ottoman Empire crushes the Venetians and takes over Cyprus. Orthodox hierarchy is restored to assist in local taxation. Some 20,000 Turks settle on the island.	Plague wipes out over 50% of the estimated population on the island. A string of bloody insurgencies against oppressive Ottoman rule are savagely quashed. Plague ends (1700).	Greek Cypriots side with Greece in a revolt against Turkish rule. The island's leading Orthodox clergy are executed as punishment, and 20,000 Christians flee the island.	Britain leases Cyprus from Turkey, as the administrator of the island. The British formally annex Cyprus in 1914. Turkey does not recognise the annexation until 1923.

RAUF DENKTAŞ: PORTRAIT OF A RENEGADE

Viewed as the bane of Cypriot society by Greeks, and saviour of the nation by many Turks, Rauf Denktaş still provokes strong feelings among Cypriots. Before he stepped down as president of the self-proclaimed independent republic in 2005, this one-time lawyer was matched in resilience and political longevity by few neighbouring Middle Eastern political leaders. He used charm and tenacity to lead the Turkish Cypriot community from well before the forced division of Cyprus in 1974. Until Mehmet Ali Talat won the 2005 election, he had been leader for 31 years.

A mercurial character, Denktaş was born near Pafos on the island's southern coast and trained as a barrister in London before commencing his long political career. As leader of the Turkish Communal Chamber from 1960, he was in and out of the spotlight – and trouble – until 1974, when he became leader of the partitioned Turkish Cypriots.

Denktaş was known for his persistence and perceived intransigence in seeking a solution for reuniting Cyprus. His drive to seek a mutually acceptable solution to the political impasse was compromised by a steadfastness and unwillingness to deviate from the long-held party line. At thrice-weekly talks held in the UN buffer zone during the spring and summer of 2002 Denktaş refused to concede any ground from the position of his Turkish-mainland backers. They insisted on a bizonal, bicommunal state, with a large degree of autonomy and separation between the two communities. These talks sputtered on into 2003 without any progress.

During that year, Denktaş made the surprise announcement that he would ease border controls between the two parts of the island, thus allowing Cypriots from both sides to cross with immediate effect. This decision marked a major point in Cyprus' history, and was a crucial step towards a different future for the island.

Echoes from the Dead Zone: Across the Cyprus Divide, by Yiannis Papadakis, is about the author's journey from the Greek to the Turkish side of the border, overcoming prejudices and finding understanding.

thrice-weekly talks aimed at reunification. Again discussions got bogged down by the intricacies of land ownership and the real number of Turkish mainland settlers.

In April 2003, TRNC President Rauf Denktaş made the surprise announcement that travel restrictions across the border would be eased, thus allowing Greek Cypriots daily access to visit the northern parts of the island. Since then, seven checkpoints have been opened and visiting periods have gone from daily restrictions to up to three months.

During this period Kofi Annan, the former UN secretary general, brokered an agreement allowing separate island-wide referenda on a reunification plan.

The 'Annan Plan', as it was known, was designed to make Cyprus a federation of two constituent states, with shared proportional power. Political leaders on both sides campaigned for a 'no' vote. Greek

1914–15	1923–25	1955–60	1963–64
Turkey sides with Germany in WWI. Britain offers Cyprus to Greece as incentive to support the British. King Constantine declines in an attempt to remain neutral.	Turkey is compensated by the British for its loss of the island. Cyprus becomes a Crown Colony (1925) and is governed by the British High Commissioner.	Ethniki Organosi tou Kypriakou Agona (EOKA; National Organisation for the Cypriot Struggle) is founded. Guerrilla warfare is directed at the British. Makarios is first president of an independent Cyprus.	President Makarios proposes constitutional changes; intercommunal fighting ensues. Turkish Cypriots withdraw and UN peacekeeping forces arrive. The Green Line is first drawn across Lefkosia.

Cypriots rejected the plan (76%), while Turkish Cypriots endorsed it (65%). The proposal was now defunct. The Greeks cited reduced legal entitlements from that of pre-1974 and Turkey's being allowed to maintain a military presence on the island as their reasons for voting 'no'.

Repairing the Damage

Many Greek Cypriots quickly regrouped after 1974, putting their energies into rebuilding their shattered nation. Within a few years the economy was on the mend and the Republic of Cyprus was recognised internationally as the only legitimate representative of the island. The economy pushed ahead through the 1980s. The opening of the Cyprus Stock Exchange, in 1999, initially absorbed vast amounts of private funds. In the early 2000s the stock exchange took a full-size nose dive and many Cypriots lost huge amounts of money.

Tourism remained buoyant, though there has been a consistent downward trend since 2002. In 2008 there were warnings that tourism was going through the worst crisis ever. This was said to be due to customer dissatisfaction with the services on offer and ever-increasing prices.

Even with its increasing economic expansion, the North is heavily dependent financially (and politically) on Ankara – to the sum of US$600 million plus a year.

HISTORY MODERN CYPRUS

BORDER BLOODSHED

On 11 August 1996, a Berlin-to-Cyprus peace ride by motorcyclists from around Europe ended at the Greek Cypriot village of Deryneia. The village adjoins the Green Line that divides Northern Cyprus from the Republic of Cyprus. Among the riders that day was a young Greek Cypriot from Protaras by the name of Tasos Isaak.

During the riders' protest at the border, to show their ongoing frustration at the continuing occupation of the North by Turkish forces, a melee ensued. Clashes between Greek Cypriots and Turkish Cypriots broke out in the UN buffer zone that separates the two communities.

In the chaos, Tasos Isaak was cut off from his fellow demonstrators, and surrounded by Turks. Despite the fact that he was unarmed, he was set upon and beaten to death. Isaak's body was later recovered by UN personnel.

Three days later, after Isaak's funeral, a crowd once more gathered at the Deryneia checkpoint, to protest against the death. Among the protesters this time was Solomos Solomou, a 26-year-old who was enraged at the death of his friend, Isaak. Despite repeated attempts to hold him back, Solomos eluded the UN peacekeepers and slipped across no-man's-land to one of the flagpoles carrying the Turkish Cypriot flag. Cigarette in mouth, he managed to climb halfway up the flagpole, before being struck by five bullets. The shots came from the nearby Turkish Cypriot guard post, and quite possibly from bushes sheltering armed soldiers. Solomos' death was captured on video, and is replayed at the viewing points that overlook the tragic site of the Deryneia deaths.

1974

Greek junta organises coup. Turkish army invades, taking a third of the island. Archbishop's Palace is the scene of much fighting. Makarios resumes presidency. Cyprus is divided thereafter.

» Archbishop's Palace

1975

Turkish Cypriots establish an independent administration, naming Rauf Denktaş as its leader. Denktaş and Clerides then agree on a population exchange between North and South.

1983

Turkish Republic of Northern Cyprus is proclaimed by its leader. Its sovereignty is only recognised by Turkey. Thousands of mainland Turks settle in the North of the island.

Turkey cannot join the EU without a settlement in Cyprus, and that would mean recognising the Greek-Cypriot government.

North of the Green Line is known by most foreigners simply as 'Northern Cyprus' and by the Greeks as the 'Occupied Territories' *(ta katehomena)*. This area, by comparison to the South, has developed at a snail's pace. An influx of Turkish mainlanders and international economic sanctions against the unrecognised Northern government has made progress difficult. It remains largely supported by its client and sponsor nation, Turkey, through direct funding and its use as a Turkish military outpost.

1977	1999	2002	2003
The first president of Cyprus, Archbishop Makarios III, dies suddenly at 63. Over 250,000 mourners pay respects during the funeral service. He is succeeded by Spyros Kyprianou.	The Republic of Cyprus starts to prosper economically and the standard of living booms. Northern Cyprus is supported largely by Turkey, in the wake of international economic sanctions.	Cyprus and Turkey both seek entry to the EU. The leaders of the Republic and the North attend intense talks, aimed at reunification. Talks stall and no agreement is reached.	The North's leader, Rauf Denktaş, announces a surprise decision to allow Cypriots from both sides to visit the opposing parts of the island. The first crossings in 29 years are peaceful.

The Cypriot Way of Life

Moulded by many centuries of rule by different nations that have coveted, fought over and possessed the island, the people of Cyprus are a blend of many races. Physically they run the gamut of appearance: some are short, stocky with a dark-complexion and tightly curled almost Moorish hair. Some are tall, slender and olive skinned, and this is attributed to the Phoenician influence. Others are pale, with fair hair and blue eyes, remnants of Achaean and Venetian settlement and conquests. Cyprus' fraught history goes some way towards explaining the unique character of its people.

Nowadays, though there remains some allegiance to mainland Greece or Turkey, most people see themselves as Cypriot first and Greek or Turkish second.

The Great Divide

The daily lives of Cypriots are still largely dominated by the domestic and international focus on the division that scores the island. Over the last 37 years, nearly two generations have grown up with partition, and many have grown immune to, or tired of, the incessant political news and discussions on both sides of the Green Line regarding the 'Cyprus problem'. The bitterness and sensitivity they feel in relation to this subject cannot be overestimated.

When the first border crossings between North and South opened in 2003, no one knew how the Cypriot people would react and what the consequences would be. Would there be riots or civil unrest? After all, no one had crossed the Green Line for 29 years save for diplomatic reasons. Many still had friends, relatives and homes they missed on the 'other side'.

The newly opened checkpoints swelled with thousands of people crossing the border. Many Turkish Cypriots who came south were enchanted by the comparative wealth and the elegant shops and restaurants in Lefkosia's streets, while many Greek Cypriots wandered the streets of North Nicosia, surprised at the way time had stood still for 30 years. Old acquaintances met and tears were shed. Some Greeks visited their former homes and properties in the North, and in some cases existing inhabitants reportedly welcomed them cordially and even invited them in for coffee and gave them gifts of citrus fruit and flowers. It is estimated that more than 35% of Cyprus' population crossed in the first two weeks, and over 25,000 Turkish Cypriots applied for a Cypriot passport (from the Republic of Cyprus) in that year alone.

The people have treated each other with studied civility and kindness, and even now, years after the openings, no major incidents have been reported. Since the attitude to crossing the border has normalised, over 20 million crossings have been recorded, with around 70% of those North

Average Life Expectancy

» Nationally: 78.2

» Men: 76.3

» Women: 80.1

Fast Facts

» Sun shines 326 days a year on average.

» Highest point is Mt Olympus at 1952m

» An ophiolite, Cyprus rose from the sea 20 million years ago to South. Indeed, many Turkish Cypriots now cross the Green Line daily to shop or work in the southern part of the island. While Greek Cypriots make up less of the border traffic, many do head over for Easter holidays and in particular to visit Apostolos Andreas church (p196) and for shopping bargains and casino visits.

While politics are discussed openly on both sides, travellers should approach the subject with tact. Both Greek and Turkish Cypriots may be forthright in discussing the issue, but it's still better to let them initiate the discussion.

Multiculturalism

Hospitable people by nature, some Cypriots regard outsiders with caution and wariness, perhaps understandably so given the island's long history of occupation and struggle for independence.

Some locals, especially those who have never left the island, consider expatriates and second-generation Cypriots from the UK, US, Canada and Australia to be *xeni* (foreigners). Over 90% of Greek Cypriots speak English, and some will show their disappointment if English-speakers can't reciprocate. Indeed, some people who have moved to the island have experienced halting acceptance from local communities if they make no effort to learn the language, and sometimes even if they do. A lasting 'Britishness' also remains from the island's colonial past and from its present-day reliance on tourism. As such, rightly or wrongly, many locals feel bombarded by outsiders.

Some feel that they are losing their traditional lifestyle and culture. While this has caused some consternation and resentment, foreigners and diversity have been welcomed by many Cypriots, especially those who have travelled and studied abroad.

Gradually most Cypriots are recognising the trend in their society towards greater multiculturalism. Indeed, this is reflected in the increasing number of Cypriots who are marrying foreigners (14% of marriages), particularly Europeans and Russians (many of whom belong to the Orthodox Church), creating a new generation of multicultural Cypriots. This phenomenon suggests that if racial and cultural barriers do linger – as some suspect they do – then their influence is diminishing.

It should be noted that most Cypriots are amazingly friendly, welcoming and kind, regardless of whether they live in cities, villages or less-developed areas.

Orthodoxy & Islam

Almost 78% of Cypriots are Greek Orthodox, 18% are Muslims and the remaining 4% are Maronite, Armenian Apostolic and other Christian denominations. Due to the island's division, Muslims predominantly live in the North while the Greek Orthodox live in the South.

Using first names alone is considered too familiar and is only done among friends. People greet each other with the title *kyrie* or *kyria* ('Mr' and 'Mrs' in Greek) before the person's name. In Turkish *bey* and *hanım* are used the same way, after naming the person.

By tradition, ultimate relaxation for a Cypriot man in his courtyard or garden requires the use of seven time-honoured wooden chairs. One for his stick, one for his coffee, one for each arm, one for each leg and of course one to sit on.

THE KAFENEIO (THE COFFEE SHOP)

In the villages, the local *kafeneio* (coffee shop) is the central meeting point. Most have two such places, distinguished by their political alignment (socialist or nationalist). They are filled with men of all generations, sitting, serving, or flipping beads. Many come and go on their way to and from work. The older men sit quietly, spread across chairs, waiting out the days like oracles, eating haloumi and olives or drinking coffee and *zivania* (fermented grape pomace). Good friends sit in pairs, smoking cigarettes and playing *tavli* (backgammon) in the shade of the vine leaves. Their dice rattle, while moves are counted and strategies are shaped in whispers. And come lunchtime, only the lingering smoke remains, as the men stampede home for their midday meal and siesta, returning in the evening to do it all again.

SUMMER SOUVLA

A favourite Cypriot pastime is enjoying a *souvla* (spit-roast) that's been roasting for hours over burning coals. It's especially fine on the beach. There's the joke that a Cypriot's favourite vehicle is a pick-up truck, because 20 chairs, a table and all the barbecue equipment can fit into the tray when the family heads out for the weekend. Indeed, part of the summer holidays for many Cypriots is often spent camping on less-touristy beaches, where the sound of batteries rotating skewers and the smell of soft lamb with herbs permeates the sea air.

The recent increase in asylum seekers from the Middle East, Africa and Central and South Asia has increased the number of practising Muslims living in the Republic, particularly Larnaka, which has one of the South's few mosques.

The presence of the Orthodox Church is ingrained in both politics and daily life, with the Cypriot year centred on the festivals, celebrations and Saints days of the Orthodox calendar. Sundays in particular are popular for visiting monasteries and the Byzantine churches in the Troödos Massif (p71).

In the North, Turkish Cypriots are mostly secular Sunni Muslims. While religion plays an important part in Turkish Cypriot culture, the more conservative Islamic and fundamentalist tradition practised elsewhere in the Middle East (and rural Turkey) is not so obvious in Cyprus. Alcohol, for example, is widely available and frequently consumed by Turkish Cypriots, and women dress far more casually than their counterparts on the Turkish mainland.

While topless bathing is generally OK, baring all is not. There are no designated nudist beaches in Cyprus, and once you leave the sand, remember that Cyprus is a traditional country, so best to put on a T-shirt.

Changing Roles

Traditional ideas about the proper role of women – cooking, cleaning and tending to house and family – persist in some sectors of Cypriot society. However, modern Cypriot women, particularly those who live in cities, like to dress in designer labels, frequent beaches in bikinis, have careers and go out on the town.

Cypriot women have freedom and independence in many areas, but more needs to be done, especially when it comes to employment, as professional positions are still very much male dominated.

Attitudes towards homosexuality have relaxed somewhat over the years, although open displays of affection are still frowned upon by many. Several gay bars and clubs can be found in cities like Lefkosia, Lemesos, Larnaka and Pafos, offering diverse and comfortable atmospheres. On the Turkish side of the island you may even see men holding hands (without any sexual connotation); however, it's still advisable to be discreet, if simply to avoid stares.

Cyprus' Natural Environment

Lie of the Land

Shaped like a swordfish surfacing from the sea with its sharp tip and flared fins, Cyprus is the third-largest island in the Mediterranean.

In the North, the 170km-long Kyrenia (Girne) Range was formed by upward-thrust masses of Mesozoic limestone. It's known locally as the Pentadaktylos (five fingers in Greek) for its five-ridged peak that runs practically parallel to the northern coastline.

A handy field companion is *Butterflies of North Cyprus* by Dr Daniel H Haines and Dr Hilary M Haines. It's a comprehensive guide available in paperback.

Directly south of these mountains is the vast Mesaoria plain (whose name means 'in between mountains' in Greek), which stretches from Morfou (Güzelyurt) in the west to Famagusta (Mağusa) in the east, with the divided capital of Lefkosia/North Nicosia situated in its middle. The plain has over 1900 sq km of irrigation and is the island's primary grain-growing area.

Further south, the island is dominated by the vast mountain range of the Troödos Massif, created millions of years ago by rising molten rock in the deep ocean. It features the imposing Mt Olympus and its lower plateaus to the east. This area is rich in minerals and natural resources like chromite, gypsum, iron pyrite, marble and copper. Mined for thousands of years, it was instrumental in the island's development during ancient times.

NATIONAL PARKS & RESERVES

The upgrading of natural areas to national-park status has steadily increased. The declared list of parks includes Akamas National Forest Park, Pafos region; Troödos National Park, declared in 1992; Cape Greco (p122) and the Peninsula Bay, east of Agia Napa; Athalassa National Forest Park, west of Lefkosia; Polemidia National Forest Park, near Lemesos; Rizoelia National Forest Park, near Larnaka; and Tripylos Natural Reserve, east of Pafos, which includes the wonderful Cedar Valley (p103).

Areas under study for inclusion include Platis Valley, near Kykkos Monastery in Troödos; Madari, east of Troödos towards Larnaka; Mavroi Kremnoi, part of Pafos state forest; and the Akrotiri Salt Lakes, on the Akrotiri Peninsula near Lemesos.

There's also one marine reserve: Lara Toxeftra Reserve, off the west coast near Lara, Pafos region, established to protect marine turtles and their nesting beaches.

In Northern Cyprus, 150 sq km of the Karpas (Kırpaşa) Peninsula has been declared a national park (p196). Environmentalists were successful in having the vulnerable and precious area protected from development. Rare marine turtles that nest in the beaches on both sides of the peninsula are now expected to benefit from this decision.

FLOWER POWER

For the best flower-spotting, enthusiasts will need to spend plenty of time trekking and searching, as many species are limited to small geographical areas. You'll need to enjoy a ramble and be patient.

Casey's larkspur This is a late-flowering species that carries a dozen or more deep-violet, long-spurred flowers atop a slender stem. Its habitat is limited to the rocky peaks 1.5km southwest of St Hilarion.

Cyprus crocus A delicate white and yellow flower from the iris family. An endangered species, it's protected by law and is generally found at high altitudes in the Troödos Massif.

Cyprus tulip Delicate and dark red, this is another rare, protected species found in the Akamas Peninsula, the Koruçam (Kormakitis) Peninsula and remote parts of the Beşparmak (Pentadaktylos) Range.

Orchids The most popular wildflowers for enthusiasts. The one endemic orchid, Kotschy's bee orchid, is an exquisite species that resembles a bee, both in its shape and patterning. While fairly rare, it's found in habitats all over the island. Other varieties found on the slopes of Mt Olympus include the slender, pink Troödos Anatolian orchid, the cone-shaped pyramidal orchid, the giant orchid and the colourful woodcock orchid.

St Hilarion cabbage This unlikely sounding beauty grows in the North, mainly on rocky outcrops near St Hilarion Castle. This large endemic cabbage flower grows to 1m in height and has spikes of creamy white flowers.

Troödos golden drop A member of the borage family, this is an endemic yellow bell-shaped flower appearing in leafy clusters. Another endangered species, it's confined to the highest peaks of the Troödos Massif.

Check out *The Floral Charm of Cyprus,* by Valerie Sinclair, for further information about the range of flora on the island.

A Plethora of Plant Life

The diversity of Cyprus' flora is not immediately obvious to first-time visitors. After the explosion of colour from endemic flora and wildflowers in spring, summer sees the island assume an arid appearance, with only a few hardy flowers and thistles.

The island is home to some 1800 species and subspecies of plants, of which about 7% are indigenous to Cyprus. Five major habitats characterise Cyprus' flora profile: pine forests, garigue and maquis (underbrush found in the Mediterranean), rocky areas, coastal areas and wetlands. One of the main places for indigenous plant species is the Troödos Massif (see p65), where around 45 endemic species can be found.

The Karpas (Kırpaşa) Peninsula (p193) has a further 19 endemic species that are found only in the North.

Over 40 species of orchids can be found on the island; many of these, such as the rare Punctate orchid, can be spotted in the lap of the Kyrenia Range (p164). The best time to see Cyprus' wildflowers is in early spring (February to March) or in late autumn (October to November), when most of the species blossom, taking advantage of the moister climate.

The island's national symbol is the Cypriot mouflon (wild sheep). Once endangered, it's now only found in the remote mountain ranges of Troödos and Pafos, with subspecies reportedly roaming parts of the uninhabited buffer zone between North and South.

Environmental Awareness

This beautiful island is unfortunately beset with environmental issues. True, some of its environmental concerns stem from tourism, but there is also the much deeper issue of littering on streets and beaches, and garbage dumping on roadsides. Industrial waste, fridges, rubble and all sorts of debris are often dumped in forests and near natural salt lakes.

In an attempt to remedy this situation, the government has responded with advertisements encouraging people to put rubbish in bins and stop discarding cigarette butts on beaches. There are new recycling points across the island. On a more grassroots level, educational programs have been launched in primary schools to encourage the next generation to be more aware of their environment and the benefits of recycling. Local councils have joined in, providing skips near and around natural habitats where dumping regularly occurs. Positive actions like these are providing new hope and putting a much-needed focus on the issue.

Water, Water, Everywhere...

The island's other significant ongoing issue, the shortage of water, has apparently been solved. Droughts and unreliable rainfall over many years had severely affected water reserves in hundreds of dams and underground reservoirs. The government's constant restrictions (especially in summer) and raised public awareness about conservation and responsibility have helped the situation somewhat, but population growth and nearly three million tourists a year have put pressure on for a permanent and sustainable solution.

Now the government Water Development Department appears to have eased concerns with the creation of more cutting-edge desalination plants. Current plants have supplied nearly 50% of domestic water over the last 10 years, and now that figure is set to rise with three new desalination units planned by 2013: one in Lemesos (2011), a second in Pafos (2012) and a third in Famagusta (2013). These will augment already existing plants located at Dekelia and near Larnaka Airport. Each of these installations is expected to produce 40,000 cubic metres of water per day, which should provide more than enough for the population.

At this stage, dams will remain the principal source of water for agricultural use while the government considers plans to set up desalination units for agricultural irrigation also. Happily for residents, water cuts have been stopped altogether, and every home in every part of the Republic of Cyprus has a constant, 24-hour supply of drinking water.

Island Animals

Mammals

While the most famous Cypriot wild animal is still the mouflon, a scattering of twitchy wild donkeys can be seen on the Karpas (Kırpaşa)

Desalination has been the answer to Cyprus' water shortage. The process is expensive and uses vast amounts of energy, however. For an up-to-date evaluation of all environmental matters in Cyprus, go to www.cypenv.info /cyprusee.

For those wanting to be immersed in the natural habitat, a growing choice of rural accommodation in the mountains and traditional villages is now available. Visit www.agrotourism .com.cy.

WHERE TO WATCH

Birds travelling between Africa and Europe use Cyprus as a stepping stone on their migratory path. Birdwatchers have an excellent window into both more exotic migratory species and local birds. Here are some of the best birdwatching locations on the island:

Larnaka Salt Lake An important migratory habitat that fills with flamingos and water fowl from February to May. There are lookout posts (with seats) at various intervals along the airport road to Larnaka. You can also walk the nature trails around the lakes past the Hala Sultan Tekke (p114).

Troödos Massif The ranges offer excellent vantage points along the many nature trails in the region. Take binoculars to catch the likes of griffon vultures, falcons and kestrels. One of the best birdwatching spots is the Kaledonia Trail, which showcases large amounts of Cyprus and Sardinian warblers and nightingales (p72).

Cape Greco Peninsula In addition to being the home of wonderful sea caves, the cape, with its scrubland and rocky outcrops, is one of the prime migration zones for birds from across the seas. Expect to see a range of birds, from chukars and spectacled warblers to pallid harriers and red-rumpled swallows (p122).

ENDANGERED SPECIES

Mouflon, the native wild mountain sheep, are timid, nimble and skilled at climbing. The males have enormous curved horns and were hunted for sport by the nobles in Lusignan times. By the early 20th century widespread shooting by farmers and hunters had nearly reduced them to extinction. However, awareness of the plight of the island's national emblem increased, and now they are protected at sites such as Stavros tis Psokas forest station, in Pafos, which shelters a small herd (see p97). In the wild, mouflon are only found in remote parts of the mountain ranges and are rarely spotted.

Green and loggerhead turtles have bred and lived on Cypriot beaches for centuries, but tourism and beach development has encroached on vital nesting areas. They nest in the soft sands of the northern beaches in particular, which are now signed and closed at night (hatching times). Look out for conservation programs in coastal areas. Follow the rules, stick to allocated swimming times, and plant your umbrellas as close to the water's edge as possible to avoid crushing eggs. See p169.

Monk seals are rarely spotted off the coast and had been considered extinct as recently as 10 years ago. However, recent sightings off the eastern coast and at Cape Greco's sea caves have revived hope. Now it's believed a very small number still survive in remote locations around the island's shores. Some conservationists campaigned to keep the location of breeding sites secret so that natural habitats where seals take refuge can avoid development. Without more awareness and a concerted effort to protect the breeding caves, these seals may truly be lost.

Peninsula. They are believed to have evolved from the domesticated donkeys that escaped or were abandoned in 1974.

In the island's differing forest environs you may also see smaller animals such as foxes, rabbits, hares, hedgehogs, squirrels and fruit bats.

Reptiles

The island's dry, hot summer landscape is a natural home for lizards, geckos, chameleons and snakes, of which only the Montpellier snake and blunt-nosed viper are poisonous.

Lizards, in particular, pop up everywhere, sunbathing on rocks, ruins and concrete walls. If you stay in any number of the wonderful agro-hotels across the island, you may even spot a gecko in your doorway out to feed on insects.

Sea Fauna

Cyprus' warm, clear waters are home to over 260 different kinds of fish, and the coves and underwater reefs along its coasts are teeming with sea-life such as corals, sponges, mussels and sea anemones, making it a haven for diving and snorkelling; see p25.

Cyprus has 140 unique flowering plants only found in the Troödos Massif, 390 different migratory bird species during spring and autumn, and over 80 nesting sites for rare and protected turtles.

CYPRUS' NATURAL ENVIRONMENT ISLAND ANIMALS

The Arts

Traditional Crafts »
Theatre »
Visual Arts »
Music & Dance »
Literature »

Folk dancing in Kissonerga

Traditional Crafts

Cyprus continues its healthy tradition of folk arts, ranging from basket making to lacework. Head for a branch of the Cyprus Handicrafts Centre to guarantee authenticity and a fair price.

Pottery

Decorative pottery is worth seeking out. You can't miss the enormous *pitharia* (earthenware storage jars), often used as stylish plant pots. Originally used for storing water, oil or wine, their sheer size renders them impossible to transport home. The village of Kornos, between Lemesos and Larnaka, is famous for its pottery, as is Pafos and the southwest region.

Below
Traditional clay pots

Basket Making

One of the oldest handicrafts, basket making was traditionally learned by everyone in the family. Today, baskets are still usually made from reeds, found growing next to streams, although in the Akamas Peninsula villages like Kritou Terra are famous for their intricately woven twig baskets. Palm leaves and straw are used for creating the distinctive brightly coloured *tsestos* (decorative 'platters' with geometric designs). These are more prevalent in Northern Cyprus, especially in the Karpasia and Mesaoria regions. Be wary of synthetic copies made from plastic, which are fortunately easy to spot.

Lacework

One of the most famous folk-art exports is the exquisite Lefkara lacework, from the same-name village, located in the southern Troödos foothills. Be wary of cheap Chinese imports. The village of Fyti in the Pafos region is also famous for its needlework, particularly woven and embroidered silk and cotton, and is, to date, not on the coach-tour trail.

LOOK DIE BILDAGENTUR DER FOTOGRAFEN GMBH/ALAMY ©

Theatre

Theatre throughout Cyprus is an important art form with a long history. Productions range from traditional Greek plays in the South to Ottoman-inspired shadow-puppet theatres in the North.

Republic of Cyprus

Theatre in the South is a flourishing industry, with the Theatre Workshop of the University of Cyprus (Thepak) and the Lefkosia Municipal Theatre very active in the performance of works written by Greeks and Cypriots.

The biannual Kypria Festival (www .kypriafestival.com) hosts performances from a variety of domestic theatre groups. Lefkosia's Eleftheria Theatre presents ancient Greek plays in local productions.

Northern Cyprus

Theatre in the North is said to have started with the arrival of the Ottomans in 1570, and with the importation from the Turkish mainland of the Karagöz puppet shadow theatre. This theatre tradition is shared by the Greeks, who call it Karagiozis. Theatre in the contemporary sense started on the island with British influence after 1878, but only really took off after independence in 1960, when amateur theatre groups were established in most Turkish Cypriot communities.

Above
Open-air festival in the ruins of Salamis

Visual Arts

The art of Cyprus has long reflected both Eastern and Western influences. Political turmoil and the division of the island have similarly had an inevitable impact.

Background

During the Neolithic age, decorative ceramics and mosaics reflected a desire for ornamentation which continued with the conversion of the island to Christianity in AD 45 and the emergence of Byzantine art. This religious expression was represented most vividly in frescos, mosaics and icons, many of which are still in evidence today. Little remains of the Frankish (1192–1489) and Venetian (1489–1571) periods, due to the looting and plundering of numerous invaders. This sorry situation continued after the conquest of the Ottomans in 1570, when physical survival took precedence over art.

The 19th century saw the emergence of folk painters and sculptors who were the forerunners of contemporary Cypriot art. They painted friezes in coffee shops and decorated glass and furniture, particularly traditional iron beds, which were adorned with plant motifs, or similar.

20th- to 21st-Century Painting & Sculpture

In the 1950s artists began to return to Cyprus after studying abroad. Important artists who emerged during this period include Christofors Savva (1924–68), who was strongly influenced by the cubist and expressionist movements, and abstract artists Costas Joachim (1936–), Nicos Kouroussis (1937–) and Andreas Ladommatos (1940–).

The 1974 division of the island had a significant influence on trends in art, with a rise in symbolism and subject matter that reflected the spiritual anguish of the time. Important artists from this period include Angelos Makrides (1942–) who represented Cyprus in the 1988 Venice Biennale, and

ROLF RICHARDSON/ALAMY ©

Clockwise from top left

1. Monastery wall mosaic 2. Byzantine mosaic, Kykkos Monastery 3. Seafront sculpture, Lemesos

Emin Chizenel (1949–), a Fulbright scholar and Turkish Cypriot who has exhibited both sides of the divide.

Female artist Haris Epaminonda was born in Lefkosia in 1980 and is known for her collages, installations and videos. She represented Cyprus in the 2007 Venice Biennale together with Turkish Cypriot Mustafa Hulusi and, in 2010, had a solo show at London's Tate Modern. Christodoulous Panayiotou (1978–) exhibits his videos and installations internationally.

For the best overview of Cypriot art, visit the State Gallery of Cypriot Contemporary Art in Lefkosia. For cutting-edge modern art, try the Nicosia Municipal Arts Centre.

Icons

Although some Cypriot churches still house magnificent Byzantine icons, many have been looted and their treasures sold on the open market. These are often unwittingly bought by collectors and, occasionally, celebrities. The singer Boy George had an icon of Jesus Christ hung proudly over his fireplace for decades before it was spotted by an expert during a televised interview.

The icon was duly returned to the Church of St Charalambos in Chorio Kythrea in 2011, from where it had been stolen in 1974.

Icons are still being produced in many monasteries today. The most famous contemporary icon painter is Father Kallinikos Stavrovounis, the aged priest of Stavrovouni Monastery, situated between the cities of Lefkosia and Lemesos. Father Kallinikos is regarded as the most superb contemporary icon painter of the Orthodox Church. The money he receives is used for the upkeep of Stavrovouni and other monasteries.

TOP CYPRIOT SCULPTORS

- » Demetris Constantinou (1924–)
- » Andreas Savvides (1930–)
- » George Sfikas (1943–)
- » Nicos Dymiotis (1930–90)
- » Kypros Perdios (1942–)
- » Leonidas Spanos (1955–)

Music & Dance

Cypriot music and dance is diverse and reflects Greek, Turkish and Arabic influences. Traditional music has an enduring appeal as evidenced by the distinctive bouzouki twanging out from all those open car windows.

Music

Greek Cypriots have tended to follow the musical preferences of mainland Greece. Conversely, Cyprus has also produced some of its own musicians who have made successful careers in Greece as well as in their homeland.

The bouzouki, which you will hear all over Cyprus, is a mandolin-like instrument similar to the Turkish *saz* and *baglama*. It's one of the main instruments of rembetika music – the Greek equivalent of American blues. Today's music scene in Cyprus is a mix of old and new, traditional and modern. Young Greek Cypriots are as happy with rembetika or *demotic* (folk) songs as they are with contemporary Greek rock music.

Cypriot singer and lyricist Evagoras Karageorgis has produced some excellent music including *Topi se Hroma Loulaki* (Places Painted in Violet); a nostalgic and painful look at the lost villages of Northern Cyprus sung in a mixture of Cypriot dialect and standard Greek, accompanied by traditional and contemporary instruments.

In the North, musical trends tend to mirror those of mainland Turkey. However, Greek music is still admired, and both cultures share a remarkable overlap in sounds and instrumentation.

Dance

Traditional Cypriot dances are commonly 'confronted pair' dances of two couples, or vigorous solo men's dances in which the dancer holds an object such as a sickle, a knife, a sieve or a tumbler. Shows at popular tourist restaurants frequently

Clockwise from top left
1. Playing the bouzouki 2. Handmade musical instruments 3. Cypriot folk dancing

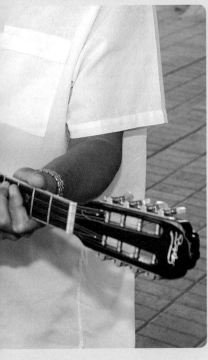

feature a dance called *datsia* where the dancer balances a stack of glasses full of wine on a sieve.

Dances in the North share very similar patterns of development and execution to those in the South, the only real difference being the names. Thus the *tsifteteli* (a style of belly dancing) is the *ciftetelli* in the North. In addition there is the *testi* and the *kozan*, both wedding dances, and the *kaşikli oyunlari*, a dance performed with wooden spoons. Restaurants with floor shows are most likely your best opportunity to sample some of the northern variants of Cypriot dancing.

Dancecyprus (www.dancecyprus.org) is Cyprus' ballet company. It produces inspiring modern and classical works to a European standard with a distinctive Cypriot influence.

TOP FIVE MUSIC FESTIVALS

» **Bellapais Music Festival**, Bellapais, Northern Cyprus (May)

» **International Famagusta Art & Culture Festival**, Famagusta, Northern Cyprus (July)

» **Paradise Jazz Festival**, Pomos, Republic of Cyprus (July)

» **International Music Festival**, Lemesos, Republic of Cyprus (July)

» **Pafos Aphrodite Festival**, Pafos, Republic of Cyprus (September)

Literature

Cyprus has produced a sprinkling of literary illuminati, and the literature scene is actively promoted and encouraged in both the Republic and Northern Cyprus.

Home-grown literary talent of the 20th century includes Loukis Akritas (1932–65), who made his mark mainly in Greece as a journalist and writer, and later championed the cause of Cypriot independence through letters, rather than violence. His works include novels, plays, short stories and essays.

Theodosis Pierides (1908–67), who wrote actively from 1928 onwards, is one of Cyprus' national and most respected poets. His *Cypriot Symphony* is considered to be the 'finest, most powerful epic written by a Greek poet about Cyprus', according to contemporary and fellow poet Tefkros Anthias (1903–68). Anthias himself was excommunicated by the Orthodox Church and internally exiled by the British administration in 1931 for his poetry collection *The Second Coming*. He was arrested during the liberation struggle of 1955–59 and imprisoned. While in prison he wrote a collection of poems called *The Diary of the CDP*, which was published in 1956.

The North supports a small but healthy literary scene with more than 30 'name' personages. Nese Yasin (1959–) is a writer, journalist and poet, and a founding member of a movement known as the '74 Generation Poetry Movement. This was a post-division literary wave of writers that sought inspiration from the climate generated after Cyprus was divided. Yasin's poems have been translated and published in magazines, newspapers, anthologies and books in Cyprus, Turkey, Greece, Yugoslavia, Hungary, the Netherlands, Germany and the UK.

Below
Holy metal book in Pareklisia, near Lemesos

Survival Guide

DIRECTORY A–Z 246

Activities 246

Business Hours 246

Climate 246

Customs Regulations . . . 246

Discount Cards 246

Electricity 247

Embassies &
Consulates 247

Food 247

Gay & Lesbian
Travellers 248

Health. 248

Insurance. 248

Internet Access. 248

Legal Matters 248

Money. 248

Photography & Video . . . 249

Post. 250

Public Holidays. 250

Safe Travel 250

Telephone 250

Time 251

Toilets. 251

Tourist Information 251

Travellers with
Disabilities. 252

Visas. 252

Volunteering 252

Women Travellers. 252

Work 252

TRANSPORT 254

GETTING THERE &
AWAY 254

Crossing the Border 254

Entering the Country. . . . 254

Air 254

Sea 257

GETTING AROUND. 257

Bicycle 257

Bus 258

Car & Motorcycle 258

Hitching 259

Local Transport. 259

Sea 260

Tours. 260

LANGUAGE 261

Glossary. 270

Directory
A–Z

Activities

See p25 for what's on offer in the activities department in Cyprus.

Business Hours

Reviews in this guidebook won't list business hours unless they differ from the following standard opening hours. These hours are for high season only and tend to decrease outside that time. They apply to both the North and South of the country, unless otherwise specified.

Banks Republic of Cyprus 8.30am-12.30pm Mon-Fri; some also open 3.15-4.45pm Mon. Northern Cyprus 8am-noon Sat & Sun, plus 2-5pm Mon-Fri

Climate

Lefkosia/North Nicosia

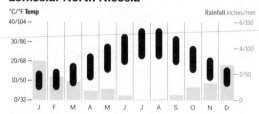

Lemesos

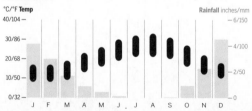

Entertainment 9pm-3am Thu-Sat

Restaurants 11am-2pm & 7.30-11pm daily

Shops 9am-7pm weekdays, closing 2pm Wed, 9am-2pm Sat

Tourist offices 8.30am-2.30pm Sat & Sun, plus 3-6.30pm Mon-Fri

Customs Regulations

Republic of Cyprus General EU customs rules apply. You are allowed to bring in or out an unrestricted amount of (legal) goods, as long as they are for your own consumption.

Northern Cyprus Limits for entering or leaving Northern Cyprus:

» 200 cigarettes

» 1L of spirits or wine

» €100 worth of other goods

The importation of agricultural products is subject to strict quarantine control and requires prior approval by the Ministry of Agriculture & Natural Resources.

When travelling, be aware that you become subject to both British and the Republic of Cyprus customs regulations when crossing the border at Pergamos (Larnaka) and Agios Nikolaos (Famagusta), as those two checkpoints are in the Dekelia Sovereign Base Area (Great Britain). The regulations are the same, but it might take a bit more time.

Discount Cards

Senior cards Reduced prices for people over 60 or 65 (depending on location) at various museums.

Student cards Discounts (usually half the normal fee) for students. You will need some kind of identification (eg an International Student Identity Card; www.isic.org) to prove student status. Not accepted everywhere.

PRACTICALITIES

Local Newspapers & Magazines

» The Republic of Cyprus' English-language newspapers are the *Cyprus Mail* and the *Cyprus Weekly*. In Northern Cyprus, look for the *Turkish Daily News* and *Cyprus Today*.

» UK dailies and German and French newspapers are widely available in the South and North.

Radio

» Cyprus Broadcasting Corporation (CyBC) has programs and news bulletins in English on Radio 2 (91.1FM). British Forces Broadcasting Services (BFBS) 1 broadcasts 24 hours a day in English on 89.7FM (Lefkosia), 92.1FM (west Cyprus) and 99.6FM (east Cyprus). BFBS 2 broadcasts on 89.9FM (Lefkosia), 91.7FM (Lemesos) and 95.3FM (Larnaka). BBC World Service is picked up 24 hours a day on 1323AM.

» Bayrak International is the voice of the North and has a lively English-language program on 87.8FM and 105FM.

TV

» CyBC TV has news in English at 8pm on Channel 2. Many hotels have CNN, BBC, Sky or NBC.

Weights & Measures

» Cyprus uses the metric system.

Smoking

» Prohibited in all bars and restaurants.

Electricity

240V/50Hz

Embassies & Consulates

Countries with diplomatic representation in the Republic of Cyprus are listed below. All missions are in Lefkosia.

Australia (☎2275 3001; www.embassy.gov.au/cy.html; cnr Leoforos Stasinou & Annis Komninis 4)

Canada (☎2277 5508; info@consulcanada.com.cy; Lambousa 1)

France (☎2277 9910; www.ambafrance-cy.org; Ploutarchou 12, Engomi)

Germany (☎2245 1145; www.nikosia.diplo.de; Nikitara 10)

Greece (☎2268 0645; www.greekembassy-cy.org; Leoforos Lordou Vyronos 8-10)

Ireland (☎2281 8183; www.embassyofireland.com.cy; Aiantas 7)

Netherlands (☎2265 3451; http://cyprus.nlembassy.org; Hilton Hotel, Leoforos Archiepiskopou Makariou III)

UK (☎2286 1100; www.ukincyprus.fco.gov.uk/en; Alexandrou Palli)

USA (☎2277 6400; www.cyprus.usembassy.gov; cnr Metohiou & Agiou Ploutarhou, Engomi)

Countries with diplomatic representation in Northern Cyprus are listed below. All are located in North Nicosia (Lefkoşa). If you're sending mail to any of these addresses in Northern Cyprus, ensure that you use the suffix 'Mersin 10, Turkey', not 'Northern Cyprus'.

Australia (☎227 7332; www.embassy.gov.au/cy.html; Güner Türkmen Sokak 20, Köşklüçiftlik)

Germany (☎227 5161; www.nikosia.diplo.de; Kasim 15)

Turkey (☎227 2314; clefkbe@cc.emu.edu.tr; Bedrettin Demirel Caddesi)

UK (☎228 3861; www.ukincyprus.fco.gov.uk/en; Mehmet Akif Caddesi 29, Köşklüçiftlik)

USA (☎227 8295; www.cyprus.usembassy.gov; Güner Türkmen Sokak 20, Köşklüçiftlik)

Food

In this book we have ordered food choices by author preference. See p37 for more information on food and drink in Cyprus. The € symbols used in the restaurant reviews refer to the following price spans:

	REPUBLIC OF CYPRUS	NORTHERN CYPRUS
€	under €7	under €5
€€	€7-12	€5-10
€€€	over €12	over €10

Gay & Lesbian Travellers

Homosexuality is legal in the Republic; contact the **Gay Liberation Movement** (☎2244 3346; PO Box 1947, Lefkosia)for more information. You will find interesting discussions, tips and contacts on anything gay in Cyprus at www.cyprusgayforum.com.

In the North, homosexuality, which has long been officially banned, was decriminalised in 2010. However, you may still find an overall conservative attitude, and overt public displays of affection may be frowned upon. To date, there are no organised support groups in Northern Cyprus.

Health

Availability & Cost of Health Care

» If you need an ambulance, call ☑119 in the Republic of Cyprus, or ☑112 in Northern Cyprus.

» Pharmacies can dispense medicines available only on prescription in most European countries, so you can consult a pharmacist for minor ailments.

» Emergency medical treatment and assistance is provided free of charge at government hospitals or medical institutions. However, payment of the prescribed fees is required for outpatient and inpatient treatment.

Drinking Water

While the tap water is perfectly safe to drink in the South, it's advisable to drink bottled water in the North.

Health Insurance

» Citizens of EU countries are entitled to free or cheaper medical care in the Republic, but not in Northern Cyprus.

» EU citizens must carry proof of their entitlement in the form of the European Health Insurance Card (EHIC).

» Citizens from other countries should find out if there is a reciprocal arrangement for free medical care between their country and Cyprus.

Recommended Vaccinations

No jabs are required to travel to Cyprus, but the World Health Organization (WHO) recommends that all travellers should be covered for diphtheria, measles, mumps, rubella and polio.

Insurance

A travel-insurance policy to cover theft, loss and medical problems and cancellation or delays to your travel arrangements is a good idea. Paying for your ticket with a credit card can often provide limited travel-accident insurance and you may be able to reclaim the payment if the operator doesn't deliver. Worldwide travel insurance is available at www.lonelyplanet.com /travel_services. You can buy, extend and claim online anytime – even if you're already on the road.

Internet Access

» Wi-fi is increasingly available at most hotels and in some cafes, restaurants and airports; generally, but not always, free. Connection speed often varies from room to room in hotels, so always ask when you check in.

» Hotels offering wi-fi are indicated throughout this book with an icon 🛜. If they have a public-access computer terminal instead, the icon is @.

» Internet cafes are fairly common, particularly in the North, but they do come and go, so check at the local tourist office. Prices per hour range from €1.50 to €3.

Legal Matters

Drinking & Driving

Driving while under the influence of alcohol is strictly controlled, and being over the limit can result in a stiff fine and a night behind bars.

Drugs

The Cypriot authorities both in Northern Cyprus and the Republic show zero tolerance towards drugs. Although, strictly speaking, a small amount of cannabis for personal use should be permissible (under EU law) in the South, it is just not worth the risk.

Money

The unit of currency in Northern Cyprus is the new Turkish lira (Yeni Turkye Lira; YTL). Exchange rates for the new Turkish lira are subject to fluctuations due to a high inflation rate and will most likely have changed by the time you read this. All prices for Northern Cyprus in this book are either in euros for accommodation and excursions, or new Turkish lira for restaurants, museum admissions and other sundry fees.

Since January 2008, the Republic's unit of currency has been the euro (€), when one Cypriot pound (CY£) was exchanged at a frozen rate of €1.68.

Banks in Cyprus exchange all major currencies in either cash or travellers cheques. Most shops and hotels in Northern Cyprus accept hard currencies such as UK pounds, US dollars and euros.

ATMs

You will find ATMs in most towns and larger villages throughout the island.

Cash

In the Republic, you can get a cash advance on Visa, MasterCard, Diners Club,

Eurocard and American Express at a number of banks, and there are plenty of ATMs. In the North, cash advances are given on Visa cards at the Vakıflar and Kooperatif banks in North Nicosia and Kyrenia; major banks (such as Iş Bankası) in large towns will have ATMs, while there is an increasing number of petrol stations with ATMs attached. Do carry some cash with you, though, especially if you're travelling up to the Karpas (Kırpaşa) Peninsula.

It's a good idea to only carry as much cash as you need for three days or so. However, a safety stash of about €100 sewn into your backpack or suitcase will see you through a temporary cash-flow problem.

Foreign-currency notes may be all right to use in major tourist centres in Cyprus, but are not much use in Troödos Massif villages. In the North, foreign currency is more likely to be widely accepted in lieu of new Turkish lira.

Currency-exchange bureaus in tourist centres operate over extended hours and most weekends.

Credit Cards

Just as popular as ATMs, credit cards can be used in stores, restaurants, supermarkets and petrol stations. In the latter, you can even buy petrol after hours with your credit card from automatic dispensers.

The Republic of Cyprus is more credit-card friendly than Northern Cyprus, though the main restaurants, hotels and car-hire companies in the North will happily take plastic.

International Transfers

If you need to access your funds, international transfers are possible from your home bank to any of Cyprus' major banks. While this method is reliable, it is usually slow – taking a week or more – and not helpful if you need a cash infusion

quickly. Telegraphic transfers are nominally quicker (and cost more) but can still take up to three working days to come through.

Private financial agencies such as Western Union are usually the best bet, as you can often obtain your transferred money the same day.

Tipping

In both parts of the island, a 10% service charge is sometimes added to a restaurant bill; if not, then a tip of a similar percentage is expected. Taxi drivers and hotel porters always appreciate a small tip. Bargaining is not normally part of the shopping scene in Cyprus, neither in the North nor the South.

Travellers Cheques

Increasingly overlooked by card-wielding travellers, travellers cheques are a dying breed. They should not, however, be written off entirely as they're an excellent form of backup, especially as you can claim a refund if they're stolen (provided you've kept a separate record of their numbers).

Amex, Visa and Travelex cheques are the easiest to cash, particularly if in US dollars, British pounds or euros. Increasingly, banks are charging hefty commissions, though, even on cheques denominated in euros. Whatever currency they are in, travellers cheques can be difficult to exchange in smaller towns. Always take your passport as identification when cashing travellers cheques.

For lost or stolen cheques call: Amex ☑800 91 49 12; MasterCard ☑800 87 08 66; Travelex ☑800 87 20 50; or Visa ☑800 87 41 55.

Photography & Video

You can buy a range of memory cards from camera stores. Film is still available,

but it can be expensive. You'll find all the gear you need in the photography shops of Lefkosia/North Nicosia and major towns.

For tips on taking great travel photos, take a look at Lonely Planet's *Travel Photography*.

Photographing People

Cypriots are often very willing subjects for photos. However, it is bad form simply to point a camera at someone without at least acknowledging your subject. A simple greeting of 'kalimera' (in the South) or 'merhaba' (in the North) or just a smile may be all that is required to break the ice and set up a potential portrait scene.

It is not culturally appropriate to take photographs in mosques when people are praying or when a service is in progress. However, outside of these restrictions, it is usually okay to take a photograph. It is less intrusive (and draws less attention) without a flash.

Restrictions

In general, you can photograph anywhere in Cyprus, with some fairly obvious exceptions. You cannot normally photograph anywhere near the Green Line. In practice, this is rarely monitored other than on both sides of the Green Line in Lefkosia/North Nicosia, where sensitivities run high. Warning signs, usually a camera with a line through it, are normally displayed prominently, so heed them.

Military camps are another no-go area and, while there are military installations in both parts of Cyprus, you will be more aware of them in the North. Do not even get a camera out if you see a warning sign.

Airports, ports and other government installations are normally touchy photo subjects, so you are advised to keep your camera out of sight near these places, too.

Museums do not normally allow you to photograph exhibits unless you have written permission.

Churches with icons do not allow the use of a flash, and, depending on the commercial value of the pictures you take, may not allow photos at all.

Post

Postal services on both sides of the island are generally very efficient. Post offices are located in all major towns and villages. Services are normally only related to selling stamps and some packing materials. Stamps can also be bought at newsagents and street kiosks. Post boxes are everywhere (in the South, they are yellow, and in the North, red).

Public Holidays

Republic of Cyprus

Holidays in the Republic of Cyprus are the same as in Greece, with the addition of Greek Cypriot Day (1 April) and Cyprus Independence Day (1 October). Kids are on holiday in August and over the New Year. Greek public holidays:

New Year's Day 1 January

Epiphany 6 January

First Sunday in Lent February

Greek Independence Day 25 March

(Orthodox) Good Friday March/April

(Orthodox) Easter Sunday March/April

Spring Festival/Labour Day 1 May

Kataklysmos June

Feast of the Assumption 15 August

Ohi Day 28 October

Christmas Day 25 December

St Stephen's Day 26 December

Northern Cyprus

Northern Cyprus observes Muslim religious holidays.

These holidays change each year, since they are calculated by the lunar system. The two major holidays are Kurban Bayramı and Şeker Bayramı, both coming at the end of the month-long Ramadan (Ramazan in Turkish) fast. The fast itself is not strictly observed in the North, and restaurants and cafes are open as normal. As in the South, kids are on holiday in August and over the New Year. Other holidays:

New Year's Day 1 January

Peace & Freedom Day 20 July

Victory Day 30 August

Turkish National Day 29 October

Proclamation of the TRNC 15 November

Safe Travel

Scams

You may well come across time-share touts if you hang around the main resorts in Cyprus and, in particular, Pafos. If you like the island enough, a time-share may be worth considering, but be careful about how and what you choose. You need to have all your rights and obligations in writing, especially where management companies promise to sell your time-share for you if you decide to

buy a new one. A number of 'free' sightseeing tours are little more than a quick trip to a theme park and then a solid round of the hard sell, as touts pressure you to buy time in a property. If you're not into this, say so up front and save yourself the hassle and always allow yourself a 'cooling off' period to consider. In other words, leave the credit cards safely at home.

Telephone

For information on ringing the North from the South, or vice versa, see the box opposite.

There are no area codes as such in Cyprus; they are an integral part of the telephone number.

In both the North and the South, mobile phones are popular. If you have an international GSM-equipped phone, check with your local service provider if global roaming is available.

You can make overseas calls from any public telephone box. However, calling from your computer using an internet-based service such as Skype is generally the cheapest option of all.

Mobile Phones

Republic of Cyprus In the South, mobile-phone

numbers begin with ☑99. If you plan to spend any time in the South, you may want to buy a SIM card for your (unlocked) mobile phone. CYTA's SoEasy pay-as-you-go mobile-phone plan is one option. For around €27, you get a start-up kit consisting of a SIM card with a new number, full connection instructions in both English and Greek, and a €5 recharge card to get you started. Visit www.cytamobile-vodafone.com for details. Note that you can top up conveniently online and top ups are valid for one year, if you are planning on returning within this period of time. MTN pay-as-you-go offers a similar plan (www.mtn.com.cy).

Northern Cyprus In the North, mobile-phone numbers commence with either ☑0542 (Telsim) or ☑0533 (Turkcell). To call a local number, you'll need to dial the full 11-digit number, ie including the Northern Cyprus code of ☑0392.

Mobile phone company Telsim has good coverage but prices are high as they are not subject to EU controls.

Pay Phones

Republic of Cyprus In the South, there are two types of public phones: those that accept prepaid phonecards and those that accept coins. Phonecard-operated phones have explanations in English and Greek. Cards to the value of €5, €10 and €15 can be purchased from banks, post offices, souvenir shops and street kiosks, and from Cyprus Telecommunications Authority (CYTA) offices in all towns.

Northern Cyprus Public telephone boxes take phone-cards (5YTL for a 100-unit card) bought at a Turkish Telecom administration office or at a post office.

Time

Time zone Cyprus is normally two hours ahead of GMT and seven hours ahead of EST.

Daylight-saving Has daylight-saving time during the summer months. Clocks go forward one hour on the last weekend in March and back one hour on the last weekend in October.

Current time A recorded time message can be heard by dialling ☑193 in the Republic of Cyprus.

Toilets

Most toilets will display a sign requesting that you do not flush toilet paper as, due to poor island-wide plumbing, this can easily cause a blockage. Wastepaper baskets are provided for this purpose. It is also a wise idea to carry a small packet of tissues with you when you are out and about.

The majority of public toilets are free, while some charge a small fee. You can also use the public facilities in a bar or cafe, although it is standard to offer a small sum or buy a drink in return.

Tourist Information

Republic of Cyprus

The main tourist organisation in the South is the **Cyprus Tourism Organisation** (CTO; ☑2233 7715; www.visitcyprus.org.cy; Leoforos Lemesou 19, Lefkosia), known in Greek as Kypriakos Organismos Tourismou (KOT). Its leaflets and free maps are adequate for getting around. The CTO's headquarters are in Lefkosia's New City, on the road to Larnaka and Lemesos. However, it's not really geared to handling over-the-counter queries from the public. The CTO has branch offices in the major towns in Cyprus (Agia Napa, Lefkosia, Lemesos, Larnaka, Pafos, Polis and Platres), where brochures and assistance can be found easily. Contact details for CTO branches are given in the regional chapters.

The CTO has branches in most European countries.

TELEPHONING BETWEEN NORTHERN CYPRUS & THE REPUBLIC

Despite the easing of border crossings from South to North and vice versa, telephoning the other side of the island is still done via half of Europe and Asia.

» Phone calls to Northern Cyprus are usually routed through Turkey. So you first dial Turkey (international access code ☑90), then the regional code for Northern Cyprus (☑392), and finally the local number.

» Note that these phone calls are billed at international rates.

» If you have a mobile phone from outside Cyprus with global roaming activated, it's possible to tune into the GSM networks of either side.

» If you have bought a pay-as-you-go Cypriot card from either side, note that it will only pick up its own network in Lefkosia/North Nicosia. Go any further away from the Green Line and you will have to revert to your international card, as roaming is not supported between the two local mobile networks.

» Also note that text messaging between the North and the South is not possible.

Northern Cyprus

The main office of the **North Cyprus Tourism Organisation** (NCTO; ☎228 1057; www.tourism.trnc.net; Bedrettin Demirel Caddesi) is located in North Nicosia. There are also branch offices in North Nicosia at Kyrenia (Girne) Gate and at the Ledra Palace Hotel crossing point. It also maintains tourist offices in Famagusta, Kyrenia and Yenierenköy (Yiallousa), which have free country and town maps, plus an increasing number of brochures.

The NCTO can be found in the UK, Belgium, the USA, Pakistan and Turkey; otherwise inquiries are handled by Turkish tourist offices.

Travellers with Disabilities

Overall Cyprus is not geared towards smooth travel for disabled people, sadly. Most restaurants, shops and tourist sights are not equipped to handle wheelchairs, although midrange and top-end accommodation options generally always have wheelchair ramps, plus rooms with appropriate facilities. Transport is tricky, although you should be able to organise a specially modified hire car from one of the international car rental companies with advance warning.

In fact, advance warning is always a good idea; start with your travel agent and see what they can offer in terms of information and assistance.

Mobility Equipment Hire

Disability Cyprus (www.disability-cyprus.com)

Mobility Abroad (www.mobilityabroad.com)

Para-Quip (www.paraquip.com.cy)

Organisations

Accessible Cyprus (www.accessible-cyprus.com) Overseen by the CTO and lists hotels with disabled facilities.

Accessible Travel & Leisure (☎01452-729739; www.accessibletravel.co.uk; Avionics House, Naas Lane, Quedgeley, Gloucester GL2 2SN) Claims to be the biggest UK travel agent dealing with travel for the disabled and encourages the disabled to travel independently.

Society for Accessible Travel & Hospitality (☎212 447 7284; www.sath.org; 347 Fifth Ave, Ste 605, New York, NY 10016) Although largely concentrated on the USA, this organisation can provide general information.

Visas

» In both the Republic of Cyprus and Northern Cyprus, nationals of the USA, Canada, Australia, New Zealand and Singapore can enter and stay for up to three months without a visa.

» Citizens of South Africa may enter for up to 30 days without a visa.

» EU citizens have no work or stay restrictions in the South, and can stay in the North for up to three months.

» When you are crossing from the South into the North, you must fill in a visa paper, which requires your personal details such as name and date of birth, and your passport number.

» You can use the same visa paper for several entries and exits, and it gets stamped each time you cross.

» You must have your passport to cross from one side to the other.

» The same border-crossing rules apply for Greek and Turkish travellers as for everyone else.

Volunteering

Possibilities for volunteering to participate in projects in Cyprus include:

Transitions Abroad (www.transitionsabroad.com) A good website to start your research.

Earthwatch Institute (www.earthwatch.org) Check to see if there are any Cypriot conservation projects on its program.

Go Abroad (www.goabroad.com) Generally has several volunteering opportunities in Cyprus.

Any Work Anywhere (www.anyworkanywhere.com) Often have volunteer openings in turtle conservation programmes, both in Northern Cyprus and the Republic.

Women Travellers

Women travellers will encounter little sexual harassment, although, you'll get more or less constant verbal 'approaches' from Cypriot men. This is common for both foreign and Cypriot women, but foreign women merit particular attention from these verbal Romeos. This can get rather tiresome, if not outright offensive. It is best to ignore the advances.

Solo women travellers should take reasonable care at rowdy nightclub resorts, such as in Agia Napa, where inebriated foreign males may be a nuisance.

Work

Nationals of EU countries, Switzerland, Norway and Iceland may freely work in the Republic of Cyprus. If you are offered a contract, your employer will normally steer you through any bureaucracy.

Virtually everyone else is supposed to obtain a work permit and, if they plan to stay more than 90 days, a residence visa. These procedures are well-nigh impossible unless you have a job contract lined up before you begin them.

Language Teaching

This type of work is a more obvious option in Northern Cyprus, where English is not as widely spoken. There is competition, however, and language teaching qualifications are a big help, namely a TEFL qualification.

Information on possible teaching work – in a school or as a private tutor – can be found in universities, foreign-language bookshops and language schools. Many have noticeboards listing opportunities or where you can place your own advert.

Tourist Resorts

Summer work at the main coastal resorts is a possibility, especially if you arrive early in the season and are prepared to stay a while. Check any local press in foreign languages, which will normally list ads for waiters, nannies, chefs, babysitters, cleaners and the like.

Yacht Crewing

It is possible to stumble upon work on yachts and cruisers although it will usually be unpaid. Ask around at the various harbours.

Transport

GETTING THERE & AWAY

Most visitors to Cyprus arrive by air. Many of them come on charter flights or inexpensive flights operated by budget airlines, particularly from the UK.

The only way to arrive in the Republic by sea is aboard a cruise boat; there are no longer any passenger ferries, but vehicles may travel unaccompanied. However, there are fast and slower passenger ferries and car-ferry services linking the Turkish mainland with Northern Cyprus.

Flights and tours can be booked online at lonely planet.com/bookings.

Crossing the Border

Travelling between the Republic and Northern Cyprus is easy nowadays, since the restrictions on crossing the border have been eased. However, you are only allowed to cross at designated checkpoints, so read the boxed text, p257, for full information.

Entering the Country

Citizens of EU member states and Switzerland can travel to the Republic with just their national identity card. Nationals of the UK have to carry a full passport (UK visitor passports are not acceptable), and all other nationalities must have a full valid passport. In Northern Cyprus, EU citizens can stay for up to three months. For exact visa requirements, see p252.

Passport

You will need a valid passport to cross between the North and South. You'll need to produce your passport or ID card every time you check into a hotel in Cyprus, and when you conduct banking transactions.

Air

There are scheduled flights and an ever-increasing number of charter and budget flights to Cyprus from most European cities and the Middle East. Flights are heavily booked in the high season (mid-summer). Tickets on scheduled flights tend to be expensive, but Europe-based travellers may be able to pick up cheaper tickets with budget companies. If you're in Greece, you can usually find reasonably priced one-way or return tickets to the Republic from travel agents in Athens, Thessaloniki or Iraklio.

Airports & Airlines

THE SOUTH

The airports in Cyprus that handle international flights are located in the Republic:

Larnaka airport (LCA; ☎2481 6130)

CLIMATE CHANGE & TRAVEL

Every form of transport that relies on carbon-based fuel generates CO_2, the main cause of human-induced climate change. Modern travel is dependent on aeroplanes, which might use less fuel per kilometre per person than most cars but travel much greater distances. The altitude at which aircraft emit gases (including CO_2) and particles also contributes to their climate change impact. Many websites offer 'carbon calculators' that allow people to estimate the carbon emissions generated by their journey and, for those who wish to do so, to offset the impact of the greenhouse gases emitted with contributions to portfolios of climate-friendly initiatives throughout the world. Lonely Planet offsets the carbon footprint of all staff and author travel.

Pafos airport (PFO/LCPH; ☎2624 0506)

Note that on most airline schedules, Larnaka is listed as 'Larnaca' and Pafos as 'Paphos'. This is particularly important to know when making online bookings.

Cyprus Airways is the national carrier of the Republic of Cyprus.

THE NORTH
Ercan airport (ECN; ☎231 4806), located 14km east of North Nicosia (Lefkoşa) in Northern Cyprus, is not recognised by the international airline authorities, so you can't fly there direct. Airlines must touch down first in Turkey and then fly on to Northern Cyprus. Ercan is smaller than Pafos airport and not particularly well-equipped with arrival facilities, such as baggage carts and other conveniences. Car hire must be arranged beforehand. Taxis are your only choice to and from the airport.

Northern Cyprus is served primarily by Turkish Airlines (Türk Hava Yolları; THY).

AIRLINES FLYING TO & FROM CYPRUS
Aegean Airlines (www.aegeanair.com; hub Athens International Airport, Athens)

Air Malta (www.airmalta.com; hub Malta Airport, Valetta)

Alitalia (www.alitalia.com; hub Rome Fiumicino Airport, Rome)

Austrian Airlines (www.aua.com; hub Vienna International Airport, Vienna)

British Airways (www.britishairways.com; hub Heathrow Airport, London)

Cyprus Airways (www.cyprusairways.com; hub Larnaka Airport, Larnaka)

Cyprus Turkish Airlines (www.kthy.net; hub Ercan Airport, Famagusta)

Easyjet (www.easyjet.com; hub Stansted & Gatwick Airports, London)

Jet2 (www.jet2.com; hub Leeds Bradford Airport, England)

Lufthansa (www.lufthansa.com; hub Frankfurt Airport, Frankfurt)

Malev (www.malev.hu; hub Budapest Ferihegy Airport, Budapest)

Monarch (www.monarch.co.uk; hub Luton & Gatwick Airports, London)

Olympic Air (www.olympicair.com; hub Athens International Airport, Athens)

Turkish Airlines (www.thy.com; hub Istanbul Ataturk Airport, Istanbul)

Tickets
Tickets to Cyprus are most expensive in August. Try picking up flight-only deals with package-holiday companies during this time or scour the budget airlines (though these are hardly budget in the summer months). Prices depend on the season, and to a lesser degree on the day of the week or even the time you fly.

CHARTER FLIGHTS
Vacant seats on charter flights block-booked to Cyprus by package-tour companies are cheap, but conditions apply. First, you can rarely get more than two weeks for your itinerary and, second, the departure and arrival times are quite inflexible once booked. That said, a percentage of all package-tour seats is given over to flight-only travellers, so give it a go.

INTERCONTINENTAL (RTW) TICKETS
Neither Cyprus Airways nor Turkish Airlines are signatories to any round-the-world (RTW) ticket agreement.

Africa
Olympic Air (www.olympicair.com) Has regular flights to the Republic from several airports, including Johannesburg and Cape Town, via Athens.

Asia
STA Travel (☎6737 7188; www.statravel.com.sg; 534a North Bridge Rd, Singapore, 188749) Reliable throughout Asia, STA Travel has branches in Hong Kong, Tokyo, Singapore, Bangkok and Kuala Lumpur and can advise on the best route and price from cities of departure throughout Asia.

Australia & New Zealand
There are no direct services from Australia or New Zealand to Cyprus, but several airlines fly with just one change of aircraft, including:

Emirates Airlines (www.emirates.com) flies more or less directly from Melbourne or Perth via Singapore, with a change of aircraft in Dubai.

Olympic Air (www.olympicair.com) flies to Athens from Melbourne and Sydney, and can usually offer good-value add-on Cyprus legs.

Singapore Airlines (www.olympicairlines.com) flies into Athens from Adelaide, Brisbane, Melbourne, Perth and Sydney three times a week, and there are daily connections with Cyprus Airways.

Local tour operators:

Axis Travel Centre (www.axistravel.com.au; 176 Glynburn Rd, Tranmere, South Australia 5073) Specialises in travel to and from the Middle East, Greece and Cyprus from Australia and New Zealand.

Flight Centre (www.flightcentre.com.au)

STA Travel (☎1300 733 035; www.statravel.com.au)

Canada
Olympic Air (www.olympicair.com) has two flights a week from Toronto to Athens via Montreal. From Athens, you can connect with a Cyprus Airways flight to Larnaka.

Continental Europe

Many European carriers fly into Larnaka airport, and some also stop in Pafos, though the bulk of the traffic is made up of charter flights.

FRANCE

Several airlines operate regular services between France and the Republic of Cyprus, including:

Air France (www.airfrance.fr) Flies to Larnaka from Paris.

Cyprus Airways (www.cyprusairways.com) Flies to Larnaka and Pafos from Paris.

Turkish Airlines (www.thy.com) links Paris with Ercan airport in Northern Cyprus daily via Istanbul.

Local tour operators:

Havas Voyages (✆01 48 51 86 19; www.havas-voyages.fr; Montreuil Cedex)

Nouvelles Frontières (✆01 49 20 65 87; (www.nouvelles-frontieres.fr; Paris)

GERMANY

Several airlines operate regular services between Germany and the Republic of Cyprus, including:

Air Berlin (www.airberlin.com) Flies to Pafos and Larnaka from Berlin, Dusseldorf, Hanover and Hamburg.

Condor (www.condor.com) Flies to Larnaka from Berlin, Stuttgart, Dusseldorf and Hamburg.

TUI Fly (www.tuifly.com) Flies to Larnaka from Nuremberg.

Lufthansa (www.lufthansa.com) Flies to Larnaka from several airports, including Frankfurt, Berlin & Munich.

KLM (www.klm.com) Flies to Larnaka and Pafos from Frankfurt.

Local tour operators:

Alternativ Tours (✆030-881 20 89; www.alternativ-tours.de; Berlin)

STA Travel (SRS Studenten Reise Service; ✆030-285 82 64; www.statravel.de; Gleimstrasse

28, Berlin) Offers special student (aged 34 or under) and youth (aged 25 or under) fares.

GREECE

Not surprisingly, Greece is well connected to both Larnaka and Pafos in the Republic of Cyprus with a comprehensive network of flights. Check the websites of the following main airlines for specific routes:

Olympic Air (www.olympicair.com)

Cyprus Airways (www.cyprusair.com)

Lufthansa (www.lufthansa.com)

German Wings (www.germanwings.com)

It's possible to fly to Northern Cyprus from Greece. Daily flights with **Turkish Airlines** (www.thy.com) from Athens to Istanbul connect with a daily evening flight to Ercan.

Local tour operators:

Aktina Travel Services (✆21-0324 9925; www.aktinatravel.gr; Nikodimou 3, Athens)

STA Travel Athens (✆21-0321 1188; www.statravelgroup.com; Voulis 31, Athens); Thessaloniki (✆231-022 1391; Tsimiski 130, Thessaloniki)

NETHERLANDS

You can fly to Cyprus from Amsterdam (the Netherlands) daily. Main airlines include:

Austrian Airlines (www.aua.com) Flies to Larnaka from Vienna.

Alitalia (www.alitalia.com) Flies to Larnaka from Vienna.

Local tour operators:

Kilroy Travels (✆020-524 51 00; www.kilroytravels.com; Singel)

Kouni (✆020-398 93 98; www.kouni.ni; Amsterdam)

Middle East

With Cyprus so close to the Middle East, transport links between the countries of the Levant and Larnaka are good, but tickets are rarely

discounted. Cyprus Airways is represented in several countries, including Lebanon, Jordan and Syria.

UK & Ireland

Discount air travel is big business in London. Check the weekend broadsheet papers for special deals, many of which include a hotel or apartment with half-board and even car rental in the final price. The following airlines have regular and relatively inexpensive flights to the Republic.

British Airways (www.ba.com) Flies to Larnaka and Pafos (summer only) from London Heathrow and Gatwick.

Easyjet (www.easyjet.com) Flies to Larnaka and Pafos from London (all airports) and several UK airports, including Manchester and Birmingham.

Monarch (www.monarch.co.uk) Flies to Larnaka and Pafos from London (Gatwick and Luton airports), Manchester and Birmingham.

Thomson Fly (www.thomson.co.uk) Flies to Larnaka and Pafos from London (all airports) and other UK airports, including Bristol, Glasgow and Manchester.

Turkish Airlines (www.thy.com) Flies to Ercan Airport from London Heathrow.

Local tour operators:

Trailfinders (✆020-7937 1234; www.trailfinders.com; 215 Kensington High St, London W8 6BD) produces a lavishly illustrated brochure that includes air-fare details.

STA Travel (✆020-7361 6161; www.statravel.co.uk; 86 Old Brompton Rd, London SW7 3LQ) has branches in the UK.

USA

You can fly to Cyprus from the USA with a number of airlines, but all involve a stop and possibly a change of airline in Europe. The *New York Times*, *LA Times*,

Chicago Tribune and *San Francisco Examiner* all produce weekly travel sections in which you can find any number of travel agents' advertisements. The magazine *Travel Unlimited* (www.travelunlimited.com) publishes details of the cheapest airfares and courier possibilities for destinations all over the world from the USA.

Local tour operator: **STA Travel** (www.sta-travel .com) Has offices in major cities nationwide.

Sea

There are currently only passenger ferry services from Turkey to Kyrenia (Girne) and Famagusta (Mağusa) in Northern Cyprus; see p167 and p187 for details.

GETTING AROUND

Cyprus is small enough for you to get around easily. Roads are good and well signposted, and traffic moves smoothly and without the excesses and unpredictability sometimes found in other countries in Mediterranean Europe.

Public transport is limited to buses and service taxis (stretch taxis that run on predetermined routes). There is no train network and no domestic air services in either the North or the South. Four-lane motorways link Lefkosia with Lemesos and Larnaka, expanding west to Pafos and east to Agia Napa. In Northern Cyprus there is only one motorway, which runs between North Nicosia and Famagusta (Mağusa).

Bicycle

Cycling is a cheap, convenient, healthy, environmentally sound and, above all, fun way of travelling. However, it's advisable to limit long-distance cycling trips to winter, spring or autumn, as high summer temperatures will make the going tough. In the Republic of Cyprus, the Cyprus Tourism Organisation (CTO) produces a very helpful brochure entitled *Cyprus for Cycling*, which lists 19 recommended mountain-bike rides around the South. These range from 2.5km to 19km from the Akamas Peninsula in the west to Cape Greco in the east. Prospective cyclists are advised to consider the following:

» It's best to stick to cycling on ordinary roads, many of which parallel motorways, where cycling is not allowed. The roads are generally good, but there is rarely extra roadside room for cyclists, so you will have to cycle with care.

» You will need a bicycle with good gears to negotiate the long hauls up and around the Troödos Massif and Kyrenia (Girne) Range.

» Towns and cities in general are much more cyclist-friendly than their counterparts in other parts of the Mediterranean. In some tourist centres, such as Protaras and Agia Napa, there are urban bicycle paths, as well as beachside boulevards that incorporate space for bike riding.

» You cannot take bicycles on all buses.

Hire

Bicycles can be hired in most areas. Rates start from around €15 a day and local tourist offices can provide you with a list of reputable local operators. Cycle hire is particularly popular in the Agia Napa resort area and the Troödos inland region.

CROSSING THE GREEN LINE

Crossing freely between the North and the South has become pretty straightforward since the easing of border restrictions in 2003. It is now possible to cross at seven points on the island, and there are ongoing negotiations between the two sides about opening more. At the time of print, you could cross at Ledra Palace Hotel and Ledra St (both pedestrians only), Agios Dometios, Pergamos, Agios Nikolaos, Limnitis-Yeşilirmak and Zodhia (vehicles). If you don't have your own transport, a taxi will take you across the border and on to anywhere you want to go.

When you cross from the South into the North, you will have to fill in a visa paper, giving your name, date of birth and passport number. You will then be issued with a 'visa' (the small piece of paper will be stamped) and you'll be allowed to stay for up to three months in Northern Cyprus. It is important to look after this piece of paper, since you will be required to show it when you leave. There are no restrictions on how many times you can cross backwards and forwards. The visa paper is enforced only in the North.

You are now also allowed to cross into the Republic of Cyprus if your point of entry into the country is in the North. All borders are open 24 hours a day, and many cross in the middle of the night, after a night's clubbing or gambling at the casinos in the North. There are no requirements for crossing from the North into the South, apart from a valid passport (see p252).

Purchase

If you are really keen on cycling, you can purchase a decent bicycle in the Republic of Cyprus. You could try one of the specialist shops in Lefkosia, such as **Zanetos Bicycles** (☑2259 0945; 34 Agiou Dometieu, Strovolos). Northern Cyprus offers less of a choice when it comes to purchasing a bike; it's better not to count on it.

Bus

Buses in the South are frequent and run from Monday to Saturday, with no services on Sunday. In 2010 the bus companies were streamlined and the ticket prices reduced (due to government subsidies). Five companies cover their respective districts and all have comprehensive websites:

» **Emel** (www.limassolbuses .com) Lemesos district.

» **Osea Buses** (www.osea buses.com) Larnaca district.

» **Osel Buses** (www.osel.com .cy) Lefkosia district.

» **Pafos Buses** (www.pafos buses.com) Pafos district.

» **Zinonas Buses** (www .zinonasbuses.com) Famagusta district.

In addition, buses that connect the cities are run by the appropriately named **InterCity Bus Company** (www.intercity-buses .com), which offers discounted fares on multiple journeys.

Buses in the North are a varied mix of old and newer privately owned buses too numerous to list here. See the regional chapters for more details.

Costs

Since 2010 fares in the Republic have been pegged at €1 per ride, €2 per day, €10 per week and €30 for a month of unlimited journeys within a district, and which includes rural villages. InterCity Buses are also government subsidised and

are surprisingly reasonable, given the distances involved.

Bus prices in the North generally cost 2.50YTL, or 5YTL to 6YTL for longer distances.

See individual city and town entries for bus frequency and departure times.

Reservations

Bus reservations are not normally required in either the South or the North.

Car & Motorcycle

Automobile Associations

In the South, there is a **Cyprus Automobile Association** (☑2231 3233; www.caa.com.cy; Hrysostomou Mylona 12, Lefkosia). The 24-hour emergency road assistance number is ☑2231 3131. There is no equivalent organisation in Northern Cyprus.

Bringing Your Own Car

Unless you intend to settle in Cyprus, there is no advantage whatsoever in bringing your own vehicle. For a stay of more than three weeks, the high cost of bringing your own vehicle to Cyprus will be outweighed by the cost of hiring a vehicle locally. You will need to send your car by ferry and take a plane for yourself, unless you are arriving in Kyrenia (p167) or Famagusta (p187) from Turkey. If you're one of the very rare visitors to bring your own vehicle, you will need registration papers and an International Insurance Certificate (or a Green Card). Your insurance company will issue this.

Driving Licence

Requirements for renting a car in Cyprus:

» Driver's licence.

» Be aged 21 or over (Republic); 18 or over (Northern Cyprus).

» For the major companies at least, have a credit or debit card.

» Smaller firms can sometimes live without a credit or debit card, although, those with a non-EU licence (in the Republic), should also have an International Driving Permit (IDP). National licences from countries like Australia, Canada, New Zealand and the USA are usually accepted.

» A licence is required for any vehicle over 50cc.

Fuel & Spare Parts

Being a nation that loves its motors, Cyprus is well equipped for all driving needs, with an abundance of petrol stations, spare parts and repairs, and usually a friendly local happy to give you a hand if your car breaks down. Normally, if you've rented a car, the rental agency will be responsible for repairs.

Hire

Cars and 4WDs are widely available for hire, and cost around €20 per day for a week's rental.

In some towns, you can also rent motorcycles (from €10) or mopeds (€10).

Rental cars are usually in good condition, but inspect your vehicle before you set off.

Open-top 4WDs are popular options (the Troödos Massif literally swarms with them on hot weekends); they offer the option of dirt-track driving, that adventure 'look' and natural air-con. If you hire a 2WD, make sure it has air-conditioning and enough power to get you up hills.

Rental cars in both the North and the South carry black on red 'Z' plates – so called because of the initial letter. Other road users normally accord a fraction more respect to 'Z' car drivers, and the police are more likely to turn a blind eye for minor infractions, but don't count on it.

If you rent a car before going to Cyprus, you'll find that it is common practice for the rental agency to leave your vehicle at the airport, unlocked, with the key waiting for you under the floor mat. Don't be surprised: with the obvious red hire-car plates and a nonexistent car theft record, the car is as safe as can be.

Insurance
The Republic of Cyprus issues full car insurance when you rent a car. The North also issues full insurance to cars rented in the North, but has a special third-party insurance for cars coming in from the South. For more information, see the boxed text, p260.

Road Rules
Blood-alcohol limit The legal limit is 0.009mg of alcohol per 100mL of blood. Random breath testing is carried out. If you are found to be over the limit you can be fined and deprived of your licence.

Front seat belts Compulsory. Children under five years of age must not sit in the front seat.

Legal driving age for cars 21 (Republic), 18 (Northern Cyprus).

Legal driving age for motorcycles and scooters 18 (80cc and over) or 17 (50cc and under). A licence is required.

Motorcyclists Must use headlights at all times and wear a helmet if riding a bike of 125cc or more.

Road distances Posted in kilometres only. Road signs are in Greek and Latin script in the Republic of Cyprus; in Northern Cyprus, destinations are given in Turkish only.

Roundabouts (traffic circles) Vehicles already in the circle have the right of way.

Side of the road Drive on the left.

Speed limits In built-up areas, 50km/h, which increases to 80km/h on major roads and up to 100km/h on motorways. Speed limits in the North are 100km/h on open roads and 50km/h in towns.

Hitching
Hitchhiking is never entirely safe in any country in the world, and we don't recommend it. Travellers who decide to hitch should understand that they are taking a small but potentially serious risk. People who do choose to hitch will be safer if they travel in pairs and let someone know where they are planning to go.

Hitching in Cyprus is relatively easy but not very common. In rural areas, where bus transport is poor, many locals hitch between their village and the city. If you do decide to hitch, stand in a prominent position with an obvious space for a ride-giver to pull in, keep your luggage to a minimum, look clean and smart, and, above all, happy. A smile goes a long way.

Hitching in the North is likely to be hampered by a lack of long-distance traffic and, in any case, public transport costs are low enough to obviate the need to hitch.

Local Transport
Bus
While urban bus services exist in Lefkosia, Lemesos, Larnaka and Famagusta, about the only two places where they are of any practical use are Larnaka (to get to and from the airport) and Lemesos, where buses go to and from the port (where cruises depart and dock). Distances between sights in most towns and cities are fairly short, so negate the need to depend on the bus service. Buses also run to and from Kourion from Lemesos Fort, though these are tourist buses designed to get travellers from Lemesos out to the sights around Kourion, rather than to move locals around.

TRAVEL IN THE LOW SEASON
All of the bus transport times in this book are for the peak season (June to October). You'll find that public transport frequency decreases, together with tourist demand, during off-peak times. This is particularly problematic with mountain destinations, where the buses sometimes don't run at all. So before departure in the quieter months be sure to check all transport times via the respective bus company's website.

Taxi
In the South, taxis are extensive and available on a 24-hour basis; they can either be hailed from the street or a taxi rank, or booked over the phone. Taxis are generally modern, air-conditioned vehicles, usually comfortable Mercedes, and, apart from outside the major centres, are equipped with meters that the taxi drivers are obliged to use.

The two tariff periods are from 6am to 8.30pm (tariff 1), and from 8.30pm to 6am (tariff 2). Tariff 1 charges are €2.40 flag fall and €0.60 per kilometre. Tariff 2 charges are €3 flag fall and €0.65 per kilometre. Luggage is charged at the rate of €0.60 for every piece weighing more than 12kg. Extra charges of €1 per fare apply during most public holidays.

'Taxi sharing', which is common in Greek cities such as Athens, is not permitted in Cyprus. Taxi drivers are normally courteous and helpful.

In the North, taxis do not sport meters, so agree on the fare with the driver beforehand. As a rough guide, expect to pay around 2.50YTL for a ride around any of the towns. A taxi ride from North Nicosia to Kyrenia will cost around 30YTL, and from North Nicosia to Famagusta, 60YTL.

SERVICE TAXI

Taking up to eight people, service taxis are a useful transport option in the South. They are run by an amalgamation of private companies called **Travel & Express** (☎07 77 477; www .travelexpress.com.cy), with one national phone number. The individual offices can also be contacted directly: **Lefkosia** (☎2273 0888), **Lemesos** (☎2536 4114), **Larnaka** (☎2466 1010) and **Pafos** (☎2693 3181).

You can get to and from Lefkosia, Lemesos and Larnaka by service taxi, but usually not directly to or from Pafos; a change in Lemesos is often required.

The fixed fares are competitive with bus travel. Either go to the service taxi office or phone to be picked up at your hotel. Note that pick-ups can often be up to 30 minutes later than booked, so build this into your plans if time is tight. Similarly, if you're departing from a service-taxi depot, expect to spend up to 30 minutes picking up other passengers before you actually get under way.

The North has minibuses (sometimes referred to as *dolmuş*) between Kyrenia, North Nicosia and Famagusta only, which cost about 6YTL per person.

TOURIST TAXI

The 'tourist' taxis that await you near the Turkish Cypriot checkpoint at the Ledra Palace Hotel in North Nicosia will take you anywhere you want to go around Northern Cyprus. A round-trip day tour to Kyrenia, Famagusta, Bellapais (Beylerbeyi), Buffavento Castle and St Hilarion Castle costs around €30 to €50. (Although euros

THE ELUSIVE INSURANCE

Since the 2003 border-crossing changes, there has been a lot of talk of the North's car insurance, issued upon entry from the Republic. And after all this talk, things are still as clear as mud. If you ask about the insurance, you are likely to get numerous reactions and conflicting information. This is because the insurance 'law' concerning vehicles and drivers from the South is full of holes and open to interpretation (mainly by the North's police force).

When you enter the North by car (privately owned or rented) at any checkpoint, your own car insurance will no longer be valid, and you will have to purchase Turkish car insurance. It is third-party cover insurance, meaning that it covers anything up to €3000 worth of damage not caused by you. If *you* crash into someone or something, you will have to pay for the entire damage amount, and until you've coughed up the cash, you won't be able to leave the North.

If you're driving a rented car, keep in mind that, while the Republic's car-rental agencies have no objections to you taking rented cars to the North (although they don't condone it), it's up to you to decide whether this risk is worth taking. Establishing who is at fault in an accident can sometimes take a lot longer than you may think and be subject to many twists and turns.

Turkish-owned cars crossing into the South have to get the standard insurance, similar to that in other EU countries. At the time of research, the North's car-rental agencies did not allow taking rented cars into the Republic.

are not in general use in the North, most people will accept them if you have no other currency; Turkish taxis at crossing points will always quote their prices in British pounds.)

Sea

Lemesos is the South's main arrival and departure port, and the port is 3km southwest of the town centre. There will be a new, flash marina by 2013 (see p56) aiming to attract tourists as well as business travellers.

Tours

Travel agencies around Cyprus offer a wide variety of pre-packaged excursions.

Some reputable tour agencies in the South: **Amathus** (☎2536 9122; www.amathus.com; Plateia Syntagmatos, Lemesos) **Salamis Tours Excursions** (☎2535 5555; www.salamis international.com; Salamis House, 28 Oktovriou, Lemesos)

Land tours in the South usually run from the main tourist centres. They include full-day tours to Troödos and the Kykkos Monastery from Pafos (from €30); day trips to Lefkosia from Agia Napa or Larnaka (from €30); boat trips to Protaras from Agia Napa (from €25); and half-day tours of Lemesos, a winery and Ancient Kourion (from €25). These kinds of tours are not available in the North.

WANT MORE?

For in-depth language information and handy phrases, check out Lonely Planet's *Greek Phrasebook* and *Turkish Phrasebook*. You'll find them at **shop.lonelyplanet.com**, or you can buy Lonely Planet's iPhone phrasebooks at the Apple App Store.

Language

Visitors to Cyprus are unlikely to encounter any serious language difficulties since many people in both the North and the South speak English. Neither Greek nor Turkish Cypriots will expect a visitor to be able to speak their respective languages – let alone the Cypriot variants. However, trying a few of the words in the local lingo will go a long way to breaking the ice. The Greek and Turkish spoken in Cyprus differs somewhat from that spoken in Greece and Turkey. However, if you use the mainland varieties – which is what we've included below – you'll be understood just fine.

GREEK

Greek is the official language of Greece and co-official language of Cyprus (alongside Turkish).

The Greek alphabet is explained on the next page, but if you read the blue pronunciation guides given with each phrase in this chapter as if they were English, you'll be understood. Note that dh is pronounced as the 'th' in 'there', gh is a softer, slightly throaty version of 'g', and kh is a throaty sound like the 'ch' in the Scottish 'loch'. All Greek words of two or more syllables have an acute accent ('), which indicates where the stress falls. In our pronunciation guides, stressed syllables are in italics.

In Greek, all nouns, articles and adjectives are either masculine, feminine or neuter – in this chapter these forms are included where necessary, separated with a slash and indicated with 'm/f/n'.

Basics

Hello.	Γειά σας.	ya·sas (polite)
	Γειά σου.	ya·su (informal)
Good morning.	Καλή μέρα.	ka·li me·ra
Good evening.	Καλή σπέρα.	ka·li spe·ra
Goodbye.	Αντίο.	an·di·o
Yes./No.	Ναι./Όχι.	ne/o·hi
Please.	Παρακαλώ.	pa·ra·ka·lo
Thank you.	Ευχαριστώ.	ef·ha·ri·sto
That's fine./	Παρακαλώ.	pa·ra·ka·lo
You're welcome.		
Sorry.	Συγγνώμη.	sigh·no·mi

What's your name?
Πώς σας λένε; pos sas le·ne

My name is ...
Με λένε ... me le·ne ...

Do you speak English?
Μιλάτε αγγλικά; mi·la·te an·gli·ka

I (don't) understand.
(Δεν) καταλαβαίνω. (dhen) ka·ta·la·ve·no

Accommodation

campsite	χώρος για κάμπινγκ	kho·ros yia kam·ping
hotel	ξενοδοχείο	kse·no·dho·khi·o
youth hostel	γιουθ χόστελ	yuth kho·stel
a ... room	ένα ... δωμάτιο	e·na ... dho·ma·ti·o
single	μονόκλινο	mo·no·kli·no
double	δίκλινο	dhi·kli·no

GREEK ALPHABET

The Greek alphabet has 24 letters, shown below in their upper- and lower-case forms. Be aware that some letters look like English letters but are pronounced very differently, such as **B**, which is pronounced 'v'; and **P**, pronounced like an 'r'. As in English, how letters are pronounced is also influenced by how they are combined, for example the **ou** combination is pronounced 'u' as in 'put', and **οι** is pronounced 'ee' as in 'feet'.

A α	a	as in 'father'		**Ξ ξ**	x	as in 'ox'
B β	v	as in 'vine'		**O o**	o	as in 'hot'
Γ γ	gh	a softer, throaty 'g'		**Π π**	p	as in 'pup'
	y	as in 'yes'		**P ρ**	r	as in 'road',
Δ δ	dh	as in 'there'				slightly trilled
E ε	e	as in 'egg'		**Σ σ, ς**	s	as in 'sand'
Z ζ	z	as in 'zoo'		**T τ**	t	as in 'tap'
H η	i	as in 'feet'		**Y υ**	i	as in 'feet'
Θ θ	th	as in 'throw'		**Φ φ**	f	as in 'find'
I ι	i	as in 'feet'		**X χ**	kh	as the 'ch' in the
K κ	k	as in 'kite'				Scottish 'loch', or
Λ λ	l	as in 'leg'				like a rough 'h'
M μ	m	as in 'man'		**Ψ ψ**	ps	as in 'lapse'
N ν	n	as in 'net'		**Ω ω**	o	as in 'hot'

Note that the letter **Σ** has two forms for the lower case – **σ** and **ς**. The second one is used at the end of words. The Greek question mark is represented with the English equivalent of a semicolon (;).

How much is it ...?	Πόσο κάνει ...;	po·so ka·ni ...
per night	τη βραδυά	ti·vra·dhya
per person	το άτομο	to a·to·mo
air-con	έρκοντίσιον	er·kon·di·si·on
bathroom	μπάνιο	ba·nio
fan	ανεμιστήρας	a·ne·mi·sti·ras
TV	τηλεόραση	ti·le·o·ra·si
window	παράθυρο	pa·ra·thi·ro

Directions

Where is ...?
Πού είναι ...; pu i·ne ...

Turn left.
Στρίψτε αριστερά. strips·te a·ri·ste·ra

Turn right.
Στρίψτε δεξιά. strips·te dhe·ksia

at the next corner
στην επόμενη γωνία stin e·po·me·ni gho·ni·a

at the traffic lights
στα φώτα sta fo·ta

behind	πίσω	pi·so
in front of	μπροστά	bro·sta
far	μακριά	ma·kri·a
near (to)	κοντά	kon·da
next to	δίπλα	dhi·pla
opposite	απέναντι	a·pe·nan·di
straight ahead	ολο ευθεία	o·lo ef·thi·a

Eating & Drinking

What would you recommend?
Τι θα συνιστούσες; ti tha si·ni·stu·ses

What's in that dish?
Τι περιέχει αυτό το φαγητό; ti pe·ri·e·hi af·to to fa·ghi·to

I'm a vegetarian.
Είμαι χορτοφάγος. i·me khor·to·fa·ghos

That was delicious.
Ήταν νοστιμότατο! i·tan no·sti·mo·ta·to

Cheers!
Εις υγείαν! is i·yi·an

Please bring the bill.
Το λογαριασμό, παρακαλώ. to lo·ghar·ya·zmo pa·ra·ka·lo

a table for ...	Ενα τραπέζι για ...	e·na tra·pe·zi ya ...
(two) people	(δύο) άτομα	(dhi·o) a·to·ma
(eight) o'clock	τις (οχτώ)	stis (okh·to)

I don't eat ...	Δεν τρώγω ...	dhen tro·gho ...
fish	ψάρι	psa·ri
(red) meat	(κόκκινο) κρέας	(ko·ki·no) kre·as
peanuts	φυστίκια	fi·sti·kia
poultry	πουλερικά	pu·le·ri·ka

Key Words

appetisers	ορεκτικά	o·rek·ti·ka
bar	μπαρ	bar
beef	βοδινό	vo·dhi·no
bottle	μπουκάλι	bu·ka·li
bowl	μπωλ	bol
bread	ψωμί	pso·mi
breakfast	πρόγευμα	pro·yev·ma
cafe	καφετέρια	ka·fe·te·ri·a
cheese	τυρί	ti·ri
chicken	κοτόπουλο	ko·to·pu·lo
cold	κρυωμένος	kri·o·me·nos
cream	κρέμα	kre·ma
delicatessen	ντελικατέσεν	de·li·ka·te·sen
desserts	επιδόρπια	e·pi·dhor·pi·a
dinner	δείπνο	dhip·no
egg	αβγό	av·gho
fish	ψάρι	psa·ri
food	φαγητό	fa·yi·to
fork	πιρούνι	pi·ru·ni
fruit	φρούτα	fru·ta
glass	ποτήρι	po·ti·ri
grocery store	οπωροπωλείο	o·po·ro·po·li·o
herb	βότανο	vo·ta·no
high chair	καρέκλα για μωρά	ka·re·kla yia mo·ro
hot	ζεστός	ze·stos
knife	μαχαίρι	ma·he·ri
lamb	αρνί	ar·ni
lunch	μεσημεριανό φαγητό	me·si·me·ria·no fa·yi·to
main courses	κύρια φαγητά	ki·ri·a fa·yi·ta
market	αγορά	a·gho·ra
menu	μενού	me·nu
nut	καρύδι	ka·ri·dhi
oil	λάδι	la·dhi

To get by in Greek, mix and match these simple patterns with words of your choice:

When's (the next bus)?
Πότε είναι (το επόμενο λεωφορείο); — *po·*te i·ne (to e·*po·*me·no le·o·fo·ri·o)

Where's (the station)?
Πού είναι (ο σταθμός); — pu i·ne (o stath·mos)

I'm looking for (...).
Ψάχνω για (...). — psakh·no yia (...)

Do you have (a local map)?
Έχετε οδικό (τοπικό χάρτη); — e·he·te o·dhi·ko (to·pi·ko khar·ti)

Is there a (lift)?
Υπάρχει (ασανσέρ); — i·par·hi (a·san·ser)

Can I (try it on)?
Μπορώ να (το προβάρω); — bo·ro na (to pro·va·ro)

I have (a reservation).
Έχω (κλείσει δωμάτιο). — e·kho (kli·si dho·ma·ti·o)

I'd like (to hire a car).
Θα ήθελα (να ενοικιάσω ένα αυτοκίνητο). — tha i·the·la (na e·ni·ki·a·so e·na af·to·ki·ni·to)

pepper	πιπέρι	pi·pe·ri
plate	πιάτο	pia·to
pork	χοιρινό	hi·ri·no
restaurant	εστιατόριο	e·sti·a·to·ri·o
salt	αλάτι	a·la·ti
souvlaki	σουβλάκι	suv·la·ki
spoon	κουτάλι	ku·ta·li
sugar	ζάχαρη	za·kha·ri
vegetable	λαχανικά	la·kha·ni·ka
vegetarian	χορτοφάγος	khor·to·fa·ghos
vinegar	ξύδι	ksi·dhi
with	με	me
without	χωρίς	kho·ris

Drinks

beer	μπύρα	bi·ra
coffee	καφές	ka·fes
juice	χυμός	hi·mos
milk	γάλα	gha·la
soft drink	αναψυκτικό	a·nap·sik·ti·ko
tea	τσάι	tsa·i
water	νερό	ne·ro
(red) wine	(κόκκινο) κρασί	(ko·ki·no) kra·si
(white) wine	(άσπρο) κρασί	(a·spro) kra·si

Emergencies

Help!	Βοήθεια!	vo·*i*·thya
Go away!	Φύγε!	*fi*·ye
I'm lost	Έχω χαθεί.	e·kho kha·*thi*
I'm ill.	Είμαι άρρωστος.	*i*·me a·ro·stos
There's been an accident.	Έγινε ατύχημα.	*ey*·i·ne a·*ti*·hi·ma
Call ...!	Φωνάξτε ...!	fo·*nak*·ste ...
a doctor	ένα γιατρό	e·na yi·a·*tro*
the police	την αστυνομία	tin a·sti·no·*mi*·a

Numbers

1	ένας/μία	e·nas/*mi*·a (m/f)
	ένα	e·na (n)
2	δύο	*dhi*·o
3	τρεις	tris (m&f)
	τρία	*tri*·a (n)
4	τέσσερεις	*te*·se·ris (m&f)
	τέσσερα	*te*·se·ra (n)
5	πέντε	*pen*·de
6	έξη	e·xi
7	επτά	ep·*ta*
8	οχτώ	oh·*to*
9	εννέα	e·*ne*·a
10	δέκα	*dhe*·ka
20	είκοσι	*ik*·o·si
30	τριάντα	tri·*an*·da
40	σαράντα	sa·*ran*·da
50	πενήντα	pe·*nin*·da
60	εξήντα	ek·*sin*·da
70	εβδομήντα	ev·dho·*min*·da
80	ογδόντα	ogh·*dhon*·da
90	ενενήντα	e·ne·*nin*·da
100	εκατό	e·ka·*to*
1000	χίλιοι/χίλιες	*hi*·li·i/*hi*·li·ez (m/f)
	χίλια	*hi*·li·a (n)

Question Words

How?	Πώς;	pos
What?	Τι;	ti
When?	Πότε;	*po*·te
Where?	Πού;	pu
Who?	Ποιος;/Ποια;	pi·os/pi·a (m/f)
	Ποιο;	pi·o (n)
Why?	Γιατί;	yi·a·*ti*

Shopping & Services

I'd like to buy ...	Θέλω ν' αγοράσω ...	the·lo na·gho·ra·so ...
I'm just looking.	Απλώς κοιτάζω.	ap·los ki·ta·zo
I don't like it.	Δεν μου αρέσει.	dhen mu a·re·si
How much is it?	Πόσο κάνει;	po·so ka·ni
It's too expensive.	Είναι πολύ ακριβό.	i·ne po·li a·kri·vo
Can you lower the price?	Μπορείς να κατεβάσεις την τιμή;	bo·ris na ka·te·va·sis tin ti·mi
ATM	αυτόματη μηχανή χρημάτων	af·to·ma·ti mi·kha·ni khri·ma·ton
bank	τράπεζα	tra·pe·za
credit card	πιστωτική κάρτα	pi·sto·ti·ki kar·ta
internet cafe	καφενείο διαδικτύου	ka·fe·ni·o dhi·a·dhik·ti·u
mobile phone	κινητό	ki·ni·to
post office	ταχυδρομείο	ta·hi·dhro·mi·o
toilet	τουαλέτα	tu·a·le·ta
tourist office	τουριστικό γραφείο	tu·ri·sti·ko ghra·fi·o

Time & Dates

What time is it?	Τι ώρα είναι;	ti o·ra i·ne
It's (2 o'clock).	είναι (δύο η ώρα).	i·ne (dhi·o i o·ra)
It's half past (10).	(Δέκα) και μισή.	(dhe·ka) ke mi·si
today	σήμερα	si·me·ra
tomorrow	αύριο	av·ri·o
yesterday	χθες	hthes
morning	πρωί	pro·i
(this) afternoon	(αυτό το) απόγευμα	(af·to to) a·po·yev·ma
evening	βράδυ	vra·dhi
Monday	Δευτέρα	dhef·te·ra
Tuesday	Τρίτη	tri·ti
Wednesday	Τετάρτη	te·tar·ti
Thursday	Πέμπτη	pemp·ti
Friday	Παρασκευή	pa·ras·ke·vi
Saturday	Σάββατο	sa·va·to
Sunday	Κυριακή	ky·ri·a·ki

Signs

ΕΙΣΟΔΟΣ	Entry
ΕΞΟΔΟΣ	Exit
ΠΛΗΡΟΦΟΡΙΕΣ	Information
ΑΝΟΙΧΤΟ	Open
ΚΛΕΙΣΤΟ	Closed
ΑΠΑΓΟΡΕΥΕΤΑΙ	Prohibited
ΑΣΤΥΝΟΜΙΑ	Police
ΑΣΤΥΝΟΜΙΚΟΣ ΣΤΑΘΜΟΣ	Police Station
ΓΥΝΑΙΚΩΝ	Toilets (women)
ΑΝΔΡΩΝ	Toilets (men)

January	Ιανουάριος	ia·nu·*ar*·i·os
February	Φεβρουάριος	fev·ru·*ar*·i·os
March	Μάρτιος	*mar*·ti·os
April	Απρίλιος	a·*pri*·li·os
May	Μάιος	*mai*·os
June	Ιούνιος	i·*u*·ni·os
July	Ιούλιος	i·*u*·li·os
August	Αύγουστος	av·ghus·tos
September	Σεπτέμβριος	sep·*tem*·vri·os
October	Οκτώβριος	ok·*to*·vri·os
November	Νοέμβριος	no·*em*·vri·os
December	Δεκέμβριος	dhe·*kem*·vri·os

Transport
Public Transport

boat	πλοίο	*pli*·o
(city) bus	αστικό	a·sti·*ko*
(intercity) bus	λεωφορείο	le·o·fo·*ri*·o
plane	αεροπλάνο	ae·ro·*pla*·no
train	τραίνο	*tre*·no

Where do I buy a ticket?
Πού αγοράζω εισιτήριο;   pu a·gho·*ra*·zo i·si·*ti*·ri·o

I want to go to ...
Θέλω να πάω στο/στη ...   the·lo na pao sto/sti...

What time does it leave?
Τι ώρα φεύγει;   ti o·ra fev·yi

Do I need to change?
Χρειάζεται να αλλάξω;   khri·a·ze·te na a·*lak*·so

Is it direct/express?
Είναι κατ'ευθείαν/   i·ne ka·tef·*thi*·an/
εξπρές;   eks·*pres*

Does it stop at (...)?
Σταματάει στο (...);   sta·ma·*ta*·i sto (...)

I'd like to get off at (...).
Θα ήθελα να κατεβώ   tha *i*·the·la na ka·te·*vo*
στο (...).   sto (...)

I'd like (a) ...
Θα ήθελα   tha *i*·the·la
(ένα) ...   (*e*·na) ...

one-way ticket	απλό εισιτήριο	a·*plo* i·si·*ti*·ri·o
return ticket	εισιτήριο με	i·si·*ti*·ri·o me
	επιστροφή	e·pi·stro·*fi*
1st class	πρώτη θέση	*pro*·ti *the*·si
2nd class	δεύτερη θέση	*def*·te·ri *the*·si

cancelled	ακυρώθηκε	a·ki·*ro*·thi·ke
delayed	καθυστέρησε	ka·thi·*ste*·ri·se
platform	πλατφόρμα f	plat·*for*·ma
ticket office	εκδοτήριο	ek·dho·*ti*·ri·o
	εισιτηρίων	i·si·ti·*ri*·on
timetable	δρομολόγιο	dhro·mo·*lo*·gio
train station	σταθμός	stath·*mos*
	τρένου	*tre*·nu

Driving & Cycling

I'd like to hire a ...
Θα ήθελα να   tha *i*·the·la na
νοικιάσω ...   ni·ki·a·so ...

car	ένα	*e*·na
	αυτοκίνητο	af·ti·*ki*·ni·to
4WD	ένα τέσσερα	*e*·na tes·se·ra
	επί τέσσερα	e·*pi* tes·se·ra
jeep	ένα τζιπ	*e*·na tzip
motorbike	μια	*mya*
	μοτοσυκλέττα	mo·to·si·*klet*·ta
bicycle	ένα	*e*·na
	ποδήλατο	po·*dhi*·la·to

Do I need a helmet?
Χρειάζομαι κράνος;   khri·a·zo·me *kra*·nos

Do you have a road map?
Έχετε οδικό χάρτη;   e·he·te o·thi·ko *khar*·ti

Is this the road to ...?
Αυτός είναι ο   af·*tos* i·ne o
δρόμος για ...   *dhro*·mos ya ...

Can I park here?
Μπορώ να παρκάρω   bo·*ro* na par·*ka*·ro
εδώ;   e·*dho*

The car/motorbike has broken down (at ...).
Το αυτοκίνητο/   to af·to·*ki*·ni·to/
η μοτοσυκλέττα   i mo·to·si·*klet*·ta
χάλασε στο ...   *kha*·la·se sto ...

I have a flat tyre.
Έπαθα λάστιχο.   e·pa·tha *la*·sti·cho

I've run out of petrol.
Έμεινα από βενζίνη.   e·mi·na a·*po* ven·*zi*·ni

Where's a petrol station?
Πού είναι ένα πρατήριο   pu *i*·ne e·na pra·*ti*·ri·o
βενζίνας;   ven·*zi*·nas

TURKISH

Turkish is the official language of Turkey and co-official language of Cyprus (alongside Greek).

Turkish pronunciation is not difficult as most sounds are also found in English. There are just a few simple things to watch out for.

The Turkish letters ı – undotted in both lower and upper case (eg Isparta uhs·par·ta) – is pronounced as uh (as sound similar to the 'i' in 'habit'), while the i –with dots in both cases (eg İzmir eez·meer) – is pronounced as ee. Similarly, o is pronounced o as in 'go', ö as er in 'her' (without 'r' sound), u as oo in 'moon' and ü as ew in 'few'. Also note that ğ is a silent letter which extends the vowel before it – it acts as the 'gh' combination in 'weigh', and is never pronounced. The letter h is always pronounced h as in 'house'. The letter j is pronounced zh (as the 's' in 'pleasure'), ç as ch in 'church', and ş as in the sh in 'ship'.

Don't worry about these spelling and pro-nuniation idiosyncracies – if you read the blue pronunciation guides given with each phrase in this chapter as if they were English, you'll be understood.

KEY PATTERNS

To get by in Turkish, mix and match these simple patterns with words of your choice:

When's (the next bus)?
(Sonraki otobüs) ne zaman? (son·ra·kee o·to·bews) ne za·man

Where's (the market)?
(Pazar yeri) nerede? (pa·zar ye·ree) ne·re·de

Do you have (a map)?
(Haritanız) var mı? (ha·ree·ta·nuhz) var muh

Is there (a toilet)?
(Tuvalet) var mı? (too·va·let) var muh

I have (a reservation).
(Rezervasyonum) var. (re·zer·vas·yo·noom) var

I'd like (the menu).
(Menüyü) istiyorum. (me·new·yew) ees·tee·yo·room

I need (assistance).
(Yardıma) ihtiyacım var. (yar·duh·ma) eeh·tee·ya·juhm var

Basics

Hello.	Merhaba.	mer·ha·ba
Hi.	Selam.	se·lam
Good morning.	İyi sabahlar.	ee·yee sa·bah·lar
Good evening.	İyi akşamlar.	ee·yee ak·sham·lar
Goodbye. (when leaving)	Hoşçakal. Hoşçakalın.	hosh·cha·kal (inf) hosh·cha·ka·luhn (pol)
Goodbye. (when staying)	Güle güle.	gew·le gew·le
Yes./No.	Evet./Hayır.	e·vet/ha·yuhr
Please.	Lütfen.	lewt·fen
Thank you (very much).	(Çok) Teşekkür ederim.	(chok) te·shek·kewr e·de·reem
Thanks.	Teşekkürler.	te·shek·kewr·ler
You're welcome.	Birşey değil.	beer·shay de·eel
Sorry.	Özür dilerim.	er·zewr dee·le·reem

What's your name?
Adınız ne? a·duh·nuhz ne (inf)
Adınız nedir? a·duh·nuhz ne·deer (pol)

My name is ...
Benim adım ... be·neem a·duhm ...

Do you speak English?
(İngilizce) konuşuyor musunuz? (een·gee·leez·je) ko·noo·shoo·yor moo·soo·nooz

I understand.
Anlıyorum. an·luh·yo·room

I don't understand.
Anlamıyorum. an·la·muh·yo·room

Accommodation

campsite	kamp yeri	kamp ye·ree
hotel	otel	o·tel
youth hostel	gençlik hosteli	gench·leek hos·te·lee

Do you have a ... room?	... odanız var mı?	... o·da·nuhz var muh
single	Tek kişilik	tek kee·shee·leek
double	İki kişilik	ee·kee kee·shee·leek

How much is it per ...?	... ne kadar?	... ne ka·dar
night	Geceliği	ge·je·lee·ee
person	Kişi başına	kee·shee ba·shuh·na

air-con	klima	klee·ma
bathroom	banyo	ban·yo
fan	fan	fan
TV	TV	te·ve
window	pencere	pen·je·re

Directions

Where is ...?	... nerede?	... ne·re·de
Turn left.	Sola dön.	so·la dern
Turn right.	Sağa dön.	sa·a dern

Its ...

behind ...	... arkasında.	... ar·ka·suhn·da
in front of ...	... önünde.	... er·newn·de
near ...	... yakınında.	... ya·kuh·nuhn·da
next to ...	... yanında.	... ya·nuhn·da
opposite ...	... karşısında.	... kar·shuh·suhn·da

Its ...

at the traffic lights	Trafik ışıklarından.	tra·feek uh·shuhk·la·ruhn·dan
close	Yakın.	ya·kuhn
here	Burada.	boo·ra·da
on the corner	Köşede.	ker·she·de
straight ahead	Tam karşıda.	tam kar·shuh·da
there	Şurada.	shoo·ra·da

Eating & Drinking

What would you recommend?
Ne tavsiye edersiniz? — ne tav·see·ye e·der·see·neez

What's in that dish?
Bu yemekte neler var? — boo ye·mek·te ne·ler var

I'm a vegetarian.
Ben vejeteryanım. — ben ve·zhe·ter·ya·nuhm

That was delicious.
Nefisti! — ne·fees·tee

Cheers!
Şerefe! — she·re·fe

Could I have the bill, please?
Lütfen hesabı getirir misiniz? — lewt·fen he·sa·buh ge·tee·reer mee·see·neez

I'd like to reserve a table for ...	... bir masa ayırtmak istiyorum.	... beer ma·sa a·yuhrt·mak ees·tee·yo·room
(two) people	(İki) kişilik	(ee·kee) kee·shee·leek
(eight) o'clock	Saat (sekiz) için	sa·at (se·keez) ee·cheen

I don't eat ...	... yemiyorum.	... ye·mee·yo·room
fish	Balık	ba·luhk
(red) meat	(Kırmızı) Et	kuhr·muh·zuh et
peanuts	Fıstığa	fuhs·tuh·a
poultry	Tavuk eti	ta·vook e·tee

Key Words

appetisers	mezeler	me·ze·ler
bar	bar	bar
beef	sığır eti	suh·uhr e·tee
bottle	şişe	shee·she
bowl	kase	ka·se
bread	ekmek	ek·mek
breakfast	kahvaltı	kah·val·tuh
cafe	kafe	ka·fe
cheese	peynir	pay·neer
chicken	tavuk	ta·vook
cold	soğuk	so·ook
cream	krema	kre·ma
delicatessen	şarküteri	shar·kew·te·ree
desserts	tatlılar	tat·luh·lar
dinner	akşam yemeği	ak·sham ye·me·ee
drinks	İçecekler	ee·che·jek·ler
egg	yumurta	yoo·moor·ta
fish	balık	ba·luhk
food	yiyecek	yee·ye·jek
fork	çatal	cha·tal
fruit	meyve	may·ve
glass	bardak	bar·dak
greengrocer	manav	ma·nav
herb	bitki	beet·kee
high chair	mama sandalyesi	ma·ma san·dal·ye·see
hot	sıcak	suh·jak
ice cream	dondurma	don·door·ma
kebab	kebab	ke·bab
knife	bıçak	buh·chak
lamb	kuzu	koo·zoo
lunch	öğle yemeği	er·le ye·me·ee
main courses	ana yemekler	a·na ye·mek·ler
market	pazar	pa·zar
menu	yemek listesi	ye·mek lees·te·see
nut	çerez	che·rez
oil	yağ	ya
pepper	kara biber	ka·ra bee·ber
plate	tabak	ta·bak
pork	domuz eti	do·mooz e·tee
restaurant	restoran	res·to·ran
salad	salata	sa·la·ta
salt	tuz	tooz
soup	çorba	chor·ba
spoon	kaşık	ka·shuhk
sugar	şeker	she·ker
vegetable	sebze	seb·ze
vegetarian	vejeteryan	ve·zhe·ter·yan
vinegar	sirke	seer·ke
with	ile	ee·le
without	-sız/-siz/ -suz/-süz	·suhz/·seez/ ·sooz/·sewz

Drinks

beer	*bira*	*bee·ra*
coffee	*kahve*	*kah·ve*
juice	*suyu*	*soo·yoo*
milk	*süt*	*sewt*
soft drink	*meşrubat*	*mesh·roo·bat*
tea	*çay*	*chai*
water	*su*	*soo*
wine	*şarap*	*sha·rap*
white	*beyaz*	*be·yaz*
red	*kırmızı*	*kuhr·muh·zuh*

Signs

Giriş	*gee·reesh*	Entrance
Çıkış	*chuh·kuhsh*	Exit
Açık	*a·chuhk*	Open
Kapalı	*ka·pa·luh*	Closed
Danışma	*da·nuhsh·ma*	Information
Yasak	*ya·sak*	Prohibited
Tuvaletler	*too·va·let·ler*	Toilets
Erkek	*er·kek*	Men
Kadın	*ka·duhn*	Women

Emergencies

Help!	*İmdat!*	*eem·dat*
Go away!	*Git burdan!*	*geet boor·dan*
I'm lost	*Kayboldum.*	*kai·bol·doom*
I'm ill.	*Hastayım.*	*has·ta·yuhm*
There's been an accident.	*Bir kaza oldu.*	*beer ka·za ol·doo*
Call ...!	*... çağırın!*	*... cha·uh·ruhn*
a doctor	*Doktor*	*dok·tor*
the police	*Polis*	*po·lees*

Numbers

0	*sıfır*	*suh·fuhr*
1	*bir*	*beer*
2	*iki*	*ee·kee*
3	*üç*	*ewch*
4	*dört*	*dert*
5	*beş*	*besh*
6	*altı*	*al·tuh*
7	*yedi*	*ye·dee*
8	*sekiz*	*se·keez*
9	*dokuz*	*do·kooz*
10	*on*	*on*
20	*yirmi*	*yeer·mee*
30	*otuz*	*o·tooz*
40	*kırk*	*kuhrk*
50	*elli*	*el·lee*
60	*altmış*	*alt·muhsh*
70	*yetmiş*	*yet·meesh*
80	*seksen*	*sek·sen*
90	*doksan*	*dok·san*
100	*yüz*	*yewz*
1000	*bin*	*been*

Shopping & Services

I'd like to buy ...
... almak istiyorum.	*... al·mak ees·tee·yo·room*

How much is it?
Ne kadar?	*ne ka·dar*

It's too expensive.
Bu çok pahalı.	*boo chok pa·ha·luh*

Do you have something cheaper?
Daha ucuz birşey var mı?	*da·ha oo·jooz beer·shay var muh*

ATM	*bankamatik*	*ban·ka·ma·teek*
bank	*banka*	*ban·ka*
credit card	*kredi kartı*	*kre·dee kar·tuh*
internet cafe	*internet kafe*	*een·ter·net ka·fe*
mobile phone	*cep telefonu*	*jep te·le·fo·noo*
post office	*postane*	*pos·ta·ne*
toilet	*tuvalet*	*too·va·let*
tourist office	*turizm bürosu*	*too·reezm bew·ro·soo*

Time & Dates

What time is it?	*Saat kaç?*	*sa·at kach*
It's (ten) o'clock.	*Saat (on).*	*sa·at (on)*
It's half past (ten).	*(On) buçuk.*	*(on) boo·chook*
today	*bugün*	*boo·gewn*
tomorrow	*yarın*	*ya·ruhn*
yesterday	*dün*	*dewn*
morning	*sabah*	*sa·bah*
(this)	*(bu)*	*(boo)*
afternoon	*öğleden sonra*	*er·le·den son·ra*
evening	*akşam*	*ak·sham*

Monday	Pazartesi	pa·zar·te·see
Tuesday	Salı	sa·luh
Wednesday	Çarşamba	char·sham·ba
Thursday	Perşembe	per·shem·be
Friday	Cuma	joo·ma
Saturday	Cumartesi	joo·mar·te·see
Sunday	Pazar	pa·zar

January	Ocak	o·jak
February	Şubat	shoo·bat
March	Mart	mart
April	Nisan	nee·san
May	Mayıs	ma·yuhs
June	Haziran	ha·zee·ran
July	Temmuz	tem·mooz
August	Ağustos	a·oos·tos
September	Eylül	ay·lewl
October	Ekim	e·keem
November	Kasım	ka·suhm
December	Aralık	a·ra·luhk

Transport
Public Transport

boat	vapur	va·poor
(city) bus	şehir otobüsü	she·heer o·to·bew·sew
(intercity) bus	şehirlerarası otobüs	she·heer·ler·a·ra·suh o·to·bews
plane	uçak	oo·chak
train	tren	tren

Where do I buy a ticket?
Nereden bilet
alabilirim?
ne·re·den bee·let
a·la·bee·lee·reem

What time does it leave?
Ne zaman kalkacak? ne za·man kal·ka·jak

Do I need to change?
Aktarma yapmam
gerekli mi?
ak·tar·ma yap·mam
ge·rek·lee mee

Does it stop at ...?
... durur mu? ... doo·roor moo

What's the next stop?
Sonraki durak
hangisi?
son·ra·kee doo·rak
han·gee·see

I'd like to get off at ...
... inmek
istiyorum.
... een·mek
ees·tee·yo·room

A one-way ticket, please.
Gidiş bileti
lütfen.
gee·deesh bee·le·tee
lewt·fen

Question Words

How?	Nasıl?	na·suhl
What?	Ne?	ne
When?	Ne zaman?	ne za·man
Where?	Nerede?	ne·re·de
Who?	Kim?	keem
Why?	Neden?	ne·den

A ... ticket, please.	... bilet lütfen.	... bee·let lewt·fen
1st-class	Birinci mevki	bee·reen·jee mev·kee
2nd-class	Ikinci mevki	ee·keen·jee mev·kee
return	Gidiş-dönüş	gee·deesh·der·newsh

cancel v	iptal etmek	eep·tal et·mek
delay n	gecikme	ge·jeek·me
platform	peron	pe·ron
ticket office	bilet gişesi	bee·let gee·she·see
timetable	tarife	ta·ree·fe
train station	tren istasyonu	tren ees·tas·yo·noo

Driving & Cycling

I'd like to hire a/an ...	Bir ... kiralamak istiyorum.	beer ... kee·ra·la·mak ees·tee·yo·room
4WD	dört çeker	dert che·ker
car	araba	a·ra·ba
motorbike	motosiklet	mo·to·seek·let
bicycle	bisiklet	bee·seek·let

Do I need a helmet?
Kask takmam
gerekli mi?
kask tak·mam
ge·rek·lee mee

Is this the road to ...?
... giden
yol bu mu?
... gee·den
yol boo moo

How long can I park here?
Buraya ne kadar
süre park
edebilirim?
boo·ra·ya ne ka·dar
sew·re park
e·de·bee·lee·reem

The car/motorbike has broken down (at ...).
Arabam/
motosikletim
... bozuldu.
a·ra·bam/
mo·to·seek·le·teem
... bo·zool·doo

I have a flat tyre.
Lastiğim patladı. las·tee·eem pat·la·duh

I've run out of petrol.
Benzinim bitti. ben·zee·neem beet·tee

For words dealing with Cypriot cuisine, see p262. Abbreviations: (Fr) = French; (Gr) = Greek; (Tr) = Turkish; (m) = masculine; (f) = feminine; (n) = neutral

agios (m), **agia** (f; Gr) – saint

bedesten (Tr) – covered market
belediye (Tr) – town hall
bulvarı (Tr) – boulevard, avenue
burnu (Tr) – cape
Byzantine Empire – Hellenistic, Christian empire lasting from AD 395 to 1453, centred on Constantinople (Istanbul)

caddesi (Tr) – road
camii (Tr) – mosque
commandery – a district under the control of a commander of an order of knights
CTO – Cyprus Tourism Organisation, the Republic of Cyprus' official tourism promotion body

dolmuş (Tr) – minibus, shared taxi (literally 'stuffed')

enosis (Gr) – union (with Greece); the frequent demand made by many Greek Cypriots before 1974
entrepôt (Fr) – commercial centre for import and export
EOKA – Ethniki Organosi tou Kypriakou Agona (National Organisation for the Cypriot Struggle); nationalist guerrilla movement that fought for independence from Britain
EOKA-B – post-independence reincarnation of EOKA, which mostly fought Turkish Cypriots

ethnarch (Gr) – leader of a nation

garigue (Fr) – low, open scrubland with evergreen shrubs, low trees, aromatic herbs and grasses, found in poor or dry soil in the Mediterranean region
Green Line – the border that divides Greek Cypriot Lefkosia from Turkish Cypriot North Nicosia (Lefkoşa); also the whole border between North and South

hammam (Tr) – public bathhouse

kafeneio (Gr) – coffee shop
kalesi (Tr) – castle
kato (Gr) – lower, eg Kato Pafos (Lower Pafos)
KKTC (Tr) – Kuzey Kıbrıs Türk Cumhuriyeti (Turkish Republic of Northern Cyprus)
KOT (Gr) – Kypriakos Organismos Tourismou; the official tourist organisation of the Republic of Cyprus; see CTO

leoforos (Gr) – avenue
Lusignan – Cypriot dynasty founded by French nobleman Guy de Lusignan in 1187, which lasted until 1489

maquis (Fr) – thick, scrubby underbrush of Mediterranean shores, particularly of the islands of Corsica and Cyprus
Maronites – ancient Christian sect from the Middle East
Mesaoria (Gr), **Mesarya** (Tr) – the large plain between the Kyrenia (Girne) Range and the Troödos Massif
meydanı (Tr) – square
meze (s), **mezedes** (pl) – literally 'appetiser'; used in Cyprus to mean dining on lots of small plates of appetisers

mouflon (Fr) – endangered indigenous wild sheep of Cyprus

narthex (Gr) – railed-off western porch in early Christian churches used by women and penitents
NCTO – North Cyprus Tourism Organisation; Northern Cyprus' tourism-promotion body
neos (m), **nea** (f), **neo** (n; Gr) – new; common prefix to place names

Ottoman Empire – Turkish empire founded in the 11th century AD, which ruled Cyprus from 1571 to 1878; it was abolished in 1922

panagia (Gr) – church
panigyri (Gr) – feast or festival
Pantokrator (Gr) – the 'Almighty'; traditional fresco of Christ, painted in the dome of Orthodox churches
paşa (Tr) – Ottoman title roughly equivalent to 'lord'
pitta (Gr) – flat, unleavened bread
plateia (Gr) – square
Ptolemies – Graeco-Macedonian rulers of Egypt in the 4th century BC

rembetika (Gr) – Greek equivalent of American blues music, believed to have emerged from 'low-life' cafes in the 1870s

sokak (Tr) – street
Sufi (Tr) – adherent of the Sufi variant of Islam

taksim (Tr) – partition (of Cyprus); demanded by Turkish Cypriots in response to Greek Cypriots' calls for enosis
taverna (Gr) – traditional restaurant that serves food and wine

tekkesi (Tr) – gathering place of the Sufi; mosque

tholos (Gr) – the dome of an Orthodox church

TRNC (Tr) – Turkish Republic of Northern Cyprus; see KKTC

Unesco – United Nations Educational, Scientific and Cultural Organization

behind the scenes

SEND US YOUR FEEDBACK

We love to hear from travellers – your comments keep us on our toes and help make our books better. Our well-travelled team reads every word on what you loved or loathed about this book. Although we cannot reply individually to postal submissions, we always guarantee that your feedback goes straight to the appropriate authors, in time for the next edition. Each person who sends us information is thanked in the next edition – and the most useful submissions are rewarded with a free book.

Visit **lonelyplanet.com/contact** to submit your updates and suggestions or to ask for help. Our award-winning website also features inspirational travel stories, news and discussions.

Note: We may edit, reproduce and incorporate your comments in Lonely Planet products such as guidebooks, websites and digital products, so let us know if you don't want your comments reproduced or your name acknowledged. For a copy of our privacy policy visit lonelyplanet.com/privacy.

OUR READERS

Many thanks to the travellers who used the last edition and wrote to us with helpful hints, useful advice and interesting anecdotes:

A Georgina Arrambide B Luciano Baracco, Noam Bleicher C Paola Cacciari, Venetia Caine, Theodoros Christophides D Richard Demeester, Marina Dodigovic G Karin Genz, Robert Gerald Bailey H Jaclyn Hadjipieris, Sue Heath, Fraser Hocking, Matt Hollingsbee, Mike Hughes J Seonaid Joynson K Angela Kennedy, David Kolecki, Katja Kriehn, Mike Komo L Bertil Linden M Jose Mari Barco, Peter Moselund, Jens Müller R Anna Raiter, Keith Reid, Elaine Robinson S Karien Schilder, Vic Sofras, Robert Soule, Dominik Spoden T Martin Taylor, Andy Thompson W Candace Weddle, Christian Wehrhahn.

AUTHOR THANKS

Josephine Quintero

Josephine would like to thank all the helpful folk in the various CTO tourist offices, in particular Alexis Christodoulides from Larnaka, Selin Feza from Lefkosia and Niki Alitoupoulou from Lemesos. She would also like to thank Athina Papadoupoulou from the Nicosia Master Plan Office for her invaluable contribution. Thanks, too, to fellow author Matt Charles and to all those involved in the title from the Lonely Planet London- and Melbourne-based offices, as well as to Robin Chapman for sharing a bottle of wine after many a long day on the road.

Matthew Charles

Special thanks go to my Stephanie and Jordan (HOF), Andreas for near-perfect advice, Anita and the Christodoulou family, Mr C Smilas and Dino Smilas, Aki and Chris Kyriacou, Parthenoula Michaels, Jason Constantine, the Florent family, Nikos Afxentiou, Viki Kyriakopoulos, Cath Lanigan, Brandon Presser, Josephine Quintero, Mum and James Botterill, Amber, Kyri (on his path), Dad and the rest of my extensive family. I owe all of you much and hope one day to square the ledger entirely.

ACKNOWLEDGMENTS

Climate map data adapted from Peel MC, Finlayson BL & McMahon TA (2007) 'Updated World Map of the Köppen-Geiger Climate Classification', Hydrology and Earth System Sciences, 11, 163344.

Cover photograph: Corinthian columns and basilica remains at Ancient Kourion,

THIS BOOK

This 5th edition of Lonely Planet's Cyprus guidebook was researched and written by Josephine Quintero and Matthew Charles. The 3rd and 4th editions were written by Vesna Marić and the 1st and 2nd editions were written by Paul Hellander. This guidebook was commissioned in Lonely Planet's London office, laid out by Cambridge Publishing Management, UK, and produced by the following:

Commissioning Editors Katie O'Connell, Glenn van der Knijff

Coordinating Editors Sarah Bailey, Kate Taylor

Coordinating Cartographer Marc Milinkovic

Coordinating Layout Designer Paul Queripel

Managing Editors Helen Christinis, Bruce Evans

Senior Editor Angela Tinson

Managing Cartographers Shahara Ahmed, Anita Banh

Managing Layout Designer Jane Hart

Assisting Editors Elisa Arduca, Kathryn Glendenning, Michala Green, Ceinwen Sinclair, Simon Williamson

Assisting Layout Designer Julie Crane

Cover Research Naomi Parker

Internal Image Research Aude Vauconsant

Colour Designer Tim Newton

Indexer Amanda Jones

Language Content Annelies Mertens

Thanks to Ryan Evans, Chris Girdler, Gerard Walker, Catherine Craddock-Carrillo, Imogen Hall, Sally Schafer, Trent Paton, Lucas Arlidge, Rebecca Skinner

NOTES

index

A

accommodation 198-212, *see also individual locations*
  agrotourism 199, 234
  apartment hotels 199-200
  camping 199
  costs 198
  hotels 199
  internet resources 199, 201
  language 261-2, 266
  private rooms (*domatia*) 199
  seasons 200
  villas 200
activities 25-32, *see also individual activities, individual locations*
Afendrika 196
Agia Marina 147
Agia Mavri Winery 76
Agia Napa 117-22, **118**
  accommodation 207-8
  activities 119-20
  beaches 119
  children 124
  climate 117
  drinking 120-1
  entertainment 121
  food 120
  sights 117-19
  tourist information 121
  travel to/from 121-2
  travel within 122
Agia Napa Cultural Winter 23
Agia Napa Monastery 117
Agia Paraskevi 87
Agia Solomoni & the Christian Catacomb 86
Agia Triada Beach 124
Agios Andronikos 97
Agios Filon Beach 194
Agios Filon Church 196
Agios Georgios Beach 93
Agios Georgios Church 196

000 Map pages
000 Photo pages

Agios Georgios Museum 88
Agios Ioannis Church 185
Agios Ioannis Lambadistis Monastery 72
Agios Lambrianos Rock-Cut Tomb 87
Agios Lazaros 105
Agios Mamas Church at Agios Sozomenos 146
Agios Mamas Orthodox Church 176
Agios Nikolaos tis Stegis 77
Agros 80, 204
agrotourism 199, 234
air travel 254-7
  airports 19, 20, 254-5
Akamas Heights 10, 93-5, 205-6
Akamas Peninsula 95-100, 206, **30**
Akritas, Loukis 244
Akrotiri Peninsula 63
Alagadı (Turtle) Beach 168-9
Alevkaya Herbarium 172, 174
Alykes Beach 90
Amathous 61
Ancient Amathous 61
Ancient Enkomi 191
Ancient Kition 107
Ancient Kourion 17, 61-2, **17**
Ancient Salamis 16, 188-91, **189**, **16**, **219**, **239**
Ancient Soloi 177-8
Ancient Tamassos 144-5
Ancient Vouni 178
animals 234-5, *see also* birds, birdwatching
  donkeys 16, 60, 68, 168, 193, 234-5, **17**
  insects 70
  monk seals 93, 235
  mouflon 97, 102, 233, 234, 235
  octopuses 27
  snakes 190, 235
  turtles 10, 93, 168-9, 193-4, 235
Annan Plan 177, 226-7
Anthias, Tefkros 244
apartment hotels 199-200
Aphrodite 60, 61, 65, 99, 100
Aphrodite Classic Car Rally 23
Aphrodite Waterpark 91
Aphrodite's Rock & Beach 13, 60-1, **2**, **13**
Apostolos Varnavas church 191
Archaeological and Natural History Museum (Morfou) 176
Archaeological Museum (Lemesos) 51
Archaeological Museum (Pafos) 87
Archaeological Museum (Polis) 97
archaeological sites 21
  Agia Solomoni & the Christian Catacomb 86

Agios Lambrianos Rock-Cut Tomb 87
Ancient Amathous 61
Ancient Enkomi 191
Ancient Kition 107
Ancient Kourion 17, 61-2, **17**
Ancient Salamis 16, 188-91, **189**, **16**, **219**, **239**
Ancient Soloi 177-8
Ancient Tamassos 144-5
Ancient Vouni 178
Choirokoitia 13, 116, **13**
Hrysopolitissa Basilica 86
Makronissos Tombs 118-19
Necropolis of Salamis 190
Pafos Archaeological Site 6, 83, 85, **7**, **22**
Sanctuary of Apollon Ylatis 62
St Paul's Pillar 86
Tombs of the Kings 85-6
Archangelos Icon 163
Archangelos Michail 71
Archbishop's Palace **227**
area codes 19, 250
art galleries, *see* museums & galleries
arts 21, 24, 240-1, *see also individual arts*
Asmalı Beach 174
ATMs 248
Avdimou Beach 58
Avgas Gorge 94-5
Avgorou 123
Ayios Elias 123-4

B

Bafra Beach 188
basket making 238
bathrooms 251
Baths of Aphrodite 99-100
Bayraktar Mosque 135
beaches 21, 231, *see also individual locations*
  Agia Triada Beach 124
  Agios Filon Beach 194
  Agios Georgios Beach 93
  Alagadı (Turtle) Beach 168-9
  Alykes Beach 90
  Aphrodite's Rock & Beach 13, 60-1, **2**, **13**
  Asmalı Beach 174
  Avdimou Beach 58
  Bafra Beach 188
  Bediz Beach 188
  Cape Kiti 113
  Çatalköy Beach 168
  Faros Beach 90
  Fig Tree Bay 124
  Finikoudes Beach 113

beaches *continued*
Glapsides Beach 186
Golden Beach (Nangomi Bay) 193-4
Governor's Beach 58
Kermia Beach 119
Kissonerga Bay 90
Konnos Beach 119
Kourion Beach 17, 58
Kumyali (Koma Tou Gialou) Beach 193
Lady's Mile Beach 58
Lara Beach 10, 93, **10**
Lara (Vakıflar) Beach 168
Louma Beach 124
Makenzy Beach 113
Melanda Beach 58, 60
Nissi Beach 119
Palm Beach 186
Perivolia 113
Pernera Beach 124
Petra tou Romiou 13, 60-1, **2**, **13**
Polis 98
Protaras 124
Silver Beach 188
Skoutari Beach 124
Vrysi (Acapulco) Beach 168
Vrysoudia Beach 90
Yavuz Çıkarma (Five Mile) Beach 168
Yedidalga Belediyesi Plaji 174
Bedesten 20, 151, 153
Bediz Beach 188
Belediye Pazarı 155
Bellapais 170-2
Bellapais Abbey 170-2
Bellapais Music Festival 23, 171, 243
bicycle travel, *see* cycling
birds 68, 72, 114, 234
birdwatching 68, 165, 186, 234
boat travel 257, 260
boat trips 22, 88, 98, 120, 164
Boğaz 193
books 214, **244**, *see also* literature
history 214, 226
plants 233
travel 223
wildlife 232
border crossings 137, 229-30, 246, 252, 254
Agios Dometios 127, 158, 257
Agios Nikolaos 257
car insurance 260
customs regulations 157, 246, 252, 257

000 Map pages
000 Photo pages

Ledra Palace Hotel 127, 131, 149, 257
Ledra St 127, 130-1, 149, 257
Limnitis-Yeşilirmak 149, 177, 257
Pergamos 257
Zodhia 174, 177, 257
bouzouki 242, **242**
budget 18
Buffavento Castle 172
bungee jumping 120
bus travel 20, 258, 259
business hours 246
Büyük Hammam 153, 155
Büyük Han 149
Byzantine Art Museum 134
Byzantine churches 14, 71, **14**, *see also* frescos
Byzantine Museum (Kalopanayiotis) 72-3
Byzantine Museum (Kykkos Monastery) 73
Byzantine Museum (Larnaka) 107
Byzantine Museum (Pafos) 88
Byzantine Museum (Pedoulas) 71

C
cabarets 57
camel rides 107
camping 199, *see also* individual locations
Canbulat Museum 186
Cape Greco 122, 234
Cape Kiti 113, 114
car travel 19, 163, 258-9, *see also* driving tours
driving licences 258
hire 259-60
insurance 259, 260
road rules 248, 259
Casey's larkspur 233
castles
Buffavento Castle 172
Kantara Castle 194-5
Kolossi Castle 62-3
Kyrenia Castle 161, 163
Lemesos Medieval Castle 49, 51
Pafos Castle 87
St Hilarion Castle 14, 169-70, **14**
Çatalköy Beach 168
caves 122, 195
Cedar Valley 103
cell phones 19, 250-1
Cellarka tombs 190
chemists 248
children, travel with 41-2
Agia Napa 124

internet resources 41
Kyrenia 172
Larnaka 107
Lefkosia 140
Lemesos 55
North Nicosia 156
Pafos 91, 92
Troödos Massif 68
Chizenel, Emin 241
Choirokoitia 13, 116, **13**
churches
Agia Paraskevi 87
Agios Andronikos 97
Agios Filon Church 196
Agios Georgios Church 196
Agios Ioannis Church 185
Agios Ioannis Lambadistis Monastery 72
Agios Lazaros 105
Agios Mamas Church at Agios Sozomenos 146
Agios Mamas Orthodox Church 176
Agios Nikolaos tis Stegis 77
Apostolos Varnavas 191
Archangelos Michail 71
Ayios Elias 123-4
Bedesten 20, 151, 153
Byzantine churches 14, 71, **14**
Church of the Transfiguration of the Saviour 81
Church of Timios Stavros 81
Faneromeni Church 133
Holy Cross Catholic Church 133
Hrysopolitissa Basilica 86
Panagia Asomatos 196
Panagia Chrysaliniotissa 134
Panagia Forviotissa 78
Panagia Khrysiotissa 196
Panagia Theotokou 78
Panagia tis Podythou 77-8
Panagia tou Araka 80-1
Panagia tou Moutoulla 73
Stavros tou Agiasmati 80
cinemas 57, 112, 141
climate 18, 23-4, 246, *see also* individual locations
climate change 254
coffee 15, 39, 40, 230, **15**
coffee shops 39, 230
Constantinou, Demetris 241
consulates 247
copper 144, 217, 218
Coral Bay 92-3
costs 18, *see also* money
accommodation 198
food 247
Countryside Documentary & Animated Film Festival 24
crafts, *see* handicrafts

credit cards 249
Cultural Centre of Occupied Ammochostos 123
culture 229-31
Curium Beach Equestrian Centre 58
currency 18, 215, 248
customs regulations 157, 246, 252, 257
cycling 29, 68, 257-8, **30**, **31**
  tours 20, 98, 110
Cyprus Classic Motorcycle Museum 140
Cyprus crocus 233
Cyprus Handicrafts Centres 12-13, 57, 238
Cyprus International 4-Day Challenge 24
Cyprus Museum 127, 129
Cyprus tulip 233
Cyprus Turkish Shadow Theatre 156
Cyprus Wine Museum 12, 51, **12**

D
dance 13, 242-3, **13**, **237**, **242**
dangers, see also emergencies, safety
  hitching 259
Dekelia Sovereign Base Area 123
Denktaŏ, Rauf 225, 226
Dervish Pasha Museum 153
Deryneia 122-3, 227
Dhrousia 94
Dipkarpaz 196
disabilities, travellers with 252
diving 11, 25-7, 60, 88, 120, 164, **11**, **26**
Domane Valassides 76
domatia, see private rooms
donkeys 16, 60, 68, 168, 193, 234-5, **17**
drinking, see individual locations
  drink driving 248
drinks 37-40, see also wine
  coffee 15, 39, 40, 230, **15**
  language 263, 268
  water 248
driving, see car travel
driving licences 258
driving tours
  Famagusta (Maǧusa) & the Karpas (Kırpaşa) Peninsula 192, **192**
  Kyrenia (Girne) & the Northern Coast 173, **173**
  Larnaka & the East 115, **115**
  Lemesos & the South Coast 59, **59**
  Pafos & the West 96, **96**
  Troödos Massif 75, 79, **75**, **79**
droughts 234
drugs 248
drugstores 248

Durrell, Lawrence 49, 131, 171
Dymiotis, Nicos 241

E
Easter 23
economy 214-15, 227-8
ecotourism, see agrotourism
electricity 247
Elies Bridge 74
embassies 247
emergencies 19
  language 264, 268
endangered species 235
Enkomi 191
enosis 74, 223
environmental issues 177, 196, 232, 233-4, 235
EOKA 74, 76, 127, 146, 149, 191, 223
Epaminonda, Haris 241
Episkopi 61
Ethnographic Museum (Lefkosia) 134
Ethnographical Museum (Pafos) 88
etiquette 132, 214, 230, 231
European Long Distance Path E4 74, 76
events, see festivals & events
exchange rates 19

F
Famagusta 45, 179-88, **180-1**, **182**, **188**
  accommodation 179, 211-12
  activities 186
  beaches 186
  climate 179
  drinking 187
  festivals & events 186
  food 179, 186-7
  highlights 180-1
  history 181-2
  shopping 187
  sights 184-6
  tourist information 184, 187
  travel to/from 187, 188
  travel within 183, 187
Fanemoreni Church 133
Faros Beach 90
Fasouri Watermania 55
Fatsa Wax Museum 117
ferry services 257
festivals & events 23-4, see also individual locations
  Bellapais Music Festival 23, 171, 243
  Green Monday 110
  International Cyprus Theatre Festival 148
  International Famagusta Art & Culture Festival 23, 24, 186, 243

Kataklysmos Festival 110
  Kypria Festival 239
  Lemesos Carnival 23, 53
  Lemesos Wine Festival 24, 53
  Pafos Aphrodite Festival 24, 88, 243
  Paradise Jazz Festival 24, 101, 243
  Solar Car Challenge 20, 88
Fig Tree Bay 124
Fikardou 147
film
  cinemas 57, 112, 141
  Countryside Documentary & Animated Film Festival 24
  Lefkosia Film Festival 24
  Nicosia International Documentary Film Festival 23
Finikoudes Beach 113
fishing 29, 164
flowers 165, 233
Foini 75
folk art, see handicrafts
Folk Art Museum (Deryneia) 123
Folk Art Museum (Fyti) 102
Folk Art Museum (Kyrenia) 163
Folk Art Museum (Pedoulas) 72
food 22, 37-40, see also individual locations
  authentic cypriot cuisine 146
  costs 247
  desserts 38
  glossary 37-8, 40
  holiday food 40
  internet resources 39, 215
  lahmacun 14, 38, 150, **15**
  language 262-3, 267
  markets 155
  meze 8, 39-40, 94, **3**, **8**
  oranges 176
  pide 14, 22, 38, 150, **15**
  restaurants 39, 40, 94, 95, 246
  seasons 37
  souvla 231
  vegetarians 37, 38
football 142
Frenaros 123
frescos 14, 71, 72, 73, 77, 78, 80-1, **14**, **223**
Fyti 102

G
Gaia Oinotechniki 76
galleries, see museums & galleries
gay travellers 231, 248
Gemikonaǧi 176
geography 232
geology 232
Geroskipou 94
Glapsides Beach 186

Golden Beach (Nangomi Bay) 193-4
golf 169
Goudi 94
Governor's Beach 58
Grand Mosque (Larnaka) 109
Grand Mosque (Lemesos) 51
Green Line 101, 137, 149, 158, 224, 225, 228, 229-30
  crossing 9, 127, 137, 149, 257
Green Monday 110
Grivas, Georgios 74, 88, 191, 223

H
Hadid, Zaha 132
Hala Sultan Tekke 114
hammams 22
  Büyük Hammam 153, 155
  Lemesos Hammam 51
  Omeriye Hammam 10, 134, **11**
handicrafts 21, 115, 135
  basket making 238
  Cyprus Handicrafts Centres 12-13, 57, 238
  lace 116-17, 238
  pottery 112, 238, **238**
  weaving 102
Haydarpasha Mosque 155
health 248
hiking 25, 29, **31**
  Akamas Peninsula 95, 97
  Aphrodite Trail 95, **30**
  Artemis Trail 65, 68
  Atalante Trail 68
  Cape Greco 122
  European Long Distance Path E4 74, 76
  Kyrenia Range 168
  Persephone Trail 68
  Pitsylia 78
  Troödos Massif 8, 65-8, **8**
  Tylliria 102
historical sites, see archaeological sites
history 216-28, see also individual locations
  ancient 216-19
  books 214, 226
  Byzantine 219-21
  Christianity 219
  city kingdoms 216-17
  enosis 74, 223
  Lusignan Dynasties 221
  Ottoman rule 221-2
  partition 127, 223-5, 229

Republic of Cyprus 224, 227
  reunification attempts 225-7
  Roman Empire 218
  Venetian rule 221-2
hitching 259
holidays 250, see also festivals & events
Holy Cross Catholic Church 133
Holy Monastery of St Nicholas of the Cats 63
horse riding 25, 32, 58, 68, 97, 124
hotels 199
House of Hatzigeorgakis Kornesios 130
Hrysopolitissa Basilica 86

I
icons 71, 73, 88, 134, 163, 191, 193, 241
immigration 254
Ineia 93
Inia 94
insects 70
insurance
  car 259, 260
  health 248
  travel 248
International Cyprus Theatre Festival 148
International Famagusta Art & Culture Festival 23, 24, 186, 243
international money transfers 249
International Music Festival, Lemesos 24, 243
internet access 248, see also individual locations
internet resources 19, 215
  accommodation 199, 201
  children 41
  food 39, 215
  government travel advice 250
  music 215
  politics 215
itineraries 33-6, **33**, **34**, **35**, **36**

J
Joachim, Costas 240

K
kafeneia (coffee shops) 39, 230
Kakopetria 76-7
Kalopanayiotis 72-3
Kamares Aqueduct 113-14
Kampos 102-3
Kantara Castle 194-5
Kapoura 147
Karageorgis, Evagoras 242
Karpas Peninsula 179, 192, 193-7, 212, **192**, **194**

Kataklysmos Festival 110
Kathikas 94
Kato Akourdalia 94
Kato Pafos, see Pafos
Kato Pyrgos 101
Kelefos Bridge 74
Kermia Beach 119
Kissonerga Bay 90
kitesurfing 11, 25, 27, 58, 113, 168
Kiti 114
Kition 107
Kleides, the 197
Kokkina 101
Kokkinohoria 123
Kolossi Castle 62-3
Kommandaria 76, 77
Konnos Beach 119
Koruçam Peninsula 175
Kourdali 81
Kourion 17, 61-2, **17**
Kourion Beach 17, 58
Kourion Museum 61
Kouroussis, Nicos 240
krasohoria 9, 65, 76, **9**
Kritou Terra 94
Ktima, see Pafos
Küçük, Faisal 223
Kumarcılar Han 149
Kumyali (Koma Tou Gialou) Beach 193
Kykkos Monastery 73
Kypria Festival 239
kypriaka 215
Kyrenia 45, 160-7, **162**, **164**
  accommodation 160, 210-11
  activities 164-5
  beaches 168-9
  children 172
  climate 160
  drinking 166
  driving tours 173, **173**
  entertainment 166
  food 160, 165-6
  highlights 162
  shopping 167
  sights 161, 163-4
  tourist information 167
  travel to/from 167
  travel within 161, 163, 167
  walking tours 164-5
Kyrenia Castle 161, 163
Kyrenia Old Harbour 6, 161, **6**
Kyrenia Olive Festival 24
Kyrenia Range 168

L
lace 116-17, 238
Ladommatos, Andreas 240

Lady's Mile Beach 58
lahmacun 14, 38, 150, **15**
Lala Mustafa Paşa 185
Laneia 61
language 18, 215, 261-70
  drinks 263
  food 262-3, 267
  Greek 261-5
  names 163, 230
  Turkish 266-9
Lanitis Art Foundation 51
Lapidary Museum 155
Lapta 174
Lara Beach 10, 93, **10**
Lara (Vakıflar) Beach 168
Larnaka 44, 104-13, **106**, **108**
  accommodation 104, 206-7
  activities 110
  beaches 113
  children 107
  climate 104
  cycling tours 20, 110
  drinking 111
  driving tours 115, **115**
  entertainment 111-12
  festivals & events 110
  food 104, 110-11
  highlights 106
  history 105
  shopping 112
  sights 105, 107-9
  tourist information 112
  travel to/from 112-13
  travel within 105, 113
  walking tours 110
Larnaka Archaeological Museum 107
Larnaka Fort & Museum 107
Larnaka Salt Lake 114, 234
Latsi 97
Lazanias 147
Ledra Palace Hotel border crossing 127, 131, 149, 257
Ledra St border crossing 127, 130-1, 149, 257
Lefkara 116
Lefke 176-7
Lefkoşa, *see* North Nicosia
Lefkosia 44, 125-44, **126**, **128**, **138**, **145**
  accommodation 125, 208-9
  children 140
  climate 125
  drinking 140-1
  entertainment 141-2
  food 125, 135-40
  highlights 126
  history 126-7
  shopping 142

  sights 127, 129-35
  tourist information 127, 134, 142-3
  travel to/from 143-4
  travel within 127, 143, 144
  walking tours 135, 136, **136**
Lefkosia Film Festival 24
legal matters 248
Lemesos 20, 43, 48-57, **50**, **52**, **240**
  accommodation 48, 200-2
  activities 51
  beaches 58, 60
  children 55
  climate 48
  drinking 55-6
  driving tours 59, **59**
  entertainment 56-7
  festivals & events 53
  food 48, 53-4
  highlights 50
  history 49
  shopping 57
  sights 49, 51
  tourist information 57
  travel to/from 57, 58
  travel within 49, 57, 58
  walking tours 51-3
Lemesos Carnival 23, 53
Lemesos Medieval Castle 49, 51
Lemesos Mini Zoo 55
Lemesos Wine Festival 24, 53
lesbian travellers 231, 248
Leventis City Museum 130
libraries 135
Limassol (Limasol), *see* Lemesos
Limassol Marina 56
Limnitis-Yeşilırmak border crossing 149, 177, 257
Liopetri 123
literature 244, *see also* books
Louma Beach 124
Lythrodontas 147

M

Magic Dancing Water 123
Maheras Monastery 146-7
Makarios III, Archbishop 73-4, 103, 223, 224, 225
Makarios Cultural Centre 103
Makarios Cultural Foundation 134
Makenzy Beach 113
Makrides, Angelos 240-1
Makronissos Tombs 118-19
Marathasa Valley 71-6, 203
marinas 20, 56
markets 155
Maronites 175
Mazotos Camel Park 107
measures 247

medical services 248, *see also individual locations*
Medieval Museum (Lemesos) 49
Mehmetcik Grape Festival 24
Melanda Beach 58, 60
Mesaoria villages 147
metric system 247
Mevlevi Order 151, 153
Mevlevi Shrine Museum 153
meze 8, 39-40, 94, **3**, **8**
mobile phones 19, 250-1
monasteries
  Agia Napa Monastery 117
  Agios Ioannis Lambadistis Monastery 72
  Bellapais Abbey 170-2
  Holy Monastery of St Nicholas of the Cats 63
  Kykkos Monastery 73
  Maheras Monastery 146-7
  Monastery of Agios Irakleidios 145-6
  Monastery of Apostolos Andreas 196-7
  Moni Timiou Stavrou 76
  Panagia Absinthiotissa Monastery 172
  Stavrovouni Monastery 114, 116
  Troöditissa Monastery 75
money 19, 215, 246, 248-9, *see also* costs
Moni Timiou Stavrou 76
monk seals 93, 235
Morfou 176
mosaics 6, 83, 85, 86, 114, 134, 196, **7**, **240**, **241**
mosques 132
  Bayraktar Mosque 135
  Grand Mosque (Larnaka) 109
  Grand Mosque (Lemesos) 51
  Hala Sultan Tekke 114
  Haydarpasha Mosque 155
  Lala Mustafa Paşa 185
  Omeriye Mosque 133-4
  Piri Osman Pasha Mosque 177
  Selimiye Mosque 149, 151
motorcycle travel 258-9
mouflon 97, 102, 233, 234, 235
mountain biking, *see* cycling
Mousio Theasis 20, 109
Moutoullas 73
Mt Olympus 8, 64, 65, 68
multiculturalism 230
Municipal Cultural Centre, Larnaka 107-9
murals 80
Museum of Barbarism 155
museums & galleries
  Agios Georgios Museum 88

museums & galleries *continued*
Archaeological and Natural History Museum (Morfou) 176
Archaeological Museum (Lemesos) 51
Archaeological Museum (Pafos) 87
Archaeological Museum (Polis) 97
Archangelos Icon 163
Byzantine Art Museum 134
Byzantine Museum (Kalopanayiotis) 72-3
Byzantine Museum (Kykkos Monastery) 73
Byzantine Museum (Larnaka) 107
Byzantine Museum (Pafos) 88
Byzantine Museum (Pedoulas) 71
Canbulat Museum 186
Cyprus Classic Motorcycle Museum 140
Cyprus Museum 127, 129
Cyprus Wine Museum 12, 51, **12**
Dervish Pasha Museum 153
Ethnographic Museum (Lefkosia) 134
Ethnographical Museum (Pafos) 88
Fatsa Wax Museum 117
Folk Art Museum (Deryneia) 123
Folk Art Museum (Fyti) 102
Folk Art Museum (Kyrenia) 163
Folk Art Museum (Pedoulas) 72
House of Hatzigeorgakis Kornesios 130
Kourion Museum 61
Lanitis Art Foundation 51
Lapidary Museum 155
Larnaka Archaeological Museum 107
Larnaka Fort & Museum 107
Leventis City Museum 130
Makarios Cultural Centre 103
Makarios Cultural Foundation 134
Medieval Museum 49
Mevlevi Shrine Museum 153
Mousio Theasis 20, 109
Municipal Cultural Centre, Larnaka 107-9
Museum of Barbarism 155
Museum of Natural History, Pomos 20, 100
Museum of Traditional Embroidery & Silver-Smithing 117
Namık Kemal Prison 185-6
National Struggle Museum 134
Natural History Museum 109
Natural Sea Sponge Exhibition Centre 55
Nicosia Municipal Arts Centre 129-30, 131
Pancyprian Gymnasium Museums 131
Pierides Archaeological Foundation 107
Shipwreck Museum 163
State Gallery of Cypriot Contemporary Art 132
Thalassa Municipal Museum of the Sea 117-18
music 242, 243, **242**, **243**
Bellapais Music Festival 23, 171, 243
International Music Festival, Lemesos 24
internet resources 215
Musical Sundays, Larnaka 110
Pafos Aphrodite Festival 24, 88, 243
Paradise Jazz Festival 24, 101, 243
Summer Nights in Polis 98

N
Namık Kemal Prison 185-6
national parks & reserves 196, 232
National Struggle Museum 134
Natural History Museum 109
Natural Sea Sponge Exhibition Centre 55
Necropolis of Salamis 190
New Year's Eve 24
newspapers 247
Nicosia, *see* Lefkosia
Nicosia International Documentary Film Festival 23
Nicosia Master Plan project 10, 131, 133
Nicosia Municipal Arts Centre 129-30, 131
Nissi Beach 119
North Nicosia 9, 44, 148-59, **150**, **152**, **9**
accommodation 148, 209-10
children 156
climate 148
drinking 156-7
entertainment 156-7
festivals & events 148
food 148, 155-6
highlights 150
history 149
shopping 155, 157
sights 149, 151, 153-5
tourist information 157-8
travel to/from 158
travel within 158-9
walking tours 154, **154**

O
Octopus Aqua Park 172
octopuses 27
Olive Mill of 'Paphitaina' 81
Omeriye Hammam 10, 134, **11**
Omeriye Mosque 133-4
Omodos 9, 76, **9**
opening hours 246
oranges 176
orchids 165, 233
Orounda 147
Ostrich Wonderland Theme Park 140
Othello's Tower (The Citadel) 184-5

P
Pafos 44, 82-103, **84**, **86**, **89**
accommodation 82, 204-5
activities 88, 92
beaches 90
children 91, 92
climate 82
drinking 90-1
driving tours 96, **96**
entertainment 91
festivals & events 88
food 82, 88-90
highlights 84
sights 83, 85-8
tourist information 91-2
travel to/from 92
travel within 83, 92
Pafos Aphrodite Festival 24, 88, 243
Pafos Archaeological Site 6, 83, 85, **7**, **22**
Pafos Bird Park 91
Pafos Castle 87
Pafos Marina 20, 88, 93
Pafos Mosaics 83, 85
Pahyammos 101
paintball 25, 32
painting 240-1, *see also* arts, frescos, icons
palaces (rock formations) 122
Palm Beach 186
Panagia Absinthiotissa Monastery 172
Panagia Asomatos 196
Panagia Chrysaliniotissa 134
Panagia Forviotissa 78
Panagia Khrysiotissa 196
Panagia Theotokou 78
Panagia tis Podythou 77-8
Panagia tou Araka 80-1
Panagia tou Moutoulla 73
Panayioto, Christodoulous 241
Pancyprian Gymnasium Museums 131
Pano Akourdalia 94

Pano Panagia 103
Paradise Jazz Festival 24, 101, 243
paragliding 164
Paralimni 122
Parko Paliasto 119-20
partition 127, 223-5, 229
passports 254, *see also* visas
Pedoulas 71-2
Pera 147
Perdios, Kypros 241
Peristerona 147
Perivolia 113, 114
Pernera 124
Petra tou Romiou 13, 60-1, **2**, **13**
pharmacies 248
phonecards 251
photography 101, 137, 158, 185, 249-50
picnicking 68, 76, 95, 102, 103, 147
pide 14, 22, 38, 150, **15**
Pierides Archaeological Foundation 107
Pierides, Theodosis 244
Pissouri Bay & Village 60
Pitsylia 78, 80
planning
  budgeting 18
  calendar of events 23-4
  children 41-2
  internet resources 19
  itineraries 33-6, **33**, **34**, **35**, **36**
  regions 43-5
  repeat visitors 20
  travel seasons 18, 23-4, 200
plants 103, 233, *see also* flowers
Plateia Eleftherias, Lefkosia 20, 132
Platres 69-70, 202-3
police 19
Polis 97-9, **98**
politics 214, 215
Pomos 100-1
population 214, 215
postal services 250
Potima 20, 88, 93
pottery 112, 238, **238**
private rooms (*domatia*) 199, *see also individual locations*
Prodromos 75
property, buying 174
Protaras 123-4
Psokas 102
public holidays 250
puppet shadow theatre 156, 239
Pyla 123

R
radio 247
religion 175, 215, 230-1

responsible travel 254
restaurants 39, 40, 94, 95, 246, *see also* food
reunification 225-7
Richard the Lionheart 49, 77, 161, 172, 194, 220-1
road rules 248, 259
Roccas Bastion 133
Roudhias Bridge 76

S
safety 215, 250, *see also* emergencies
  road 248, 260
  scams 250
Salamis 16, 188-91, **189**, **16**, **219**, **239**
Sanctuary of Apollon Ylatis 62
Santa Marina Retreat 55
Savva, Christofors 240
Savvides, Andreas 241
scams 250
scuba diving, *see* diving
sculpture 240-1
sea caves 93, 122
Selimiye Mosque 149, 151
senior travellers 246
Sfikas, George 241
Shacolas Tower Observatory 131
Shipwreck Museum 163
shipwrecks 11, 25, 27
shopping 12, *see also individual locations*
  language 264, 268
  opening hours 246
Silver Beach 188
Sipahi 195
skiing 29, 32, 68-9
Skordokefalos 147
Skoutari Beach 124
smoking 247
snakes 190, 235
snorkelling 27, *see also* diving
soccer 142
Solar Car Challenge 20, 88
Solea Valley 76-8, 203
Soloi 177-8
Sotira 123
souvla 231
Spanos, Leonidas 241
spas 22
Spilia 81
sports 142
St Hilarion cabbage 233
St Hilarion Castle 14, 169-70, **14**
St Hilarion winery 22
St Paul's Pillar 86
stand-up paddle surfing 27, 29
State Gallery of Cypriot Contemporary Art 132

Stavros tis Psokas 102
Stavros tou Agiasmati 80
Stavrovouni Monastery 114, 116
Stavrovounis, Father Kallinikos 241
sulphur springs 72, 74
sustainable travel 254

T
taksim 74, 223
Tamassos 144-5
taxis 259-60
telephone services 250-1
Tenta (Kalavasos) 116
Thalassa Municipal Museum of the Sea 117-18
theatre 57, 141-2, 239
theme parks
  Aphrodite Waterpark 91
  Fasouri Watermania 55
  Octopus Aqua Park 172
  Ostrich Wonderland Theme Park 140
  Pafos Bird Park 91
  Water World 119
Throni Shrine 73
time 251
tipping 249
toilets 251
tombs 85, 195
  Agios Lambrianos Rock-Cut Tomb 87
  cave tombs 195
  Cellarka tombs 190
  Makronissos Tombs 118-19
  Necropolis of Salamis 190
  Tomb of Archbishop Makarios III 73-4
  Tomb of Lazarus 105
  Tombs of the Kings 85-6
Toumazis, Yiannis 131
tourist information 251-2, *see also individual locations*
tours 260, *see also* driving tours, walking tours, *individual locations*
  cycling 20, 98, 110
  wine 79, 96, **79**, **96**
travel seasons 18, 23-4, 200
travel to/from Cyprus 254-7
travel within Cyprus 257-60
travellers cheques 249
Tree of Idleness 171
Treis Elies 74, 76
trekking, *see* hiking
TRNC 225, 226
Troöditissa Monastery 75
Troödos 65-9, 202
Troödos Byzantine churches 14, 71, **14**

Troödos golden drop 233
Troödos Massif 8, 43, 64-81, **66-7**, **8**, **28**
  accommodation 64, 202-4
  activities 65-9, 70, 76, 78, 234
  children 68
  climate 64
  driving tours 75, 79, **75**, **79**
  food 64, 69, 70, 72, 77, 80
  highlights 66
  hiking 8, 65-8
  history 65
  shopping 80, 81
  sights 69-70, 71-3, 80
  tourist information 70
  travel to/from 69, 70, 72, 77, 80
  travel within 65, 69
turtles 10, 93, 168-9, 193-4, 235
TV 247
Tylliria 100-3, 206

U

Unesco World Heritage Sites
  Agios Ioannis Lambadistis
    Monastery 72
  Agios Nikolaos tis Stegis 77
  Archangelos Michail 71
  Choirokoitia 13, 116, **13**
  Church of the Transfiguration of
    the Saviour 81
  Church of Timios Stavros 81
  Panagia Forviotissa 78
  Panagia tis Podythou 77-8
  Panagia tou Araka 80-1
  Panagia tou Moutoulla 73
  Stavros tou Agiasmati 80

Tombs of the Kings 85-6
Troödos Byzantine churches 14,
  71, **14**

V

vacations 250
vaccinations 248
Varosia 185
vegetarian travellers 37, 38
Venetian walls 130, 184
villas 200
visas 19, 252, see also passports
volunteering 252
Vouni 178
Vouni Donkey Sanctuary 16, 60, **17**
Vrysi (Acapulco) Beach 168
Vrysoudia Beach 90

W

walking, see hiking
walking tours
  Kyrenia (Girne) & the Northern
    Coast 164-5
  Larnaka & the East 110
  Lefkosia (Nicosia) 135, 136, **136**
  Lemesos & the South Coast 51-3
  North Nicosia (Lefkoşa) 154, **154**
water, drinking 248
water parks, see theme parks
water shortages 234
Water World 119
waterfalls 72
weather 18, 23-4, 246, see also
  individual locations
weaving 102
websites, see internet resources

weights 247
Western Troödos 103, 206
whirling dervishes 151, 153
wildflowers, see flowers
wildlife, see animals, birds, plants
windsurfing 11, 25, 27, 58, 113, **11**, **26**
wine 22, 80
  Cyprus Wine Museum 12, 51, **12**
  driving tours 79, 96, **79**, **96**
  Kommandaria 76, 77
  krasohoria 9, 65, 76, **9**
  Lemesos Wine Festival 24, 53
  Mehmetcik Grape Festival 24
  wineries 9, 22, 59, 76, 77, 79, **9**
women in Cyprus 231
women travellers 252
work 252-3

X

Xyliatos Dam 147
Xylofagou 123

Y

Yasin, Nese 244
Yavuz Çıkarma (Five Mile) Beach
  168
Yedidalga Belediyesi Plaji 174
Yenierenköy 195
Yiaskouris Winery 76
yoga 110
Ýskele 191, 193

Z

Zafer Burnu 197
zoos 55, 91

000 Map pages
000 Photo pages